Praise for Memoir ork

"Thus, McManus became Britain's nemesis in America, the driving force that would eventually erode Britain's influence within the U.S. government."—Joseph E. Thompson. *American Policy and Northern Ireland: A Saga of Peacebuilding.* 2001.

"Advising Congressman [Richard Ottinger, D-NY], and helping him in the talks [in Belfast] was Fr. Sean McManus, the Washington-based Redemptorist priest ordained in England and now a scourge of the British Government. The lime-and-soda drinking cleric is not liked by British diplomats in the American capital, where he leads the Irish National Caucus, a lobbying group aimed at influencing American foreign policy with the target of Irish unity, freedom, and peace."—"Americans in Ulster Maelstrom." Daily Telegraph. London. August 18, 1983.

"The [MacBride] campaign is being run by the Irish National Caucus... The move, inspired by Father Sean McManus, who has been consistently opposed to British policy, is particularly well timed. For even if the law is never passed, it provides an opportunity to link, however, tenuously, the issues of South Africa and Northern Ireland. The MacBride Principles also call for the same kind of affirmative action programs for Catholics which American companies already use in the employment of women and blacks in the U.S.A"—"New York Threat of Ulster Snares Boycott." Will Ellsworth-Jones. *The Times.* London. January 6, 1985.

"Fr. Sean McManus is the man who put Northern Ireland on the map in America. As head of Washington-based lobby group the Irish National Caucus, which he founded in 1974, he continues to fight the fight over sectarianism and justice—British governments have been and gone, Fr. Sean is still here. He famously championed the MacBride Principles which called on US companies investing in Northern Ireland to operate a fair employment practice. It made him a hate figure for Unionists and a constant prick in the side of the British."—Richard Sullivan. Sunday World. Belfast. January 4, 2018.

"After being 'transported' out of London 1972, [Church and State] sent Fr. McManus to far-flung America. ...They thought it was a safe enough place to banish him after he attacked the British Government and its policies in [Northern Ireland] in the early 1970s. But how wrong [they] were. Some political observers in America say he was light years ahead of his time when he set up the Irish National Caucus to fight for justice and rights for [Catholics] back home in Northern Ireland."—John Cassidy, Sunday World. Belfast. March 18, 2007.

"No one has done more than Father McManus to keep the U.S. Congress on track regarding justice and peace in Ireland. Indeed, I believe historians will record that no one since John Devoy (1842–1928) has done more to organize American pressure for justice in Ireland."—Congressman Ben Gilman (R-NY), Chairman, House International Relations Committee. 2003.

"My American Struggle for Justice in Northern Ireland, and this Third Edition, is a hugely important book. It is probably the most significant memoir in the historiography of Irish-American nationalism since Recollections of an Irish Rebel (1929) by John Devoy." Washington Irish Committee.

"For the past nearly 50 years Fr. Sean McManus has been championing, almost single-handedly, the struggle for peace with justice for the partitioned six counties of "Northern Ireland." His has been the constant voice keeping the U.S. Congress, international media and the entire Irish-American community, informed

and constantly up to date with the truth. He withstood attacks of the English Government for his relentless efforts in fighting for the ultimate adoption of the MacBride Principles. Fr. Sean's ongoing work and efforts on behalf of Mr. Raymond McCord, a Protestant from Belfast, has become another example of his vital role in the search for peace with JUSTICE irrespective of one's religion."
—Bob Bateman, Past National Historian, Ancient Order of Hibernians. AOH Liaison to the Irish National Caucus and Congressional Ad Hoc Committee for Irish Affairs (1976-1982). (Great-grandnephew of the Fenian Captain Timothy Deasy).

"[Fr. McManus] stood out against powerful forces in a fight for justice and fairness. I didn't always agree with the causes he supported, but I admired his persistence, his courage, his relentlessness. And admiration that one person, almost alone, could make such impact on public policy in the United States."—Vincent Browne's speech at book launch in Dublin. 2011.

"Fr. Sean knows the history of the struggle for justice in Northern Ireland as well as anyone—he lived it. A very important book."—Ray Flynn, former mayor of Boston and U.S. ambassador to the Vatican. 2011.

"Fr. Sean McManus has spent a lifetime leading the fight to achieve a peaceful solution to the conflict in Northern Ireland. That so many Americans and, particularly those in American government leadership roles, joined in the effort to achieve a peaceful resolution of the conflict is a credit to his courageous and inspiring leadership."—Bill Flynn, Chairman Emeritus, Mutual of America chairman, National Committee on American Foreign Policy. 2011.

"A spiritual and magnanimous man, McManus is undeniably a brilliant tactician. His fine book chronicles a long and vibrant journey of an astute, intelligent and politically committed mind in action. ...Many elected American officials of all ethnic backgrounds were convinced by McManus of the urgency and legitimacy of the issue and became supporters of his unceasing efforts. His crowning achievement came when after a laborious campaign the MacBride Principles were signed into law by President Clinton."—Joe Martin. Real Change. October 27, 2011.

"So, from Kinawley to the halls of Congress, your story—which I thank you for—is hard to put down. May this year be one of deepening justice and peace for Ireland."—Jim Douglass, noted author on nonviolence. January 8, 2012.

"Fr. McManus ... has released this must-read tome for anyone interested in the long struggle for full Irish freedom ... The book documents the priest's successful struggle to incorporate the MacBride Principles (business ethics for American companies doing business in the north of Ireland) into U.S. law. This is not a work of fiction, though the herculean task Fr. McManus set for himself and his Irish National Caucus lobbying effort on Capitol Hill would appear to qualify as such."—Bryan T. McMahon. *The Ponchatoula Times*. Florida. June 28, 2013.

"As a writer, singer and performer of Irish ballads, I know the value of voice, words, and thoughts that expose injustice (as this book does). Over the last 40 years Fr. McManus has been the powerful voice that has kept the U.S. Congress involved in the struggle for justice and peace in Ireland."—Derek Warfield, (Young) Wolfe Tones. 2011.

"The intrepid Fermanagh-born battler for justice, Fr. Sean McManus, has published the definitive book on Irish-America's fight for justice in the North of Ireland, including the epic MacBride Principles campaign."—Máirtín ÓMuilleoir, Belfast Media, President of *The Irish Echo*. 2011.

No ... U.S. initiative ... [on Northern Ireland] would have come about had it not been for the activities of the Irish National Caucus.—*Sunday News* (Belfast), 1979.

"Perhaps the Caucus' boldest success has been its efforts to create ... The Committee for Irish Affairs."—*The New York Times*. 1979.

"...The Irish National Caucus ... has been influential in getting Congress to see Northern Ireland as a human rights issue."—*The Washington Post*. 1981.

"The MacBride campaign, directed by the Irish National Caucus won the support of the AFL-CIO and of several religious institutional shareholders including several Catholic orders and several major Protestant denominations."—*The Wall Street Journal*.1988.

"It all started with Father McManus. When he came over here, we were all sympathetic to him."—House Speaker Tip O'Neill (Irish America). 1986.

"I support the Irish National Caucus because it represents a compelling voice for fair employment, legal justice, and lasting peace in Northern Ireland."—Rep. Joseph P. Kennedy II (D-MA) 1988.

"Dear Fr. McManus ... I would be honored to be a Congressional Friend of the Irish National Caucus. I support your nonviolent work for justice and peace in Northern Ireland with full equality for the Catholic minority. Additionally, I support continued

American involvement in the Irish peace-process."—Rep. Joseph P. Kennedy, III, December13, 2012.

"As Chairman of the Ad Hoc Committee for Irish Affairs, I ... commend the Irish National Caucus for your steadfast advocacy on behalf of human rights ...Fr. McManus is 'The Apostle of Human Rights for Northern Ireland.'"—Rep. Mario Biaggi (D-NY). 1980.

"Thank-you [Fr. McManus] for your gracious invitation to become a 'Congressional Friend' of the Irish National Caucus. The warm welcome that I have received from the Irish people on my visits there has gladdened my heart and made me always hopeful that people throughout Ireland will live in a climate of peace and nonviolence."—Senator Hillary Rodham Clinton (D-NY). 2003; appointed U.S. secretary of state by President Obama in 2009.

"I am a Protestant (which normally I would not mention). However, I had to turn to a Catholic priest, Father Sean McManus, to seek justice for the murder of my son, Raymond Jr. Father McManus helped me get a powerful Congressional hearing into young Raymond's murder and expose state collusion in his murder."—Raymond McCord Sr., Belfast. 2011.

"Fr. McManus, from his Capitol Hill office, has been a prominent and influential figure in the quest for progress and peace with justice in Northern Ireland, blending knowledge of his native land with experience drawn from his years of dealing with the intricacies of the political system in his adopted one. His has been a unique role. Long may it continue."—Ray O'Hanlon. editor of *The Irish Echo*. New York. 2011.

"Fr. Sean McManus is a man to be reckoned with when it comes to advocating causes. His espousal of the MacBride

Principles back in the 1980s caused fits for the British government ... McManus has also been a constant watchdog in Washington on Irish affairs and has been hugely successful in setting the Irish-American agenda over the past 30 years."
—Niall O'Dowd. Editor of *The Irish Voice*, New York. 1990.

"The master ... in publicity terms, is Father Sean McManus, a burly, plausible charmer whose Irish National Caucus has taken center stage ... the good Father has made himself expert in congressional lobbying techniques ... I spent a long and, to be perfectly frank, rather enjoyable afternoon with Father McManus in his Capitol Hill office ... and it became clear that he hadn't been raised as a clerical apologist for nothing."
—Christopher Hitchens, public intellectual, author of *God Is Not Great* and *The Missionary Position*: Mother Teresa in Theory and Practice. The Spectator. England. October 5, 1985.

"We did not take him [INC President, Fr. Sean McManus] very seriously at first, but the MacBride Principles have caused serious problems and cost millions to try to counteract."—A Senior British official in Northern Ireland—Sunday Life. Belfast).1992.

"The fanfare of publicity about new and tougher action against job discrimination, for example, is designed, at least in part, to help the British Government to counter the extremely effective campaign on the MacBride Principles which is being waged by the Irish National Caucus in the United States."—*The Irish Times*. Dublin. 1987.

"I support the Irish National Caucus in its important work for justice and peace in Northern Ireland and would be proud to be associated with this worthy organization."—Rep. Peter T. King (R-NY) 1994.

MY AMERICAN STRUGGLE FOR JUSTICE IN NORTHERN IRELAND

MY AMERICAN STRUGGLE FOR JUSTICE IN NORTHERN IRELAND

By Fr. Sean McManus

© 2012 Sean McManus
Second US Edition 2014
Third US Edition 2019
All Rights Reserved.

This book may not be reproduced in whole or in part by any means without the expressed, written consent of the author.

MY AMERICAN STRUGGLE FOR JUSTICE IN NORTHERN IRELAND

Third US Edition 2019 Published by
Irish National Caucus Publications
P.O. Box 15128 Washington, D.C. 20003-0849
www.irishnationalcaucus.org

MY AMERICAN STRUGGLE FOR JUSTICE IN NORTHERN IRELAND
Third US Edition 2019

ISBN: 9781096876588

KDP, Columbia, SC

Cover Photographs
Front and Spine: Author photo (courtesy of author)
Capitol Hill: (iStock photo) Back: Speaker Nancy Pelosi with author
(courtesy of author)

Fr. Sean McManus, president of the Capitol Hill-based Irish National Caucus, was born in 1944 in County Fermanagh, one of the six counties in Northern Ireland—in a parish, significantly, divided by the British-imposed Border, declared in 1920.

In 1972, Church and State exiled him from Britain to the U.S. because he refused to be silent about injustice in Northern Ireland. In 1974, he founded the Capitol Hill-based Irish National Caucus: "Thus McManus became Britain's nemesis in America, the driving force that would eventually erode Britain's influence within the U.S. government." (American Policy and Northern Ireland. Professor Joseph E. Thompson).

My American Struggle for Justice in Northern Ireland is widely acclaimed. It has been declared a classic, a masterpiece, a must-read, and a hugely important book. There is simply no other book like it because no one has done what Fr. McManus has done on Capitol Hill for almost 50 years regarding justice and peace in Ireland. Therefore, nobody else could have written such a book. It is unique and original: "No one has done more than Father McManus to keep the U.S. Congress on track regarding justice and peace in Ireland. Indeed, I believe historians will record that no one since John Devoy (1842–1928) has done more to organize American pressure for justice in Ireland." Congressman Ben Gilman (R-NY), Chairman, House International Relations Committee. 2003.

The Sunday World of Belfast says: "After being "transported" out of London 1972, [Church and State] sent Fr. McManus to far-flung America. ...They thought it was a safe enough place to banish him after he attacked the British Government and its policies in [Northern Ireland] in the early 1970s. But how wrong [they] were. Some political observers in America say he was light years ahead of his time when he set up the Irish National Caucus to fight for justice and rights for [Catholics] back home in Northern Ireland." March 18, 2007.

And the same newspaper declares: "Fr. Sean McManus is the man who put Northern Ireland on the map in America." (January 4, 2018).

Famed Dublin journalist and broadcaster Vincent Browne says: "[Fr. McManus] stood out against powerful forces in a fight for justice and fairness. I didn't always agree with the causes he supported, but I admired his persistence, his courage, his relentlessness. And admiration that one person, almost alone, could make such impact on public policy in the United States." (2011).

Dedicated to the memory of my patriot brother Patrick McManus (1929–1958)

In him it seems the ancient clans combined
In pagan strength and Holy Rood;
The unsheathed swords of proud and bitter kings,
Marched and mingled in his blood.
Brave Spirit, when of you Freedom sings
At the exultant gates of God,
Your passing serves to illumine the Cause;
You are not dead but lack a mortal robe.
Epitaph for Patrick McManus by P.J. Madigan. 1958.

TABLE OF CONTENTS

Foreword		xix
Introduction		1
Chapter 1	Bonny Banks of Lough Erne	5
Chapter 2	The Day Celia Was Married and Patrick Was Killed	18
Chapter 3	The Call	27
Chapter 4	Kinnoull and Hawkstone Years	39
Chapter 5	The Troubles Come Back to Haunt	55
Chapter 6	Bound for America	79
Chapter 7	Formation of the Irish National Caucus	93
Chapter 8	Caucus Baptized in Blood at British Embassy	104
Chapter 9	All the News That's Fit to Print–Or Not	116
Chapter 10	The Caucus and Jimmy Carter	127
Chapter 11	The Long Knives of the Dublin Government	141
Chapter 12	Move to Washington	165
Chapter 13	The Old Sow that Eats Its Own Farrow	185
Chapter 14	Capitol Hill Struggle	218
Chapter 15	The MacBride Principles: Genesis and History	247
Chapter 16	Anti-MacBride Campaign	276
Chapter 17	Forcing Clinton to Sign MacBride	304
Chapter 18	"A Protestant Boy" on Capitol Hill	327
Chapter 19	World Peace Prize	333
Chapter 20	Irish American Peace Prize Announced	344
Chapter 21	Changing My Sky, Not My Soul	347
Epilogue		355
APPENDIX A		361
APPENDIX B		364
APPENDIX C		367
APPENDIX D		371
APPENDIX E		377

APPENDIX F · 381
APPENDIX G · 384
APPENDIX H · 399
APPENDIX I · 404
APPENDIX J · 405
APPENDIX K · 408
ENDNOTES · 419
INDEX · 445

Fr. McManus' Partitioned Parish and Partitioned Country

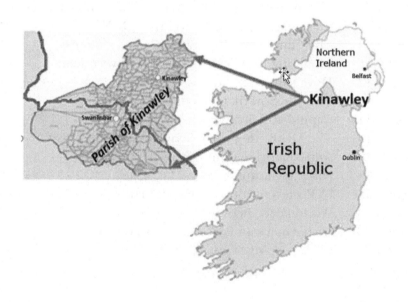

Foreword

This book was first published in Ireland by Collins Press, Cork in 2011.

The Irish Edition told the story up to 2009. The First US Edition brought the story up to 2012; the Second US Edition brought the story up to 2014—with many additions throughout both books, including fifty additional pages and twenty-two more photos.

The Third US Edition brings the story up to 2019. It is also larger in dimensions (6 x 9) whereas the 2014 Second Edition is smaller in dimensions (5x 7.5). Furthermore, this Third Edition adds an extra 125 (larger) pages and 41 additional photos.

This book covers a lot of ground, and many years, so it is impossible to thank every one who should be thanked.

In the first place, I want to thank my brothers and sisters who read the early chapters that dealt with our entire family.

I also want to express my heartfelt and humble gratitude to all those good and decent Irish-Americans who made my work for Irish justice possible. Without them, there would have been no Irish National Caucus—and no book, either. God bless each and every one of them. While all their names cannot be recorded in this book, they will be surely recorded in The Book of Life.

In particular, I must thank my colleague Barbara Flaherty who made the writing and the production of the book so much easier. She showed remarkable commitment to the project, which was immensely encouraging to me.

Furthermore, since the publication of the Irish edition, she has devoted great time and energy to each edition of this book and its promotion. Her daughter Barbara Maureen Corkery provided invaluable legal help and advice to the Irish National Caucus.

Any mistake or error is my own.

Fr. Sean McManus, October 2019

Introduction

The letter, dated Friday, April 15, 1972, from my Religious Superior got right to the point in the very first sentence:

> "Will you please pack up all your own belongings and leave everything ready to be sent on later without your having to return to Scotland. When this is done, I would like to see you here in Clapham [London], please, as soon as possible afterwords [sic], and not later than Thursday night [April 21]."

Even if he had not said anything else, I knew the writing was on the wall (not just in his typed letter). But he continued and, after the polite, very proper English opening, he let loose:

> You will understand that we cannot any longer tolerate the harm you are doing to yourself, the Church, and the Congregation through your stupid and stubborn persistence in writing to newspapers. I do not want anyone to know your immediate destination, nor your proposed transfer from Perth [Scotland]. I once again forbid you to make any communications to the Press or Media either per se or per alium, or to call on anyone en route or before departure. You have had just enough public notice, and it is time you thought about your own confreres and your apostolate. Please inform your superior, present or future, when you leave, of my permission for you

to do so, and ask them for the time being to regard it as confidential.

With sincere regards,

Yours JMJA

Charles Shepherd, CSsR[1]

There was a train strike at the time, so I phoned Fr. Shepherd to let him know. "Then fly down," he huffed and slammed down the phone. In those days it would have been most unusual for a young Redemptorist to fly from Scotland to London, so I knew I was in serious trouble.

And what was my offense? Had I mistreated people, preached heresy, denied the Real Presence of Christ in the Holy Eucharist? No, none of these. But worse still, in the eyes of some, I had broken about the only remaining taboo in Britain, especially for a young Irish priest: I had the temerity to criticize what Her Majesty's government and army were doing in the North of Ireland. Never from the pulpit, mind you, but just a few times in the press and on TV.

As I packed my bag (singular) I knew my life would never be the same again. But I also knew, come what may, I would be true to my conscience, or else something would die in my soul. I would not, through my silence, collaborate with England's oppression of my country. I prayed for a steady hand and a true heart. I was worried and anxious, with no idea I was embarking on the first leg of my journey to America. But now, almost fifty years later, I can smile and "with malice toward none, charity for all,"[2] thank God that instead of silencing me, they—the Church and State sent me to the one place on the planet where I was better able to work for justice and peace in Ireland. Charlie Shepherd, from his now high place in Heaven, must be echoing the famous words of Margaret Thatcher, when her Party ousted her from office in 1990, "It's a strange old world."

But more importantly still—and the thing that has given me the most peace of mind and spiritual consolation over all these years—is that I was able to carve out a way to reconcile my struggle for justice and peace in Ireland with my vocation as a priest. And what would provide me with the solid theological foundation for my work in America with the Irish National Caucus was the official teaching of the Catholic Church: "Action on behalf of justice ... [is] a constitutive dimension of the preaching of the Gospel ... and [a constitutive of dimension] of the Church's mission for the redemption of the human race and its liberation from every oppressive situation[3]

This groundbreaking document could not have come at a more providential time for me. Unfortunately, it is still very little known, and certainly, the Bishops of Ireland, Britain and the United States[4] never seemed to stress it in regard to Northern Ireland. I am not sure if Fr. Shepherd had ever read this prophetic document, but even if he had, it would never have occurred to him that it just might trump his own apparent narcissistic obsession to be obeyed. More perhaps about his own will rather than God's will, plus, of course, his wanting to do the will of the British government.

But for me "Justice in the World" would "a lamp to my feet, and a light to my path" (Psalm 119: 105).

I knew I had to choose between Pax Britannica and Pax Christi, to do what Psalm 40 urges, and which is part of the liturgy of the Mass for the Feast Day of The Annunciation (my favorite Feast Day) "I announced your justice ... I did not restrain my lips ...Your justice I kept not hid within my heart..."

In other words, I had to do the exact opposite of what Fr. Shepherd demanded: to never again to criticize England's rule in Ireland.

And later, when I became more familiar with the "Social Gospel"[5] as preached and practiced by Blessed Martin Luther King, Jr., I knew with God's grace nothing was going to turn me around.

"Ain't gonna let nobody turn me 'roun.'
Turn me 'roun'
Ain't gonna let nobody turn me 'roun'
I'm gonna wait until my change comes."
(Old Negro Spiritual)

However, that did not mean I was free from the burden that results from a crisis of conscience. "Religious obedience" is deeply ingrained in members of religious orders and refusing to obey a Religious Superior is a most serious issue, and carries a price—like, to some degree, "civil disobedience" can carry a price in the secular world. I carried that burden for a number of years. But in time, I came to be fully at peace with my decision knowing that, in this case, Fr. Shepherd's voice was not "the voice of God." The voice of God, instead, demanded I speak up, that I should not be not be silent. And the official teaching of the Catholic Church on social justice made clear I should not be complicit with British government oppression, injustice, systematic human rights violations, and state-sponsored sectarianism, state-sponsored anti-Catholicism, and state-sponsored terrorism in my country. And it was a wonderful grace and blessing for me to receive, and for which I thank God every day.

CHAPTER 1

Bonny Banks of Lough Erne

*And for all this, nature is never spent;
There lives the dearest freshness deep down things.*
"God's Grandeur."
Gerard Manley Hopkins

AMERICAN CATHOLICS WHO WERE VERY PROUD of their "historic" parishes used to be astonished whenever I told them that I came from a parish that had essentially existed since the sixth century—the parish of Kinawley in Fermanagh.

I was born on February 6, 1944, in the townland of Clonliff, which is about three miles from the village of Kinawley, which in turn is about two miles from the Cavan border near Swanlinbar. The historic parish of Kinawley is actually divided by the British-imposed border. So, I grew up extremely conscious that the British government had partitioned not only my country but also my own ancient parish. The name in Irish, "Cill Naile," means Church of St. Naile, a famous saint who ministered in the area in the sixth century.[1]

I was the tenth child in a family of twelve. Our parents owned a small farm of twenty-three acres, on which our father, Patrick Sr., was born (January 28, 1877—January 21, 1962). Our mother, Celia McMullen-McManus (September 30, 1903—June 28, 1991) came from nearby Carn Mountain. Well, not much of a mountain, truth be told. In America, it would be considered more of a hill. Carn townland is on the side of Molly Mountain, which peaks at nine hundred thirty feet. Mother's home was almost seven hundred feet above sea level. In America, a hill is seen to be any natural elevation of the earth's surface up to two thousand feet, with a mountain's height starting higher than that.

When they got married, my father was forty-nine and my mother twenty-two. My mother explained that she first met Daddy at a dance in Cleary's—a small thatched house "across the bog," as we would say—in Clondaval, the next townland to Clonliff. She also explained, with still evident delight, that Daddy affectionately referred to her at the dance as a "moor hen"—referring to the fact she was from Carn mountain. So, in the movie *Jerry Maguire*, Tom Cruise was told by his love interest that "He had her at 'hello,'" Patrick McManus obviously had the fair Celia McMullen at "moor hen." However, instead of being made in Hollywood, our parents' marriage was made in heaven.

The back of the farm is lapped by the waters of Upper Lough Erne, and the front is bounded by the Cladagh River[2], which empties into Lough Erne. Our home was a small thatched house. Because Clonliff Lane was entirely Catholic (nine families then), it was not provided with running water or electricity until 1960.

No memoirs of mine would make sense without full acknowledgment of my brothers and sisters, for it was my whole family that shaped me. All that is good in me, I owe, under God, to them. My faults and sins I owe to myself alone: Mary Kate (born in 1927), twins Patrick and Terence (born in 1929; Terence died before he was three years old); Celia (born in 1931), Thomas (born in 1933), Alice (born in 1934), Terence (the second, born in 1937), Jim, who also became a priest (born in 1938), Frank (born in 1942), and finally, my two younger brothers, Myles (born in1948) and Arthur (born in 1949, died in May 1950).

My father was sixty-seven when I was born so, obviously, I never knew him when he was a young man—indeed none of us did. Yet, I never felt I missed out on that account—probably because there were so many of us and because our father was always there. He would never have been absent or away from home overnight in his entire life. Because my father was himself old, I grew up revering old people, and that reverence has never left me. For me, God is almost tangibly present around the very old and very young. I don't suppose any father was loved more by his children. And that was always evident sixty years later when we all would get together and reminisce. Smiles would always break out when we talked about him.

Your Father Was A Saint

About thirty years ago, when I was home from America on vacation, I was chatting to one of our nearest and dearest neighbors, the late Matthew Mc Hugh, who was twenty-eight years older than I. He, therefore, would have known Daddy (as the family always called him, and still does) when Daddy was still fairly young. I asked Matthew what was the thing he most remembered about Daddy, as a younger man. I was expecting him to say that he was strong, funny, or something like that—to mention some such physical quality that stood out. But Matthew took me totally aback by saying, "Your father was a saint." I asked him why he said that. He told me that whenever he worked with Daddy in the fields, at the end of the day when they would walk up to where the spades were stored, Daddy would bless himself with the Sign of the Cross (invoking the name of the Holy Trinity—Father, Son and Holy Spirit) and say three Hail Marys for a good day's work. It was the first time I had ever heard that, and I was touched by the sweetness of it—and the grace of it. My father knew that humble work blessed by God was "more precious than rubies." And he certainly knew that that was even truer of his bride, the fair Celia McMullen-McManus: "Who can find a virtuous woman? For her price is far above rubies. She opens her mouth with wisdom: and in her tongue is the law of kindness. Her children rise up and call her blessed; her husband also, and he praises her." (Proverbs 31:10, 26, 28). My mother was a remarkably strong, independent and resilient woman—patriotic to the core with a profound trust in God. This will become very evident later in the story. In later life, she really blossomed and enjoyed her old age immensely.

There were a lot of us for a small house. Yet, I don't ever remember feeling crowded and needing my own space. But, of course, not all of us lived in the house at the same time. You can see the closeness in age of some of the children, and the great age difference between the youngest and oldest. In that sense, as far as growing up together, we were like three different families. Mary Kate, Patrick, Celia, Thomas and Alice grew up together. Terence and Jim were the second crop. And, finally, Frankie, Myles, and I sprouted up. There is a seventeen-year difference between Mary Kate and me, and twenty-one years between her and Myles.

Mary Kate left home for Omagh, Portadown and later England when she was nineteen (when I was only two years old). Alice went to school in the convent when she was thirteen (and I was three) and stayed in Enniskillen with our Aunt Lizzie, Daddy's sister, who had inherited a house in the town. Essentially, she never lived full-time at home after that. Thomas left for England at nineteen (when I was eight) and in the same year Jim left (aged fourteen) for the Presentation Brothers in Cork, only to defect later to the Redemptorists; Terence left at seventeen (when I was ten) to work and stay in Enniskillen.

So, for most of my growing up, the only permanent dwellers in Macs were my parents and Patrick and Celia, who were both adults. Frankie, Myles and I were the cubs. But we cubs also grew up with another almost-brother—our first cousin Patrick Maguire who is two years younger than I am.

Patrick with his parents, John James and Maggie, lived nearby. Maggie was my mother's older sister and they were very close. Patrick hung out with us a lot and is still like a brother to this day. In 2002—inspired by showing the old Mc Mullen ruins on Carn to long-lost cousins from America—Patrick crafted a moving poem (part elegy, part paean), "The Carn Lintel," the only thing left standing:

*Tired and hungry fields, receding, as the gorse reclaims its space,
Our ancestral tracks have vanished, footprints faded beyond trace. Vengeful bramble, angry briar, that for long were held at bay, Boldly colonize the meadow where my mother trampled hay ...*

*Nettles, tall as were my uncles, stretch up from the strewn floor
And yet, the stubborn lintel sullenly protects the door. Persevering through the decades,* **(See full poem on Appendix A and on the web at IrishNationalCaucus.org).**

I guess I knew we were not rich but again I don't remember feeling deprived although I was conscious that Francie Reilly across the bog had a bicycle and I didn't. But then none of the McManus children ever had a bike, so it was no big deal.

Country poverty, at least as I experienced it, is vastly different from city poverty. We had twenty-three acres of our own land to roam, not to mention the entire countryside, in perfect safety as long as we stayed away from the river because the monster, Terry McGrath, lived there. Nobody seemed to know the origins of the story behind this bogeyman, but it certainly kept us away until we were big enough. Amazingly, although we were surrounded by water, hardly anyone in our area could swim. But then, how could they? They were all scared of Terry McGrath!

Ironically, one time the river did not seem to hold fear for any of us, not even for Mother. It was during the Big Snow of 1947 from the end of February well into March when the Cladagh River was frozen over (and therefore presumably keeping Terry McGrath frozen below). I remember clearly holding Mother's hand and walking on the ice with a group of neighbors. I can also still see in my mind's eye the little snow house that my father and older brothers built on the back street, as we called it, which was really sort of a back yard. I was only three at the time, but my recollection is vivid.

Now by American standards, the Big Snow may not have been all that big, but for Ireland it was. Newspapers at the time reported "huge snow-drifts, some up to fifteen feet high were common in many areas." And *The Swanlinbar News* reported "that it had been estimated that over 1,000 sheep had been lost in the snow..."[3]

Anyway, the Macs, as we were called locally, all survived the Big Snow, and without thermal clothing!

Fishing in the Blood

But when we were big enough and no longer scared of Teddy McGrath, the Cladagh River became a beloved fishing spot—especially "Murphy's Hole."

The Murphys lived one field across from us to the left. Charles (always pronounced "CHARL-es") (1877-1967), was a colorful and legendary figure and a lifelong friend of our father. We got such a kick out of him. He could be a quite fearsome spectacle as he supported Kinawley against Derrylin. But he was always kind and gentle to us—unless we just went too far in annoying him. Even then he would just chase us away for awhile. He never hit me. He had been a good footballer in his day, but when I was growing up, he was in his late seventies. He was a fanatic fisherman, fishing almost every morning during fishing season, and at the ungodly hour of 5: am. Clonliff Lane and indeed all of Kinawley was a late-starting zone. People stayed up late and got up late. Not the intrepid Charles. He would be in bed before nine o'clock at night, and by dawn's first light, the fish better watch out. He always fished with three rods (cut out of the hedge), and he would land the roach and perch on the river-bank with amazing rapidity.

Charles would feed "Murphy's Hole" each night with all sorts of stuff: wheat, bread, anything at all. He didn't keep pigs, so all sorts of slops went into the fishing hole. And boy, did his strategy work. The fish practically begged to be caught. Pike would be caught by leaving a line out overnight. Bream were also in the river but were no way as abundant as perch and roach.

Charles would awaken us at that ungodly hour, and we would fish to our hearts' content with rods also cut from the hedge and string for our lines. I often think of that now when I'm using my fancy fly rod and all my sophisticated tackle. Charles would not have been impressed by any of it. Indeed, one day my brother-in-law, Michael Ferguson (Celia's husband), joined Charles at the river bank with a brand-new spinning rod. Charles cast a suspicious eye on this new-fangled article and said, "That's a dangerous looking weapon."

One Sunday afternoon, Frankie and I went fishing with Charles in his boat, kept at the bottom of his land, which like our land, was on the edge of Lough Erne. Charles rowed to Kipping, a very small island about twenty minutes away from our adjoining farms. We stopped just off Kipping and in a few hours, we had caught thirteen dozen fish. I never forgot thenumber.

The fishing was so great that we could skim the hook/worm just above the water and the fish would jump up to grab it. I have never witnessed that phenomenon again. In those days, we could still actually see the fish a little bit under the water even though Lough Erne is naturally dark. One of my great laments is that the Cladagh and Lough Erne are so polluted—like my own present-day fishing-hole—the mighty Chesapeake Bay. In the 1600's, Native Americans could see a fish thirty feet below the waters of the Chesapeake. Now, one cannot see the tiniest fraction of an inch below the water. So much for progress. We have destroyed the waters of the world with "progress." It would have broken Charles Murphy's stout heart.

LIFE ON THE RANCH

Out of the twenty-three acres of land, probably only about fifteen were arable. The remainder was bog and bottomland along the edge of Lough Erne, and only good for growing bulrushes. Frankie, Myles and I used to pull the bulrushes and use them as a floatation device when we were trying to learn to swim in the shallow waters of the Lough (Terry McGrath did not inhabit Lough Erne). In fact, the bulrushes were only an obstacle, a water-crutch that only delayed proper learning. Indeed, I could never really swim until at the age of sixteen, I went to the Redemptorist junior seminary in Birmingham, England, in 1960. We were allowed to visit the local public swimming pool once a week. And I was so embarrassed to see all the little English kids jump into the pool and swim like fish, and there was I, a big Paddy, standing at the edge of the pool like a proper eejit. I watched how they were doing it, and patriotic pride took over. "Says I to myself, if these English cubs can do it, so can I." And with that, I dove in and swam, quite well. "Bulrushes, how are ye?" I thought to myself.

On the farm we grew potatoes, turnips, lettuce, carrots, cabbage, and wheat—enough to keep us well fed, with chicken, hen eggs, duck eggs and bacon from our pigs that Johnny Mc Caffery, our neighbor out the lane, would slaughter in the backyard. Plus, our diet was amply supplemented with fresh fish we caught and rabbits and hares we snared or caught with our dogs.

Not one of us was ever sick, apart from the usual stuff, except baby Arthur who had a hole in his heart—fatal in those days.

We made hay in the summer (and I never had hay fever until I came to Washington, DC) for our four to five cows, and cut turf, peat, to keep the home fires burning. Turf was our only fuel in the open hearth and our only source of heat. The Macs were truly ahead of their time: green, all the way. No machinery of any kind. All farm work was done by shovel, spade, pitchfork, and grape. Al Gore would have been proud of us.

When I was too small to spread fertilizer (a posh word for cow dung) with the grape, I spread it with my hands. Once you have done that, no job is beneath you, and you come to know what holy men and women have taught from the beginning: that creation is sacred, and all work has an inherent dignity.

School for all the Macs was Drumbroughas National School—one classroom, two teachers and a dry-toilet across the road. The younger children sat facing Miss McManus (no relation), and the older children sat in the opposite direction, facing Miss McHugh.

The school was about three miles from our house and, naturally, we walked there and back each day. In the summer we walked in our bare feet, not because we did not have shoes but because it was the custom. By the end of the summer, the soles of our feet were as tough as leather.

Drumbroughas School was almost all Catholic, except for the odd Protestant. During religion class, the Protestants got to go outside, and there were times I wished I were a Protestant.

GAA IN THE BLOOD

School never turned me on—that was the preserve of the GAA (Gaelic Athletic Association). All seven brothers were devoted to the game. Indeed, one of the family treasures is a photograph of all seven brothers togged out in football uniforms, posing proudly on the "hill" outside the house. We had, at least in our minds, our own seven-a-side team. The photograph was taken in 1956 when all ten children were home. Mary Kate remembers Mother saying it would never happen again that all ten of us would be home at the same time. Sadly, she was right.

Patrick had played a key role in reviving the Kinawley Football Club, the Brian Borus, for which he served as Secretary. The Fermanagh GAA County Secretary, Tom Fee, would later recall: "I remember making ... a number of trips to the [Kinawley] parish in 1950 in an effort to have the club resurrected ... We were fortunate enough to find the very man in Patrick McManus ... he was the vital part ..."[4] Patrick, however, did not play much himself but did occasionally act as referee. Thomas was a good player, although I never actually remember him playing. I do, however, clearly remember Celia cheering, "Come on our Thomas" at a game in the old field at Carron's Gap. Thomas played on the county minors, with his buddy across the field, Patrick Murphy, Charles' eldest son. But forced emigration cut short Thomas' football career. Terence, God rest him, was a strong player, if not the most genteel. Jim left too early to play for Kinawley, and there was no Under-Fourteen team then. But while he was in Cork from 1952 to 1955, he got hooked on hurling. When he came home on holidays, I remember he would strut his stuff on the hill with his camán (hurling stick) and sliotar (the ball), probably thinking he was Christy Ring[5] or one of the famous Cork players. But hurling was a "foreign" game in Kinawley. Frankie and Myles played for the county, but I left for the Redemptorists just as I was beginning to peak: "I coulda been a contender" as Marlon Brando famously lamented in *On the Waterfront*.

However, I did have my share of glory playing on the Under Fourteens on a joint Kinawley–Swanlinbar team in the league. We won the cup for the Under-Fourteen County Cavan League in 1956 and 1958. Frankie was the captain in 1956, and I was captain in 1958.

It was a huge thrill for us Fermanagh boys to win in Breffni Park—home pitch of the once-famed Cavan footballers. Also, I was the Kinawley captain when we won the Fermanagh Schoolboy Cup in 1959. When I left for the Redemptorists in Birmingham, England, in 1960, the only material things of value I had were the medals from those victories—and I still have them today.

While I was still under fourteen, I not only played for the Under-Fourteens, but also for the minors (Under-Eighteen) and the senior team. Which meant I was going up against big bruisers from Derrylin and elsewhere in their twenties and thirties. But I had a back-up strategy: while I played center-left, Terence was center-half, Frankie was center-right, and to top it off, my brother-in-law, Big Mick Ferguson, was full-back, so if "them Derrylin boys" wanted trouble, they had come to the right place.

SPIRITUALITY IN THE BLOOD

Our home was a devout one though we would never have been considered "churchy." Indeed, I never remember seeing the priest in our home until Patrick was killed. However, no night passed without Mother gathering us all around and saying the Rosary, with all the trimmings. She would recite the Litany of the Saints by heart without falter—unless one of us misbehaved and distracted her. Then she would have to stop, go back to the beginning and take another run at it. The only time my father ever "cuffed me in the ear" (a gentle touch with his hand) was during the Rosary when he wrongly blamed me for something Frankie or Myles would do.

The spiritual world—God, the Incarnation, Death, and Resurrection of Jesus Christ, The Word and The Sacraments, Heaven and Hell—was as real to us as the land and the sky.

It was even more real because we knew the material world would pass, but God's Word would last forever. Our theology and cosmology may have been overly simple, but compared to the shallowness and emptiness of much in today's culture we had the essentials right. And we have all been sustained by an unshakeable trust in God's abiding love for each one of us and the entire world.

"May God's holy will be done" was the constant refrain of my mother both in good times and bad—and bad times did come.

At the time, none of us would have seen that "worldview" as Celtic spirituality, but today it's almost quite fashionably seen as that. Deacon Owen F. Cummings, a professor of theology in Oregon, frames the issue quite well: "[The second characteristic of Celtic spirituality] is the Celtic emphasis on the place of nature within the Christian revelation. The natural world has come from God and is, therefore, a place where God may be found. There is no principled dichotomy between nature and supernature, the world of nature and the world of grace, but rather they are best seen as a continuum. This attitude gives rise to a permeative sense of God's presence so that the Celt was very much a God-intoxicated man whose life was embraced on all sides by the divine Being. But this presence was always mediated through some finite, worldly reality. So, it would be difficult to imagine spirituality more down to earth than this one. For the Celt, there is no distance from the Divine."[6]

Religious vocabulary infused our culture. As a very young child, I used to think when the Gospel was read about Jesus being "wrapped in swaddling clothes" (Luke2:12) that it meant "Swanlinbar clothing." You see clothing in Swad, as we called it, was much cheaper in than in the North. And Hugh Cullen, a draper in Swad, had a second-hand shop in Kinawley, from which we all were clothed. So naturally enough, being a budding theologian, I reasoned that just as we depended on Swad clothing, so did Jesus because He was poor just like us.

I guess almost every child in Ireland had a memory like that.

The redoubtable Malachy McCourt, brother of Frank (*Angela's Ashes'* author[7]) recounts in his book "A Monk Swimming" that he thought for a long time that, "amongst women" in the Hail Mary was "a monk swimming."[7]

I remember one day when I was about ten, I was all by myself clamping turf (building them in little crisscrossed blocks so they would dry) on Murphy's Bank. I was fed up and lonely. I laid down at the edge of the turf bank staring into the bog hole thinking, "Badcest (bad luck) to Adam and Eve. If they had not sinned, I would not have to work 'by the sweat of my brow.'" The Book of Genesis (3:19) says one of the consequences of sin is hard work.

And they say Catholic kids didn't know their Bible!

It seems fashionable these days for writers to deplore and complain about their Catholic childhood. I recognize that *Angela's Ashes* is a classic, but I must beg to differ with Frank Mc Court's much-quoted line: "Worse than the ordinary miserable childhood is the miserable Irish childhood, and worse yet is the miserable Irish Catholic childhood...."[8]

The *New York Times* loves that sort of thing. Frank may have said it tongue in cheek, of course, but it has perniciously promoted an ugly stereotype. I must confess that my experience was totally different from Mc Court's. I never had one ugly incident in my childhood, which was as Irish and as Catholic as any on the planet, and which I would not change for anything in this world.

I was surrounded and protected by loving parents and devoted brothers and sisters, and the greatest neighbors in the world. I know that won't make any headlines, but it is true—and its value is more precious than rubies.

That is why I was so deeply shocked and furious to read, it seemed like every day in the nineties, about all the sexual abuse of children in Ireland and America. I used to be scared to pick up a newspaper because I knew it would smash me in the face like a fist. It has forever harmed the Catholic Church. It is a demented sickness and a criminal betrayal of the worst possible kind. But I know that, after the victims and their families, the ones most outraged are the decent Catholic priests, 95 percent of whom have never harmed a child.

However, five percent, four percent, or whatever percent, is still too much and is a crime that calls out to Heaven.

CHAPTER 2

The Day Celia Was Married and Patrick Was Killed

Your joy is your sorrow unmasked.
And the self-same well from which your laughter rises
was often times filled with your tears.
Khalil Gibran, *The Prophet*

BUT MY HAPPY AND CAREFREE CHILDHOOD would soon end, on July 15, 1958: the day Celia was married, and Patrick was killed. Our lives would never be the same again. But let me go back to Sunday, December 9, 1956, to set the scene for Patrick's death, at the age of twenty-nine.

The family, in general, was not aware of Patrick's involvement in the IRA until the night before "he went on the run." That Sunday night there had been a parish bazaar. When the family came home (those who were still living there), Patrick sat us all down. Mother said she would stand, but he insisted she sit down. He stood in the middle of the small kitchen and announced that he had something very important to tell us, which we had to keep secret—that in the morning he was leaving home as a soldier of the IRA, that we would not see him again until Ireland was free, and that, if necessary, he was prepared to die for The Cause. He warned us that the police would harass us, that we could suffer reprisals and that we might be put under curfew. He stressed that the fight was against the

British government and that the family should continue to be friendly with our Protestant neighbors. He ended by explaining that nineteen-year-old Terence (the second), who had agreed in advance, would quit his job as a barman in Enniskillen and work the farm. Terence's life and career were, therefore, drastically changed but no one ever heard him complain. To Terence, who died in 2000, it was something he had to do for his family and country. He, too, was an Irish patriot. (Jim, the next oldest at eighteen, was already in the Redemptorist Novitiate in Perth, Scotland.) Patrick then told us what reason to give to the police and indeed everyone as to why he had gone away: he had gone on a holiday to one of his uncles in Athlone (Mother's brother, Terence) and because war had broken out, he was afraid to return. What double irony! Patrick was fearless and never had a day's holiday in his life.

The family was shocked and stunned at Patrick's dramatic announcement, but amazingly, Mother expressed relief, as she was scared he was going to tell us he had done something bad that would disgrace the family. My father, then seventy-nine, only said one thing, "You will not be halfway out the lane until the police know"—expressing the age-old fear of informers.

The following morning, Monday, December 10, 1956, is still as clear in my mind as yesterday. Patrick was getting ready to take off. I remember him patching up his knapsack, putting in a blanket and ponger (tin cup). He told me to go and fodder the cows and followed me out. I had two armfuls of hay and let some drop. Patrick told me to pick it up, just like our father would have directed. I noticed he was wearing big boots and walking in a different way. I later understood he was in full military mode, marching along the street (the backyard of the farm).

Back inside, Patrick would say goodbye. Mother was standing behind the back door (which opened to the inside of the kitchen) to hide her tears and sobbing. He left quickly so as not to prolong the anguish. I followed him up to the top lane, and by the chestnut tree, tearfully watched him march out Clonliff Lane for the last time, his big boots stomping on the road. I felt I would never see him again, but I did, once. In the spring of 1958, I went to a football game in Swanlinbar, at which I was not playing. On my way, I stopped at a "safe house" in Swad to pick up a letter Patrick would leave there for our Mother. I was sitting in the room, waiting for the letter when, lo and behold, Patrick himself walked in. I couldn't believe it. I almost did not recognize him. He was looking fantastic, had put on about fourteen pounds (which he badly needed), and he was dressed impeccably: sports coat, shirt and tie, and slacks. I had never seen Patrick so spruced up, and I was struck by how handsome he was, something of which I had never been aware. Being dressed in a professional manner was obviously the disguise that worked best for this country boy on the run.

Patrick bought me a lemonade and asked all about the family. He gave me his famous "big-brother talk"—study hard, look after my young brother Myles, then eight ... that Frankie and I should stay away from bad company and not give our parents any trouble, etc. And, of course, I was not to tell anyone outside the family that I had seen him. Mother would have seen him a number of times, at the same safe house but our father never did see him again—something that weighed very heavily on his elderly shoulders.

Patrick was quite right when he warned us the police would harass us. They raided our home often. The typical tactic was to reverse their open-backed vehicles to both the front and back doors of our little house. So, when we opened the doors, we would see them sitting with their guns pointing right at us. It was meant to frighten us, but it never took a flinch out of us. I remember one evening they were up in the loft, where Patrick used to sleep, going through everything. One Special Branch man made a big show of carefully examining a stamp. My lovely sister Celia, normally the least combative of the entire family, said to him in exasperation, "What do you expect to find in that stamp—a machine gun?" Later when he went down the ladder from the loft, the same Special Branch man told us the next time we saw Patrick would be "when they carried him in, feet first and dead." Another Branch man in a gabardine overcoat told Mother the best thing she could do was to turn Patrick in for his own good. Expecting our mother to be an informer was a hilarious notion.

Other times, the Royal Ulster Constabulary (RUC) would take Frankie and me off the bus at Montiagh Cross (a couple of miles from home), handcuff us and search us. Again, if it was meant to scare us, they didn't know the Macs. We never experienced one moment of fear. Patrick's own defiance had put steel in our backbone, and there was no way we would allow ourselves to be intimidated by servants of the Crown.

PATRICK AT HOME

Let me now talk a bit about Patrick before he went on the run. Patrick left Drumbroughas school when he was fourteen and worked the farm with Father. Being the eldest boy in a large family, and with an elderly father, Patrick assumed a lot of responsibility. Though not well educated in the formal sense, he became a knowledgeable man, especially in Irish history. He believed strongly that his much younger brothers should have the education he himself and the older members of the family were not able to have.

Patrick grew to be about five feet, nine inches, with a thin, wiry frame and flaming red hair. Years later, an IRA colleague would remember he "had a great smile," though of serious disposition. He had a healthy self-confidence and could turn his hand to many things. For example, the grandfather clock in the home had stopped for many a year. He believed that he could fix it. Without ever having seen the inside of a clock in his life, he took the inner workings apart, spread them out on the table, figured out what was wrong and restored it to perfect working order. And he went from clockmaker to boat builder. He felt a new rowing boat was needed, as the one our father had used all his life to row up and down the lough was no longer seaworthy. Patrick persuaded his father that together they could build a new and bigger boat. They worked at it for months. The maiden voyage of "Mac's new boat" was a major event for the family and the children in Clonliff Lane.

Patrick could even turn to poetry, using it years later to pay tribute to his two IRA comrades in arms, Seán South and Feargal O'Hanlon who were killed on New Year's Eve 1957, in an attack on Brookeborough Barracks, County Fermanagh:

> May God be with those noble hearts
> May Heaven be their home
> For they never feared the RUC
> Or B-Specials on patrol;
> In Brookeborough town they were shot down,
> In a cabin they lay cold:
> O'h-Annluain from old Monaghan town
> And Sabhat from Garryowen

The same analytical and practical mind that led him to mend clocks and build boats led him to accurately analyze and clearly discern the root causes of oppression, division, and discrimination in the North of Ireland. He took his religion from Rome and his politics from Tone. With Wolfe Tone, Patrick believed in "breaking the connection with England, the never-failing source of all our political evils."

He became active in the anti-partition campaign of the late 1940s and early 1950s. There were rallies in the parish hall and rousing speeches from local politicians including Cahir Healy, the Member of Parliament (MP) for South Fermanagh at Stormont. The family always remembered with pride how Patrick defiantly flew the tricolor from a tree. The whole parish was talking about it. But then, as expected, the RUC arrived in force to tear it down.

Patrick remained "on the run" until the night he was killed, July 15, 1958, in a premature explosion of a bomb he was transporting. He was the Officer Commanding (OC) for South Fermanagh, and in the Spring of 1958, he was appointed to the Army Council.

Sean Cronin, future Chief of Staff, would later write in the *United Irishman*, "He must have escaped death or capture a score of times. And it is ironic that when death came, in the end, it should come in the way it did to a man so wise, so cautious, so experienced. There was iron in his soul as well as in his body, and he passed it on to those who came in contact with him ..."[1]

And, J. Bowyer Bell, in his classic history, *The Secret Army: the IRA, 1916–1970*, describes Patrick as follows: "He was the only active IRA leader to escape arrest during the period. An intrepid guerrilla fighter, he preferred the mountains to the towns and disliked leaving his own area for meetings in strange places. Operating mostly from dugouts—a string of which he had built right across Fermanagh—he rarely slept in a house. His death was a major blow to the struggle ..."[2]

But the family now knows that Patrick did, in fact, go to "strange places," even openly campaigning, under the pseudonym of Tumulty, for a Sinn Féin Abstentionist Candidate, Pádraig Kelly, in County Galway in the spring of 1957. He was, in fact, safer away from his home base, where everybody would have recognized him.

KILLED IN ACTION

Patrick was killed at around 9:45 p.m. while handing over a bomb to colleagues who were waiting on an isolated country road in the townland of Derryrealt, about two miles outside Swanlinbar. He had constructed the gelignite bomb himself—"in a five-gallon gas drum with the head cut off it." Patrick came across a field, carrying the container-bomb, stopping on the inside of the ditch below where the car was waiting. As he lifted up the container to hand it to his colleagues, the bomb exploded. Patrick was killed instantly, blown to pieces. Two of his colleagues were injured. The Republican Movement would later build a fine monument on the exact spot where Patrick was killed.

To make his death even worse, Celia had been married that very day. She heard the tragic news when RTÉ announced it the following day on the radio, as she and her husband Michael Ferguson were on their honeymoon in Salthill, Galway.

The following morning after Celia's joyous wedding, the first in the family, I was woken by crying. I rushed into the kitchen and saw the local curate, Fr. Gilmartin, there. I knew immediately that Patrick had been killed. It remains to this day my most vivid, traumatic moment. Jim was rushed home from the Redemptorist Major Seminary in England, and he, Terence and Michael Ferguson had to go and try to identify the "remains," which did not really exist. No family could have been more devastated, yet no family could have been more defiantly proud. Patrick had died for Irish freedom and that, along with our deep faith, sustained us as a family and as individuals.

What the family remembers most about Patrick was his spiritual side. While never wearing his religion on his sleeve, he was deeply religious, never failing to get on his knees before he went to sleep no matter how late he came home. Patrick meditated daily through the Rosary, on the incarnation, life, death and resurrection of Jesus Christ, his Most Holy Redeemer. His colleagues later in the Republican Movement all recall Patrick's devotion to prayer. One remembers: "He'd kneel down and give out the Rosary to us. I'd have to recite the Rosary along with him... He was a religious man. He was a very great man ... he was loyal to his country and his people ... and the people were loyal to him."

Another IRA colleague recounts how one night he and Patrick were pinned down by the RUC and British Army in a field just inside the border near the village of Kinawley. While the police spotlight beamed all across the field, Patrick and his colleague were hugging the ground. The colleague tried to cover his cough with his coat-collar, and Patrick whispered, "What are you doing?" The colleague explained about the cough, and then asked Patrick, "What are you doing?"

"I'm on my third Rosary," he replied.

Patrick had made it clear that should he die, he did not want to be buried "under the Union Jack," i.e., buried in the North. So, he was buried across the border in Swanlinbar, but still part of the parish of Kinawley. Even at the funeral Mass, Fr. Fox, the curate in Swanlinbar, commented on Patrick's deep faith and his devotion to Our Blessed Lady. Thousands attended his funeral and, after the Mass, the funeral cortege marched to Killaduff Cemetery, about two miles outside Swad. The cortege was led by a lone piper. It was the most heart-rending sound

I had ever heard. To this day, every time I hear the bagpipes, even see them played on TV or in the movies, I can choke up.

I distinctly remember as the cortège passed through the village, a garda saluted Patrick's coffin. As a consequence of that gesture of respect, I always had a friendly attitude towards the gardaí—no matter what I may have thought of their political bosses.

Seán Ó Brádaigh, Ruairi's brother, gave the graveside oration:

"This place where we stand will henceforth be a place of pilgrimage. Now is the time for all the Irish people to unite behind the Republican Movement and make Patrick McManus's ideal a living reality." The following Easter (1959) a memorial was unveiled at the spot where Patrick was killed. Seán Cronin, recently released from jail in the Curragh Camp, performed the unveiling. And 1966, the 50th Anniversary year of the 1916 Rising, a memorial headstone was erected at Patrick's grave, and unveiled by Daithí Ó Conaill.

At the cemetery, I remember being profoundly impressed by the first two men who stepped out of the crowd of mourners, with liturgical dignity and solemnity, to begin filling in the grave with spades: Terry Baxter, Sr., Kinawley, and Jimmy Gilheaney, and Bellanaleck. I saw it as a wonderful and special act of solidarity (even though, of course, I would not have used that word in 1958)—but it is the perfect word for what those two men did. And from that moment, until now, I remember both men fondly and with great respect and gratitude. God rest their noble souls.

After Patrick's death, I naturally assumed I would stop playing football for an extended mourning period as was the custom then. But Fr. Fox—backed up by Fr. Gilmartin—with great pastoral wisdom, convinced my mother that I should continue playing. Now, of course, one could say he also wanted to win the upcoming final in Breffni Park. Either way, it was sound advice as football helped me to cope with our devastating loss.

Shortly after Patrick's death, I was playing in County Cavan on our joint Kinawley–Swanlinbar team. A fight started, and a general free-for-all ensued, with spectators storming the pitch, bringing the game to a halt. Frankie and a big lump of a lad got into a punch up. As they were pulled and held apart, another fellow, a non-player, from the edge of the crowd that had invaded the pitch, shouted at Frankie: "Your brother thought he was a tough guy and see what happened to him." Well, that did it. Up until then, I had not been really involved in the fracas as I was more focused on winning the game. I rounded on the fellow, who was probably about nineteen or older and charged with such fury that he took off running. I followed him to the corner of the field, where he was trapped. I let loose with the perfect upper cut (Rocky-Marciano-style against Jersey Joe Walcott) with my full body weight behind my punch, hitting him under the chin.[3] He went straight down on the flat of his back. Out for the count. Out cold.

I would hear much later that, ironically, his own family was very Republican, so the poor guy probably caught hell when he got home for disrespecting the name of an Irish patriot. I often wonder what became of him, and I wish him well wherever he is. The "big lump of a lad" would years later be parish priest in Derrylin and he and Frankie would be good friends.

Today, in his native parish of Kinawley–Swanlinbar, the esteem in which Patrick, the Irish patriot, is held is demonstrated by five public honors: the monument at his grave; a monument at the spot where he was killed; a monument at the end of Clonliff Lane, close to the Derrylin-Enniskillen road; a monument just across the border in Cavan; and the Kinawley GAA stadium, named "Patrick McManus Memorial Park." The stadium was officially opened on Sunday, August 26, 1984, and proudly attended by Patrick's mother, his six brothers, and two sisters. Mary Kate, who was then in New Zealand, could not make it.

Our family has always remained very proud of Patrick, regarding him as the quintessential Irish patriot. And even over sixty years later, when we are all together as a family, we can still get choked up and tearful when we talk about him.

CHAPTER 3

The Call

*An unfulfilled vocation drains the color
From a man's entire existence.*
Honoré de Balzac (1841)

ON MONDAY, SEPTEMBER 2, 1957, at age thirteen years and seven months, I began my less than illustrious career at St. Michael's School in Enniskillen, an all-Catholic school. Patrick Maguire started on the same date; Frankie had started in 1953. Myles, still only nine, continued at Drumbroughas. I would remain at that school until September 1960, when I went off to the Redemptorist Juvenate in Birmingham, England.

St. Michael's was run by the priests of the Diocese of Clogher, and I certainly do not owe my vocation to them because I did not like any of them, except Fr. Sean Clerkin. He was the only priest who called me aside to inquire about how my parents were doing after Patrick was killed. Imagine that! The place was full of priests, and yet they did not have the decency or pastoral concern to minister to a young boy deeply traumatized by his brother's death. They were more concerned about being politically correct—they did not want to be seen showing any sympathy to an "IRA-family." If my faith had depended on those priests, I would have become a crusading atheist or joined Paisley's emerging church. But my faith was grounded on my parent's example, on the Word of God and on the tradition and doctrine of the universal Catholic Church.

I am the first to admit that I was not a model student. My entire focus, apart from football, was chasing the fair girls at the convent school and fighting the "townies."

FIGHTING TOWNIES AND TEDDY BOYS

People may think the big divide in Northern Ireland was between Protestants and Catholics, but to me, in those days the big divide was between the townies and the country boys. The townies liked to see themselves as Teddy Boys—slicked-back hair combed like Elvis, leather jackets and tight blue jeans. I almost felt a moral obligation to "modify their thinking." There was one period I could not walk through the town without Frankie, who was a fearsome and mighty fighter. All the Teddy Boys were scared of his deadly right hand.

There was one fellow who was the epitome of the Teddy Boy and fancied himself as something of a legend. He was older than I was (I never fought anyone younger than myself) and for some inexplicable reason, he did not seem to fully appreciate my fine Kinawley qualities. He was determined to give me the mother of all beatings and equally determined to let everyone know about it.

Anyway, I knew I was going to be back in town on a Saturday (to celebrate my birthday, February 6th, which fell earlier in the week). So, in "High Noon" fashion, I made an appointment with my adversary in the Broad Meadows, then a public park by the water in Enniskillen. I had not told Frankie about it because I wanted to fight this battle on my own.

When I showed up, Mr. Teddy Boy was there with a group of townies all eagerly awaiting with evident relish the impending humiliation of this poor country boy from Kinawley. Mr.Teddy Boy began with a great display of bravado and showmanship, ducking this way and that, bobbing and weaving, doing the Ali shuffle even before it had been invented by Muhammad Ali—but in a mishmash of judo and heaven knows what. He would swipe at me with his right hand and then when I countered his swipe, he would duck immediately and try to grab my legs. Big mistake. I let him try it a few more times and then finally let him grab me by the hips. Then I reached over his bent back, as his head was rammed into my stomach, and I hoisted him up and held him in that position for quite a while demanding that he give up. He refused. I then carried him—in the same locked position, backside and heels up in the air—to a barbed-wire fence, hoisted him above it and held him about a foot above the wire. "Don't drop me," he pleaded, "these are the only pair of jeans I have." "You have only one pair (of something else) that you should be more worried about," I retorted (that's the cleaned-up version I use for my sisters). I had, of course, no intention of dropping him. But I found it hard not to laugh. There he was being held over a barbed-wire fence—his belly facing down close to the wire—and the only thing he was worried about was his blue jeans!

I asked him if he gave up; he said yes. I asked him to promise not to bother me again, and he did. So, I put him down, hurting neither him nor his blue jeans.

Another time, I was up on Fort Hill—a wooded town park in the middle of Enniskillen—standing up on a park bench waving to the girls in the Convent School. There was a hedge right in front of me. All of a sudden, I was pushed in the back and shot right into the hedge. When I got up, I saw a group of townies, bursting for a fight. One small skinny guy squared up to me. I knew I could knock him into the middle of next week, but I was concerned about the five or six other townies—especially one much older guy, with a totally bald head (when shaved heads were not in fashion). Baldy had a bit of a reputation, and he was sporting a studded belt, sure sign of a tough guy. I whispered to Patrick Maguire, "Go and get Frankie," and I played for time. The moment I saw Frankie's head appear over the brow of the hill, I said to my would-be slayer, "So, you want a piece of me, eh?" Just kidding; Kinawley boys didn't talk like that, at least in my day. But I did immediately light into him, and by the time Frankie arrived, my unworthy opponent was lying bleeding under a tree.

Baldy then challenged Frankie. Big mistake. Baldy pulled off his prized studded belt and with deliberate and ostentatious slowness began to wrap it around his fist, all the while looking hard and menacing. He must have thought our Frankie had been born yesterday, that Frankie would stand idly by and allow Baldy to arm himself. No way. Frankie charged him with a body slam, flattened him, grabbed his bald head and kept bouncing it up and down on the ground like a basketball until Baldy begged for mercy. Then we went back to class as if nothing had happened. But the word did go out: Don't mess with the Macs. And from then on, the townies left us alone.

Old St. Michael's Grammar School (L) and Convent School (R).

Out of all my fights, only one was with a Protestant, and it had nothing to do with sectarianism. Years later, in 1968, that same Protestant was at Matthew Mc Hugh's house, two fields below our home. I had just been ordained. He gestured up to our house and said, "So I hear Sean McManus got ordained?" Matthew proudly and enthusiastically affirmed it. And the Protestant man said: "He was the right cross hoor of a cub." Matthew, God rest him, would regale us with that story for years—and it got better with each telling. Our family loved Matthew. To us, he was the nicest and funniest man in Ireland. Yet he never told jokes, only "bits,"—funny anecdotes, which may or may not have "gained in the telling." We loved to see him come up for a cheilde (social visit) where he would light up the room with his "bits," which were never unkind. When we saw him tilt his head back and say, "I mind the time...," we all knew we were in for a classic Matthew story.

All this took place before my conversion to nonviolence, and none of it would have been approved by Martin Luther King, Jr. But even

Martin himself in his early days– during the Montgomery, Alabama, Bus Boycott (December 1, 1955—December 20, 1956)—had a gun. Bayard Rustin had to convince him to get rid of it, as it was a contradiction of Gandhi's nonviolence that Martin was propounding.[1]

I continued to be a poor student at St. Michael's and continued to chase the bonny Fermanagh lassies (and some from Tyrone and Cavan). But I was never sectarian. I dated bonny Protestant lassies, too. One of the girls would later join the Ulster Defense Regiment (UDR) and would be killed in an IRA attack on her barracks in the 1970s. I was deeply saddened to hear it.

BE STILL AND KNOW THAT I AM GOD (PSALM 46:10)

As the summer of 1960 progressed, a "small, still voice" kept whispering in my soul. There must be more to your life; you must commit yourself to a cause greater than yourself. I kept shutting it out. But finally, it got the better of me. I was coming home one night from Aunt Maggie's. The bike got a flat tire, and somehow, I didn't mind. It was a beautiful, starry night. I was walking along Graffey Lane, going up the brae at Phil Murphy's big house, staring at the stars. Suddenly, softly, sweetly, a feeling of transcendence swept over me. And in a split second, I knew I was being called to be a priest.

My next immediate realization was, "Sean, that means you will have to give up marriage, playing football and you will not be able to join the IRA and finish the job Patrick set out to do." It was a moment of total clarity, no drama, no thunderclaps, no gnashing of teeth. Just the profound peacefulness that comes when God makes the way clear. And, fundamentally, I have never looked back since that moment outside Phil Murphy's. I don't mean that there have not been ups and downs, nor that I have led a perfect Christian life. But I have never doubted my calling, despite my sins and failures.

In the Catholic tradition—at least up to that time—when a person had such a religious experience, it normally was seen as a call to the priesthood or the religious life. In the Protestant tradition, it is seen as "being born again"—a deeper commitment to Christ, but not necessarily a call to ministry. Well, of course, I had been "born again" at baptism, with water and the Holy Spirit, confirmed in the Spirit at Confirmation and nourished on the "Bread of Life and the Cup of Eternal Salvation" in the Holy Eucharist. So, to me, the only next step was the priesthood. Today, however, I am sure that some Catholics have similar experiences as I had but see it as a call to more closely follow Christ, but not a call to the priesthood or the religious life. I am sure there is a lot to be discussed and developed in this area of Catholic spirituality, but I will leave that to my big brother, Fr. Jim, the spiritual guru in the family.

I realized that I would have to give up Gaelic football because I knew I would naturally follow Jim and join the London Province of Redemptorists. Pus, there was that tradition: Ireland had already too many priests (little did we know how that would change), and anyway, it was heathen England that needed priests!

I never said a thing to Mother when I got home that night. I slept on it, and in the morning, it was still as clear as ever. So, I told Mother. She nearly fell off the chair with shock. My father seemed very pleased. I think Frankie took a pain in his side from laughing. But the transition period went very smoothly.

Jim, a student at this time in Hawkstone, the Redemptorist Major Seminary in Shropshire, made all the necessary contacts for me.

Off to England

Sean with Irish couple in Erdington Abbey parish who took him to a GAA game in Birmingham. 1960.

On Wednesday, September 28, 1960, Fr. Joe Hanton, CSsR, Director of the Juvenate, the minor seminary in Birmingham, wrote to me: "I am happy to inform you that you have been accepted as a candidate for the priesthood and ... you will be welcome to come to Erdington (a section of Birmingham) as soon as you can make arrangements." Thus began a whole new phase in my life.

It says something wonderful about the tradition that I was raised in that despite our absolute opposition to English rule in the North of Ireland, we never held it against the English people and never hesitated to minister to them, working for them without pay of any kind. Equally, it says something wonderful about the British Redemptorists for never holding Patrick against Jim and me. Sure, my activities, later on, would cause Charlie Shepherd serious heartburn, but that is a different issue from the point I'm making here.

I will never forget my voyage from Belfast to Liverpool. It was my first-time leaving Ireland and my first time on a ship. Although full of religious zeal, I was nonetheless homesick. On board, I was so relieved to see a Kinawley man, John Anderson. He gave me great advice: "Don't be frightened if you think your stomach is going to come out of your body when the sea gets rough——and it always does." Man, did it ever. I got as sick as a dog.

The following morning, I arrived in Liverpool, sleep-deprived and still sick, only to be confronted by what I thought was the terrible smell of Liverpool—my first sniff of a big city. My country nose could not take it. My spirits were buoyed when Jim met me at the train and accompanied me to Birmingham. Mary Kate, who was also in England, supported me by sending me money weekly.

My first culture shock in the Juvenate was the breakfast—fried bread and beans. Baked beans sloshed onto bread dipped in frying fat. The taste was abominable. And to make matters worse, we had to wash it down with coffee made from liquid from a bottle. Where were my porridge, my fresh egg, and my fadge (soda) bread? What barbarians had I come among?

There were about forty boys in the Juvenate. I went into the senior class and for the first time in my life hit the books and studied hard. Fr. James Mythen would soon amaze me by complimenting me on my Latin. In English Literature, we had to study Wordsworth. My teacher, Fr. Hanton, was not too good as he was just filling in and did not really know Wordsworth. But I knew who did—Master O'Shea back in St. Michael's, a lay teacher whom I liked. I wrote to him, told him I needed help to prepare for an exam and he wrote me a number of pages about how Wordsworth changed English poetry, by taking it out of its baroque setting into the open countryside, etc. I aced the exam, and I have never forgotten Master O'Shea who later became a priest himself. And, thus began my lifelong affection for Wordsworth, who after Shakespeare, is the most worthy of all the British writers.

I was delighted to discover in my Religious Knowledge class that I was far more advanced than anyone else.

I trained myself to wake up at night to say one Rosary, thereby completing the goal I had set myself of three rosaries per day—the Five Joyful Mysteries, the Five Sorrowful Mysteries, the Five Glorious Mysteries. (Pope John Paul II would later add the Five Luminous Mysteries in 2002).

I enjoyed the Juvenate, even though the change of lifestyle was quite dramatic. I knew the one thing that could quickly get me into trouble was my tendency to settle things with my fists. I was helped by the fact that I was one of the biggest and certainly the strongest boys in the Juvenate, and nobody would mess with me, and I knew I would never hit anyone younger or smaller than I.

Indeed, even when I was at home, I never hit anyone smaller, except if they had bullied Myles when they were much bigger than he was. Then my self-imposed law did not apply. To this day, Myles still recounts his alarm at the fact that Frankie and I left home around the same time—he to Belfast University, I to Birmingham. Suddenly, Myles was without defenders. But he would soon develop a formidable right hand of his own.

The other drastic change was football—no longer Gaelic but soccer. Yet I quickly got to like it while never mastering it. I played right-full-back. Later in Hawkstone, I would play in goals and really come into my own, just as Jim did.

Fr. McManus's parents, Celia and Patrick McManus (1929).

Patrick McManus, Fr. McManus' eldest brother, who was killed in 1958.

7-Aside Team. Back (l-r): Frankie, Patrick, Sean
Middle (l-r): Jim, Terence, Thomas. Front: Myles. Clonliff, 1956.

Author's Mother and three sisters (l-r): Alice, Celia, Mother, and Mary Kate. Clonliff, 1958.

Six brothers. Back (l-r): Myles, Terence, and Frankie; front (l-r): Sean, Thomas and Jim. Enniskillen, 1984.

Fr. McManus (far right) with his family (l-r): Myles, Frankie, Celia, Jim, Mary Kate, Alice. Kinnoull, Perth, Scotland, 2007.

CHAPTER 4

Kinnoull and Hawkstone Years

Prayer without study would be empty.
Study without prayer would be blind.
Karl Barth[1]

In September 1961, I went to the Redemptorist Novitiate in Saint Mary's Monastery, high up on Kinnoull Hill, Perth, Scotland. I pulled up in front of the monastery in a taxi. Gave a packet of cigarettes to the driver, saying. "I'll never use these here," and I never did.

The Novitiate, in those years, was a "religious boot camp"—a year of unrelenting self-discipline, penance, prayer, religious training, religious lectures, long periods of total silence and manual labor.

The Novice Master (in charge of spiritual formation) was Fr. Shepherd—the aforementioned Fr. Shepherd, who would later pack me off to America.

The monastery had a small farm and, when needed, I had to do the milking as I was the only novice with that skill. Brother John was the farmer, and I was utterly amazed to see him using gloves while making hay. My first thought was, "What would Daddy and Charles Murphy think of a man wearing gloves to use a pitchfork?" I was also amazed to see Brother John "ruck" the hay (build it in large cone-shaped stacks) while it was still damp. My father would have chased him out of the meadow, as you daren't ruck the hay until it was bone dry. "It will rot," I kept telling Brother John but, in fact, it turned out fine.

Once a year the novices were allowed a bus trip to St. Andrews, not to play at the famous golf course, but to spend a day at the gusty beach. As the bus took off from the Novitiate, the Rector of Kinnoull, Fr. Vincent Lucas, brother of the Provincial Fr. George Lucas, sat beside me and said, "So, Brother McManus, what part of Ireland are you from?"

"From British-occupied Ireland," I defiantly responded. He collapsed in laughter, as he thought it was the funniest thing he had ever heard. It was my first insight into how little the average Englishman knows about Britain's involvement in Northern Ireland.

Despite the Spartan regime, I loved the Novitiate and experienced a deep sense of spiritual tranquility ... no angst, no turmoil, no anguish.

Father's Death

But there was great sadness because my father died in January 1962. I was reading in the refectory from the pulpit- like dais (at evening meals the novices would take turns at reading aloud from some spiritual book to the entire community—the other novices, plus the priests who were giving Missions throughout Scotland). The Novice Master came over and asked me to stop, so I knew there was bad news. I had been aware that my father was failing. The Novice Master asked me to come outside the refectory and told me that my father was very ill and that I should prepare to go home immediately.

When I arrived home in Clonliff, I found my father near death. But I took great consolation in the way his eyes brightened up when he saw me, as he clearly recognized me. The last conscious action I saw him make was when he raised up his mouth to kiss the small crucifix I held to his lips. If dying a holy death, after leading a good life, is the supreme Christian goal, then my father surely went straight home to the Father, through Christ, by the power of the Holy Spirit and into Eternal Life. I spent about a week at home and then returned to the Novitiate.

In September 1962, after two weeks of intense retreat and total silence, which I never once broke, I took my First Vows with four others. My mother and a few of my family came for the event. Then, it was off to the pleasant fields of Shropshire for seven years at Hawkstone Hall, then the Redemptorist Major Seminary. (Later, Jim would develop it into a major international center for spirituality[2]).

HAWKSTONE

There were about forty students at Hawkstone. I loved all my seven years there and went after my studies with gusto, especially logic, philosophy, and theology. Most of the available books, of course, stuck rigidly to the abstract, non-historical, neo-scholastic line. Neo-Scholasticism was the philosophical theology that was taught in seminaries from 1860 until Vatican II. The *Encyclopedia of Catholicism* explains: "Neo-Thomism, in turn, is a development within neo-scholasticism, the revival of Scholastic, that is, medieval theology. Modern neo-Thomism (rarely discussed outside of Catholicism and mandated by papal documents like

Pope Leo XIII's encyclical *Aeterni Patris* of 1879) sought to transcend the Enlightenment and Reformation by proposing that the thought-world of medieval Scholasticism, and particularly that of Thomas Aquinas, could hold solutions to contemporary problems."[3]

The American theologian, Fr. Thomas F. O'Meara, OP, wonderfully recreates the atmosphere of those seminary days: "During my first week in the seminary [the Dominican seminary near Chicago] the professor introducing us to philosophy made[a] startling observation[s]: Everything a priest needed to know was found in the writings of Aristotle [384–322BC...During the first half of the twentieth century, most priests in America [and in Britain and Ireland, he could have added] received some neo-scholastic indoctrination in philosophy and theology. That simple philosophy with a black and white logic emphasized laws that had no exceptions: the laws of logic, administration of the church, abstract moral rules, and obscure rubrics for liturgy. The Church had somewhat exchanged the Gospel for Greek antiquity, and its Aristotelianism held no interest for scientific America or ordinary Catholics."[4]

Nonetheless, neo-scholasticism taught me how to reason logically and think analytically. And I have maintained an abiding reverence for the great St. Thomas Aquinas, whom we now know should not have been pigeonholed the way some neo-Thomists tried to do: "Many sought through Vatican power a monopolistic and dictatorial control over Catholic thinking, and, in the name of Thomism, warred against modern philosophy, science, and politics as well as ecumenism, vernacular liturgy and modern art. This monopoly of thought ended when Vatican II (1962–1965) affirmed modern biblical, patristic, systematic, and pastoral theologies, many of which were rooted in Aquinas' historical openness and positive depiction of God and humans."[5]

In time, I would come to realize that the best way to understand the change brought about by the Second Vatican Council was to see it in terms of a paradigm shift: a shift from classicism to historical consciousness—from a classicist to a historically conscious Weltanschauung (world view).

Classicism views reality in terms of the immutable, the never changing. It uses the deductive method of reasoning: from the universal to the particular. This is best illustrated by the following syllogism, which was taught in Scholastic logic to every student for the priesthood, up to the mid-1960s:

"All human beings are rational.
Seamus is a human being. Ergo
(therefore) Seamus is rational."

Classicism uses the deductive method of reasoning. It seeks conclusions that are always true, in all situations: if it was true in 1962, it is true in 2062. Historical consciousness uses the *inductive method* of reasoning: from the particular to the universal. The conclusions it reaches (from the ground up, so to speak) will be based on changing circumstances and history. It does not seek absolute, dogmatic certitude but settles for moral, practical certitude. Vatican II would attempt to explain the faith, not just hand down authoritarian decrees, as in the style of Vatican I (December 8, 1869–October 20, 1870)—the foundational style of teaching as opposed to the apologetic.

My greatest regret is that the Scripture classes were so poor. Most of the teachers were inadequate. In fact, Jim was the only really good teacher, and that is not a matter of standing up for my big brother. Every student would agree with me. Jim had been ordained on January 12, 1964. Most of the family, many of our relatives and neighbors from home came to Hawkstone for his ordination. It was a most special day in the life of our family. After ordination, Jim went to Rome for further study for four years. He taught Moral Theology for my last year in Hawkstone.

Despite the poor quality of the teachers, Jim excepted, it was still a great time to be embarking on theological training.

Vatican II started on October 11, 1962, and soon seminarians would no longer have to be taught in Latin or read the Divine Office in Latin, the Mass could be said in English, the "new theology" would emerge, etc.

It was really an exciting time—the ecclesiastical version of the Sixties! But no long hair, no dope, and no sex.

EUCHARIST, LUTHER, AND PIUS IX

Eucharistic theology became my particular interest, and I have kept up my study of this subject over the years. While I have always been prepared to question Church teaching on a variety of subjects, I've always been very careful on Eucharistic Doctrine which is, in a uniquely special way, the ultimate responsibility of the Magisterium. Get the Eucharist wrong, and you get the Church wrong—and vice versa. The age-old maxim nails it: "The Eucharist makes the Church and the Church make the Eucharist."

But I also came to believe that every good Catholic needs a good dose of Protestantism. So, I developed a great interest in Martin Luther and his "Justification by Faith alone." I soon came to believe that Rome and he were just talking at cross-purposes and that, as in all fights, as the rhetoric heated up, the positions unnecessarily hardened when a resolution was possible. Fr. Shepherd (yes, the same, now the Rector at Hawkstone, and the teacher of Church history) cautioned me about my enthusiasm for the heretic Luther. It was, therefore, a very happy and emotional day for me when, over thirty years later, I attended the National Cathedral (Episcopal) in Washington in 1999, to celebrate the signing of The Joint Declaration on Justification by the Vatican and the World Lutheran Federation. Yet, for me, the occasion was tinged with sadness as I reflected on how easy it is for leaders to change, leaving their followers hung out to dry: "Oops, it was all a misunderstanding, now let's move on."

I was also very disappointed that the historic Joint Declaration did not receive proper attention. For goodness' sake, here was the wedge issue, the leading cause of the Reformation being essentially agreed on by the Pope and the Lutherans, yet Northern Ireland, of all places, did not give it due attention. What's wrong with that picture?

Fr. Shepherd even taught the notorious Syllabus of Errors, issued by Pope Pius IX in conjunction with his encyclical *Quanta Cura* (How Much Concern) (1864) as if they were revealed truth, instead of being, in part, the paranoid fears of an emotionally unbalanced pope. Among other things, they condemned freedom of conscience, freedom of religion, freedom of speech and the separation of Church and State. And here Scottish theologian, Fr. Fergus Kerr, OP, is not far off the mark when he says, "The history of twentieth-century Catholic theology is the history of the attempted elimination of theological modernism, by censorship, sackings, and excommunication ..."[6]

However, I have other issues with Pope Pius IX. On January 12, 1870, at the urgings of the British government and sycophantic Irish Bishops, Pius IX excommunicated the Fenians, not only in Ireland but also in America: "The American or Irish society called Fenian," as the decree of condemnation put it.[7] Had Pope Pius IX condemned the Fenians because he believed in the philosophy of nonviolence, that would have been a different matter. But that Pope did not believe in nonviolence. He had his own papal armed force, and he had earlier called on Irishmen to come and fight for his Papal States. Hundreds of Irishmen—including Fenians—answered his call. So, it was OK for Irishmen to fight for the Papal States, but it was a sin for them to fight for Ireland. Years later in Washington, I would write to the Papal Nuncio objecting to the proposed canonization of this anti-Fenian, anti-semitic and anti-freedom pope.

But my reading in Hawkstone was not just Scholastic. I set out to read all the great Irish writers, starting with Edna O'Brien. I read James Joyce's *Ulysses* three times in Hawkstone. These books were still on the forbidden index, but a traveling library (a van) would come regularly to the end of the Hawkstone road, and I would go out there to meet it each week. No matter how hard I tried, I could not make head or tail of *Finnegans Wake*. William Trevor became one of my favorite Irish writers.

FROM GAA TO SOCCER

Life at Hawkstone was not just all spiritual and intellectual for me. We played soccer three times a week and had some fine players. After Jim left, I took his place in goals and was in my element. I could soar like an eagle and catch the ball knowing none of the other players could touch it with their hands (except the other goalie at the far end of the pitch), and that no big bruiser from Derrylin would be spoiling my catch. In this way, the Gaelic footballer was in heaven playing goalie in soccer. It spoiled you rotten. However, diving on the ball at the players' feet was a skill that had to be mastered. When I first saw Jim do it in Hawkstone, I was amazed and wondered how he could do it without getting his skull split open. But I soon got the hang of it. In the latter years, we were allowed to play "outside" (non-seminarians) teams.

I remember once a local team came to play us at Hawkstone. I could tell immediately that they had a condescending attitude to "us monks," that they thought we were a crowd of sissies ... and that they had an anti-Catholic attitude (my Northern Ireland background gave me an unerring nose for that).

They were several years older than we were, and they clearly thought they were masters of the game.

In the first minutes of the game, the ball came into me, and I charged out to get it. One of their forwards blatantly jumped into me with both knees. When I cleared the ball, I turned to him, and for the first time in years I reverted to type—to the Kinawley footballer—and told him: "Do not come back like that again." He sniggered and replied, "Every time, mate."

The ball soon came back in at chest level. At this level, the goalie has a great advantage from the point of physical contact (although the invading forward has the opportunity to take a low ball away from you). I saw our friend charge me and, as I grabbed the ball firmly to my chest, I swung my left shoulder hard to meet him. I knocked him a couple of feet off the ground, landing him flat on his back. His fellow-forward roared at me, "You're supposed to be a preacher." I replied, "And I have given him a sermon he'll remember for the rest of the game." And he did too. He never came near me for the rest of the game.

Well, we went on to beat them in a ridiculous fashion, 7–nil. They were the worst team I had ever seen in my life—absolutely hopeless. All hat and no cattle. Now to be fair, they were probably up late drinking beer the night before and rejoicing how they would thrash "the monks." None of our team smoked or drank. We were young and fit, and we sent them "homeward, tae think again."[8] One thing is certain, none of them were ever recruited by Manchester United.

From Pioneer to Poteen Maker

The students did not drink alcohol, except for a glass of very ordinary wine with meals on special and rare feast days. Ironically, I was a Pioneer (had taken the pledge not to drink) until I arrived in Hawkstone. When the newly professed novices arrived from the Novitiate at Hawkstone, the tradition was to give them a glass of sherry. I was told that my religious vows superseded all other pledges and that I could break my pledge. I would later come to see that as "religious imperialism" and always regretted breaking my Pioneer Pledge. (In 1988 I redeemed my pledge and stopped drinking completely).

But while in Hawkstone, I became a winemaker, and a moonshiner—a maker of poteen!

There was an elderly couple that lived on the Hawkstone property in an old gatehouse to the former Victorian mansion that Hawkstone was. My mother used to stay there when she came to visit Jim and me. One day the man of the house served Mother and me a glass of white wine. It was delicious. I had never tasted anything like it. "What is that, Harry?" I inquired. "It's rhubarb wine," he replied, "and if you like it, wait till you taste my elderberry wine," I asked him where he had got it. "Made it myself," he said proudly.

I was instantly hooked. Not on the wine, but on vinification, the process of making wine. I picked Harry's brain, and he was only too pleased to enlighten me. I went back to the monastery and immediately went to see the Rector, then Fr. Nolan, who was originally from Dublin. (He was a wonderful man, and I had huge respect for him. Years later, he would pass on to me, through a trusted courier, Jim, an IRA belt that was used in the GPO in 1916. It is a brown leather belt with a heavy brass buckle, which is inscribed with Óglaigh na h-Éireann, "soldiers of Ireland." The other end of the belt, also brass that inserts into the buckle has a harp embossed on it.) In retrospect, I now see that my visit to Fr. Nolan was my first lobbying job. I proposed to him that he give me permission to start making homemade wine to be used on Feast Days ... that there was a long tradition of monasteries doing so, and that we had a very fine, classically built wine cellar. In fact, the wine cellar was so good that even Winston Churchill wanted to buy Hawkstone for that reason alone but could not afford the taxes. (After the Second World War, a lot of the great mansions were bought by religious or educational institutions because individuals could no longer afford them).

Fr. Nolan, in his great voice and with a trademark slap of his hands, said it was a splendid idea and told me to go right ahead. Thus my life as an oenologist (wine "expert") began. At that stage, I had no idea of trying to make poteen and so had not mentioned it to Fr. Nolan. Anyway, there was no way he could give me permission to do something that was, ahem, well, not quite legal.

I began as I always begin: by studying the subject. I got dozens of books from my friendly traveling library at the end of Hawkstone lane and boned up on the quite surprisingly popular English tradition of brewing homemade wine.

I scoured the countryside looking for the right containers. In an antique shop in Shrewsbury, I ferreted out three amazing five- gallon pottery vats, like something out of Sinbad the Sailor. The vats, wide at the bottom, tapered into narrow necks—perfect for my mission. I fermented (the science of which is called zymology) rhubarb and elderberries, separately, in my prized vats and after the allotted time, I drained the contents, put in isinglass to bring all the impurities to the top, and tied the opening off tightly with a heavy cloth.

At the appropriate time, I bottled the wine, put it safely away in one large cubicle in the wine cellar, built a little door and put it all under lock and key. I would occasionally check the door to make sure none of my brothers-in-Christ had been tempted. None of them were. In due time, the wine was served to great acclaim.

Now the great philosophers teach us that knowledge should always be progressing and advancing. So, in that grand tradition, I says to meself: I wonder how poteen is made. Wouldn't it be a worthy project to make it, purely for the science of it, you understand?

So, I wrote to Frankie and asked him to find out the recipe and to mail it to me. There was no tradition in Clonliff of making poteen. If you wanted it, you had to go to the law-breakers across the river in Knockninny–Derrylin.

Frankie duly wrote back to me with the recipe, warning me to drink only the most "infinitesimal amount" (the actual words, I still remember). In fact, I drank only two teaspoonfuls.

Then began my second scouring of the countryside. How to find a "still" (the pot or container used for distilling poteen), without calling it that? Again, my Guardian Angel led me to a shop in Shrewsbury that had the perfect container: a five-gallon copper pot with an airtight lid. (One needs a copper pot to avoid the danger of poisoning. Even though the big bruisers in Derrylin used tar-barrels).

Then I would need to solder a copper pipe or tube, with a small opening, into the still. That was no bother. But how to make the copper pipe into a "worm"—the coiled pipe, in which the vapor would be cooled and condensed, under cold running water? That stumped me. Now, bear in mind there was no Internet in those days, and I could not go around asking people for help in making a still. Only one other person knew about my secret project. Finally, I turned to a man I admired and trusted—Eddie Corish. He had been a Brother in the Irish Province and as an older man decided to become a Redemptorist priest in the London Province.

Eddie was a man for all seasons, deeply spiritual but with a very practical mechanical bent. "How can I, Eddie, twist this copper pipe into a coil without closing the air flow?" "Very simple," responded the intrepid Eddie. "Fill it with sand and twist it around a metal bar, horizontal to the ground, then shake the sand out." "You are a genius, Eddie," says I.

My first attempts did not work out too well. I started with the normal Irish method, fermenting potatoes. But I soon discovered it was much easier and far better to distill the rhubarb wine. It was a real thrill to see the first bubble of distilled liquid shyly emanate from the end of the worm, linger a moment, then gently plop into the container below. To add to the thrill, I ran my still in an unused room next to the room of the Professor of Moral Theology (not Jim) who was totally unaware. Unlike the big bruisers from Derrylin who used a turf fire in the bogs to do their distilling, I used a little gas stove. I sent a bottle of the poteen to Terence in London, and he told me it was the best he had ever tasted.

I kept four bottles of poteen in my room—and never touched it—waiting for Christmas. After Christmas dinner, I invited a select few whom I knew I could trust, and who regarded themselves as guys who could hold their drink, to a classroom at the back of the building. I produced a bottle, and quoting my older brother Frankie, cautioned them to only consume the "most infinitesimal amount." I demonstrated its potency by first putting some in a teaspoon and setting it alight. I poured each person less than half a shot. Some sipped it straight; some drank it with orange juice. I demonstrated my caution by only sipping two teaspoonfuls. Then they claimed I had exaggerated the strength of the poteen and called for a refill. I remonstrated with them again, but George said, "Enough of the Irish baloney [or some such word that implied the Irish like to exaggerate], Sean, give us more poteen." So, I relented.

Now, the classroom that was doing double duty as a monastic shebeen was about three lengths of a football field—up a long corridor, past the individual rooms of the revelers—from the students' common room. We knew we had to be there before too long as that was the only night, Christmas night, that the Rector would visit our common room—which was very large, with a stage, billiard ball table, TV, etc. The Rector now was Fr. Shepherd (yes, *that* Fr. Shepherd). On the way up the corridor, I lost five of the lads who "could hold their drink." They went down like logs, and I had to carry them to their beds.

I went into the common room and Fr. Shepherd was sitting in a large circle talking to the students. I took my place, wondering what had happened to Pat. He had not fallen down, so, where was he? I didn't have to wait long. Pat was seen as an ascetic, who spent long hours in prayer. He had Bedouin blood in him. In a short time, the bold Pat burst into the common room, still dressed in his habit but with a white bath towel wrapped around his head, Bedouin-style, and without further ado exploded into a Bedouin dance for about ten minutes. I was sure our game was up, that Charlie Shepherd would be on to us, but there he was doubled over, convulsed in laughter, like everyone else, at the extraordinary spectacle.

When I was leaving Hawkstone, I destroyed the still and refused to pass on my esoteric skills as a moonshiner. I was scared if it was done wrongly, it could poison someone. Thus, ended my career as a poteen-maker, a bootlegger. I was about to say that I had never touched the stuff again, but I did.

In 1977, the American Ancient Order of Hibernians (AOH) was holding its convention in Killarney. I was traveling down from Fermanagh to it and stopped overnight in the home of a high-up Republican and teetotaler. I had a terrible, awful cold, with my chest totally congested. I worried about how I could make the convention. To my amazement, this teetotaler, who was regularly raided and harassed by the Special Branch, produced a bottle of the illegal substance. He made me a very large hot toddy, told me to drink it all down, and in the morning, I would be as right as rain. And, honest to goodness, when I woke up the following morning, it was if my cold had been a dream. It was gone completely, no congestion, no cough, and I felt terrific! No wonder poteen was the universal cure for farm animals in those days in my part of County Fermanagh.

OLD–IRA FATHER CONFESSOR

The Sam Browne belt that Fr. Nolan had passed on to me was not the only Hawkstone connection with IRA history. There was a much closer link—a living, breathing one: the students' Confessor, the saintly Fr. Liam Pilkington (1894–1977). "Pilkie" as we affectionately called him, had been the Commandant of the Third Western Division, IRA, who took the Republican side in the Civil War. In 1924, he joined the Redemptorists in the English Province. In his seventies, he became the Confessor for the students. We would line up at his door, and when my turn would come he would say, "Come on in, Brother McManus and I'll clean your skillet (absolve your sins)."

He never talked about his IRA years (1913–1924) except to Jim and me. When he used to talk to me, after a while, his hands would shake, as is common with many old soldiers, and he would end the conversation. He knew Liam Mellows, who swore him into the Irish Republican Brotherhood (IRB), Michael Collins, Éamon de Valera, etc.

I think he was a bit prudish. He said he was appalled by Collins' bad language, "The foulest mouth of any man he ever knew." And he never politically forgave de Valera. On one occasion Dev went to Cape Town, South Africa, where Pilkie was stationed at the time. Dev went to the monastery to see him, but Pilkie refused to meet him. He always believed that they did not need to sign the Treaty (that lead to the partition of Ireland), that they could have kept fighting because they were at their very strongest. Yet he mentioned that years later as a priest when he was someplace in England, walking around "acres and acres of munitions" he thought to himself, "We must have been mad to think we could beat them."

He showed me a prayer book (which I wished I had got) that was given to him when he was a political prisoner by the Catholic chaplain, an English priest. Pilkie had told him that when Ireland was free, he was going to become a priest. The chaplain jokingly inscribed it: "May you achieve the goal you desire, instead of the gaol [deliberate old English spelling] you deserve." Pilkie still got a great kick out of that and would smile with delight.

Sometimes in Hawkstone, Pilkie used to preside at the "preaching academy"—weekly, a student had to preach a memorized sermon from an approved source, in front of all the other students, while an older, experienced priest would sit in to evaluate the performance. Well, one day it was my turn to "preach." I had memorized a sermon and had entitled it "The Last Day by Father James Joyce." (In fact, it was my own editing of Joyce's famous "sermon" by the Retreat Master in *A Portrait of the Artist as a Young Man*—hardly an "approved" source, as Joyce was still on the Index, the list of books banned by the Church.) My thinking was that these English blokes would not recognize Joyce's "sermon." But, ah man, didn't Pilkie come in to preside over my sermon? There was nothing, however, I could do but plough ahead as I had nothing else prepared. So, I gave the sermon, announcing that the author was Fr. James Joyce:

> The last day had come. The doomsday was at hand ...And lo, the supreme judge is coming! No longer the lowly Lamb of God, no longer the meek Jesus of Nazareth, no longer the Man of Sorrows, no longer the Good Shepherd, He is seen now coming upon the clouds, in great power and majesty, attended by nine choirs of angels, angels and archangels, principalities, powers and virtues, thrones and dominations, cherubim and seraphim, God Omnipotent, God Everlasting. He speaks and His voice is heard even at the farthest limits of space, even in the bottomless abyss. Supreme Judge, from His sentence there will be and can be no appeal ...

On the way back, I walked down the corridor with Pilkie, and he told me it was the best sermon on The Last Day he had ever heard in his life. He then asked me about the "priest" who had written it (he clearly had not connected "Fr. Joyce" with *the* James Joyce). I certainly was not going to tell a lie to my confessor, so I leveled with him. I thought he was going to have a heart attack. "That blackguard," he hissed. "He was as bad as Yeats, who couldn't believe in Jesus Christ but did believe in fairies." And with that, he turned on his heel and strode off in righteous exasperation, his military step more pronounced than usual.

I was ordained on September 1, 1968. That was another very special day for our family, most of whom came to the Ordination with relatives and neighbors from Kinawley.

Our class stayed on in Hawkstone until the following summer, finishing our studies. Then it was off to Bishop's Stortford in Hertfordshire, southeast England, for our Second Novitiate—a six-month period for writing sermons for the parish missions. Even this quiet town had an IRA connection. In 1953, Cathal Goulding and Seán Mac Stíofáin, each of whom would later become Chief of Staff of the IRA, were arrested there with a van-load of weapons stolen from "the officers training corps armory of Felsted School in Essex."[9]

Our class then went to different areas. I first went to Birmingham, back to Erdington Abbey, and then to the Redemptorist House in Liverpool, as part of a Parish Missions team. I preached missions and school retreats in a number of places in England and Scotland, thinking this was what I would be doing for the rest of my life. I had no idea what lay ahead.

CHAPTER 5

The Troubles Come Back to Haunt

But just as I thought I was out, they pull me back in.[1]

MEANWHILE, I HAD BEEN KEEPING AN EYE on the developing political situation in Northern Ireland. Civil rights marches had begun in 1968 only to be met, inevitably and predictably, by the brute forces of the deeply sectarian and anti-Catholic State that the British government had violently and undemocratically created in 1920. **(For more detail, please see Appendix B).**

This artificial State had a two-fold purpose: to ensure a continuation of Britain's foothold on the island of Ireland and to place the Unionists/Loyalist/Protestants in a permanent position of supremacy. Protestant supremacy would be guaranteed by discrimination, repressive legislation and a deeply sectarian and bigoted police force, the RUC and their auxiliaries, the B Specials. The "credit" for this masterstroke goes to Winston Churchill who in July 1920 posed the question, "What if the Protestants in the six counties were given weapons and ... charged with maintaining law and order and policing the country?" The British government then proceeded to set up the new police force and recruited the Ulster Volunteer Force (a fascist Protestant militia that had threatened armed rebellion against the Crown) wholesale into it.[2]

The peaceful, nonviolent marches were beaten off the streets by Protestant mobs, incited by the demagoguery of Protestant politicians and clergymen, and facilitated by the RUC and the B Specials. Think Bull Connors and his racist police "keeping uppity blacks in their place" in Birmingham, Alabama, in 1963, and you've essentially got the picture. In 1969, Bombay Street, a Catholic street in Belfast, was burned out by mobs, while the police looked on and the B Specials participated in the burning.

From the outset, my brother Frank was in the thick of the civil rights struggle, becoming chairman of the Fermanagh Civil Rights Association. On June 18, 1970, he was elected, as Unity Candidate, MP for Fermanagh and South Tyrone. For the next four years, he was hardly out of the news, and never out of danger. On January 18, 1971, he was jailed for six months for leading a proscribed civil rights march. In May 1971 there was a national census in Britain and Northern Ireland, and the Catholic community, including a number of priests and teachers, refused to comply with the census in order to protest against the corruption of the judicial process and the systematic violation of human and civil rights.

Meanwhile, I was tormented by all of this. I was safe in Liverpool and feeling guilty. Women and children were putting their lives on the line while I was safe and secure preaching from nice, cozy pulpits all across England—the country responsible for the injustices in Northern Ireland. But what could I do? Hadn't I abandoned all patriotic duty when I became a Redemptorist? Wasn't there the cardinal Redemptorist rule, that a young priest did not rock the boat—on anything?

Some may find it hard to understand why it was so difficult for a young priest to speak out in those days. As I look back now, I even find it hard to believe it myself. But the ecclesiastical, religious climate then was almost cult-like in its control on individuals and in the blind obedience it demanded. "Blind obedience" was seen as following the will of God. But what if God was not blind to injustice? (God "is a God of justice", Isaiah 30:6 and "hates injustice," Isaiah 61:8).

What if God demands of all his followers, especially priests, to work for justice? ("This is what Yahweh asks of you: only this, to do justice, to love tenderly, and to walk humbly with your God." Micah 6:8).

How could the Catholic Church wash its hands of "the Irish problem"? What if silence in the face of injustice is complicity with that very injustice?

Census Protest in Britain

I knew I could not live in denial. After much prayer and the most serious reflection I had ever done since my decision to become a priest, I decided not to comply with the census. I released the following statement (which, on reading now, does not seem that much of a big deal but it was for me at that time):

> "I have refused to cooperate with the census. I have refused to fill in the form sent to me. I have done so as a means of protest against the general injustices perpetrated by the Unionist Government in the North of Ireland. More specifically, it is a protest against the Northern Ireland judiciary who blatantly apply a double standard in the administration of justice: one of ridiculous leniency for the Unionists; and one of vigorous severity for the non-Unionists. The latter is exemplified not only in the well-known cases of my brother, Frank McManus, M.P. and of Frank Gogarty, Vice Chairman of the Civil Rights Association, but also in numerous recent but less publicized convictions.
>
> I want this carefully considered gesture of mine to be an expression of solidarity with those priests and teachers and others in the North of Ireland who have taken similar action. The fact that I lived in Britain and received a somewhat different census than the one issued

in the North of Ireland does not negate or diminish the intelligibility of my protest, because—to state the painfully obvious—Britain and the North of Ireland are not unconnected. Moreover, the above-mentioned people in the North of Ireland are not opposed to the census in itself; they are, like me, simply using it as a means of protest.

I want to make it perfectly clear that I am not opposed to the census. I neither resent nor do I object to any single question asked in the census form which I received. I find it perfectly reasonable. In fact, I consider it a social necessity, and I truly regret that I am forced to refuse my cooperation.

Furthermore, because I am a priest, I find it embarrassing that I should have to make such a public protest ... but then a Christian conscience or sense of justice is not always a comfortable commodity."

I was the only priest in Britain—indeed, the only person in Britain, period—to make such a protest. The papers gave it small coverage. But poor Charlie Shepherd reacted as if I had called for the abolition of both the Papacy and the Monarchy. He telephoned me in utter panic and told me to pack my bag and go immediately to Kinnoull. I did. (I had to wait 44 years to fully discover the chain of events my simple protest set in motion. And how a fellow Redemptorist turned informer and enlisted the help of the racist Enoch Powell to oppose me. For more details, see **Appendix C**.)

On May 18, Frankie was released from prison, saying defiantly that it didn't do him "a damn bit of harm"—in the sense that it had not intimidated him in the slightest, as the authorities had hoped.

Frankie then set his wedding to the fair Carmel Doherty of Lisnaskea, County Fermanagh, for August 11, 1971, and asked me to perform the ceremony, as Jim had a few years earlier performed Terence's wedding.

Two days before the planned wedding, on August 9, 1971, the British government reintroduced their favorite weapon for keeping uppity Catholics in their place: internment, imprisonment without charge or trial.

Frankie was sure he would be interned, but he was determined to get married first. I drove him over the border to a safe house in Swanlinbar the night before. He came back the following day for his wedding in Lisnaskea. The British did not arrest him—perhaps they thought it would be stretching it a bit, even for them, to intern a Member of Parliament. Frank left for London on his honeymoon, and to attend parliament to condemn the introduction of internment.

Anti-Internment Protest and Arrest

On August 13, a large march was quickly organized in Enniskillen to protest against internment. Naturally, Terence, Jim, Myles, and my brother-in-law, Michael Ferguson attended. And so did I.

The RUC and British Army were clearly out for blood. They bullied and harassed the peaceful crowd and inevitably the young men were not going to take it. A riot broke out. Tear gas was fired into the crowd. I did my best to calm things down, even pulling a brick from the hand of a very agitated young man from Kinawley, whom I knew well, now deceased.

Then I spotted a group of RUC men laying into another young guy. I went over and said, "Come on now, there is no need for that" and non-violently interposed my body between the young man and his police attackers, as I had read the civil right activists in the American Deep South had been taught to do.

An eyewitness to my arrest, Martin O'Brien, who would later become a reporter and producer for the BBC, recounted in the Fermanagh Herald: "Then, Fr. Sean McManus CSsR who had ben trying to restrain the crowd was arrested."3 (Later in court the policeman who arrested me alleged I had broken his hold on a person he was arresting. That was not the case. Furthermore, had I wanted to use physical force, it is not his "hold" I would have broken!)I was immediately arrested, which I did not resist, and frogmarched to a police van. I was unceremoniously dumped into the van, landing on a young lad crying on the floor.

Immediately, another young man whom I could not properly see, as the inside of the van was dark, gave me a black beret and asked me if I would keep it because if it was found on him, the police would use it as "proof" that he was in the IRA. I put the beret in my pocket.

The next thing, my young brother Myles was tossed in on top of me. Eventually, the van took off for the nearby Enniskillen Barracks. It was somehow obstructed and had to stop, and the two policemen jumped out of the front. Suddenly, the back door of the police van was swung open with a mighty heave. Big brother Terence, always the rescuer of his younger brothers, commanded: "Out yous get."

With that, several young lads bounded like hares out of the van. I grabbed Myles and stopped him from jumping out, in case it would only make matters worse for him. It is an action I have often questioned. Could he have gotten away, free and clear? Overall, I doubt it. It is almost certain the police knew who he was and that is why they had arrested him. Even if they did not know him, they would have quickly found out because of the informers and agents they had interspersed throughout the crowd. Then they would probably have put out a warrant for Myles' arrest for escaping from police custody, thereby increasing the seriousness of the charge. Myles then might have been tempted to slip across the border, and in no time would have been on the most wanted list, not because he was a member of the IRA but because he was a brother of the local MP, Frank, whom they took glee in harassing.

And of course, had Terence been caught freeing the prisoners, he would have been in serious trouble. Eventually, the police van made it to the barracks. When I walked into the holding room, there were dozens of young men lined up before a policeman sitting at a makeshift desk in the middle of the room, taking down statements. Now I was glad I had been arrested as I could see someone had to stand up for these worried young lads. In a very loud, commanding voice (well trained by years of elocution in Hawkstone) I said, "Do not tell them anything until you are first advised of your rights." That seemed to steady the young men, and they all looked relieved, as the room fell silent. Then a short, mean-looking British soldier, in full infantry regalia (I think), got in my face and pulled me over to the corner of the room. He was the very embodiment of Synge's "loosed khaki cutthroat."[4] Sticking his finger in my face, and glaring up at me, he spat, "You have no rights, and that's what's killing you." I told him that though he had no idea, he was doing it, he had just summed up British rule in Ireland—we had no rights, and it was killing us. He gasped and stared at me helplessly.

I then said, "Now you come with me," and motioned to him to follow me back to the policeman behind the desk. I said to him, "This soldier tells me we have no rights, is that right? Do you agree with him?" The RUC man had the decency to lower his head and not say a word. It was very clear who was in charge—the British Army, not the police. I had been told once before by another Englishman that I had no rights. In my last year in Hawkstone, while I was ordained, I went to see the Prefect of Students, Barty Meehan, to ask if we could stay up to watch an Irish film on TV (I think it was *The Informer* or *Shake Hands with the Devil*). Barty said no. I pressed the case and said we should have the right to watch it. "As a Redemptorist, you have no rights. You gave them all up when you took your vows."

I was beginning to get fed up with Englishmen telling me I had no rights.

At 2.00 a.m., the police tossed me out on the street, not caring that my home was eight miles away. I would later learn from my study of the Black Freedom Struggle in the U.S. that it was a favorite tactic of the racist police—dump the blacks on the street late at night and tip off the Ku Klux Klan. But before I left the barracks, I got—or so I thought—the assurance from the Enniskillen RUC Chief Inspector, H. J. Currie, who had been previously stationed in Kinawley, that neither Myles nor any of the other young lads arrested would be mistreated. Nonetheless, after I left, the police would point their guns through the spyhole in the door of Myles' cell, and say, "Shall we shoot him now, or later?" They would keep switching the lights on and off, go into the cell and give him a good whacking. That went on throughout the night. Remember, this was only at the start of the Troubles. Can you imagine what the police did when the Catholic community really rose up in rebellion, and when they captured actual members of the IRA, which Myles was not? The following morning, Myles was brought to court, fined and released.

Meanwhile, while the rioting was still going on and while Myles and I were still at the barracks, Frankie got a telephone call in London from the wife of a local Catholic politician: "Come home, Frank, the town's in flames, and ALL your family has been arrested." Hell of a way to begin a honeymoon.

One of my in-laws, an elderly lady, on learning that her priest-relative had been arrested by the hated RUC, flew into a righteous rage and declared that the arm of the arresting officer (a Constable Frederick Scott) would "rot from the shoulder down" and to back up her prediction she quoted scripture: "Touch not my anointed..." (1 Chronicles 16:22). Who says Catholics don't know their Bible? I hope Constable Scott did not lose his arm. I often wonder what happened to him and I wish him well.

The British soldiers and the RUC did not scare me, but Charlie Shepherd did. What would he do now that I had been arrested in a riot situation? He would certainly have no precedence to go on as I was almost certainly the only Redemptorist from the English Province to have been arrested.

I Refuse to Recognize the Court

I returned to Kinnoull and waited to hear from the police. I was summoned to appear in the Enniskillen Magistrates Court on September 6, 1971, charged with "obstructing a Constable in the due execution of his duty." When the Resident Magistrate, Mr. John W. Adams, asked me how I pleaded, I responded: "I do not recognize the authority of the court." Fighting words and a characteristic tactic of the IRA.

The Magistrate imposed a fine of £20 to be paid in fifteen days and, "in default of payment to be imprisoned in the Prison of Belfast for the period of three months unless the said sum be sooner paid." I also refused to pay the fine.

I had not told my brother Frankie, who sat with me, that I was going to refuse to recognize the Court. I did not want to implicate him so that he could truthfully tell the media that he was not involved in my decision. I was also concerned that there was some parliamentary rule in the House of Commons which the British could use to expel Frankie for being complicit in such "treasonable" language.

I had, however, given an advance copy of my statement to Sinn Féin's office in Dublin for release the moment the hearing was over. My statement got wide coverage. *The Irish Times* not only wrote a report on the court hearing but also printed my lengthy statement, word for word, which, given the history of that paper, amazed me. My statement was as follows:

> [I] refused to recognize the Court because it has no legitimate authority. But that is only the tip of the iceberg. I do not, I never have, and I never will recognize the colonial State of British Occupied Ireland. This State exists because of a morally and politically criminal action. It was illegally imposed by force, and it is illegally sustained by force, against the will of the Irish people. Therefore, its institutions, its laws, and its legal and political expressions are invalid.
>
> The creation and maintenance of this State blatantly violate God's laws and the natural law, because its fundamental principle is "ownership by the right of conquest," i.e., ownership through violence and the gun, and by violence and the gun it is maintained. And those who created it, and those who sustain it, are the real men

of violence—they are the gunmen, they alone are the terrorists

This terrorist State I reject in its entirety. I reject in particular its judiciary. In principle it is illegitimate, in practice, it has a despicable record of injustice, corruption, and sectarianism.

Refusing to recognize the court is the policy of the Irish Republican army. I will immediately be suspected of being in sympathy with the IRA. Well, let's clear up this "suspicion." I want to state publicly and unequivocally that I am in sympathy with the IRA. Indeed, sympathy is too weak a word.

Many people may wonder why I should want to publicly proclaim my convictions. The answer is simple. My conscience forbids me to be silent, and if I did not now speak out, I could never live with myself because for the rest of my life I would know that I had been a coward ... no matter how hard I tried to justify my silence as prudence. I would know that I had been deceitful and treacherous to the patriots who were sacrificing their lives for the freedom of Ireland. I cannot join them in the fight for the freedom of my country, but the very least I can do is to speak up for them when they are being slandered and vilified by unscrupulously vicious propaganda.

The oppressors of Irish freedom call the IRA terrorists and murderers, but I call them by their proper titles: I call them freedom fighters, I call them heroes, and I venerate their dead as martyrs for Ireland. And I know that any true Irishman or indeed any informed, honest and fair-minded person thinks and feels the same way.

I could not live with myself if by my silence, I traitorously stabbed these patriots in the back. I abhor the deceit and hypocrisy that condemns these men and women who are sacrificing lives for the freedom of Ireland. I could not bear to be even remotely associated with such deceit and hypocrisy—and my silence would associate me. It is only expected that the violent men who are opposing Irish freedom should condemn the IRA freedom fighters, but it is unforgivable when many so-called Nationalist spokesmen also condemn them.

Yet, in the light of history, condemnation from the latter is not surprising for every struggle for Irish freedom has been traitorously condemned by this sort of people. (And yet our patriots, despite "this unkindest cut of all," still fought on because they were, and are, men and women of courage, integrity and dedication.) And of this I am certain: that when our patriots free Ireland, and free it, they surely will, these very people will be the very first to jump on the bandwagon and salute the men and women they now condemn. They did it before, and they will do it again.

To praise Tone, Pearse, Connolly, Sean Treacy, and Cathal Brugha and all the others, on the one hand, while on the other, condemning those (and here I make no distinction between the Provisionals and the Officials) is treachery and deceit of the lowest kind. How I detest such chicanery. It revolts and disgusts me, and I will have no part of it.

I finalized my decision to speak out as I stood by a lonely grave. It is the grave of a man who was the personification of nobility, courage, and integrity: a typical member of the IRA. He is a man whose memory I honor and of whom I am deeply proud: my brother Patrick who died for Ireland in 1958.

The day before the court hearing, I was being driven by the late Dave O'Connell, a top IRA man, and political strategist, from Dublin to Monaghan. I read my statement out loud for him to hear. When I had finished, he pulled the car off the road, clearly very moved. "I never thought I'd see the day when a priest would have the balls to say what you have said." And with great embarrassment, he silently sobbed for about five minutes.

If nothing else, it's worth it, just for this, I thought, as memories flooded back into my mind about how the priests at St. Michael's were so scared of being associated with the IRA that they would not even perform a basic act of Christian charity or human decency, except Fr. Clerkin. Dave pulled himself together and in his signature Cork accent—at once authoritative, yet almost roguish—said, "Don't tell anyone I cried. It would be bad for my image if the Brits knew." His secret was safe with me. Dave died in Dublin in January 1991, age fifty-three. Sadly, Sinn Féin split in 1986 and Dave broke from Gerry Adams and Martin McGuinness, both of whom would go on to do truly historic work. However, no one can diminish Dave's stature, integrity, and heroism. I had deep respect for him and held him in great affection. On my annual pilgrimage to Glasnevin Cemetery, "where the Fenians sleep," I always kneel and say a prayer at his grave in the Republican Plot.

When Frankie saw my statement, he told me I would be interned, which I was quite prepared for. In fact, I would have welcomed it, for as Thoreau said: "Under a government, which imprisons any unjustly, the true place for a just man is also a prison."[5] But I was neither interned for my statement nor imprisoned for not paying the fine.

I knew that the British government and its whole intelligence operations would not stand idly by, even though they had not publicly moved against me. I knew they would exert huge pressure on the Catholic hierarchy in Britain and Ireland, and through them on Fr. Shepherd. After all, the British government had succeeded in 1870 in getting Pope Pius IX to excommunicate the Fenians, both in Ireland and America. No matter how badly the British treated Irish Catholics, the Vatican always listened to them on Ireland with the aid of the Irish Bishops. 'Twas enough to make a Kinawleyman a Protestant!

However, I continued to speak out but, again, never from the pulpit. Finally, that letter, dated Friday, April 15, 1972, with which this book opened, arrived from Fr. Shepherd telling me to pack my bag for Clapham in London. "I do not want anyone to know your immediate destination, nor your proposed transfer from Perth. I once again forbid you to make any communications to the Press or Media either per se or per alium, or to call on anyone en route or before departure."

I was blessed with the insight to see that for what it was: an unconscionable, almost racist missive, which in fact meant: do not fraternize with any Irish person on the way to your ecclesiastical house arrest, on behalf, in effect, of Her Majesty's government.

The racist implication becomes clear if one imagines a white church superior telling Martin Luther King, Jr. (not that I'm comparing myself to that great man) that he must not associate with any black person, especially one engaged in the Black Freedom Struggle. James Joyce said of Ireland that "Christ and Caesar are hand in glove," but that applies even more so to England, as I was soon about to learn.

I felt no moral obligation to obey this patently unjust and politicized diktat. Charlie Shepherd was simply implementing that British soldier's ignorant decree: "You have no rights ..." I am sure Charlie saw himself as protecting the Redemptorist Order, but the only way he could do that was by pleasing the British government. So, the end result was the same.

PROTESTANT SOLIDARITY

But let me contrast Charlie's letter with the one I received on April 19 from a local Episcopalian priest in Perth. You be the judge as to which is the more Christian:

Fr. Sean McManus

Dear Father,

Whilst I was at the altar celebrating the Liturgy this morning, I thought about you and the difficult situation in which you find yourself at present. I would like you to know that this vivid thought prompted me to include you in my prayers and intention in the Eucharist.

I would also like you to know that I think that I can sense—and to some extent share—the anguish which you feel about the situation in Ireland. I suppose it will always be difficult for the priest transfixed by the knowledge that he must be an [intermediary] representing God to his people and the people to God—and yet, burning within with a great desire to move into an area of what seems like worldly action for a cause which he knows in his heart of hearts is right. I use the word transfixed for it seems to me that in this kind of situation, the priest is nailed to the cross, a cross which is that well-nigh unbearable tension between his priesthood, as conceived of in spiritual terms, and his (dare I use the word?) priesthood as he sees it in worldly terms. But of course, this is what the priesthood is all about. It is surely more than offering the Eucharistic sacrifice and preaching the Word (though it is that too)—but a living of this tension between the spiritual and the physical, between this world and the "other" world. The priest who lives this tension in his own life is stretched on the Cross with his Master.

Take heart, Father. There are many who will understand and pray for you—as I do. I hope that when "things are blown over" you will be able to come to visit me and have another "natter."

On Friday, I will be celebrating the Liturgy at our cathedral at 8 a.m. I will pray especially for you. In our calendar and Ordo, it is the double feast of St. Maelrubha (Abbot of Applecross and Bangor) and St. Anselm, Archbishop of Canterbury—a Celtic saint and one from an English See: perhaps there might be some significance in that—reconciliation?

With every prayer and blessing.

Yours in Christ,

Reverend John Ross.

I flew down to London. Frankie was in Parliament, and, naturally, I needed to talk to him about the whole thing. Incredibly even at that period (the week of April 16, 1972), I was able to check in my bag at the House of Commons cloakroom. Then I remembered that in my bag there was an alarm clock set to go off at 5.30 a.m., and it was now nearly 5:30 p.m., and I was concerned my clock would not distinguish between a.m. and p.m. So, I hurried back to the clerk and told him not to worry if the alarm went off. "Don't worry, Reverend, that will be no problem," said the very nice Englishman.

It was there I met Bernadette Devlin, MP, for the first time. She had been elected the year before Frankie, and he and she fought the good fight in "the belly of the beast." I had, of course, great admiration for her fearlessness, courage, and eloquence. But I was not expecting someone with such a formidable public persona to be so charming and gracious. And thus, she has been each time I've met her over the years. She and Frankie (and sometimes Gerry Fitt, MP for West Belfast) had to fight lonely battles. The day after Bloody Sunday (January 30, 1972, when British paratroopers killed thirteen innocents at a nonviolent march in Derry) Bernadette punched out the Foreign Secretary, Reginald Maudling, in the House of Commons for trying to cover up the act of

State terrorism. Years later, in an interview with the London magazine, *The Big Issue*, Bernadette would recall: "I walked over and clattered Maudling ... Big Davison, a conservative, hit me and Frank McManus floored him."[6]

That evening I went to St. Mary's, Clapham, the Provincial's headquarters. Fr. Shepherd told me he wanted to see me first thing in the morning. At the appointed time, I went to his office (which, ironically, my brother Jim would later occupy as Provincial for three terms, 1990 -1999). Charlie was in no mood for chit- chat. He got right to the point: "Unless you give a promise, without mental reservation or equivocation, never to criticize the government again on Northern Ireland, I will suspend you from all public priestly work."

I deliberately paused for a very long time before replying so that he would know that I was as serious as he was. My reply was slow and steady: "Father, in conscience and with all due respect, I cannot make such a promise. While I do not intend to speak out all the time, I cannot make a promise be silent in the face of injustice because that would make me as guilty as the British government and British army." Then he lost it: "You are in the English Province, and you will not criticize the English government." Well, despite my intention to maintain a controlled demeanor, the Kinawleyman reasserted itself, and I gave it back to him in kind: "For as long as your government oppresses my country, I will not be silent."

He jumped out of his chair, declared he had not called me in for a discussion and told me to pack my bag for Chawton (to Alphonsus House, the Redemptorist publishing house, which had no parish) in Hampshire, about fifty-six miles southwest of London.

As I headed for the door, I turned and said, "Does this mean I am being silenced [in the canonical sense of not being able to function as a priest]?" He snapped, "Nobody said anything about silencing."

ECCLESIASTICAL LONG KESH

So that meant I could say a private Mass in Alphonsus House and, as there was no parish attached, the issue of public Masses did not apply.

I would come to refer to Chawton as "my ecclesiastical Long Kesh," after the prison of that name the British were operating in the North.

Charlie Shepherd would telephone me every week or so to see if I would recant. "In good conscience, and with all due respect, Father, I cannot ..." But he would often slam down the phone before I could complete my mantra.

The fact that Chawton had no parish seemed a logical place to sequester me, but it had one ironic disadvantage: it was only about nine miles from Aldershot. On February 22, 1972, the Official IRA had bombed the Sixteenth Parachute Brigade headquarters at Aldershot in retaliation for the Parachute Regiment's murderous attack on the peaceful march on January 30, 1972, in Derry—the atrocity and act of State terrorism known as Bloody Sunday. Five women and one Catholic priest, a chaplain, were tragically killed in the IRA attack. The priest, Fr. Gerry Weston, thirty-seven, had been a regular visitor to Alphonus House and was a good friend of all the Redemptorists there. So, that made the situation very poignant for all of us. Yet, I must say everyone in Alphonsus House treated me very kindly, though they must have wondered what they had done to deserve this turn of events.

However, my forced ecclesiastical quarantine gave me time for serious reflection and prayer. The library wasn't too bad. It had a copy of *Justice in the World* (mentioned in the Introduction). I went to the local library and got a copy of Martin Luther King, Jr.'s "Letter from Birmingham Jail"—his magisterial response to the top eight Birmingham Church leaders, including the Catholic Bishop of Birmingham, who had publicly censored his protest actions:

> I have almost reached the regrettable conclusion that the Negro's great stumbling block in his stride toward freedom is not the White Citizen's Councilor or the Ku Klux Klanner, but the white moderate, who is more devoted to

order than to justice; who prefers a negative peace which is the absence of tension to a positive peace which is the presence of justice; who constantly says: "I agree with you in the goal you seek, but I cannot agree with your methods of direct action;" who paternalistically believes he can set the timetable for another man's freedom; who lives by a mythical concept of time and who constantly advises the Negro to wait for a "more convenient season." Shallow understanding from people of good will is more frustrating than absolute misunderstanding from people of ill will. Lukewarm acceptance is much more bewildering than outright rejection ... Before closing, I feel impelled to mention one other point in your statement that has troubled me profoundly. You warmly commended Birmingham police force for keeping "order" and "preventing violence." I doubt that you would have so warmly commended the police force if you had seen its dogs sinking their teeth into unarmed, nonviolent Negroes. I doubt that you would so quickly commend the policemen if you were to observe their ugly and inhumane treatment of Negroes here in the city jail; if you were to watch them push and curse old Negro women and young Negro girls; if you were to see them slap and kick old Negro men and young boys; if you were to observe them, as they did on two occasions, refuse to give us food because we wanted to sing our grace together. I cannot join you in your praise of the Birmingham police department."[7]

I am still amazed, almost fifty years later, how comparable the Black Freedom Struggle is to the Irish struggle.

PAX CHRISTI OR PAX BRITANNICA

I also decided to contact one of the priests who had taught me "the new theology" in Hawkstone. So, on May 9, 1972, I wrote asking him for his guidance on the theology concerning the "conflict of conscience"—the possible conflict between conscience and authority. I stressed I did not want him to take a position on my stand, nor make judgments about the Irish situation, but to clearly explicate the theological principle. He wrote back saying that a good Redemptorist can never have a conflict of conscience! That was a total contradiction of both the new and the "old" theology. Not Pax Christi, but Pax Britannica. Rule Britannia. And I was supposed to be the one being political.

Because of my rather unique position, I had to make a serious study of the subject. I knew that first of all: one had an obligation to have an informed conscience—to seek out all the available teaching on the issue, to study it sincerely and objectively, and, above all, pray that one was not deceiving oneself because all of us can have a "self-serving" conscience. The Second Vatican Council, in its document *Gaudium et Spes* (Joy and Hope), told me that "conscience is the man's most secret core and his sanctuary." So, I knew if I betrayed my conscience, I would be betraying my truest self—the inner me who stands naked before the all-seeing eye of God.

I knew very well how the deal would go down: some good Catholic MPs (and I hoped it wasn't Frankie or Bernadette Devlin!) would contact Cardinal Heenan saying it was very bad for the Church to have a young priest accusing the British government of such awful things and wasn't there something His Eminence could do about it? The Cardinal would then call Charlie. Indeed, Charlie admitted as much to me—well, he let it slip out and then couldn't take it back.

I also knew there was another fundamental principle involved in making a conscientious protest: you take your punishment without whining, and you do not, after the fact, unfairly look to involve others in the consequences of your action. Again, I found solace in Martin Luther King, Jr.: "An individual who breaks a law that conscience tells him is unjust, and who willingly accepts the penalty of imprisonment in order to arouse the conscience of the community over its injustice, is, in reality, expressing the highest respect for the law."

I finally wrote to Fr. Shepherd on May 16, 1972:

> I have thought things over—but, it was all well-charted ground. I am unable to see things in a different light. The actions I took were not impetuous: they were studied and calculated and prayed about. I am totally convinced that what I did was right and that I was bound to do it. Therefore, in principle, I could never give an absolute unconditional promise never to speak out again ... Before God, I do not believe that my actions were motivated by anything base or ulterior. In fact, from the very nature of the case, I have patently nothing to gain but everything to lose. Indeed, from the way things look at present, I know that I may very well have (if I may speak like this for a moment) ruined my "personal career."

I went on to acknowledge that I had put him in a difficult position but stressed that any apparent clash between my loyalty to the Province and my conscience was only that, i.e., apparent: "... Because when a man stands up for what he knows is right, then he is not being disloyal to any side: he is being loyal to the truth, which can never 'compete' against any value or good." But I knew the die was cast. There was no way I would be allowed to continue working in Britain or Ireland.

I would have liked for Fr. Shepherd to acknowledge the moral integrity of my conscientious protest, but he never did. He insisted as seeing it "formal disobedience," maybe because it was easier that way for him, or because he was just plain scared or because he was incapable of respecting a conscience that disagreed with his. Religious superiors can easily fall into the sin of thinking they speak for God at all times and in all ways. They don't. That's why we have this thing called conscience. No authority, no superior, can take its place.

Soon the whole world was my parish. Fr. Shepherd gave me all sorts of choices: go to Rome for further studies in Eucharistic theology, or any place in continental Europe, Canada or America. South Africa would have been the usual "dumping ground" for the English Province. But an Anglican priest had recently been deported back to England for speaking out against the apartheid system. And there was no way someone like me would be allowed into that country.

I chose America. I checked out which Redemptorist Province in America was the most Irish. If I was going to be "transported" (the very resonant word that was used for the exiling of political prisoners to Australia, up until 1868), then I might as well go to an area where I could do the most good. I chose the Baltimore Province because that included New York, Boston and, most importantly of all, the nation's capital, Washington, DC.

Charlie now became very cooperative, doing everything in his power to facilitate my "transportation." On June 16, 1972, he wrote to the Provincial of the Baltimore Province, Fr. Joseph L. Kerins, at his headquarters in Brooklyn, New York.

"Fr. Sean McManus aged 29 [sic]. This young man is an excellent priest and a very promising missionary on the Parish Mission. Unfortunately, owing to his Irish origins, he has foolishly become implicated through newspaper articles & a TV appearance in the very sad political impasse in N. Ireland ... Would it be at all possible for you to take him and let him work on the Parish Mission band in the Baltimore Province? ... I am not trying to unload a bad priest on anyone, but one who has been foolish and stubborn in this particular Irish problem." [Notice here, the strange distancing, probably unconscious, but typically British ... "the Irish problem"—as if it had no connection to Britain or that the British Army was not in the North doing terrible things.]

I acknowledged earlier that the average British person knows little about Northern Ireland. But is that really a good enough excuse? How long can a well-educated people be excused for not knowing what their government, army and "tax dollars" are doing in another country? Is it ignorance or indifference? And how could the churches in Britain ignore the mistreatment of Catholics in Northern Ireland? Is it because they did not want to become "involved in politics" or is it because they were being profoundly political? Was their silence prudence or betrayal? How could ecclesiastical silence be reconciled with the clarion call of *Gaudium et Spes* issued by the Second Vatican Council in its very opening lines: "The joys and the hopes, the griefs and the anxieties of the men of this age, especially those who are poor or in any way afflicted, these are the joys and hopes, the griefs and anxieties of the followers of Christ. Indeed, nothing genuinely human fails to raise an echo in their hearts."

ATTEMPT TO KILL MOTHER

In August I went home to Clonliff to prepare for my exile to America. So far, 1972 was proving to be one of the worst years of the Troubles. Danger was palpable all over the North. And it visited Mother. She was home alone one night. A gunman blasted her bedroom window, but mercifully she escaped injury. She was sixty-nine at the time. And to make it all the more painful, the man who tried to kill her was a local Protestant whom we had known all our lives, and whom we had always treated with friendliness and kindness (as we had treated all our Protestant neighbors). Now let me tell you the follow-up to this incident in two parts. The first and most important part is about my Mother's forgiveness, and the second is about the nature of the State of Northern Ireland.

About two nights after the shooting (while we still did not know who the shooter was) I was sitting home with my mother. There was a knock on the door, and as we were not expecting any visitors, I signaled to my Mother not to move and went to the door. Outside there was standing the tallest policeman I had ever seen in my life, indeed the tallest person I had ever seen. I then saw there was someone hiding behind him whom the policeman then brought forward. The policeman said: "[first and last name] has come to apologize for shooting at Mrs. McManus."

The man then, sheepishly said, "Hello, Fr. Sean," casting his eyes down.

I brought them both into the kitchen, and the Protestant gunman said, "Mrs. McManus, I am sorry for shooting at you. Will you forgive me?"

Without hesitating a split second, Mother reached out, grabbed his hand in hers and said, "Of course, I will [first name]. God love you."

I have told that story to very few outside the family because it is so profoundly personal and precious, and also because it is difficult for me to get through it without crying.

And now to the second, less edifying, part of the story: can you imagine that had a Catholic tried to kill the mother of a Protestant MP, the police would have brought him to that woman's house to apologize? Nothing can tell you more about the nature of the State of Northern Ireland than this. Why would the police do such a thing? Certainly, it had to come from the very top, as no local policeman would take it upon himself to do such an extraordinary thing. Local people immediately saw it as an attempt to get the court to go easy on the gunman. But the far more serious question was why would the police go so far out on a limb for an ordinary working-class Protestant? What was the purpose of their damage control? What were they trying to contain or hide?

We have never been given an explanation. But we all, like Mother, forgave the gunman, whom we felt had been used as a patsy, like so many other working-class Protestant gunmen.

The first night after the shooting, mother and I were alone in the house. She was asleep in her room upstairs. I was across the hall in my room.

Pounding on the front door woke me up. I sprang out of bed, fearing we were under attack again. I charged out of my room to the top of the stairs, thinking "If they have guns, we are done for." I braced myself at the top of the stairs in the dark as the front door was forced open. "If I hurl myself on top of them at least I will slow them down," I thought, as I prepared to jump at a shape at the bottom of the stairs. And then the "shape" began to scamper up the stairs yelping with delight to be inside. It was Judy, Mother's big, much-loved black Labrador dog. She had learned the trick of pouncing on the front door until the simple "Yale lock" eased open.

I was never so pleased to see any dog in my life.

A final note on this episode: shortly after I arrived in New York, I learned more about the shooting incident. I discovered that a prominent IRA leader in the Leitrim-Cavan area had taken grave exception to the attempted shooting of "the mother of Patrick McManus." He dispatched two men to cross The Border "to go looking for" the Protestant gunman. They spent two nights trying to find him but could not. That Protestant man never knew how lucky he was. Then again, the police would have expected the IRA to retaliate and would have taken the gunman into protective custody.

CHAPTER 6

Bound for America

I know how men in exile feed on dreams.
Aeschylus

I HAVE NEVER MET AN EMIGRANT FROM IRELAND who did not know the exact date of his or her arrival in America. It is a big day in their lives—truly a transitional moment in every sense. My big day was October 2, 1972. The older I get, the more conscious I have become of that date being the Feast Day of the Guardian Angel.

I flew out from Dublin on Aer Lingus with a stop in Shannon Airport. At the airport, I telephoned Celia to get the momentous news that Carmel, Frankie's wife, had just given birth to a lovely baby girl, Emer. I ran back to the plane, my homesickness abated by the good news. Needless to say, I never have a problem remembering Emer's birthday.

Ironically, I wasn't back on the plane ten minutes before the woman sitting next to me brought up Frankie's name, of her own accord, having no idea who I was. When she heard I was from the North, she immediately started talking about the Troubles. I knew immediately she had to be living in America because most people from southern Ireland did not want to talk about the North. She was a nice, middle-aged woman, originally from Dublin, who had spent most of her life in America but was now living six months in Ireland and six months in America. "God bless us," I thought, "she must be a millionaire." Anyway, she proceeded to tell me something which was not "generally known": that Frank McManus and Bernadette Devlin were secretly married, and that there was nothing wrong with that, and that they were properly married in the Church (an acknowledgment of my clerical collar), but the marriage had to be secret because a husband and wife could not serve in the British Parliament at the same time.

Keeping a straight face, I asked her the source of her information. She implied she knew some very well-connected people. "Well, now, I don't think that's quite right," I said, looking for a way to let her down gently. But she would have none of it, and dismissed my mild protestations with a wave of the hand and changed the subject. It was my first introduction to how some Irish-Americans (even Irish born) have very definite views about Ireland that may not be exactly correct.

I will never forget my arrival at JFK Airport in New York. I was a little apprehensive. I had never seen so many people, racing like crazy. I saw some sort of uniform, a gun in a holster and instinctively I tightened. Then I saw it was a black man in uniform and somehow that made it all right. It had been my first sight of an armed policeman, other than the RUC.

I got a cab and headed for the Redemptorist headquarters on Shore Road, Brooklyn. And, would you believe it? The cab broke down, in the worst looking area I had ever seen in my life. I immediately thought it was a set-up. I was relieved the driver was an African American, but what if the British had paid him to "break down"? That may all sound melodramatic now, and it may have all been in my head, but the reality was that the British were regularly setting up people for assassination in the North.

But my driver waved down a passing cab, and I made it safely to the Redemptorist headquarters. When I had settled in, I went to the common room where about five or six Redemptorists were watching TV news. They welcomed me kindly and offered me a seat. I took out a pack of cigarettes, and in my good mannerly way, offered one to each priest. They laughed and declined. I had learned my first etiquette lesson in America: it is not considered cheap if you do not offer a cigarette, as everyone smokes their own, but you better unlearn that when you are back in Ireland.

As we watched the news (each smoking his own cigarette), Kissinger came on. He had just returned from the Middle East. He was asked if America has plans to take over the Arab oil fields. That would only be done if America's national interest were at stake, he droned. I wanted to shout back at the TV, but I was just off the boat, so to speak. I glanced around the room expecting a reaction to Kissinger's British-imperialist-type declaration, but it hadn't even raised an eyebrow. I had learned my first political lesson: America is permanently in danger of making the same mistakes as the British—the hubris of empire.

My most vivid first impressions of America came the following morning as I jumped into the shower in my room. The water took lumps out of me. I couldn't believe its force. In the Redemptorists' showers in Britain, you almost had to beg the water to trickle out. When I grabbed the towel, I couldn't believe its size, softness, and absorbency. The towels in the London Province, by contrast, were like glorified dishcloths that became soaked on the first contact with your wet back. When I stepped out of the bathroom, it appeared that my feet almost sank up to my ankles in the lush carpet. Coming out of the showers (individual little brick cubicles) in Hawkstone was always the worst part. You stepped on cold cement floor and froze until you had dressed again. Not in the good old USA. I could have been quite comfortable in my room with just the big towel around my waist. (Mind you, the rooms in the Redemptorist houses throughout the Baltimore Province were not as nice and did not have their own bathroom.) After Mass and breakfast, I met with the Provincial, Fr. Joe Kerins. I knew immediately I was in the presence of a remarkably fine man. Things even got better when he knowingly said, "One of my uncles in Kerry was in the IRA." (*Put that in your pipe, Charlie Shepherd, and smoke it*, I thought to myself).

Then he completely bowled me over when he said, "Here's your file."

"What do you mean?" I asked. "It is a copy of all correspondence regarding you—including Fr. Shepherd's letters," he explained.

"And do I get to keep this file?"

"Yes, in this Province, we have a policy of total openness. It is the right of every Redemptorist to see every letter that is written about him."

To me, this was extraordinary and revolutionary. I had been so used to Englishmen telling me I had no rights. *God bless us*, I thought, *this is a great country altogether.*

And that is how I got a copy of the letter from Charlie Shepherd, to Fr. Kerins, that I quoted earlier. Over the next few years, Fr. Kerins would keep sending me copies of letters Fr. Shepherd would write about me, as I kept denouncing the British government—the more I denounced, the angrier and more personal Shepherd's letter became. And, I'm sure he had no idea I was being given copies of his letters.

Fr. Kerins told me they badly needed a young priest in Sacred Heart of Jesus parish, in Baltimore, especially for youth work. I suspected that Baltimore was selected because it was not as Irish as New York or Boston. He told me to take some time for myself and visit my brother Thomas in upstate New York and my sister Alice in Reading, Pennsylvania.

He also told me that he was sure I would want "to meet my many admirers in New York City." And with a big smile, he handed me a copy of *The Irish People*, which I had never heard of, but which announced to great acclaim there was "an Irish rebel priest" in town.

Ardent New York Irish

A delegation of ardent Irish men and women came to Shore Road to escort me into the city. I stayed in the apartment of a man from Ballinamore, County Leitrim, who had been in the IRA with Patrick and had soldiered alongside him. He was a laboring man yet, when he showed me into my room, he pulled out two drawers from a cabinet and said if I needed any vests (T-shirts), there were plenty there. And was there ever! I had never seen so many gleaming white T-shirts, all neatly folded, maybe even pressed. Now, I had come to America wearing one T-shirt and one in my bag. "God bless us," I thought, "this man must be rich indeed."

My Ballinamore host could not wait to take me to meet Seán Cronin, who was Chief of Staff of the IRA after Patrick was killed. He was then a journalist in New York City. Seán was very pleased to meet me as he had great respect for Patrick. He told me I could do a lot of good work for the Cause, but to watch my back, as both the London and Dublin governments would try to bring me down. I soon met all the leaders and activists in Irish Northern Aid, AOH and general Irish organizations in New York City. They were fiercely anti-British and furious at the quisling attitude of the Free State government. Suddenly, I felt very much at home.

When I arrived at Sacred Heart of Jesus, in the section of Baltimore called Highlandtown, the first thing that struck me was that there were absolutely no people on the streets, although it was midafternoon. The next thing I spotted were the famous marble steps that lead up to each row house, and which the housewives kept as clean as their own very white teeth. Highlandtown was mostly German and Polish, hardly any Irish.

After the Masses on Sunday, my reaction was that apart from superficial differences, Sacred Heart could have been like any city parish in Belfast, Dublin or London. I was sad, however, to see only a few black faces—the great weakness in the American Catholic Church. How often over the years would I reflect on that telling quote of Martin Luther King, Jr. about eleven o'clock on a Sunday morning being the most segregated hour of the week!

Right away, I arranged a meeting with the officers of the parish Catholic Youth Organization (CYO), a group of lovely young girls, aged fifteen to seventeen, I guess. They were delighted to have a young priest for their group. The TV show *Charlie's Angels* was very popular at the time, so they took to calling themselves "Fr. Sean's Angels." When I told them I was from Ireland, they nodded their heads. But at the end of the meeting, the president, a very bright young lady, said, "Fr. Sean, where is Ireland? Near Canada?" This was my first lesson about Americans and geography. And there was I thinking Ireland was the center of the world, with everybody knowing about it.

I quickly got the run of the parish and did my work with gusto.

There was hardly any Irish activity in Baltimore and none on the North. But I was determined to quickly change that. The word got out that I was in town and a group wanted me to speak to them. I made them feel guilty that they were ignoring their homeland and told them they were aiding British oppression in Ireland by their silence. Soon there was an active chapter of Irish Northern Aid in Baltimore and Washington.

As the only young priest, I was doing a lot of good work in the parish. All the other priests were over fifty, with most in their seventies. I loved the people. I had never met any nicer people than these German and Polish folk—all patriotic Americans and deeply committed Catholics. I was humbled by their devout Catholicism and surprised at how strongly Catholic this big country was.

I was getting on with my work, reinvigorating the parish with no thought that I would see Ireland in the near future. But just as I thought I was out, they pulled me back in.

MacStiofain Hunger Strike

A month after I arrived in Baltimore, Seán MacStíofáin, Chief of Staff of the IRA, was arrested in Dublin on November 19, 1972, and immediately began a hunger and thirst strike. On November 25, he was sentenced to six months imprisonment. The previous day, Irish Northern Aid leaders in New York had appealed to me to come and speak at protest meetings in New York and to go to Ireland because Mac Stíofáin had asked for me.

I tried to reach both my Rector at Sacred Heart and Father Provincial in New York. They were unavailable, so I left a message for them that "I had presumed permission" (the theological principle that states one can, in an emergency, legitimately and in good faith presume the superior would grant permission if he were present). I traveled to New York and spoke at the hastily called public meeting at the Irish Institute. The other two speakers were Seán Cronin and Congressman Biaggi. The meeting was followed by an all-night vigil outside the Irish Consulate.

Jack McCarthy, the crusty but admirable leader of Irish Northern Aid, arranged my flight to Dublin.

When I picked up my luggage at Dublin airport, I asked the luggage handler if MacStíofáin was still alive. "Unfortunately, he is. It would be far better for the country if he died." He clearly thought because I had a clerical collar on that I would be supporting the Dublin government. I gave him such a withering look he scurried off. I stayed at the home of friends, a fine elderly couple from Kerry. Their house was a veritable hotel for IRA leaders like the late Joe Cahill.

I spoke at a massive rally, which my brother Frank also attended. On Sunday afternoon, November 26, I visited Mac Stíofáin in the Mater Hospital, to which he had been transferred from prison because of his deteriorating condition. As I walked into the hospital ward, a group of Special Branch men grabbed me and pinned me with my back to the wall. I had never seen such fury or hatred in anybody's eyes as the man who held me by the throat. I said, "You fellows are worse than the British Army. Why are you doing this?"

The lead guy hissed, "One of you f—kers tried to shoot me."

"What do you mean one of us f—kers tried to shoot you?" I demanded.

Then I learned why they were so (understandably) agitated. A short time before I had arrived, an IRA team, disguised as priests, had tried to rescue MacStíofáin and had got into a shoot-out with the Special Branch. Two IRA men were wounded, and four caught. I had been oblivious to all of this and had innocently blundered into an explosive setting. IRA leaders had known in advance that I was going to be visiting MacStíofáin but had not said a word to me—and I guess that was also understandable.

Finally—with bruised neck, but none the worse for wear—I got into MacStíofáin's room. I was stunned to see how terrible he looked on his eighth day of hunger and thirst strike. The last time I saw him, he was a vigorous, strong man. But now he was a shadow of his former self. It was evident he was in a most critical condition.

That night or early morning the following day—to avoid any further rescue attempts—MacStíofáin was transferred by helicopter to the Irish Army's main barracks in the Curragh, about thirty miles from Dublin. Dave O'Connell, a top IRA man, told me it was vital that I got into the

Curragh to see Mac Stíofáin, as the Republican Movement would have no other point of contact.

Friends drove me to the Curragh, and I tried to see Mac Stíofáin the evening of Monday, November 27, as it was getting dark. The Free State Army had the entire area cordoned off. I asked to speak to the lead soldier, a surprisingly young man. He was absolute: It didn't matter if I were the pope. I was not getting through, he told me with just too much relish. "How does it feel to be doing England's dirty work?" I blasted. Sticking out his chest he boasted, "It feels great. It feels great." I think if I had not been a priest, I would have decked him on the spot.

The following morning, I returned to the Curragh military hospital and waited outside with Mrs. MacStíofáin and her daughter, Marie. They were eventually allowed in.

Then I went to a soldier guarding the door and asked him if I could use the bathroom. He refused. I told him it was an emergency and if I could not use the bathroom, I would go behind the trees at the bottom of the field. He then earnestly pleaded, "Father, please don't. We have orders to shoot anything that moves down there." *At least he's a decent sort*, I thought, *compared to the blackguard from the night before.*

Sometime later, the top brass summoned me in: "It's an emergency." They rushed me to where MacStíofáin was caged, literally: his bed was inside a huge cage. From inside the bars, MacStíofáin's daughter was screaming, "Fr. Sean, Fr. Sean, my father is dying." MacStíofáin was having some sort of seizure, shaking violently. However, he survived and came off his thirst strike, and afterward off his hunger strike.

Later on, when the emotion and high drama had subsided, I slipped up to Fermanagh to see my mother. In retrospect, it was probably a risky thing to have done as the Orangemen were out for my blood.

When I was returning to America, Dave O'Connell drove me to the Dublin airport. He assured me he had given a full report to Irish Northern Aid leaders in New York about all the details of my efforts.

The same luggage handler was there. I had been on TV so much that he could not fail to recognize me. A look of sheer terror came over his face, scared that I might have passed on his vicious comment about

MacStíofáin to the IRA. I had not, of course, as I did not want him to suffer any retaliation. I went over to him and assured that I had not told anyone. "Oh, thank you, Father, thank you, Father. I didn't mean it. I'm a good Republican meself." You've never seen a more relieved man.

Years later, a Redemptorist friend told Jim and me this story in Washington. He was based in Clapham with Charlie Shepherd during the MacStíofáin hunger strike. They were in the common room watching the TV news, and the hunger strike was covered. Charlie turned around and intoned to all in the room, "Thank goodness Sean McManus is safely in America." And at that very instant, I appear on the TV, large as life, not safely in America but in Dublin. Charlie got such a shock he almost fainted.

When I arrived back in Baltimore, I wasn't sure of the reception I would receive at Sacred Heart of Jesus. The national and Baltimore media had covered my activities, and everyone in the parish had been excited to read about their "young new Irish priest." I did not receive one negative comment from the parishioners, only, "right on, Father, way to go" from those lovely German and Polish Catholics.

Parishioners are one thing, but what about the powers that be? Fr. Kerns—the noblest of them all—would provide me with another file of all correspondences relating to my Irish visit. God bless us, I thought to myself yet again, *this is a great country altogether.*

On December 1, while I was still in Ireland, the Rector of Sacred Heart had written to Fr. Kerins: "My reaction about this whole affair [the MacStíofáin hunger strike] is that Sean is welcome back here at Sacred Heart, as far as I am concerned. My motives for saying this perhaps are not unselfish in that he is filling a need here for someone in the younger age brackets ... I honestly don't think he has caused any serious embarrassment or problem to us here."

Fr. Kerins replied on December 6: "I certainly would have no objections to his return to our Province. I would agree with you that he had a valid reason for going to Ireland ..." And then this splendid human being instructed the Rector: "It might be well if you ask [Sean] if he had to borrow the money for his travels. I would not want him to be saddled with a debt or have to approach his own Provincial [Charlie Shepherd] for funds in this situation ..."

Then on December 10, (ironically, International Human Rights Day), Charlie Shepherd wrote a letter to Fr. Kerins decrying my disobedience in "presuming permission" and the harm I had done to both the English and Irish Provinces. I did not mind his attack on me. I was fair game. But Shepherd—abandoning even the slightest pretense at objectivity and fairness—took out his anger on my brother Jim. He complained: "I have heard his brother, Fr. Jim ([at] Hawkstone) has been in touch with Baltimore [Sacred Heart]. He is just as politically minded as Sean, but more cautious in the way he goes about things. The point of the matter is that at least 75% of this Province are heartily fed up with the two of them, especially with Sean, in the complete disregard they show for the feelings of the people of this country, where they received the opportunity of their priesthood and the chance of exercising it."

Let's examine the bit about England being "the opportunity of their priesthood." A bit like telling Martin Luther King, Jr., a native of the state of Georgia, that if he wanted to exercise his ministry in Alabama or Mississippi, he would have to be silent. The analogy is even more apt if one accepts, for the sake of the argument, Maggie Thatcher's dictum "Northern Ireland is as British as Finchley."

And there you have it, the classic blackmail. You must not oppose England's injustice in Ireland lest you upset the feelings of the English people. So, forget human rights. Forget democracy. Forget even the teaching of the Catholic Church on justice. Anything that disturbs order in Her Majesty's realm is sinful, inconsiderate and to be crushed. Remember that quote, given earlier, from Martin Luther King, Jr. about how the greatest stumbling block to justice is the nice, respectable "moderate, who is more devoted to 'order' than to justice; who prefers a negative peace which is the absence of tension to a positive peace which is the presence of justice."

Contrast Fr. Shepherd's myopic moral view with that of the greatest Redemptorist moral authority, after St. Alphonsus, the famed German moral theologian, Fr. Bernard Haring: "One of the most important criteria for determining a genuine priestly vocation is a deep rootedness in, and practice of, the virtue of nonviolence.If strength and resolve to become witnesses to justice, peace and nonviolence do not flow from our Eucharistic celebrations, then we must fearfully and sadly conclude that far too many priestly and lay Christian vocations are not sufficiently authentic."[1]

As regarding Fr. Shepherd's gratuitous swipe at my brother: Jim was and is one of the most respected and productive members of the London Province and would go on to be himself elected Provincial, not just once but three times for a total of nine years (1990–1999).

The ever-unflappable Fr. Kerins replied to Shepherd on December 18: "Despite your own evident displeasure at this development in his life, I would have to frankly let you know that in my judgment the presumption on his part was valid." Still, Charlie Shepherd would not let it go. He must have thought the natives in the former colony (these United States of America) were getting uppity. On January 17, 1973, he replied to Fr. Kerins: "I do understand that in your country you have learned to live with protest, especially made in the name of conscience, which over here is still something of a novelty." A novelty? Charlie was here personifying what Thomas Merton (1915–1968)—the Trappist monk who was at the time one of the most incisive spiritual thinkers and prophetic voices—deplored: "One of the grave problems of religion in our time is posed by the almost total lack of protest on the part of religious people and clergy in the face of enormous social evils. It is not that these people are wicked or perverse ... but simply that they are no longer fully capable of seeing and evaluating certain evils as they truly are: as crimes against God and as betrayals of the Christian ethic of love."[2]

Fr. Shepherd concluded his letter with a parting shot: "Let us hope that Fr. Sean won't want to dash over—on the grounds of conscience—to console other leaders of the IRA if the Dublin legislation puts more under restraint."

This from the man who was supposed to be nonpolitical! This from the man who warned me never to express political opinions!

Status Quo Clericalism Brits' Best Friend

The "Dublin legislation," so blithely referred to, allowed the imprisonment of any suspected IRA member just on the word of a senior policeman.

This type of double standard has, unfortunately, a long history in the Catholic Church, and ranks, in my mind, as almost a heresy. It is the belief that the politics with which the religious superior agrees –i.e., the status quo—is not politics at all but in effect, the divine order. Therefore, the Churchmen conclude (and always on behalf of God) that a person is only political if he opposes this "order."

To give another perfect example, jumping ahead some years: Two members of the Irish National Caucus from Kentucky, a nun, and a social worker, made a fact-finding trip to Northern Ireland. They called on the bishop of Derry, Edward Daly, and he, too, was an honorable man. When my name came up, the good Bishop said, "But you realize he's from a VERY POLITICAL family?" He failed to point out (or, I guess the point here is that it never occurred to him) to mention that so was he himself from a very political family. For at that very time, his brother was Chairman of the SDLP in County Fermanagh, while my brother Frank was Chairman of the Irish Independence Party … Frankie was of course "political," and the Bishop's brother was not!

I have often heard authors say that they had no idea where their writing would take them. I never fully understood that until I started writing this book. All these years, I have been giving Charlie Shepherd a pass—making excuses for him, that I had put him in a difficult position, that it was impossible for him to understand, that he was timid and scared, etc.

But now as I read these letters almost fifty years later (and it's at least twenty years since I've gone into my files), I think the objective reader would find it hard to recognize the spirit of The Gospel in any of Charlie's letters: no concern for justice (only "order"), no charity, no compassion, no solidarity with brother Redemptorists. Just personal spleen that his hectoring will is not enforced, and that his personal comfort zone is disturbed. No thought of the sufferings of Catholics in North of Ireland. No mention that the British government was running a racist, sectarian undemocratic regime there. No concern for "the poor and abandoned" for whose sake the great St. Alphonsus founded the Order... I had not expected my writing to take me there, but it has. And so be it. That, however, is not to say I think my own actions were always without fault. And yet I still retain affection for Charlie. He was a prisoner of an introverted system, which can rob some clerics of true freedom.

Charlie also suffered from the all too common "Irish in England syndrome"—the anxiety that because they are Irish and Catholic, they will not be fully accepted as loyal Brits. This can apply particularly with certain types of Catholic priests. And I think Charlie is a good example of this because he had the extra "burden" of having been born in Dublin. Had Charlie been of impeccable English heritage, with unquestionable patriotic credentials, he would have been much better able to deal with the issue.

For example, Fr. Edward Lumley-Holmes, with whom I was stationed in Liverpool, was such a perfectly credentialed Englishman. His sister had been Churchill's personal secretary. Lumley used to type my anti-British government letters. I would always apologize for asking him to do that, but he shrugged it off, merrily announcing he had always known England had treated Ireland badly, and that he always believed Ireland should be free. Then he would chuckle that whereas his sister was secretary to Churchill, he was secretary to the IRA.

But I am led to this somber reflection: How often have churchmen practiced the abuse of authority over the centuries? How often have they used the "voice of God" for their own comfort and agenda? My own case is very minor, and I will never play the victim. But what about those priests (in all sorts of different contexts), who were not as strong as I, who were forced into silence and their spirits crushed because it was "the will of God"? After all, I had the example of my brother Patrick's heroism to sustain me, and the desire for Ireland's freedom to steel me. What resources did they have to withstand the capricious, often bullying, tactics of superiors claiming to speak for God?

If a priest, as a sacrifice/penance/fast to God, obeys his superior then such obedience is pleasing to God. But he must always remember the words of the Prophet Isaiah: "Is not this the fast that I have chosen? …to loose the bands of injustice, to undo the heavy burdens, and to let the oppressed go free, and that you break every yoke?" (Isaiah 58:6). "God's will," therefore, can never be invoked to cover up injustice. It can never be for the good of the Church to cover up injustice, no matter what "prudent" churchmen say.

But the priest can never just resort to blind obedience: "No one can or may delegate this responsibility in a 'blind' obedience—so to speak—to the official Church and her teaching office. Obedience of faith against one's own understanding would be an immoral act." That is how the renowned theologian, Walter Kasper, later cardinal, in 1969, stressed the importance of conscience.[3] And an even better-known theologian, explains the central role of conscience in this most unequivocal way: "At the same time … conscience represents the inner complement and limit of the Church principle. Over the pope as the expression of the binding claim of ecclesiastical authority, there still stands one's own conscience, which must be obeyed before all else, if necessary, even against the requirement of ecclesiastical authority." That young theologian was Joseph Ratzinger, the future Pope Benedict XVI, speaking immediately after Vatican II (October 11, 1962—December 8, 1965).

I thank God (the real God, the God of justice, the God who "hates injustice") that I was able to distinguish the will of God from the will of the British government. What if Martin Luther King, Jr. had listened to what white churchmen in the Deep South were telling him "the will of God" was? Again, I am not trying to compare myself to that great man, just holding him up as a model for all who work for justice.

And what about all the Irish-American priests, especially the Irish-born? Why were ninety percent of them silent? Some from Southern Ireland were even known to tell Americans that Northern Ireland is an internal matter for the British government! What pathology is at work there? What explains such self-loathing gombeenism? It was enough to make a man become a Protestant. History will not forgive them—neither will biblical theology.

CHAPTER 7

Formation of the Irish National Caucus

The imagination, courage and energy of an immigrant Northern Ireland Catholic priest made the dream of an Irish-American lobby a reality.
Joseph E. Thompson[1]

ONCE THE HULLABALOO OVER MY VISIT to Ireland for the MacStíofáin hunger strike died down, I was back to my good work in the parish. I said Mass, preached, administered the sacraments, visited the sick, comforted the dying and instructed the young—all the ordinary, wonderful work of any parish.

But the Baltimore media kept me in the news. I gave interviews on TV, radio, spoke at colleges and to all sorts of groups.

The months sped by and it was soon the summer of 1973. I was entitled to go home vacation but gave it up to go on a speaking tour for Irish Northern Aid. On July 8 I went to Cleveland, Ohio; July 10 to Detroit, Michigan; July 12 to Chicago, Illinois; July 14 to St. Paul, Minnesota; July 15 to Portland, Oregon; July 17 to San Francisco, California; July 18 to Los Angeles, California; July 19 to Saint Louis, Missouri; July 21 to Dayton, Ohio; July 23-27 back to New York to speak all over the city and state. I was so impressed and touched by the dedication of Irish-Americans. And that feeling has never left me.

THE LONG MARCH: BALTIMORE TO WASHINGTON

Irish Freedom March from Baltimore to Washington, D.C., October 13, 1973. Fr. McManus and marchers rested at St. Mary's Church, Laurel, Maryland. Trusty bullhorn to the right on the ground.

Fr. McManus speaking in front of the White House at end of Irish Freedom March. Oct. 14, 1973.

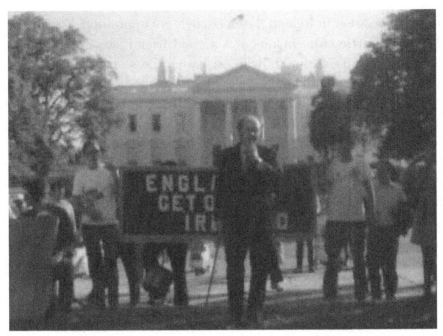

Frank McManus, brother of Fr. Sean, speaks in front of the White House at the end of Irish Freedom March, October 14, 1975.

I wanted to put Baltimore on the map as an Irish city. All the publicity I had received greatly helped. But I wanted to get the Irish on the move. What better way than a march to the nation's capital, forty-five miles away? So, I announced we were going to have "An Irish Freedom March," and then set to organizing it with a small group of very enthusiastic men and women. The bets started immediately on who would be able to walk the full forty-five miles.

And here is when I established a principle that would be the guiding one for the rest of my work with the Irish National Caucus. Others immediately thought I would be leading them to the British Embassy. No, I insisted, Irish-Americans have no influence with the British Embassy, but they do have with their own government. The proper role of Irish-Americans is to change American foreign policy, to end the historic "hands off Northern Ireland" policy. So, the march would be to the White House to protest the silence of the American government about

British oppression in Ireland. I immediately got opposition. The intrepid Jack McCarthy, who by now was a good friend, was on the phone in high panic: "Fr. Sean, Fr. Sean, we cannot be seen to be criticizing America. We should only criticize England."

I explained that if we only criticized a foreign government, we would be giving a pass to all politicians in America, and they need never listen to us: "Jack, if you were still living in County Cork, you could criticize England. What is the point of being an American unless you mobilize America to put pressure on England?" But Jack was really scared that the march would be seen as anti-American. And of course, he would be right, if marching on the White House was anti-American. (In the same way, Jack was right to tell Republican speakers from Ireland not to confuse Americans by mentioning "socialism" as they would be branded communist.) "Jack, there is nothing more American than petitioning your government for help, and for having input into its foreign policy. We will march from Fort McHenry, birthplace of the star-spangled banner and site of a famous victory against the Brits, with both American and Irish flags flying proudly for forty-five miles. I will be the only one with the bullhorn, calling out the question: 'What do we want?' And all of you will respond: 'England out of Ireland.' What better message, Jack, to carry to the White House?"

I could feel Jack was softening up. And I clinched it by asking him to be in charge of supplying American flags. He was delighted. It was as if he was back in his youth and being given his first assignment to go and fight the Black and Tans, "like the boys from the County Cork." And that great-hearted Irish patriot went on to deliver two busloads of people for the last leg of the march to the White House.

I invited Bishop Thomas Drury of Corpus Christi to attend one of the planning meetings—a small group of about ten. He urged us to see the march as a pilgrimage that the Irish should be proud to march in, "even with pebbles in their shoes." Years later, when I got my FBI file, through the Freedom of Information Act, the exact quote from the Bishop is filed in the report, by the informant at the meeting. Needless to say, with my background, I was totally conscious that there would be informers everywher—FBI, British government, Irish government, etc. I was equally aware that there was nothing I could do about it, except to make sure they would never gain control of my work.

The plan was to split the journey into two. We would stay overnight on Saturday, October 13, 1973 in Laurel, Maryland, the halfway point, in Saint Mary's church hall, sleeping on the floor in sleeping bags. The pastor, an Irish-born priest, insisted that I would use the spare room in the rectory. I was a bit concerned about this, as I did not want it to affect the morale of the "troops"—seeing the leader defecting to a comfortable bed while they slept on the floor. But once they all assured me that I should accept the courtesy of the parish priest, I agreed I would.

We had invited my brother Frank to speak at the rally outside the White House. One morning my sister Alice woke me with a phone call: "Frankie has been shot." Alice had forgotten how back home when people said someone was shot, it meant shot dead. And for one terrible moment, that's what I thought she was telling me. "But, he's OK, just a slight wound in the leg," she added. I'll let Frankie tell the story himself: "At about 10.30 p.m. on the night of September 18, 1973, I was traveling home alone. I was not paying any particular attention to road users behind me. As I turned left off the main road, I heard my car being hit. Road works were taking place at the time, and I immediately thought that I had hit loose stones at the side of the road, and I did the one thing that I should not have done, I stopped and got out of my car. It was only then that I realized that I had been shot. As I turned left, the car behind me carried on, effectively creating the two long sides of a triangle. The gunman was obviously an expert. He fired three shots, two of which hit the car and one of which hit the front of our new home. One of the shots pierced the driver's door and shot me just where my right thigh made contact with the seat, causing an unpleasant but essentially a superficial flesh wound."[2]

I assumed that Frankie would not be able to travel to Washington. But he did, marching a good distance, with limp and walking stick, which added to the urgency and drama of what we were about.

The Washington Post gave the march reasonable coverage under the headline "Irish-Americans Urged to Enlist Aid of Countrymen Against British": "With sore feet and soaring enthusiasm, 250 persons ended a 45-mile 'Irish Freedom Walk' at Lafayette Park yesterday, where they were urged by [Frank McManus] a member of the British Parliament to enlist the support of other Irish-Americans in their quest to oust British troops from Ulster." (Monday, October 15, 1973).

The following year, as promised, we had another Irish Freedom March, this time to the British Embassy. The Embassy sent word that they would receive a delegation, but I refused to accept their offer, which was meant to co-opt the march and show how reasonable they were.

WHY NO IRISH LOBBY?

Any chance I could get I would go into Washington to speak to Members of Congress to tell them about the great injustices Her Majesty's government was inflicting on the Catholics in Northern Ireland. As I walked through the Halls of Congress, I would run into all sorts of ethnic groups lobbying for their homelands—Jewish Americans, African Americans, the Poles, the Greeks, etc. But there was one group noticeably absent. And they were one of the largest, best educated, affluent and politically connected: Irish-Americans.

I just could not believe it. There was no Irish lobby or office on Capitol Hill. I knew that would have to change. In the meantime, my immediate priority was to get Congress to officially show concern for the violation of human rights in Northern Ireland.

One of the very first people who offered her help and expertise was Bernadette O'Reilly (later McAuliffe) whose parents were from County Cavan. Bernadette was the personal secretary for Silvio O. Conte (R-MA) and, therefore, was very familiar with the workings of Congress. Fred O'Brien, an attorney with U.S. Customs also offered to help.

My First Congressional Hearing

One of our first efforts was to arrange for my brother Frank to be called to testify before the House Foreign Relations Subcommittee on Human Rights, chaired by Congressman Donald M. Fraser (D-MN). We met with the Director of the Subcommittee. He explained that the practice was not to have someone testify for a foreign government: "Don't worry," I said, "Frankie will not be testifying for, but *against*, the British government." That sealed the deal. Then we convinced him to invite Ruairí ÓBrádaigh, then president of Sinn Féin (like Dave O'Connell, Ruairí, unfortunately, would split from Gerry Adams in 1986 and form Republican Sinn Féin, of which he became president. Ruairí was in the IRA with my brother Patrick, and they soldiered together, so I have always had respect for him)

The Hearing took place on October 10, 1973. Frank and ÓBrádaigh gave powerful testimonies—much to the shock and chagrin of both the British and Irish Embassies. Congressman Conte and Tip O'Neill, then Democratic Majority Leader, held a reception in their honor, which Bishop Drury also attended. Before the reception, Tip chaired a press conference with Frank and ÓBrádaigh. He complained bitterly that he never got information about the Troubles from the Irish Embassy and promised "if the good Father [yours truly]" kept him informed, he would do everything he could to help. That, of course, was proof to me that an Irish lobby had to be launched on Capitol Hill.

By now I was getting to know Tip quite well. He was very friendly in the way all Catholic Boston politicians are to priests. I remember later when he called a number of congressmen together in his office for a publicity photograph for the Irish National Caucus, he put his hand on my right shoulder and said to the late Congressman Joe Moakley (D-MA): "Look at those big shoulders, Joe. He's got them from loading guns in the coffins they ship to Ireland." And they had a great laugh at that. Personally, I resented it but did not say anything. I have always hated frivolous stereotyping of the Troubles—a sure sign of superficiality, with no sensitivity for the deep pain and anguish.

But I would quickly learn a basic Washington law "For every action, there is an equal and opposite reaction." It may be Newton's third law of motion, but it is Capitol Hill's first law. Our initial successful foray in Congress would now force the Irish Embassy to organize against us. Isn't that ironic? They had not been lobbying to get the Congress to put pressure on the British, but they would lobby against us. And of course, so would the British Embassy, but it would let the Irish Embassy lead the public charge, as would be later admitted by Ambassador Peter Jay, son-in-law of James Callaghan, Britain's Labor Prime Minister from 1976 to 1979.

Tip would later, as Speaker of the House, give me the cold shoulder but in the meantime, the Irish Embassy provided him with the perfect cover. He would put that big hand on my shoulder and say, "Fr. Sean, how can I be more patriotic than the Prime Minister of Ireland?" My response was always the same, "That wouldn't be hard, Tip."

Caucus Launched on My Birthday

But anyway, buoyed up by the success of the Congressional hearing, I knew I had to give a name to the work I was doing, which was simply not being done by any other Irish group, no matter how worthy. My basic conviction was that the primary role of Irish-Americans should be to influence American foreign policy on Ireland—to change the long-standing "hands off Ireland because we must not offend the British." My operating principle was: "Human Rights for Ireland is an American Issue." It became one of the first mottos of the Irish National Caucus. Our job would not be to raise funds for Ireland or to relate to a particular group, party or government in Ireland. And we would most certainly not be controlled by any entity in Ireland, North or South. In other words, we would have "no foreign principal."

My initial thought was to get others to head up the new organization, but I quickly realized that if I did not do it, it would not be done. So, on my birthday, February 6, 1974, I founded the Irish National Caucus and signed up, as officers, Bishop Drury, Bernadette O'Reilly, and Fred

O'Brien. Bernadette did invaluable work for us until the opening of the Caucus office on Capitol Hill on December 10, 1978.

Amazingly, some books have said the Caucus' origins were unclear, yet no organization ever had such clear origins. I founded it and put out a press release announcing it. The late Jack Holland in his book *The American Connection* states, "Though the Caucus' beginnings are a matter of dispute, even among its own members..." Strangely, Holland, who had taken up residence in the U.S. by that time, never called me to ask how the Caucus started. Even more oddly, in over thirty years of writing about Irish-American activity, Holland never called me except once—on the death of Seán Mac Stíofáin in 2001. Holland then proceeded to make the ridiculous claim that, "Mike Flannery, the founding father of Irish Northern Aid ... was among those involved in its formation."[3]

Nothing could be further from the truth. Indeed, Flannery was always opposed to the formation of the Irish National Caucus, feeling that there was no need for any other Irish organization because Irish Northern Aid could do it all—something that most evidently was not true. Also, he seemed to be always concerned that I might overshadow him—a silly fear that seemed to motivate some others in Irish groups. Petty jealousy was always something I could not abide especially since we were supposed to be about a noble and selfless cause.

I then turned my attention to the Ancient Order of Hibernians (AOH), which by this time was very familiar with me. Up until 1974, the AOH was only nominally involved in the Northern Ireland issue. It followed the Dublin government line, which was "do not support the IRA and do not criticize the British lest it gives aid and comfort to the IRA." A nonpolicy, which, in fact, aided and comforted the British government.

But there were many members of the AOH who vehemently disagreed with this appeasement of the British government, and they wanted me to "convert" the AOH. In 1974, two AOH stalwarts, the late Dave Burke from Massachusetts and Liam Murphy from New York, arranged for me to address the AOH National Board meeting in Washington, DC in advance of the National Convention in Anaheim, California. I spoke very strongly, denouncing the weakness of the Irish government and urged them as proud Americans to stand up for American values in Ireland. "I believe," I told them, "that Ireland too has the right to be one nation under God, indivisible, with liberty and justice for all."

Dave Burke and Liam Murphy were ecstatic—they could see the AOH change before their eyes as I spoke. Jack Keane, who was running to be the new AOH president, was particularly moved, and immediately proposed that I would be invited to give the keynote address at the National Convention. His proposal was unanimously accepted.

Reminiscing on those days, Jack Keane, on May 30, 2008, said: "At that time I was trying to get the AOH to take a firmer stand on the North of Ireland. The perfect instrument came along in the person of Father McManus. He electrified the National Board Meeting and then the entire Convention. From that moment we made sure the AOH would be intensely involved."[4] Jack Keane was elected president. He appointed Bishop Drury to be the National Chaplain and appointed me Deputy National Chaplain. It would be safe to say that now the AOH had indeed been officially converted. Liam became the editor of the AOH paper, *Hibernian Digest,* and kept up a steady Irish Republican drumbeat. Dave, God rest him, went on to become, without a doubt, one of the most dedicated and productive leaders the AOH ever had. Tom McNabb, New York, would follow Jack Keane as president. Tom was as good as Jack, and both men have been the two most important National Presidents the AOH has had in the past one hundred years. I feel a particular debt of gratitude to these two fine Irish-Americans. They deserve great credit. They showed real courage and leadership, setting the proper course for the AOH. God rest them both. Since that time, the AOH has retained an activist and excellent position on Northern Ireland.

On September 28, 1974, Jack, in keeping with a promise made to me if he were elected AOH president, called a meeting in New York of all the major Irish organizations and they unanimously endorsed the Irish National Caucus—seven months after the founding of the Caucus.

However, while I appreciated their endorsement, I made it clear that the Irish National Caucus would continue to be an independent organization—hat they had endorsed us but we had not endorsed them, and we would not be getting involved in their internal business (or feuds). I also made it crystal clear that while they could have reasonable input, they could not control us in any way. I knew, of course, there would be immediate attempts to destabilize and marginalize us—by the Irish and British governments, and maybe the American government. I knew what to expect—agents, informers, "useful idiots" (those who would be helping the British without even knowing it), malcontents, people who simply did not like me or people whom, through my own fault, I rubbed the wrong way. But hey, welcome to Irish-American politics!

Later the following year, on February 18, 1975, the Executive Council of the American Federation of Labor and Congress of Industrial Organizations (AFL-CIO) endorsed the Irish National Caucus after I addressed a luncheon meeting of about three hundred union members in Bal Harbour, Florida. The then president, the famed George Meany, sent Lane Kirkland, secretary-treasurer, to deliver the endorsement.

CHAPTER 8

Caucus Baptized in Blood at British Embassy

To sin by silence when they should protest makes cowards of men.
Abraham Lincoln

ORGANIZING POLITICALLY DID NOT MEAN that I would cease my activist "street politics." Both were needed—and necessitated by developing circumstances. I decided that the first action of the Irish National Caucus should be symbolically at the British Embassy.

In Baltimore, I got to know the late Phil Berrigan (1923–2002), the former Josephite priest and anti-war activist, and his wife Liz McAllister who had founded Jonah House. Phil was one of the most remarkable men I have ever met. He was a bigger, better-looking version of Paul Newman. I've never known a man with such physical presence. I confided in them that I wanted to do a nonviolent action at the British Embassy in Washington, and I needed their advice on how to pour blood all over the premises, and how to contain things in a nonviolent manner so that nobody would get hurt—except the pride of Her Majesty's government. I could not have consulted a more wise or seasoned source than Phil. He tutored me in the technique—and nonviolent resistance is most certainly a technique as well as a principle. He explained it was vital for me at all times to maintain control of the situation—through the unique calmness that descends on one if nonviolence is done correctly. I had explained to him that the British tended to lead with their guns, and I was concerned that things could spiral out of control, and lead to one of my group being shot by Embassy security or the many British agents housed there. Phil explained that the more I knew about the layout of the British Embassy the better, so as to minimize surprises or confusion.

One of his group, a mother of a four-year-old boy, kindly offered "to case the joint"—to visit the British Embassy and give me an intelligence report. When she visited the Embassy, she would prod her son to send him to different corners of the embassy so that she would have an excuse to follow him. What a gal! And she didn't have one drop of Irish blood. She then drew a perfect sketch of the layout of the inside of the Embassy.

Now about the blood. How were we to get it? "Leave that to me," said Phil, "I know a doctor who does that for us when needed."

The doctor drew two pints of blood from me, on two separate occasions. A local man gave another pint. And the late Mitch Snyder (1946–1990) gave one pint. Mitch, a Vietnam vet, had been converted (back to active Catholicism) in Danbury Prison, Connecticut, by Phil Berrigan and his Jesuit brother, Dan. And he would go on to dedicate his life to the poor and homeless in Washington as the driving force in the Community for Creative Nonviolence (CCNV). In a celebrated hunger strike, he forced President Reagan to hand over a federal building for the homeless, now called Mitch Snyder Place. In 1986, Martin Sheen, also a disciple of the Berrigan brothers, would make a TV biopic about him, *Samaritan: The Mitch Snyder Story*. Sadly, this great man who had "given his blood for Ireland," hanged himself on July 5, 1990.

I decided I needed only three colleagues, as anything more than four people would be a bit unwieldy. I felt there should be two men and two women. And I knew I would have to pick carefully and diligently. They would have to be totally reliable and prepared to go to prison, maybe for several years, without regrets or recriminations. I was proud of my choice: the late Maureen Armstrong of New York, from County Monaghan, a grandmother in her late fifties; Joe Mitchell, John Molloy, sixty, a warehouseman of Queens, NY, from County Meath; and Mary

Baggarly, twenty-eight, of Maryland, a housewife and mother of two, from the Bogside, Derry. Mary was a "Stickie"[1] when I met her, but I converted her from the error of her ways.

We were all set. But there was no point in having a protest in the British Embassy if nobody knew about it. So, I alerted trusted reporters, telling them they could enter a few minutes after us.

At exactly 11:58 a.m., Friday, April 24, 1974, Jack O'Brien[2] of Maryland (who also had been a Stickie until I converted him), drove the four of us to the front of the British Embassy (chancery, technically; the embassy is the residence of the ambassador, a bit farther down Massachusetts Avenue, NW).[3]

IN THE BELLY OF THE BEAST

I jumped out of the car, and immediately a young man headed towards me. I thought he was on to us. In an exaggerated display of coolness, I looked up at the sky and said, "What a beautiful day."

"Indeed," the young man replied with a smile.

We headed for the big glass doors, and again I was alarmed as another young man hurried to the door—But only for us to open it.

"Good morning, lovely day," I said, and with that, all four of us made it safely into the Embassy.

Phil Berrigan had drilled it into me to immediately "disarm" the first point of contact—to engage the guy at the security desk in a friendly, one-to-one, eye-to-eye dialogue. I headed straight for the desk, while the other three remained by the inside of the door.

"Good afternoon," I beamed, "'Tis a grand day."

"Indeed, it is," he replied

"My name is Father McManus."

"Oh, yes, Father."

"I'm based in a parish in Baltimore."

He folded his arms and looked very interested.

"I have come with some friends to the Embassy ..."

"Yes, good."

To express our concern about Northern Ireland."

That changed everything. He unfolded his arms, shot up in his chair and grabbed the telephone. He had the phone up to about his shoulder when I positioned our statement right in front of his face, and urged, "Please read this"—never once breaking the eye contact that Berrigan had warned me was so crucial.

He put the phone down and read the opening sentence: "Our action—the pouring of blood ..." His mouth fell open. He jumped to his feet, put one foot up on the chair behind him and held the arms of the chair with both hands and sank back staring at me. "Just a moment, just a moment," he gasped and grabbed the phone. I leaned over toward him, and in my best Confessional manner, I whispered: "Look, it is very important that you remain cool: otherwise, you will cause panic. Remain calm. Do not be afraid. We are nonviolent people. We will not hurt anybody; I assure you."

I gently motioned with both hands for him to sit down and he did, never taking his eyes off me, in sort of a trance. Berrigan and his people told me to be prepared for that to happen. I then told the man I was going to open my coat and for him not to be afraid. "In this pocket," I said, "there is a bottle, which I am now going to slowly take out." His eyes followed my hands. "In the bottle is some blood. My friends and I are going to pour blood all over the Embassy. But stay calm and do not scare people."

I then turned to Joe, Mary, and Maureen and gave them the signal to begin pouring blood.

SPILLING IRISH BLOOD

And then for the first time, I think, the man realized what was happening. He jumped up and shouted: "Stop there, sir. That is forbidden. I am sorry I cannot allow you. This is an embassy." As I turned away from him, he shouted, "Get someone. It's the Irish." (You're damn right, I thought to myself. *It is the Irish*).

It is amazing how quickly blood diffuses and spreads. Squirted methodically from "squeeze" bottles, Mary and I had the entire front of the glass building covered in no time. (The night before I had called Mary to express concern that we did not have enough blood and asked her to make some blood-substitute—ketchup, etc. and that we would explain to the media that we had made some extra blood substitute as a backup.)

Meanwhile, Maureen and Joe were doing their thing, as planned. The *Baltimore Sun*'s reporter, whom I had brought with us, would describe Maureen as, "... neat as a pin, no make-up, and no-nonsense grandmother." Joe, he wrote, was "a soft-spoken law-abiding ... man with a steady hand and a narrow tie."[4]

Both stood in the middle of the Embassy holding a Union Jack and proceeded to pour blood all over that flag, which for centuries has been soaked in Irish blood.

COWARDLY BRITISH ASSAULT

Suddenly, the head of the chancery, John Graham, probably in his fifties, charged Maureen from the back, bowled her over, grabbed the flag and ran part of the way up the stairway, stopped and turned around, clutching the flag to his chest. It was a cowardly, violent British assault on a nonviolent Irish grandmother.

As Maureen lay moaning on the ground, we knelt beside her, and I grabbed hold of all of them and said, "Remember, we had vowed nothing would make us retaliate. If we do, we will destroy our entire protest." We had role-played and mentally disciplined ourselves that no matter what happened we would not be violent. We helped Maureen to her feet and continued our business, calmly and serenely.

Mary and I opened the glass doors and poured blood on the outside and on the doorsteps. As I stepped back in, a distinguished grey-haired man came towards me to usher me out. "You can't, you can't possibly ... this is the British Embassy," he said. I gently patted him on the shoulder and ever so soothingly said, "You do not understand. This is a nonviolent protest, and it is precisely to do this that we came." He stared at me in complete astonishment. Then he saw that Mary was still outside, so he ran and held the doors closed against her. I tapped him on the shoulder, and with complete authority in my voice, ordered, "Excuse me, let the lady into the Embassy." And incredibly, he did. He looked at me apologetically and said, "OK, OK," and then walked away. Again, the amazing power of nonviolence!

When we had finished pouring the blood, we calmly reassembled in the middle of the embassy. We quietly stood there while all around us the Embassy was in chaos. A feeling of complete harmony and tranquility descended upon me. It was a beautiful moment, which the Berrigan people had told me to expect if our motives and techniques were pure. The other three, I could tell, were experiencing the same serenity, although flushed and smiling from our success.

We waited for the confrontation. It had been agreed that I would do the talking, no matter what happened so we could contain the situation in a disciplined manner—another essential ingredient of the successful nonviolent action. If each of us were tricked into speaking to different members of the embassy the coherence of our protest would be shattered.

While we waited, embassy people started pouring out from everywhere. Employees were hanging over the banisters of the big spiral staircase in the lobby, staring down. Dozens of people began forming a semicircle around us.

In a calm but loud voice (well trained in Hawkstone for the parish missions in Britain), I called out. "Would you all be quiet, please?" There was instant silence, a palpable hush. "Please do not be alarmed. This is a nonviolent protest. We come in peace. We will not do you any harm." They all stared in astonishment. Then a pompous little man in a dark suit pushed his way through the crowd. His face was deathly white, and he was bubbling with venom.

"Mister, are you in charge?" he fairly spat at me.

I calmly demanded, again with authority, "Who are you?" It had the expected result. He was astonished at the temerity of this intruder asking him who he was. He prodded both hands to his chest and in complete exasperation spluttered, "Who... who am I? I'm the head of security."

"Fine," I replied, "I will talk to you. My name is Fr. McManus. This is Joe Mitchell, this is Mary Baggarly, and this is the lady whom one of the embassy officials assaulted, Maureen Armstrong." The three courteously nodded.

"There was no assault here," shouted an official to my left.

"Yes, there was," said a reporter, "and we have a photo to prove it." Then an embassy official tried to grab the camera. "Take your f—ing hands off my camera, buddy," the reporter said with explosive force, and for a moment I thought there was going to be a fistfight. I remember thinking: wouldn't it be ironic if, after all our nonviolent role-playing, the press starts a riot in the embassy? I turned back to the little security man who was wailing away.

"I have got a responsibility ... I have got to do my duty."

"We understand; no need to give explanations. Of course, do your duty, and we will do ours," I said reassuringly and softly. He just could not handle it and was going to start wailing again. "No, no," I said, "it's all right, be calm, there is no need to worry. This is a nonviolent protest, and we will not harm anyone."

He made an obvious effort to control himself, then very officiously pulled out a little notebook and said to Mary, "OK, madam, what's your address in Ireland?"

"Do not answer that, Mary," I directed.

He almost pleadingly said, "But I've got to have... I've got to have—."

I gently leaned toward him and said, "We are not answering any of your questions like that. We will answer all questions at the appropriate time and place." The poor guy just gave up. He put his little book into his little pocket and walked off, dejected and defeated.

An ashen-faced individual was hovering around the periphery of the semicircle going nuts. "He is sheltering behind his collar," he was screaming.

I turned to him and demanded, "Do you want to speak to me?" It stopped him dead. Then he started up again, arms flailing.

"He's a priest. He does not have to tell the truth."
"Do you work here?" I asked.
"Yes," he hissed.

"It appears you are giving vent to religious prejudice, which ill becomes the British Embassy. And how could I be sheltering behind my collar when I'm completely at your mercy?" He stared at me in total exasperation and then darted off.

HAVE YOU BEEN TO IRELAND?

Then I began to address the crowd again: I realize that we have caused you embarrassment," I began. "We are not embarrassed," someone shouted from my right. I turned around. A tall, well-groomed young man was glowering at me. "What nationality are you?" he asked. I quietly stared him in the eye and wondered if the same tactic would work again. "Who are you?" I asked. The simple question stunned him by its impertinence. I could see he was trying to regain his poise. "I am Baker Bates, the embassy information officer," he said. "What are you doing here?"

I replied we were conducting a nonviolent protest against British mistreatment of political prisoners and the assassination campaign of the British Army. Thinking he had a trump card, he shot back, in a perfect English accent, "I am from Northern Ireland. Have you ever been to Ireland?"

(There was I thinking the British Embassy would know all about me!) "My home is in British-occupied Ireland," I conversationally replied. He was not expecting that. "Well, it's a pity you just missed John Hume," he sniffed. "Was this done to offset the good John Hume did here? Did you know he was here?"

We, of course, had no idea Hume had just been there and I told him so. He very illogically responded, "So you're saying this was not a planned protest?" I replied, "Not at all. It was a very planned protest."

"Yes, indeed," he shouted. "You even brought your own hired press." Then whirling on his heels, he snapped, "OK, Jack, you have made your point."

"Thank you," I replied, "you are most courteous."

Then I turned to the next official, a young man with fairly long, well-styled hair, who clearly wanted to have a go at me. "Now it's your turn," I said to him. He let loose.

"I suppose you also brought rubber bullets with you, Fr. McManus?" (I had shown rubber bullets on TV all over America to illustrate that they were not harmless little pellets but six-inch projectiles of hard rubber that had killed children and blinded people in Northern Ireland).

"So, you know me?" I said.

"Yes, I've seen you on TV, and I read *The Irish People* every week," he said. Then he, too, started up about John Hume: "John Hume says that all the money of the Irish Northern Aid Committee goes to the IRA. It all goes direct to Joe Cahill."

I asked, "What has the IRA and Northern Aid got to do with this protest?"

He replied, "This is an Irish Northern Aid protest."

"Please don't speculate. Read our statement, and you will see what it is." He would have none of it.

"You are the spokesman for Irish Northern Aid," he persisted. "No, I am not," I said. "But I've heard you speak on their behalf," he shouted.

"Yes, I have spoken on their behalf, but I'm not their spokesman," I tried to reason.

He finally agreed to read our statement. When he came to the part about political prisoners, he went on again about John Hume. (The British Embassy for years always paraded out John Hume to cover up their misdeeds.) "John Hume says there are no political prisoners in Northern Ireland.

I looked him straight in the eye and earnestly said: "I am prepared to discuss Northern Ireland with someone in the embassy who knows something about it, but you quite obviously know nothing about it." The gentleness with which I said it puzzled him, I could tell. I kept calmly looking him in the eye until he felt uncomfortable and finally walked away.

Baker Bates came back, a little bit more in control of himself: "Fr. McManus, you have made your statement. Now, why don't you leave?"

This was unexpected. And the Berrigan people had warned me about the unexpected, as that is when things can unravel. We had expected to be immediately arrested, and clearly the embassy did not want that. I needed to play for time so as to be able to talk to my three colleagues. I glanced admiringly around the fine building, and said to Baker Bates, "I've never been in the British Embassy before. I think I will stay a while."

"So, it's a sit-in, is it?" he snapped and took off like a scalded cat.

Standing Up—By Sitting Down

I huddled with Joe, Mary, and Maureen and explained we would have to do a sit-in, which we had not planned because they were not going to have us arrested. I told them to do exactly as I did.

The Executive Protective Service, the uniformed branch of the Secret Service, soon arrived. The moment the lead officer saw me he smiled broadly. I immediately knew he was Irish Catholic. I told them that we were concluding our nonviolent protest by a sit-in. We would not resist in any way, but they would have to carry us out. I then signaled to Maureen, Joe, and Mary to sit down. The smiling officer said to me as he and another lifted me off the floor, "I had a nice pint of Guinness in your country, Father, a few months ago."

"Which part?" I asked.

"Mayo," he grunted as he held me. "My mother is from Mayo, and my father is from Galway."

It was only in the police station that we realized the extent to which Maureen had been hurt. Her left arm and back were badly bruised by the body-slam of the embassy official. She did not want to go to the hospital and leave Mary in prison by herself. But we insisted.

We refused to sign the citation form, which would have entitled us to get out. Instead, in solidarity with the political prisoners, we spent the night in prison—Mary in the Women's House of Detention and Joe and I in the DC Central Cell Block. I got on the metal bed, no blanket, put my shoes under my head and slept soundly throughout the night. The following morning, I was handed a sandwich through the bars of my cell. It was just a piece of ham between dry bread, but no food ever tasted so good (I had not eaten for several hours before being arrested and was now starving.)

Afterward, I was moved from my cell to a holding area—a huge cage-like structure with dozens of young black men. I think I was the only white man in the cage (although I never think of myself as white, just Irish). They were astonished to see me, in my black suit and clerical collar. "Hey, Preacher-man/Rev./ Father what you in for?" They swarmed around me all excited. I was in high spirits, so I decided to have some fun with them.

"Well, you see, I work in a poor all-black parish in Baltimore. I just got tired and angry at the poverty of the poor people, so, I went and robbed a bank, and I gave thousands of dollars to the black parishioners." Well, they went crazy, cheering and whooping and giving me high fives. When I told them I was just kidding, they were visibly disappointed.

MORE PROTESTANT SOLIDARITY

Before arraignment, I was greeted by a nice surprise, a press release from the Fellowship of Reconciliation, one of the oldest Christian non-violent movements. It read:

> "The following is the text of the statement that two leading representatives of the organization Fellowship of Reconciliation (F.O.R.) issued in response to the non-violent blood-protest that Fr. Sean McManus led at the British Embassy on Friday, April 24. The statement was hand delivered to Fr. McManus while he was in prison. "We British visitors to Washington welcome such

dramatic nonviolent protest against the military policy of the British Government in Ireland."

"Blood given for justice in Ireland is a supremely good investment."

This statement was released by Rev. David Harding, a Methodist minister, who is secretary general for Fellowship of Reconciliation in Britain; and by Mr. Guy Otten, who is a member of the International Executive of Fellowship of Reconciliation.

Later that morning, we were arraigned, charged with "protesting within five hundred feet of an Embassy." The British Embassy did not press charges, and the judge told us we were free to go.

We were well pleased by our good work. It sublimely confirmed to me the transcendent power of nonviolent action—and demonstrated that the British government cannot simply handle it, as Gandhi knew so well.

I will be eternally grateful to Phil Berrigan and Mitch Snyder. May God rest their noble souls.

CHAPTER 9

All the News That's Fit to Print— Or Not

In wartime, truth is so precious that she should always be attended by a bodyguard of lies.
Winston Churchill

MY ARREST AT THE BRITISH EMBASSY—plus all the previous publicity and consciousness raising my activity had generated—gained huge support for my work all across the United States. Therefore, when I stressed the need for the new approach of the Irish National Caucus, people listened and trusted my judgment. Furthermore, the new approach could not be dismissed as being "soft" because, as the action at the British Embassy proved, we were prepared to go to prison. I was, of course, aware that my actions could be seen as "radical"—a real taboo among many Irish-Americans. Being "radical" was almost as bad as being a communist. So, I had to walk a fine line, which some very conservative folk believed I crossed often.

But without resources and money, I knew of no other way to spread the word. One had to break the unbelievable conspiracy of silence in the media and U.S. Congress.

To give one passing example of media bias: After my brother Frank was shot, *The New York Times* reported that he had been shot by the IRA because he was not sufficiently militant. Now, how do you suppose they got that ridiculous piece of information? I called the *Times* from Sacred Heart Church in Baltimore and asked to speak to one of the editors responsible for publishing the item. I began by protesting the story, and he countered by saying, "What would a priest in Baltimore know about the incident?" I told him I was Frank's brother. He countered by saying their information was good and that they were standing by the story. If such a prestigious newspaper as *The New York Times* can be so obtuse on Northern Ireland, what could one expect from the general American media that simply kept churning out the same old British line?

In fact, my very first letter to the American media was to the Baltimore archdiocesan newspaper, *The Catholic Review*. The well-known priest, sociologist, and novelist, Fr. Andrew Greely, had written in his column that the IRA was in business for the thrill of killing and being killed—this from a man who prided himself on his Irishness and knowledge of all things Irish. Just how do you suppose he came by that conviction? Years later, Greely would become an outright defender of the IRA. A few years ago, I met him on two occasions at the White House for Saint Patrick's Day celebrations. On both occasions, I reminded him of his ridiculous letter, and each time he totally ignored what I said, making absolutely no response.

And in speaking of *The Catholic Review*, I recently checked its website where it reviews its own history and its "campaign against the Ku Klux Klan in the 1920s or its calls for justice in Central America in the 1980s. What about justice for Catholics in Northern Ireland? No campaign for them! It was not just the secular media that was complicit in British oppression of Catholics, so were the Catholic media, with some exceptions—and so were the U.S. Catholic bishops, with very few exceptions. More of that later.

So, with that sort of media indifference, what could one do? If the American media were not going to announce the news, I would have to announce it myself. A case in point: on October 15, 1974, the political prisoners—incarcerated without charge or trial—burned Long Kesh to the ground in protest at the inhumane conditions. That did receive media attention, but the resulting British punitive action, including forcing the prisoners to sleep in the open air, covered only by sheets of polythene did not. I tried, to no avail, to get the media to cover that inhumanity. So, I decided if they were not going to announce it, I would do it for them.

At that time, ABC nationwide news was announced live, at least in part, from its studio in Washington, DC by Howard K. Smith. I decided to interrupt the live newscast and tell America, all one hundred million of the estimated viewers, about the mistreatment of prisoners in Long Kesh.

Again, I decided four was a good number for the action. I selected Mary Baggarly and a young woman from Baltimore, Cathy Fogarty, who, with her father, had become very active. The third person was Sean Walsh of Washington who had recently joined the Irish National Caucus. Naturally, we had to "case the joint." In particular, I had to know exactly when Howard K. Smith was broadcasting live otherwise my protest would not be carried.

Days well in advance, I went to the ABC studio and introduced myself to the appropriate persons. I told them that I was visiting from Ireland, where I was in religious broadcasting, and I wanted to learn from the real professionals of ABC, and could I perhaps come back and observe from within the studio how these great experts did it? They graciously accepted. While I was talking to them, Sean Walsh was casing the joint, even using his credit card to slip the lock to enter the broadcasting room, then not in use. He even made a date with the young receptionist who would have to buzz us in when we came back for our action. He took her to dinner the night before the action.

ANNOUNCING THE NEWS OURSELVES

On Tuesday, October 22, 1974, the four of us headed to ABC News. They recognized Sean and me and brought us in. At first, I was escorted into the glass control booth, with all the TV monitors, etc. I was initially concerned because it cordoned me off from the actual studio where

Howard K. Smith was seated. But I quickly realized it was a blessing as it enabled me to know exactly what was going on, with the very helpful control-team giving me a blow-by-blow account. Otherwise, I would have no idea when Smith was going out live. The control team told me there was a commercial break coming up and that right after it, Howard K. Smith would be broadcasting. I made my move, quickly telling my three colleagues to follow me. I walked into the actual broadcast room. A technician looked momentarily alarmed, I put my finger to my lips, in the silence gesture, and nodded reassuringly that I was just going to stand nearby. He nodded back, understandingly.

I was now in a perfect position to see and to interrupt Howard K. Smith. I had given the others the exact same sentence which each of us would say, knowing we would have only a split second to get it out before we were cut off.

At exactly 6:16 p.m., I mounted the raised dais from which Howard K. Smith was reading the news live. I walked right behind him (and felt guilty at the way the poor man jumped off his chair in real shock) and proceeded to say my lines: "Will someone please help? The British are torturing political prisoners in Northern Ireland." Every word went out as clear as a bell, all across the United States. I then moved on, as planned, to let the three others walking behind in single file, say the same words. But they were cut off, as I feared they would.

The allegedly unflappable media went flapping like crazy. These folks, who demand that others keep their cool under the most trying circumstances, were like headless chickens. I walked out of the main newsroom, to wait for the police, reassuringly holding out my hands saying, "Don't worry. This is a nonviolent protest. We will cause no harm."

A small guy with longish hair, in his late thirties, and obviously in some position of authority in ABC, tried to confront me, saying he was not going to let me leave. I told him not to worry; we were not leaving but waiting for the police because we wanted to be arrested in completion of our nonviolent act. He then got a bit hysterical, screaming at me that I was protected by my collar. I quietly asked him if it did not occur to him that my collar might be protecting him. "What do you mean?" he incredulously asked. "Well, if I were not a priest, I might have punched you out for your abusiveness," I gently responded. That seemed to steady him up.

Then a group gathered around, all complaining about our action. I asked which of them were reporters as opposed to technicians, producers, etc. A few indicated they were. I then made the point that the first question a real newsperson should be asking is "Why did we do it?" Not just berating us for doing it. I further explained that we were fed up with the news always presenting the problem in Northern Ireland as a senseless conflict between Protestants and Catholics with no explanation of the vicious role of the British government. One newsman defiantly said ABC did not present the problem in simple Protestant-Catholic terms. And just as he said it, Howard K. Smith stormed among us, incandescent with rage. He roared at me: "What are you—Protestant or Catholic?"

I gave a knowing sweep of my hand to the previous newsman who had just been speaking and said: "The top ABC man has just confirmed my point."

Smith rounded on and said, "What the hell does that mean? What are you talking about?" I explained to him that the other newsman had denied my charge that ABC presents the Northern Ireland problem as just a religious squabble.

"And Mr. Smith," I said, "you just proved my argument." Then he spluttered that he gave money to both Protestant and Catholic charities. "Very commendable," I said, "but that is not the point. You have not exposed British government violation of human rights in Northern Ireland." He waved his hands dismissively and stormed off to his inner sanctum.

The police finally arrived, a hefty black officer of about 40-years old, in the lead. He immediately gave me a huge smile. He's Catholic, I said to myself. "OK, OK, settle down, you all. What's going on?" I waited for ABC to explain what happened. The officer then inquired if the intruders had a knife or anything or attacked anybody. No, he was told. Then he burst into a huge smile and asked what all the commotion was about. He then turned to me and said, "Father, what's going on?"

"Well, Officer, in the tradition of Martin Luther King, Jr."—here he broke into the biggest smile I had ever seen, "we have done a nonviolent action to protest ABC covering up British oppression in Northern Ireland. We interrupted Mr. Smith's live broadcast. And in the spirit of Martin Luther King, Jr., we waited for you to come and arrest us."

It was clear that the officer was enjoying all of this. "Do you want me to arrest the good Father?" he asked the ABC officials. They huddled for a moment.

"No," was their firm answer.

"OK, Padre," said the smiling cop, "you and your friends are free to go." And, so ended my stint as an ABC newscaster.

I got hundreds of letters, even three marriage proposals! For years later people would say to me, "Oh, you're the priest that made Howard K. Smith jump out of his chair."

RICHARD HARRIS: MOVIE STAR AND IRISH PATRIOT

One of the last things I did in Baltimore before moving to Boston was to organize with Ed Brady and others an Irish Testimonial Dinner on June 21, 1975, for Irish Northern Aid with Limerick-born movie star, Richard Harris, as the guest speaker.

About a year before the event, I had met Harris for the first time after a live performance at a local university. After the performance, I waited for him to come out from the stage area. Out he comes, with the longest overcoat I had ever seen on a man—down to his heels—and with a stunning lady on his arm, Ann Turkel. She was the most glamorous woman I had ever seen, almost as tall as Richard and with a smile as wide as the ocean. I gingerly approached this super-couple, excused myself for interrupting, but explained I was desperately trying to help The North of Ireland, and if he were interested, as rumored, I would like to meet with him. "I'm fiercely interested, absolutely, passionately," he declaimed in his best King Arthur voice. "Annie, let's cancel our appointments for tomorrow and meet with Fr. Sean for breakfast."

Richard was intensely patriotic. And we got on very well. Before the Baltimore dinner, I had him as the guest speaker for the big Irish Northern Aid Dinner in New York. He recited the poem, "The Fool" by Patrick Pearse and concluded by singing, without any accompaniment, "Kevin Barry." Needless to say, that brought the house down. Ann was especially pleased as she told me she had never seen such an outpouring of love and respect for Richard.

Ann was a lovely lady and though not Catholic, had an exaggerated respect for priests, as is shown by the following story. At the time, the horror movie *The Exorcist* was all the rage. I had seen it in Baltimore. One evening I called Richard from Sacred Heart Church at their New York apartment. Ann answered the phone. "It's Fr. Sean, Ann," I said. Well, she let out a bloodcurdling shriek.

I heard Richard shout, "Annie, Annie, it's all right." Richard then came on and said he would have to call me back as Anne was almost fainting.

I was really worried and didn't know what to do. Anyway, a short time later Ann called back, very apologetic. "Don't worry," I said. "What happened?"

She explained that they had just come in from seeing *The Exorcist*, which had deeply troubled her, and on the way back Richard was increasing her fear by telling her even worse stories that happened in Ireland—bigger and scarier, of course. Ann kept fretting that if diabolic possession could happen to anyone, might it happen to her? By the time she was walking in the door, she had worked herself into somewhat of a frenzy. She said to Richard, "I've got to call Fr. Sean, or I will go insane." She grabbed the phone to dial my number, and at that very split second, I said, "It's Father Sean." It scared the living daylights out of the poor woman.

OFF TO MISSION CHURCH, BOSTON

In the summer of 1975, the Baltimore Province of Redemptorists was making the periodic new appointments. I was assigned to Mission

Church in Boston. That surprised me. Had my superiors been unduly concerned about my escalating activity, they would have hardly sent me to the most Irish city in the most Irish state of all.

I was given the same room that de Valera used when he visited Mission Church to meet with his half-brother who was stationed there, Fr. Thomas Wheelwright. (That was during the period 1919–1920). Down the street from Mission Church was the funeral parlor owned by Gene Sheehan, an old IRA man who was a close friend of Dev and the last man on the run in the Civil War (according to Gene).

I loved Boston. What a city! No Irishman could feel unwelcome there. However, the Irish in Boston were not as militant as the New York Irish regarding Northern Ireland.

I had spoken several times in Boston, so I was already well known by all the Irish with an interest in the Troubles. Mission Church parish itself was no longer strongly Irish. The neighborhood had changed and was now predominantly black and Hispanic. I welcomed the chance to work for them, as there had been very few blacks or Hispanics in Sacred Heart Church in Baltimore. I got to know many of them, especially those involved in social work and community activism. Some were really radical, in the good sense. And boy, did they stand by me when the Irish consulate in Boston tried to have me silenced or moved! More of that later.

Shortly after I arrived, an old Irish-born man came to see me. He said it was great to have a young Irish priest again in the parish, that it would be like old times and that I should use the parish halls for Irish dances—not the newfangled stuff, mind you, no bands, just a man sitting in the corner, playing a fiddle.

I was touched by the wistfulness of the moment, but acutely conscious of how he was living in the past. That day was gone. The parish would never be like that again—when fifty thousand people attended the Masses on Sunday during the Second World War and practically every newly arrived Irish person in Boston wanted to get married at Mission Church. I have since used this as a parable to illustrate how the status of Unionism in Northern Ireland has changed (even if some Unionists are still in a state of denial): there is no going back to "big house Unionism," where Unionists rule supreme. That day, too, has gone forever.

But I did have some Irish dances in the hall. And I took the theatre—yes, the theatre—out of mothballs. It had the best acoustics in all of Boston, and a local Irish drama group put it to fine use. One of my jobs was looking after the parish's primary school, which was run by Notre Dame Nun—all of them walking saints. All except one were over fifty. They were a group of dedicated, loving and joyful women, so totally different from the often ignorant, cruel and sexist stereotype of nuns in the media. It was a terrific school, totally integrated, black, white and Hispanic. And I loved the kids. I became good friends of the Sheehan family, who had three girls at the school. The father, Mossie, God rest him, was an ardent Kerryman, who loved to sing and was GAA mad; the mother, Pat (Patricia) is a wonderful Irish-American lady.

TRICIA—LITTLE KERRY ANGEL

Their youngest girl, Tricia, was out sick for a while. One day I was walking back to Mission Church from my hospital- chaplain rounds, and as I passed the local pharmacy, I spotted a cute teddy bear in the window. And a strange thing happened, which I've never been able to explain, and which has never happened since. I found myself thinking, *"Why should I rush to New York to meet a politician*—some politician had asked to meet with me—*when little Tricia is sick?"* I decided to cancel my New York visit, bought the teddy bear, went to the Sheehan's house, and gave it to a delighted Tricia. It was on her hospital bed the day she died. In a heartbreakingly short time, we discovered Tricia did not have the flu, but leukemia. I was in her hospital room with her parents when her heartbeat started to fail. The doctors swooped into the room and practically lifted the parents out, leaving me inside as they desperately attempted to revive her. I could feel death descend on the room almost like a wind, while Tricia's soul soared to God.

Even now, after all these years, I tear up as I write this. My sorrow at Tricia's death was made all the more acute because my sister Celia and her husband, Michael, had lost their young daughter Caroline to the same dreaded disease. Tricia was a special child, with beautiful, golden-blonde hair and a personality that lit up the room. I preached at her funeral Mass, and I think it was the most difficult thing I have ever done. But I made it through without breaking down, buoying up the grieving congregation with my tribute to Tricia, aged eleven. The power of the funeral Mass, with its message of hope and resurrection, remains one of the most visible sacramental graces of the Catholic Church. It has healed and helped millions to recover from the most awful human suffering and bereavement.

Lobbying the Vatican

My campaigning for justice and peace in Northern Ireland did not appear as sensational as it had in a German–Polish parish in Baltimore. I continued to speak and organize chapters of the Irish National Caucus all across the United States. And then we made a surprise move. I organized an Irish National Caucus delegation to the Vatican.

Through the assistance of an Irish nun from Belfast, I was put in touch with a priest involved with the Pontifical Commission for Justice and Peace at the Vatican, Monsignor Maurice Bonneric, who felt it would help to raise the profile of the Troubles if an American group was to visit specifically for that reason. He guaranteed a meeting with Archbishop Giovanni Benelli, Substitute Secretary of State. *The Sunday Telegraph* said the Archbishop had "in effect become the Pope's [Paul VI] chief executive."[1] He was made a Cardinal in 1977. He was also on most *papabili* lists—shortlists of likely future popes. But he died suddenly in 1982 at the age of sixty-one.

We traveled to Rome during the week of December 7, 1975. The delegation I headed up was composed of Bishop Drury, Jack Keane (president of the AOH), Brendan McCusker (chairman of Irish Northern Aid Committee), Sean Walsh and Fred O'Brien of the Irish National Caucus. Cardinal Wright of Boston welcomed us to the Eternal City by giving us dinner in his apartment. Wright, who was the Prefect of the

Congregation for the Clergy, was the highest-ranking American in the Roman Curia.

Archbishop Benelli gave us a very attentive and gracious hearing. I spoke very strongly and urgently, but very respectfully. The Cardinal seemed to be very sympathetic and emphasized the importance of America putting pressure on Britain. As we were leaving, he grasped my hand and whispered earnestly, "The Irish National Caucus must be nonviolent. In the Lord's name, I beseech you to follow the path of nonviolence."

When a top Vatican official, so close to the Pope, and in the Vatican to boot, says that to a young priest, it has to register. And it did. The fact that the Archbishop listened carefully and did not automatically take the side of the British made his appeal more authentic. He was preaching Pax Christi, not Pax Britannica. In that instance, I just knew the Irish National Caucus would have to formally adopt the position of nonviolence. The Caucus was, in fact, nonviolent, as our actions showed, plus we had no foreign principal, but we had not formally taken a position of nonviolence. I knew it was one thing for me as an individual to say the IRA had as much right to fight for freedom as the British or Americans had, but if I were to head up an organization as a priest, then I would have to formally adopt a policy of nonviolence. This became even more compelling later on when I realized I would have to go full-time into a special ministry of justice and peace if the Irish National Caucus was to succeed in its mission. I issued a press release saying we were well pleased with our visit.[2]

After the Vatican visit, we went to Dublin. Ruairí ÓBrádaigh and Joe Cahill met us at the airport. And the Special Branch went crazy. They were scurrying about the place as if aliens had arrived. We filled in Republican leaders on our Vatican visit. I gave interviews to the Irish media and told them that since the Caucus was now well established, we would be making Ireland an issue in the 1976 presidential elections. I slipped up to Fermanagh to see my family and then returned to the United States.

CHAPTER 10

The Caucus and Jimmy Carter

*The Irish National Caucus ... achieved its first major mark
... when it obtained an "Irish justice statement
from candidate Jimmy Carter."*
Professor Paul Power[1]

As mentioned in the previous chapter, I was determined that the Irish National Caucus would flex its muscles in the 1976 presidential election. The first Democratic candidate who made contact with me was Senator Henry "Scoop" Jackson of Washington State. I traveled to meet Jackson in New York. The first thing he said to me was, "Well, Father, I'm of Viking stock so the Irish cannot be mad at me." With a totally straight face, I said, "You guys killed Brian Boru in 1014, and we haven't forgotten it." He almost fell off his chair thinking he had made the classic and much-dreaded candidate faux pas. Then I laughed and told him I was kidding. I urged him to make a strong statement, no wishy-washy nonsense, condemning the violation of human rights, internment and calling for British withdrawal. He did exactly that in January 1976.

Then one of Jackson's top operators made contact with me during the hunger strike of Frank Stagg (1942–1976), who died in a British prison on February 12, 1976, after sixty-two days on hunger strike. I explained that Stagg's hunger strike was making a huge impact on the Irish in Massachusetts and that Jackson should campaign vigorously among them on his Irish position. Finally, when Stagg died, I invited Jackson's man to the public Mass I was saying at Mission Church for Stagg. We had put on a special effort to have a suitable turnout for the Mass. Thousands flocked to honor and pray for that young Irish hero who sacrificed his life for Irish freedom.

I preached a moving tribute to Stagg. I was careful not to be "political" as this was the Mass, not a political rally. I have always been scrupulously correct in this matter. Nonetheless, I could not preach a proper funeral Mass homily unless I properly explained who Stagg was, what his values were, and why he had sacrificed his young life.

After the Mass, Jackson's man told me I was "a master" at presenting a difficult subject, expressed amazement at the size of the congregation and how they responded to my words. I replied that it "was the song, not the singer" that the Irish felt deeply about The Troubles and all politicians ignored that at their peril. "I bet you're now glad that Senator Jackson put out that strong statement," I added.

Jackson went on to win the Massachusetts Democratic primary on March 2. On March 16, he wrote me a personal letter of thanks:

"Let me personally thank you and the Irish National Caucus for your efforts with the Irish voters on my behalf ... Let me reaffirm my commitment to the cause of Irish Freedom so closely related to the founding of our great nation. As stated previously, I support a declaration of intent from the British Government regarding their withdrawal from Ireland, and I believe that will be a concrete step towards peace with justice in Ireland, a cause for which an Irishman, Frank Stagg, died recently in a nonviolent, peaceful protest in an English prison."

That from a Cold War anticommunist senator! You knew it had to get the attention of the British (and that of the Irish government). But more importantly, it got the attention of the man who beat out Jackson for the Democratic nomination—Jimmy Carter. (Jackson won the New York primary on April 6 but dropped out on May 1 after Carter beat him in Pennsylvania.) I sent the Jackson letter to the Carter people through Senator Joe Timilty of Boston, a good friend of mine and an ardent Irishman, who was a key man in the Carter campaign. I told Joe we wanted to meet Carter, and that we would not support him unless he met with us.

Irish "Welcome" for Queen

But here let me digress a bit, to take care of the Queen of England. She visited Boston on Sunday, July 11, and I had to make sure she got an Irish welcome. Tommy and Agnes Clifford, two good friends, and I organized the protest. Tommy drove me around the city for weeks so that I could speak to every possible Irish grouping. We had a pretty good turnout for the protest. The *New York Times* carried a photograph of Her Majesty surrounded by placards saying: "America 1776. Ireland?" "Ireland Unfree Shall Never Be at Peace." "Tyranny Is Not Easily Conquered, But We Will Conquer" and "England Out of Ireland."[2] To my own astonishment, I was able to get right up beside the queen—only Mayor Kevin White was between us. Sometime later when I arranged for the mayor to meet Nora Connolly O'Brien, daughter of Irish patriot-martyr James Connolly, when she visited Boston, he smiled and said, "Seems like I always see you, Father, when we greet famous ladies from across the Atlantic."

Carter Meeting

Just when it seemed that a meeting was in the works, Carter's people got nervous and admitted that the British were going crazy and putting a lot of pressure on them to cancel the meeting. "How is it going to look if Carter is seen to back down because he is scared of the Brits. How many votes will that get him?" I retorted.

Then Al Stern, first assistant to Stu Eizenstat, Carter's top adviser, sent a telegram to us: "Urgent ... Trying to reach you. Please call."[3]

I called Stern, and he assured me that Carter was not scared of the British and that the meeting was still on, even though the Irish Embassy was also opposed to the meeting. The meeting was finally and hurriedly scheduled for Wednesday, October 27, 1976, in Pittsburgh—just six days before the presidential election. I discussed with Stern, line by line, the opening statement I would make on behalf of the thirty four member Caucus delegation. And I had sent him a copy well in advance of the meeting; with the assurance, not a syllable would be changed:

> Irish National Caucus statement to Governor Jimmy Carter, Pittsburgh Hilton Hotel, Pittsburgh, Pennsylvania. October 27, 1976.
>
> Governor Carter,
>
> On behalf of the Irish National Caucus, may we say that it is an honor to meet the next President of the United States. The Irish National Caucus represents all the major Irish-American organizations in the United States and is their official voice on justice and peace in Ireland.
>
> We are deeply saddened by the ongoing tragedy in Ireland; and as Irish-Americans, we are deeply hurt by the stonewalling silence of the Nixon-Ford Administration. But we are greatly encouraged by the Irish plank in the Democratic Platform which states: "The voice of the United States should be heard in Northern Ireland against violence and terror, against the discrimination, repression, and deprivation which brought about that civil strife and for the efforts of the parties towards a peaceful resolution of the future of Northern Ireland.
>
> The United States should encourage the formation of a united Ireland, pertinent alliances such as NATO and international organizations such as the United Nations should be fully apprised of the interest of the United States with respect to the status of Ireland in the international community of nations.

We are even more encouraged, Governor Carter, by your words in your recent address at the University of Notre Dame: "We have watched passively as human rights are violated in Ireland. We should begin by having it understood that if any nation, whatever its political system, deprives its people of basic human rights, that fact will help shape our people's attitude towards that nation's government. If other nations want our friendship and support, they must understand that we want to see basic human rights respected."

We welcome this, Governor Carter, as a reinforcement of the Democratic Party Platform which also states "a primary object of American aid, both military and economic, is first of all to enhance the condition of freedom in the world. The United States should not provide aid to any government—anywhere in the world—which uses secret police detention without charges, and torture to enforce its power. Exceptions to this policy should be rare, and the aid provided should be limited to that which is absolutely necessary. The United States should be open and unashamed in its exercise of diplomatic efforts to encourage the observance of human rights in countries which receive American aid."

Governor Carter, in a recent letter to the National President of the Ancient Order of Hibernians, you stated: "I am sympathetic with those who seek to promote a stable and free Ireland with full civil and human rights for all citizens."

"A stable and free Ireland with full civil and human rights for all citizens, Governor Carter, is precisely what we in the Irish National Caucus stand for. We thank you for meeting with us, and we look forward to meeting you again as President of the United States.

Not only did Stern have a copy in advance, but he also suggested I would add the word "Stonewalling" before "silence" in the third paragraph.

Then Jimmy Carter made his statement. And for the record, here it is, word for word:

> President-Elect Jimmy Carter's Statement to Irish National Caucus in Pittsburgh, on Oct. 27, 1976.
>
> It is a great honor to me to come here this afternoon to be with you who come to meet with me from a major part of this nation.
>
> I don't disavow my own Irish heritage. As I said, in a speech earlier today, it does not matter when our ancestors came here, two years ago or twenty years ago or two hundred years ago or more ... It is why we came here and what we do after we arrive to make our nation great.
>
> It would be a mistake for all of us to forget that we have a dual commitment; first and foremost, of course, to our country, here, the United States. But then secondly, and very importantly, to the nations from which our families came.
>
> When I was in Notre Dame two weeks ago last Sunday with Father Hesburgh and just a few moments ago, as a matter of fact, with Cardinal Cooke in New York, we talked about the need for the establishment of a Commission on International Peace, to pursue in the multitude of

places around the world, the concept of our country's standing firm in its commitment to human rights.

We see or come on the evening television news and in the national headlines every now and then, specific instances where human rights are subjugated and where quite often our nation as was pointed out by Father [McManus], stands mute and doesn't speak.

The Democratic National Convention Platform Plank was written jointly, by my own staff and by Mayor Daley from Chicago, to be sure that the world knows that the Democratic Party understands the special problems in Ireland and that it is a mistake for our country's Government to stand quiet on the struggle of the Irish for peace for the respect of human rights and for unifying Ireland.

I would like to say that I almost feel like I am a member of the Ancient Order of Hibernians as well. For six years in a row, I was honored to go to Savannah on Saint Patrick's Day, and if any of you have ever been to Savannah on Saint Patrick's Day, you know that it is one of the fine and wonderful events in the life of a human being, and those who go there from Boston and other major cities in the world say that they have never seen anything like it. Although Savannah is a fairly small city, we have two hundred and fifty thousand people participating in the parade and the beer is green, the grits are green, the streets are green, everything is painted green; in fact, one year we dyed the entire Savannah River green. So, Georgia has an awful lot of Irish settlers including my own family. To some degree, I know the heartache that you feel to see the bloodshed and the disharmony and deprivation in

Ireland. And I am very honored that you come to let me feel a part of a hope that will never be extinguished that we can have a redressing of grievances, and a realization for hopes of our brave, unfortunate mankind in Ireland.

Needless to say, we were delighted by that statement. And the British were not. *The Guardian*, supposed to be a moderate and reasonable paper, sniffed in an editorial: "And now, a few days from what may be his elevation to the Presidency of the United States, along comes Jimmy Carter, sharing a platform with Seán Mac Stíofáin's confessor and pledging himself to a United Ireland."[4]

Carter was roundly condemned by the British media and by British and Unionist politicians. Mr. Roy Mason, the British Secretary of State for Northern Ireland told the House of Commons that Carter was, "giving aid and succor to Ulster terrorists." Nothing surprising there.

FITZGERALD RALLIES TO BRITS

What would surprise many Americans (but not this Fermanagh man) was the hysterical reaction of the obsequious Dublin government of that time. (The *Boston Globe* would later report: "Irish embassy officials protested vehemently to Carter aides. Carter, under pressure, agreed to send a telegram of clarification ... Carter, the next day, telegrammed Irish Foreign Minister FitzGerald": "... I have been informed that certain news reports concerning my meeting yesterday with Irish-American leaders have misrepresented both my position and my statements ... I do not favor violence as part of a solution to the Irish question."[5] No one, of course, had reported Carter had favored violence. But this was classic Dublin government tactic—scare people from speaking out for justice in Northern Ireland lest they be accused of supporting violence. It was unconscionable to do that to Carter. Yet the media establishment in Ireland never objected to FitzGerald's inexcusable and disgraceful actions. Years later, when candidate Bill Clinton, on April 5, 1992, in New York City, made promises to a group of us (some who also had been at the

Carter meeting in Pittsburgh), the huge difference was that Taoiseach Albert Reynolds welcomed Clinton's statement—and the rest is history. I am haunted by this thought: Had FitzGerald welcomed Carter's statement, how much sooner the peace process could have started, how many lives might have been saved and how so much suffering could have been spared? And I am not alone in thinking this way. Well-known author and journalist Tim Pat Coogan says in his memoirs, "During the 1974—7 coalition period the voice of the Dublin component of the Toffs" Brigade [pro-British elite] was particularly strong, powerful and continuous. I would blame Dublin's attitude in these years for helping to create a mindset that deepened the political vacuum and helped to prolong the Troubles."[6]

But I had inadvertently given some of Carter's people an opportunity to make specious excuses. In my hurry to prepare my statement for the Carter meeting, I quoted the Irish plank in the Democratic Platform, as given by *The Guardian*. But that paper quoted a previous draft that had been changed. The phrase, "The United States should encourage the formation of a united Ireland," was not, in fact, in the final version. It was a genuine mistake, which even the Carter people themselves missed, even though they had an advance copy and had approved every word.

Al Stern quite disingenuously went on to allege that I had tricked Carter into talking about "unifying Ireland." My response was if a simple man from Fermanagh could do that, what would the Soviets do to him, for goodness' sake. But Stern in the same *Globe* article was forced to admit that I had made an honest mistake. "Stern said he telephoned Fr. McManus after the flap and accused the priest of having tricked Carter into using the phrase [unifying Ireland.]" The presidential aide subsequently accepted McManus' explanation that it had been an honest mistake based on an incorrect version of the platform as reported in the Manchester *Guardian* ... But Stern added: 'I have reason to believe he (McManus) was delighted.'"[7] Stern could also have added that he himself did not catch the error even though he was intimately involved in the drafting of my statement, and was in possession of an advance copy, and had approved every word—even adding one. Stern also told the

National Catholic News Service that he was satisfied that what happened "was not done deliberately or maliciously."

But in fairness to Carter, he himself never withdrew his words, which were recorded. And it's his words that count, not my misquote.

But FitzGerald's apparatchiks at the Irish Embassy were instructed to continue the misinformation campaign so as to discredit the Caucus and make Carter back off. The *Jack Anderson Column*—then one of the largest syndicated columns in the United States—regurgitated the FitzGerald misinformation: "At the height of the presidential campaign, Jimmy Carter inadvertently stirred up a tempest in Great Britain ... He met in Pittsburgh with Irish-American leaders, many of them dogmatically anti-British. A militant priest read Carter what purported to be a copy of the Democratic platform on Ireland and asked whether he supported it

...But the priest spiked the non-controversial platitudes with some language of his own ... The unsuspecting Carter, groggy from the grueling campaign, overlooked the inflammatory sentence."[8]

Whitten, a writer for the *Anderson Column*, had never contacted me and clearly allowed himself to be used to do a hatchet job. He came to realize that, and later he and the paper would do some fine pieces on British human rights violations in Northern Ireland.

PAUL O'DWYER RALLIES TO IRISH CAUSE

Irish-Americans were appalled by the unfairness of it all, so they took their grievance to the ultimate court of appeal—the late, intrepid Paul O'Dwyer, then President of New York City Council, who had the zeal for justice of an Old Testament prophet. On November 17, 1976, Paul wrote to president-elect Carter:

> "An article appearing in The Jack Anderson syndicated column ... has greatly disturbed members of the Irish-American community. It charges a most respectable clergyman with having played a vile trick on you ... Leaders

of the Irish-American community have requested me to make my own inquiry into the facts ... I found the following to be the facts ... The Carter campaign leadership in Atlanta, very properly, insisted that the leader spokesman of the delegation, long in advance of the meeting, present a written script which would contain the delegation's position. The delegation adhered to the rules with meticulous care ... From the facts and circumstances, I believe that the Anderson column is a garbled distortion carrying a scurrilous and unfounded accusation against a prestigious clergyman which has angered a whole community."[9]

With that letter Paul O'Dwyer—in his own right, an important figure in the Democratic Party—was steadying President Carter and at the same time "the Lion of Bohola," as I called him, was sending a message to the Irish government and Irish Embassy that he was on to them.

Despite the Irish Embassy's concentrated campaign to discredit me with the Carter White House, I was given about a dozen tickets to the Carter Inaugural Ball and continued to be invited to the White House—although the smear campaign against me did inevitably limit my access to Carter's policymakers.

However, for the record, I must correct one peculiar, false story about how my access was blocked. In the book *John Hume in America* by Maurice Fitzpatrick,[10] it is recounted that a Robert Hunter in the White House canceled—at the urging of Michael Lillis of the Irish Embassy—my meeting with him as I was about to enter the White House. That never happened. I was never blocked from the White House as I was about to enter, and I never had an appointment with a Mr. Hunter. It is pure fiction, like other things in the same book. A responsible author would have called me to double-check the story. Mr. Fitzpatrick never double-checked with me any of the things he says about the Irish National Caucus or me—because that did not suit his agenda of "alternative facts." What's up with that?

Nonetheless, on February 24, 1977, I met for two hours with Marilyn Haft, Carter's associate director of public liaison, who specialized in advising the president on international human rights.

On March 16, 1977, Carter paid a visit to Clinton, a very Irish town in Massachusetts. Hours before, FitzGerald met with Carter and implored him not to refer to human rights in Northern Ireland, only to condemn IRA violence. Despite FitzGerald's plea, "the President defended his policies on human rights, and said he would speak out on human rights in Northern Ireland, without saying why."[11] Now you know "why" ... because FitzGerald tried to stop him, and Carter did not appreciate it.

Neither was the Irish Embassy able to stop my meeting with Andrew Young while he was US ambassador to the United Nations (1977–1979). It was just after the State Department had made Young apologize for saying that if England had not actually invented racism, she had institutionalized it around the world. Despite his forced apology, Young was in high good spirits, and with delight showed me some of the irate letters he had received from people in Britain. Andy had no doubt about who was the oppressed and who was the oppressor in Ireland.

And in face of the ongoing campaign by the Irish Embassy to blackball me, I was still invited to the Carter White House on two occasions. On Friday, April 11, 1980, I was invited "to join the President at a meeting for ethnic fraternal leaders."[12] When I met the president for a handshake and photograph, I smilingly asked him if he remembered me from Pittsburgh. "Oh, how could I forget?" He chuckled. I then said, "Please don't forget human rights in Northern Ireland." He replied, "I shan't. I promise you."[13]

Of course, I knew my meeting, and warm handshake with President Carter would cause panic in the British Embassy. But I didn't know the half of it until thirty-three years later in 2013. In that year, I would get my hands on a copy of a telegram sent by the British ambassador to "Dublin, Belfast and British Information, New York." A handwritten note, "Prime Minister," indicates it was also sent to Maggie Thatcher, then the prime minister. The two-paged typed telegram consists of a rant about how shocking it was that I had been invited to the White

House, and it outlines the Ambassador's frantic attempts to have me disinvited. It also reveals the British Embassy's first line of attack: co-opting the then Irish Ambassador, Sean Donlon, whom he states was equally upset. He states Donlon was also going to complain to the White House.

(**Please see full text of the British Ambassador's telegram in Appendix D and the article by Ray O'Hanlon of the *Irish Echo*.**)

But FitzGerald was obsessed by the success of the Caucus and was ridiculously concerned that the Caucus would be seen as having any influence with Carter. For example, he told the *New York Times* that "... the Irish Government had been anxious about American policy involving Ulster in the aftermath of widespread publicity in Ireland and Britain that the Irish National Caucus ... had access to the White House. [The Caucus] has had a propaganda campaign suggesting that they had access to the White House, that they were influential."

Apparently, according to FitzGerald, Americans should not have the right to free speech or the right to petition their government. But even FitzGerald cannot rewrite history. It was the Irish National Caucus that first got Carter speaking about the Troubles and that nobody can deny. As Professor Paul Power says, "The Irish National Caucus ... achieved its first major mark in October 1977, when it obtained an 'Irish justice' statement from candidate Jimmy Carter, providing the INC with a basis for claiming a seminal role in the later Carter statement on Northern Ireland."[14]

The significance of that assessment is all the more apparent when it is realized that in the 1970s, Professor Power of the University of Cincinnati was "the only American political science academic researching Northern Ireland affairs."[15] "The later Carter Statement" to which Power refers—also known as the Carter initiative—was made by the president on August 30, 1977.[16] Power states that it was "the first, explicit comment on Irish political issues of any kind ever made by an incumbent President." That is why it was so important to the Irish National Caucus—not so much for what it said, but that it was said at all.

But it did also contain the key points we had been pressing on the Carter White House. In fact, *The Sunday Press* (Dublin) on September

4 claimed that "some hours before the long-expected Carter initiative was finally announced ... the text of the statement was released word for word to an Irish newspaper [by the Irish National Caucus]."[17]

The key part of the statement said: "The United States wholeheartedly supports peaceful means for finding a just solution that involves both parts of the community of Northern Ireland and protects human rights and guarantees freedom from discrimination—a solution that the people of Northern Ireland, as well as the Governments of Great Britain and Ireland, can support. Violence cannot resolve Northern Ireland's problem: it only increases them and solves nothing."

The Irish Times, the day after the Carter statement was released, carried the following headline: "Irish Caucus cued Carter: McManus":

The Rev. Sean McManus, of the Irish National Caucus in the United States, said yesterday that it was the Caucus that first initiated President Carter's involvement in Ireland by making human rights, justice and peace in Ireland an issue in the Presidential election. In so doing, he said, the Caucus made such matters an international issue for which it was criticized by the British Government, and the previous Coalition Government, and leading SDLP members. Ultimately, Father McManus said in a statement, the real significance of the President's interest was that it would formally, and at the highest level, "internationalize" British involvement in Ireland, thus making it clear to the world that Northern Ireland was not just a British internal matter.[18]

CHAPTER 11

The Long Knives of the Dublin Government

*The Dublin Government will fight Irish-Americans
but not the Brits*[1]

IN THE PREVIOUS CHAPTER, I QUOTED the thank-you letter that Senator "Scoop" Jackson had sent me with his very respectful reference to Frank Stagg who had died for "peace with justice in Ireland."

There you have a non-Irish, non-Catholic "Viking" paying deep respect to that young Irish martyr. What respect did the Irish government show this heroic young Mayo man? When his body was flown from England back to Ireland, the Irish government kidnapped the body, in a frightfully ugly fascist display, to stop Stagg being given a Republican burial, as he had requested. The Irish government, on February 21, 1976, had Stagg buried under six feet of concrete, in a grave seventy yards from the Republican Plot in Leigue Cemetery, Ballina, County Mayo. The grave was guarded twenty-four hours a day by armed Special Branch men to stop the Republican Movement from reinterring their martyred comrade. But on November 6, the IRA succeeded in burying Stagg's remains in the Republican Plot.

Mrs. Stagg, Frank's mother, had written me a beautiful letter to thank me for the Mass we celebrated for her son. I promised her I would visit his grave in Ballina and say a prayer there. In the summer of 1976, I went to his grave, not wearing my clerical collar. I started to take a photo and was immediately surrounded by Special Branch men. "Stop, that's not allowed," they barked.

"What do you mean, it's not allowed? Has the Irish Constitution been changed to forbid photos?" Then in that bullying way that seems special to the Special Branch, they told me if I took photos, they would confiscate my camera and place me under arrest. "Am I allowed to say a prayer or is that, too, forbidden?" I snapped.

Can you imagine anything more guaranteed to recruit members for the IRA than the barbaric way the Dublin government treated the body of a dead hunger striker? Even the British did not do that to Bobby Sands and his nine comrades when they died in Long Kesh in 1981.

So, you can imagine that when I returned to Boston, my condemnations of the Dublin government grew stronger. Then came the shameful sandbagging of Jimmy Carter by Garret FitzGerald and all my Fermanagh contempt for the Dublin government was mightily reinforced. There was simply no way of avoiding it. The Dublin government was collaborating with Britain in its dirty war in the North.

Now fast-forward again to March 1977. The Saint Patrick's Day statement of Senator Teddy Kennedy, Speaker Tip O'Neill, Senator Pat Moynihan, and Governor Hugh Carey further indicated proof that FitzGerald had tried to muzzle President Carter from speaking about human rights in Northern Ireland. To explain what I mean, it is important here to give their statement in full:

JOINT SAINT PATRICK'S DAY APPEAL FOR PEACE IN NORTHERN IRELAND
For Release on Thursday a.m., March 17, 1977.
"The world has looked with increasing concern over the past eight years on the continuing tragedy that afflicts the people of Northern Ireland. Each of us has tried in the past to use our good offices to help see that

the underlying injustices at the heart of the Northern Ireland tragedy are ended so that a just and peaceful settlement may be secured.

It is evident to us as it is to concerned people everywhere, that continued violence cannot assist the achievement of such a settlement but can only exacerbate the wounds that divide the people of Northern Ireland.

We, therefore, join together in this appeal, which we make in a spirit of compassion and concern for the suffering people in the troubled part of Ireland. We appeal to all those organizations engaged in violence to renounce their campaign of death and destruction and return to the path of life and peace. And we appeal as well to our fellow Americans to embrace this goal of peace, and to renounce any action that promotes the current violence or provides support or encouragement for organizations engaged in violence.

We make this appeal on St. Patrick's Day 1977, a day on which Irish peoples of all traditions everywhere should feel proud to rejoice in our common heritage. And a year in which peace should come at last to Northern Ireland."

Edward M. Kennedy
Thomas P. O'Neill Jr.
Daniel Patrick Moynihan
Hugh L. Carey

Not a word about British violence, repressive legislation, or mistreatment of political prisoners. Not a whisper about how British security forces and the RUC were colluding with, arming and controlling Protestant murder gangs. Not a scintilla of mention about the deep-seated, all-pervasive, anti-Catholic sectarianism—the State religion of Northern Ireland. The "Four Horsemen" (well versed in how the media, which had christened them thusly, operates) had to know how their statement would play. The headline in The *New York Times* makes my case: "Four Top Democrats Urge Halt in Support for the IRA."[2]

In fact, the statement did nothing to stop those who were supporting the IRA. I never met an Irish-American who stopped supporting the

IRA because of Tip O'Neill or Teddy Kennedy. The statement just gave the British carte blanche.

My collision course with the Dublin government was further escalated by a nasty development in Croke Park on Sunday, April 17, 1977, before the Kerry–Dublin National Football League final. Before the game began, a group of human rights activists ran on to the pitch with banners protesting the treatment of hunger strikers in Portlaoise Prison. Two of the Dublin team—David Hickey, a medical doctor, and John McCarthy, a Dublin-based garda—attacked the protesters in an unseemly and unnecessary manner. My brother Frank, a most ardent attendee of all matches in Croke Park, alerted me to the outrage, pictures of which were prominently carried in all the papers. I was especially offended that a doctor and a garda were involved. I lobbied the two American GAA governing bodies, the New York GAA Board and the North American Board, urging them to ban the two offending Dublin players from playing in upcoming games in America. I knew most of the key members of both boards who were also members of the Irish National Caucus. In no time both boards authorized me to make the following statement, which was carried in all the Irish newspapers: "These two players [Hickey and McCarthy] will not be allowed to play in any part of the US. They disgraced the uniform of the Dublin team and the spirit of the GAA by using Croke Park to violently express their political hostility to the hunger strikers. Hickey and McCarthy in the most sordid manner introduced politics into Croke Park. Therefore, the leadership of the GAA in the U.S. is banning Hickey and McCarthy from playing with the Dublin team on their upcoming tour."[3]

Well, as they say, all hell broke out. I was told by an insider that Seán O'Síocháin, GAA Director General, erupted wanting to know, "When the f—did Father McManus and the Provos gain control of the GAA in America?" There they go again ... Any time a stand for justice is taken, it has to be the IRA!

Anyway, the hunger strike in Portlaoise Prison was settled, and we called off the ban. Prominent GAA writer Paddy Downey reported: "News that the ban had been lifted was announced by the Boston-based priest, the Rev. Sean McManus, after his brother, Mr. Frank McManus, the former Westminster MP for Fermanagh and South Tyrone, had informed him that the Portlaoise prisoners had ended their hunger-strike ... The North American Board of the GAA is now expected to follow the lead of the Caucus—as they had followed it originally when imposing the ban."[4]

BOSTON IRISH CONSUL TRIES TO SILENCE ME

But as I said, the GAA ban would speed up the Irish government campaign against me.

On April 18, 1977, *The Boston Globe* ran a front-page story on me, with photograph, "Hub priest denies he backs IRA,"[5] by top reporter David Nyhan. It told the story of how the Irish government, Irish Embassy in Washington and Irish consulate in Boston were out to squash me. A month later, Nyhan had another front-page story on me, with a photograph of me without my clerical collar demonstrating at City Hall Plaza for political prisoners in Ireland, North and South: "'Ireland putting heat on me,' says priest."[6] It reported how the Irish Consul in Boston, Carmel Heaney, had approached the chancellor of the archdiocese, Bishop Thomas V. Dailey, to try and get him to silence me. And how, in turn, Bishop Dailey called my Rector, Fr. Jim Foley, to a meeting at the Chancery. Nyhan wrote: "Heaney said, 'I certainly have not made any approach of the kind described by Fr. McManus. I really can't discuss what I may or may not do ... Obviously, I have conversations with all kinds of people in the course of my job. In some cases, they can be regarded as public, and in other cases as private.'" Heaney's words give her away.

Nyhan's story continues: "Last night Fr. Foley said in an interview that Bishop Dailey had 'mentioned his interest' in Fr. McManus' activities ... I told him what a wonderful priest Fr. McManus is. We had absolutely nothing but the highest regard for him here. Asked if Bishop Dailey had told him of being approached by Heaney, Fr. Foley replied, 'I don't want to comment on the various details. It was a private conversation.' Bishop Dailey was unavailable for comment."

Naturally, many other US papers picked up the front-page story. *The Boston Herald American* ran with the headline, "Hub priest charges Irish consul with 'dirty trick'":

> Mission Church priest yesterday accused Irish Consul Carmel Heaney here of "running forcover behind a wall of equivocation and diplomatic immunity" after working her "dirty trick" ... In response to his latest criticism of her, she said, "it would be counter-productive to get into a debate at second-hand or indirectly with Fr. McManus'... The priest, who has been accused of terrorist activities by the Irish government in Dublin, said he learned of the "dirty trick" from the Mission Church rector ... Fr. McManus said, "I am opposed to violence, whether it be British or the IRA ... I believe the fundamental violence in Ireland is institutionalized by the British government with its army, its enforced unemployment, its sectarianism, and its discrimination."[7]

The Irish Post in London—published by the late Brendan MacLua—went right to the source of the Heaney's dirty trick: "A few weeks ago the Irish Minister for Foreign Affairs, Dr. Garret FitzGerald, singled [Fr. McManus] out for special attention and condemned his activities in the U.S."[8] The National Catholic News Service (the news wire service of the U.S. Conference of Catholic Bishops) filed the following syndicated report:

"Boston priest will not be silenced on his Irish views, pastor says." "There is no danger of Father McManus being silenced—either by the Archdiocese or the Redemptorist Order." Father Foley told National Catholic News. "I'm not going to report on the details of a very private and cordial conversation with Bishop Dailey ... but I backed up Father McManus as a good priest and a good school prefect. As far as his priestly work, he's tremendous. He has every right to talk out on human rights violations as long as he's doing it nonviolently."[9]

There was huge outpouring of support for me, not only in the parish but throughout Boston. The principal of the local public school, Charles H. Gibbons, Jr., wrote to *The Boston Globe*: "I can personally attest to [Fr. McManus'] commitment and humanitarian concern for the people of Mission Hill—black, white and Hispanic... Perhaps the Irish government would suggest someone else to help us in Mission Hill. If not, I would appreciate their concerning themselves with other affairs since the most impressive priest I have seen operating in Mission Hill is Fr. Sean McManus."[10]

A middle-aged black woman, not a Catholic, became a fierce defender. This lady was a social worker dealing with great deprivation in the area. She was a force of nature and as tough as nails. She phoned Carmel Heaney and bawled her out: "You [expletive deleted], leave Fr. McManus alone. How dare you say he's collecting guns for the IRA? In Mission Hill, we keep our own damn guns."

So, there you have it. In Britain, the government tried to have me silenced. In America, the Dublin government tried to have me silenced. And I am quite convinced that had it not been for David Nyhan, God rest him, and the other journalists, they might have got Bishop Dailey to move against me. Dailey never gave me any further trouble. He was scared of *The Boston Globe*.

But here's the rub—the moral, if you wish—of the story: the Irish Embassy and consulates only really escalated their attacks on me after the Irish National Caucus formally adapted nonviolence and wrote it into our constitution. Instead of welcoming this development, the Embassy and consulates were frightened by it. Why?

I have mentioned that after Archbishop Benelli's plea to me at the Vatican, I knew we would have to formally adopt a policy of nonviolence even though I have been practicing it since I decided at sixteen to become a priest. That did not mean that I could no longer understand what made the IRA fight. It meant that I personally could not join them in that struggle. It meant that I personally had to accept nonviolence as a way of life. It did not mean I had to tell lies to cover up British injustice in Ireland, or to collaborate by my silence with that injustice.

Nonviolence does not mean doing nothing. It is short for "nonviolent resistance" to injustice and oppression.

In 1976, I went home for Christmas. *The Irish Press* interviewed me on my position on violence: "In an exclusive interview with *The Irish Press*, Fr. McManus said he was convinced that the only long-term solution to the problem was one of nonviolence ... [He] said he disagreed with many things the Provisional IRA had done. 'I disagree with the whole broad use of violence, but I must honestly say, I understand why they turned to these acts.'"[11]

In 1977, I declared that the "subtitle" of the Irish National Caucus would be, "The nonviolent pursuit of justice and peace for Ireland." That appeared under our name in all our literature—and I should know, as I wrote all our position papers and announcements.

> "The Irish National Caucus is totally opposed to the use of violence to achieve political objectives in Ireland. It is, therefore, logically and necessarily opposed in the very first place to British policy in Ireland because the British government historically and currently and par excellence, uses violence to achieve political objectives in Ireland. But the Caucus is opposed to all forms of violence, whether it is British or Irish, State or civilian. It is an exclusively American-based organization and does not support any party or organization in Ireland. It has no foreign principal, and it does not, and never has sent funds to any part of Ireland for any reason—least of all for violence."

Could anything be clearer and more unambiguous? Why did the Irish government not welcome that unequivocal nonviolent declaration? Why were they not as happy as the IRA was unhappy about it?

Irish Embassy Out to Destroy Me

But there would be no let-up in the Irish Embassy's campaign of character assassination. In 1977, Doubleday published a book, *The Power Peddlers*, by Russell Warren Howe and Sarah Hays Trott. The book, about foreign-policy lobbies in Washington, has a section on the Irish National Caucus. On page 391 it says, "Father McManus' Irish Embassy file card bears the mention 'homicidal tendencies.'"

Paul O'Dwyer's law firm initiated a libel lawsuit on my behalf against Doubleday and the authors. My Provincial, the admirable Father Joe Kerins, totally backed my lawsuit and offered to sign on as a co-defendant. He also wrote to the then Irish ambassador in Washington, John Molloy, expressing outrage and demanding an explanation. On December 8, 1978, an embassy counselor replied for the ambassador, denying that such a file card existed and that "... no representative of the Embassy has at any time suggested ... that such a card existed or that Father McManus had such tendencies."

Howe, a British subject, was ordered by a federal judge to reveal his source in the Irish Embassy. He refused: "He indicated," said *The New York Times*, "that the source could face retaliation by the Irish Republican Army because of the criticism of Father McManus."[12] He was threatened with contempt, and the embassy official whom the Irish ambassador had denied existed offered to appear before the judge "in camera" (in the judge's chambers, hidden from the public) so his identity could never be revealed, as he was allegedly scared the IRA would kill him and his family! In other words, they piled on the libel against me, making it even more outrageous.

Anyway, the case was eventually dropped. Later Howe would write about the case in an article, "Reveal the Name or go to Jail," in the *Washington Journalism Review*: "During an interview in New York, an Irish diplomat read me the priest's address and telephone numbers from an Embassy file card. He chuckled and cited a cheeky comment that someone had written on the card: homicidal tendencies."[13] Howe then continues:

"My source felt wretched about my case ... He said his ambassador would not allow him to testify, in any case. He had considered bypassing me and 'going public' on his own (although he feared IRA reprisals against his wife and children or his family in Ireland). However, his Ambassador had rejected that, saying waiving immunity would set a bad precedent. The source appealed to Irish foreign minister, Garret FitzGerald; although sympathetic, the minister decided against overruling his envoy ... 'The irony of it,' said the source, 'is that I'm sure they've guessed it's me because the IRA knows I'm the Embassy member who keeps tabs on them here.'"

All that from a person who did not exist, and from an embassy that always denied it was spying on American citizens.

Howe then explains that when the "source" appeared in camera before the judge, he "produced photos of his endangered wife and children. [Judge] Weinfeld looked at them and nodded sympathetically."

I hope all this shows I was not exaggerating when I say the Irish Embassy was conducting a character assassination campaign against me and was out to destroy me.

FORMATION OF AD HOC CONGRESSIONAL COMMITTEE FOR IRISH AFFAIRS

But the Irish Embassy would have even more reason to be concerned by what *The New York Times*, in a front-page article, described was, up until that time, "the Caucus' boldest success"—the formation of the Ad Hoc Congressional Committee for Irish Affairs.[14]

On Tuesday, September 27, 1977, I chaired the press conference on Capitol Hill at which we appointed Congressman Mario Biaggi (D-NY) as chairman: "Congressman Biaggi was selected by us," Fr. McManus said, "because he has truly distinguished himself by his consistent and outspoken concern for my country. Although his ancestry is not from

Cork, Kerry or Fermanagh, the Congressman has shown more compassion than some congressional leaders with Irish names. On behalf of the Irish National Caucus, the National President of the AOH and all Irish-American organizations, it gives me great pleasure to appoint you, Congressman Biaggi, Chairman of the Ad Hoc Congressional Committee for Irish Affairs."[15]

Then I announced the Committee's threefold purpose: (1) To seek full congressional hearings on violations of human rights in Ireland; (2) to reverse the U.S. policy of refusing visas to Irish Republicans; and (3) to represent the views of Irish-Americans to the President of the US.

The one acid test that I had given Mario before we asked him to chair the committee was, "Are you prepared to stand up to the Dublin government?"

Mario had responded, "Absolutely."

Is it not it pathetic that we had to have this concern? Is it not shameful that this highly decorated police hero, and proud son of Italy, had to not only take on the British government but to watch his back with the Irish government as well? But that's the way it was. One could see Dublin's real policy towards the North far more clearly in America than it could be seen in Ireland.

Mario (October 26, 1917—June 25, 2015) deserves huge credit and must never be forgotten by Irish-Americans who are dedicated to justice and peace. He was a truly great man; God rest his soul.

The Irish Embassy had been telling Members of Congress that Congress had no role to play in Northern Ireland—that it should be left to the British and Irish governments and to diplomats. In a very short time, we had signed up over one hundred Members—Republicans, Democrats, Liberals, Conservatives, Protestants, Jews, Catholics, etc.

On September 28, the Religious News Service filed a report: "In an interview [after the press conference] ... Father McManus said, 'We are disappointed with Sen. Edward Kennedy (D-MA) and Rep. Thomas P. O'Neill, Jr. (D-MA)—the most powerful politicians in the United States, and both Roman Catholics. They condemn violence in Northern Ireland but do not condemn British violence and torture ... The American

Catholic hierarchy has made several comments about violence in South Africa, Rhodesia and Chile, and quite rightly so. But they are silent about British violence in Ireland—with only one honorable exception, Bishop Thomas J. Drury of Corpus Christi, Texas."[16]

Over the years certain elements would try to deny the Caucus' pivotal role in forming the ad hoc committee. However, the intrepid Tom McNabb, who was actually present (as the photo in this book shows) when I Chaired the launching of the Committee, would set the record straight. As National Editor of *The Hibernian Digest* Tom declared in an Editorial: "It was through the Irish National Caucus that the important Ad Hoc Congressional Committee for Irish Affairs came into existence within the National Congress."[17]

JACK LYNCH TRIES TO DESTROY BIAGGI AND INC
AOH CONVENTION IN KILLARNEY

In February 1978, I was tipped off that the Irish Embassy was planning something big against us for Saint Patrick's Day. My informant heard one of the Irish Embassy staff boast: "Come Saint Patrick's Day, only McManus and Biaggi will be left standing." So, we braced ourselves for the gathering storm, and it came on February 17, 1978. On that date, Taoiseach Jack Lynch wrote to Congressman Mario Biaggi, denouncing him and the Irish National Caucus. But before sending it to Biaggi, Lynch made it public to *The New York Times, The Washington Post* and all the major American media. The intention was clear: to put the Ad Hoc Congressional Committee for Irish Affairs and the Irish National Caucus out of business. The Irish Embassy genuinely thought the Members of Congress we had signed up for the Committee would resign en masse. When Lynch made his attack, we had ninety-three Members of Congress signed up for the Committee for Irish Affairs. Only 2 resigned, and we went on to recruit a total of 133 Members of Congress. (Years later, I would discover that Mrs. Jack Lynch had written to Fr. Shepherd. She urged him to silence me, and stop me from criticizing her husband, whom she described as a great Irish patriot!)

The conflict with the Irish Embassy would be carried across the Atlantic to Killarney when the AOH held its annual convention there from June 27—29, 1978. The Irish Embassy had engineered Division 36 of the AOH in Shrewsbury, Massachusetts, to submit a resolution to the convention: "... that the Convention record itself as in favor of the goals and directions of the government of the Republic of Ireland, and further, that the Convention repudiate all groups advocating violence in Northern Ireland."

The Irish Embassy had simultaneously arranged for Teddy Kennedy to send a telegram to the convention supporting the resolution. Well, one did not need a degree in political science to know what was going on here. I made a statement to the convention that if Senator Kennedy and Division 36 would amend the resolution to include British violence—the violence of the British government, British army, RUC, etc.—I would support it. No such amendment was offered.

The chairman of the Resolutions Committee felt the pressure would be too much for him, so he called in sick and asked me to act as chairman. When the resolution came up, I ruled it out of order on the grounds that the AOH had no "foreign principal" and therefore could not support a foreign government. All hell broke loose, and the establishment media went crazy.

The Irish Times screamed, "AOH refuses to back government."[18] I thought one journalist was going to assault me. "How the f—k is the Irish government a foreign government?" he snarled at me. (And he was a "religious" reporter.)

I patiently explained, "Any government outside the USA is a foreign government to an American organization." Then I really set him off by adding, "Besides it is not the government of Ireland, only of twenty-six counties." He would later write that there were angry scenes between Jack Keane (AOH president) and me, when, in fact, he was the one causing the angry scene. Jack only got angry because the reporter had used the F-word to a priest.

One of the most disappointing things for me about the Irish media was how they allowed themselves to be co-opted, with some honorable exceptions, by the Dublin and British governments. They were scared stiff of deviating from the party line on the North. Oh yes, they could take on the governments on all sorts of issues, but on the North they were docile.

The convention would go on to pass resolutions calling for "the absolute independence of Ireland and urged the US government to work for the reunification of Ireland." It also passed resolutions endorsing the Ad Hoc Committee and the Irish National Caucus, and our initiative for the Ad Hoc Committee to host an Irish Peace Forum in Washington, to which "all parties could come without preconditions or compromise."

During the convention, I went to a private location for a meeting with Ruairí Ó Brádaigh, Dave O'Connell and Joe Cahill. They were clearly concerned about my emphasis on nonviolence and expressed great concern about Fred O'Brien (of whose affiliations they were suspicious). Each of them asked me a series of questions and played a recording of an interview I had given to RTÉ radio on why I had ruled out of order the resolution calling for support of the Dublin government. At the end of the meeting, Ó Brádaigh very formally asked O'Connell and Cahill if they were satisfied with my answers and both said they were. Then he, again very formally, summed up the discussion and pronounced that he, too, was satisfied. Later, he told me I had been "in a Sinn Féin court."

Irish Peace Forum

After the convention, Fred O'Brien, Bob Bateman and I traveled up to the North to sound out all the groups and parties on the Irish Peace Forum. We checked into a hotel in a strong Loyalist part of East Belfast for three nights. The UDA put a guard outside our door so that no freelancer would "shoot the priest"—at least, while I was under safe passage. In one amusing incident, when a UVF man came into our room, he challenged me very aggressively about the armed guard. But he calmed down when I told him it was UDA, as he had suspected it was IRA.

One of the first things one of the Loyalists said to me was, "I've always wanted to see you, Sean—down the barrel of a gun."

"Isn't much nicer this way, at least from my point of view?" I replied.

We met with all the Loyalist paramilitary groups—UDA, UVF, Red Hand Commandos, etc.

John McKeague, leader of the Red Hand Commandos, told me that he could always tell when Rev. Ian Paisley was going to tell a lie: he would remove his collar. He sent one of his top commandos to meet me so that "I could see his men were of better mettle than either the UDA or UVF." After I talked to that young man, he started to cry as he said goodbye. He said I was the first priest he had ever met, and that maybe he had been told lies about priests. I don't remember his name, and I often wonder what became of him.

The late Paddy Reynolds, Northern Editor of *The Irish Press*, came to see me in a panic: "Fr. Sean, the only way you are going to get out of this hotel alive is if I call RTÉ to come over and cover your exit with their cameras." I appreciated his concern but told him I was in no danger. Years later, I tended to think he may have had good reason for his concern.

All the Loyalists were in favor of the Peace Forum and so was the Republican Movement, at first. They later turned against the idea because the British would not attend. The Dublin government, as expected, was totally opposed to the idea of giving "terrorists a platform."

However, although the forum did not happen, I believe it helped to further our concept that Washington held the key to unlocking the stalemate in the North. It also made nonsense out of the Dublin government's allegation that the Caucus was supporting violence when we were trying to organize a Peace Forum in Washington.

Back in Boston, I concentrated on making preparations for my move to Washington. But, before that, a couple of things should be mentioned. I began to finalize the naturalization process of becoming a US citizen. When I went for my final interview, the official had a copy of *Trinity* by Leon Uris sitting on his desk. He was an Irish Catholic, and proud of it. He conducted all the questioning, and I got all the answers right—until he came to the part about my being prepared to bear arms in defense of the United States. "Catholic priests do not bear arms," I responded.

He sat up in the chair and with obvious relish said, "So, Father, tell me where in the US Constitution does it exempt Catholic priests from bearing arms?" I told him I had a problem with that. Then he told me that I would have to help him out because if I did not give the right answer, I would be denied citizenship. So, he said, "Father, I'm going to ask you that question again, and I can only ask it once. I am going to make it easy for you and ask, "If the communists invaded Boston would you bear arms to defend Boston?" I asked him not to say that but instead to ask me if the British invaded. He did, and I said yes.

When the interview was over, he confided that my file was the largest he had ever seen, indicating with his hands that it was about three feet tall. And me in the Land of the Free only five years! I became a US citizen on May 8, 1979.

THE VISA ISSUE

But back to the Peace Forum: if the forum were going to work, then Irish Republicans would have to be allowed to enter the United States, from which they had been banned for a number of years. Opposing the visa double standard had been one of our main campaigns: Loyalist paramilitaries were given visas to enter the US, and Irish Republicans were not. I had asked my good friend Congressman Hamilton Fish (R-NY) to take the lead on the visa issue. Congressman Fish was the very first member I had signed up for the Ad Hoc Committee in 1977. Of course, Mario Biaggi had also asked him to join, but as Mario stressed, it was important that the Ad Hoc Committee members be invited to join by me as the committee was meant to be representing the Irish-American community.

I had become very close to Fish. Indeed, before I had moved to Washington, he telephoned me in Boston to tell me that because I had spoken so highly of him in his Congressional District, the Irish groups wanted to honor him at an event. He told them he would accept, on one condition: "that Fr. McManus was the speaker." And he was telephoning me with that request. Needless to say, I agreed to speak.

Congressman Fish was the ranking Republican on the Subcommittee on Immigration, Citizenship and International Law (which came under the full Judiciary Committee). The Chairman of the Subcommittee was Joshua Eilberg (D-PA), also a good supporter of the Irish cause. Both of them got the Judiciary Committee Chairman, Peter Rodino (D-NJ)—famous for chairing the impeachment proceedings against Richard Nixon—to commission them to investigate the issue. He directed them thus: "Respected members of the Irish-American community [i.e., the Irish National Caucus] have indicated that U.S. consular officers at posts in London, Belfast and Dublin have recently been more reluctant to issue non-immigrant visas ... I believe the interests of the Committee on the Judiciary would be well served if you would... interview ... the officials ... to determine whether their decisions are arbitrary ..."[19]

Congressman Fish was really insistent that I travel with them, but I could not, so I sent Fred O'Brien instead. Their visit to Ireland and London took place from August 28 to September 1, 1978. It was a major coup for the Irish National Caucus, and their report of 675 pages totally exposed the double standard of the visa policy: "The delegation feels that the Department of State may have acted unfairly ... the delegation failed to understand the rationale of labeling only the individuals in the Provisional IRA as terrorists and exonerating individuals in Loyalist paramilitary organizations ..."[20]

The London and Dublin governments were furious at the report and, of course, they blamed me and the Irish National Caucus.

And how did the Republican Movement show their gratitude to me for orchestrating this major indictment of the visa policy that excluded them from the US? On September 27, 1978, the IRA made a most unusual statement: "The Irish Republican Army would like to put on record that Dr. Fred Burns O'Brien is persona non grata. Signed, P. O'Neill."[21]

Because they had given me no advance notice, which would have been the decent thing to do, I knew the statement was a way of getting at me, and not really about attacking Fred. And sure enough, when I later met with Ruairí Ó Brádaigh, Dave O'Connell and Joe Cahill in the Sinn Féin office in Dublin in December 1979, I asked them if the statement was meant as much for me as for Fred. "About sixty : forty," said Ó Brádaigh, sternly.

"Who's the sixty and who's the forty?" I asked.

"You're the sixty, Fr. Sean," said O'Connell in his great Cork accent, but no twinkle in his eye this time.

They obviously thought Fred was much more important to the workings of the Caucus than he really was, and that without him I would be handicapped. In truth, Fred did very little actual work for the Caucus and was mostly only seen in my company. The ironic thing was that since they were trying to "crack the big whip and keep me in line," there was no way I could be seen to accept that. As a consequence, I kept Fred on much longer than I would have otherwise done.

I made a public statement that "My response is to simply point out that it is irrelevant what group or party in Ireland finds Fred O'Brien acceptable or unacceptable."[22]

Gerry Adams was also supposed to be at that meeting in the Sinn Féin office. The other three leaders were noticeably concerned that he did not show. And I realized something was wrong—my first glimpse of the brewing problem between ÓBrádaigh and Adams.

Later in the Caucus office on Capitol Hill, a BBC correspondent from Belfast told me that a Republican spokesman was able to tell him that the IRA could not be seen to be attacking a brother of Patrick McManus, so instead, they had a slap at Fred O'Brien to bring me into line. But that, too, would change—soon the IRA would have no scruples about attacking me.

There is, however, a peculiar corollary to Fred O' Brien being formally declared "persona non grata" by the IRA. Years later—after I got rid of him—he re-emerged as a hysterical critic of mine, in an interesting capacity, on an interesting platform. He is "the Washington correspondent" (even though it's years since he lived in this city) for the Dublin newspaper, *Saoirse*, under the name, Peadar Mac Fhínín. *Saoirse* is the organ of Republican Sinn Fein, which has until recently been led by Ruairí Ó Brádaigh, former president of Sinn Fein. Ó Brádaigh—along with the late Dave O'Connel—would have been in key positions of influence when the IRA declared Fred "persona non grata." And yet, Fred is now given this platform. When Ó Brádaigh was asked what happened to the IRA's declaration, he simply replied: "It lapsed."

But can such a declaration simply lapse? Must it not be lifted? And who decided it lapsed? Now, remember here that Republican Sinn Fein split from Sinn Fein and the IRA in 1986. It sees itself as the true Irish Republican Movement.

Why would Ó Brádaigh have an interest in giving O'Brien a platform from which to attack me? For example, O'Brien in the July and October 2011 issues of *Saoirse* makes the bizarre and crazy charge that I did not even know Congressman Fish until a long time after Fish got involved in the Irish issue, and that I was opposed at that time to Irish Republicans getting visas!

Ó Brádaigh, who died in 2013, first used O'Brien as an excuse to attack the Irish National Caucus; now he was using O'Brien himself to attack the Caucus. What is going on here? Who is pulling the strings? Furthermore, did *Saoirse* ever even inform its readers that the IRA had declared their "Washington correspondent" "persona non grata?"

Furthermore, O'Brien is now in cahoots with a malcontent in New Jersey who has opposed the Irish National Caucus virtually from the beginning. That individual has never built up, just torn down, and I never trusted him. From the moment I met him, my Kinawley antenna went into overdrive. He has allegedly done ÓBrádaigh's bidding for many years (or could it be the other way around?). Ironically, he is the same guy who plotted to have the IRA declare O'Brien persona non grata. And now they are both plotting together. For what ends and for whose benefit? Again, what is going on here? Perhaps *Saoirse* can enlighten its readers.

I will return to this subject (who was really behind the attacks on me and the Irish National Caucus?) later on in this book.

Sean MacBride and Fr. McManus, New York, 1976

Fr. McManus At Sean MacBride's funeral. Dublin, 1988.

Fr. McManus with Irish Northern Aid Leaders.
(l-r): Matt Higgins, Jack McCarthy, Mike Flannery,
Mattie Reilly, Tommy Enright, Danny Crawford,
Sean Cronin is the Figure partially cut off. New York, 1972.

Fr. McManus with Tip O'Neill, then Majority Leader of the
US House Representatives. Washington, DC., 1974.

Tip O'Neill at the Hearing regarding the International Fund for Ireland. Fr. McManus (left), and Congressman Biaggi (center) keep a close eye on him. Washington, D.C. 1986

Fr. McManus Chairs launching of Ad Hoc Committee (l-r): Tomm Mc Nabb, Deputy National President, AOH; Congressman Edward P. Beard (D-RI); Congressman Mario Biaggi (D-NY); and Congressman Leo C. Zeferetti (D-NY). Washington, D.C. 1977.

Fr. McManus with Teddy Gleason, International President, ILA and George Meany, AFL- CIO President. Florida, 1975.

Bob Blancato (left), Fr. McManus and Mario Biaggi (right). Washington, DC. 1987.

Fr. McManus and presidential candidate Jimmy Carter. Pittsburgh, PA, 1976.

CHAPTER 12

Move to Washington

Thus, McManus became Britain's nemesis in America, the driving force that would eventually erode Britain's influence within the U.S. government.
Joseph E. Thompson[1]

I MENTIONED PREVIOUSLY THAT WHILE AT the Vatican I felt I was being drawn to the ineluctable conclusion that if we were going to get the job done (whatever that might eventually be), I knew I would probably have to "go full time."

When we had finished our business at the Vatican, Bishop Drury and I broke away from the rest of the delegation to pray in Saint Peter's. When we finished praying, I told the Bishop I wanted to talk to him in confidence. We sat in the pews, and I told him about a recurring dream I was having: "I am rushing back from some Irish activity to the Redemptorist rectory to check the assignment board only to discover I'm late for some assigned duty. I wake up in a panic."

Bishop Drury listened very sympathetically. And, of course, one didn't have to be a dream interpreter to see what was going on. "You shouldn't have to feel so torn," he said. "I must see how I can help."

With that, I knelt down and asked for his blessing. When I got up, it was as if a huge weight had been lifted off my shoulders. Bishop Drury was seen in his Diocese of Corpus Christi as a very conservative man. And he certainly would have eschewed all talk about charismatic blessings or healings. But something happened to me when he blessed me there in Saint Peter's. I was confirmed in the peace of Christ—I don't know how else to put it. And man, would I need that peace as the attacks from all sides would keep escalating: from the British, the Irish government, SDLP and finally from the IRA and Sinn Féin—almost as if directed by the same hand.

Over the next two years, Bishop Drury and I talked about how I could be less "torn." He then made the remarkably generous offer that if the Redemptorists would agree, I could come under his jurisdiction and he would appoint me to a Special Ministry of Justice and Peace for Ireland. What a courageous gesture from a conservative Bishop! And here is where praxis trumps theory every time: the Bishop was born in 1902. His experience of the Black and Tans was real. And he had not forgotten.

With Vatican II, the Catholic Church had begun to recognize the validity and importance of the "Special Ministry." And with the new stress that "action on behalf of justice was a constitutive dimension of the preaching of the Gospel" (*Justice in the World*), why should there not be a Special Ministry for that? Bishop Drury was not scared of the British government. And so, in December 1978, he appointed me to a full-time Special Ministry of Justice and Peace for Ireland.

Before I left Mission Church, I met with the Archbishop of Boston, Cardinal Medeiros, to ask for his blessing on my new Special Ministry. He provided me with a warm letter of introduction to Cardinal Baum of Washington, so despite the efforts of the Irish Consul in Boston to get me silenced, the Cardinal was giving me his blessings. Indeed, I am firmly convinced—and so was Bishop Drury—that one of the main reasons why the Irish Consul escalated her attacks so strongly was to sabotage my appointment to the Special Ministry. The word had somehow leaked out, leading the Bishop to wonder, "Sean, do you think the buzzards have our phones tapped?" "Buzzard" was the strongest word I ever heard him use for the British government.

In a press release announcing my appointment, dated December 11, 1978, Bishop Drury said:

"I have been deeply impressed by [Fr. McManus'] dedication to human rights, justice, and peace in Ireland. The Catholic Church teaches that certain priests are given special charisms or 'gifts' for special work. I recognize that Father McManus has been given by God a 'charism' for this work. He has truly distinguished himself by his total commitment to peace in his country. Anyone who has met Father McManus or has heard him speak must have been deeply impressed by his determination and zeal. He is uniquely suited for this Special Ministry. For the past several years, in the face of disappointments and frustration, he has worked with true Christian Charity. Father McManus is committed to nonviolence, reconciliation, and freedom in Ireland. I ask people to pray hard that his work will be blessed."

OPENING OF CAPITOL HILL OFFICE

On December 10, 1978, International Human Rights Day, the Irish National Caucus opened its National Office on Capitol Hill. December 10 was also the date Patrick went on the run in 1956. This would be the first time in Irish-American history that the Irish had an office on Capitol Hill to lobby for justice and peace in Ireland. (The Friends of Irish Freedom opened an office in 1919, not on Capitol Hill but downtown. It lasted only a few years.)

I had moved down to Washington without a red cent to my name. But I had called a dear old friend, Howard Smith (not the Howard K. Smith whose broadcast I had interrupted) and he gave me five thousand dollars for the first month's and last month's rent of the office on Capitol Hill.

Now we were perfectly positioned to increase our influence on Capitol Hill. The Washington Bureau of *The Boston Globe* predicted that "with the arrival of McManus here, one thing is certain, [Tip] O'Neill will probably feel at least two thorns on that issue." The other "thorn" was Congressman Biaggi.

Now that I had moved to Capitol Hill to lobby full time, the roles of Bernadette O'Reilly-McAuliffe and Fred O'Brien petered out. Rita Mullan, who had arrived in the US from Belfast in May 1977, became Executive Director—almost five years after the formation of the Irish National Caucus. She did a lot of fine work until she became ill in 1983.

I immediately went to work on an eighteen-hour daily schedule. I knocked on the door of virtually every Member of Congress, building up goodwill for the Irish cause, signing them up as members of the Ad Hoc Committee for Irish Affairs, putting pressure where needed, but always politely and respectfully. I made sure I would never mislead the members or give them wrong information. I immediately leveled with them that the Irish government was bitterly opposed to me, not to mention the British. I acknowledged that I had in the past, as a private individual, expressed support for the IRA but that the Irish National Caucus was nonviolent, and that we would never compromise them— that we would only seek to get Members of Congress to support nonviolent projects. I also emphasized that we would not seek any special favors for Ireland, only for America to apply a single, not a double, standard in its policy of promoting international human rights; that the "hands-off Northern Ireland lest we offend the Brits policy" had to end; that left to the triangle of Belfast, Dublin, and London, no solution could emerge; that an outside catalyst was needed, and that it was only possible and proper for America to be that catalyst.

Knowing that we could not depend on Senator Kennedy and Speaker O'Neill, whom the Irish Embassy, working in cahoots with the British Embassy, had scared off, I concentrated on non-Irish and non-Catholic Members of Congress. And to further broaden and "mainstream" the Irish issue, I made a point of enlisting the support of Republican Members of Congress. The Washington correspondent for *The Irish Times*, Sean Cronin, would write, "The 'Irish question' was almost exclusively a Democratic Party matter up to recently when the Irish National Caucus ... began to make inroads in Republican ranks."[2]

As we began to make impact on Capitol Hill, the media in Northern Ireland sent reporters to check us out. The well-known journalist David McKittrick would describe our approach thus: "The Caucus has done some effective lobbying in the past few years, achieving its propaganda successes simply by doing it the American way—playing the lobbying game according to Washington's rules, making contacts and friends in Congress, presenting the human rights case convincingly. It has become the Madison Avenue of Irish Republicanism ..."[3] And another equally well-known journalist, Barry White of the *Belfast Telegraph*, wrote, "from there [the Caucus office] Fr. McManus is just two and a half minutes from the Capitol building, where he is becoming one of the best-known faces among the lobbyists ... the way the British and Irish Embassies react to what they see as the twin menace of the Caucus and the Ad Hoc Committee of Congressman Biaggi demonstrate its potential."[4]

One of the first signs that we were beginning to have an impact was—according to a senior *Boston Globe* writer—the change in tone of Teddy Kennedy and Tip O'Neill.

On March 15, 1979, *Boston Globe* journalist Ken Harnett telephoned me and told me he had no hesitation in believing the Caucus was responsible for the change in the upcoming Saint Patrick's Day statement critical of the British. I immediately told him that I never even had a meeting with Kennedy. Harnett persisted, explaining he had checked it out and because of the pressure the Caucus was putting on Congress, Tipp and Kennedy had been forced to move to "cover their asses."

Two days later, Harnett would write:

> The leader of the Irish National Caucus listened as the long statement from the "Big Four"—Senators Kennedy and Moynihan, Speaker O'Neill and Gov. Carey—was read to him over the telephone, and for a moment, Fr. Sean McManus was almost at a loss for words. "I'm a little inarticulate right now," said the Ulster-born priest. "God, I'm elated. I welcome that statement enormously." ... The conventional wisdom, as reflected in the "Big Four's"

earlier statements, was to stress the responsibility of the Irish Republican Army for the violence in the North, and to warn Irish-Americans against giving either financial or psychological support ...

[McManus] felt frustrated trying to get across the idea of British culpability for the violence and stalemate in the North ... But suddenly, this year, someone listened... It was not that McManus had changed, or the IRA, or the perception of the IRA ... Rather, it was a variety of changes in the Irish situation itself, not the least of which was the growth in the awareness of the human-rights violations ...

And so, the annual Saint Patrick's Day proclamation had its obligatory condemnation of sectarian violence again this year, but it had much more. It had a scolding of the British government, not just for its political lassitude but for its acquiescence in "official brutality and violation of human rights." The pressure on the British was being raised by several degrees, and Sean McManus couldn't hide his great enjoyment. "Everyone was saying we were terrorists last year for saying these things. Now it's the popular, respectable thing."[5]

But not everyone would be pleased with our success, as my first Saint Patrick's Day Parade in Washington would show.

Sean Donlon–FitzGerald's Protégé "Refuses to shake my hand"

Grand Marshal Matt Hannon escorts Fr. McManus to reviewing stand. St. Patrick's Day Parade, Washington, DC. 1979.

The late Matt Hannon, an ardent Irishman and very active member of the Irish National Caucus, was the chairman of the parade. Matt insisted that I would lead the Caucus contingent seated in a fancy limousine, with the name "Irish National Caucus" emblazoned on both sides. When the limousine arrived at the reviewing stand, Matt announced me with great theatricality, and with aplomb escorted me up on the reviewing stand. I was seated next to a local bishop, so naturally, I stood and shook his hand. Then I realized that Sean Donlon, Irish Ambassador to Washington (1978–1981) was seated next to the bishop. I knew he was hostile to me, but I did the well-mannered thing, held out my hand and said: "Happy Saint Patrick's Day, Mr. Ambassador." With the entire reviewing stand looking on, Donlon burrowed himself deeper in his chair and refused to shake my hand. I kept my hand extended for a long while until everyone could plainly see what was happening.

Donlon was a protégé of Garret FitzGerald. FitzGerald claims he had got Taoiseach Jack Lynch to appoint Donlon as Ambassador to Washington.[6]

Donlon would go on to be a bitter and hysterical opponent. The ever-colorful Con Howard, at that time an official of the Irish Embassy, recounted this story to me: Donlon was speaking to him in the Irish Embassy, giving out about us. "In six weeks, I will have stomped out the Irish National Caucus," he said as he stomped the floor with his foot.

Con told me he responded to Donlon with, "You will in my arse."

Mind you, the same Con Howard did not hesitate to attack us when so directed. On the night of that same Saint Patrick's Day, I was in his home for a party. He hoisted a glass of champagne, drank it down and then with great flourish smashed it into the giant fireplace, vowing with patriotic fervor never to say a bad word about the Caucus, no matter who ordered him. A few days later, he had a letter in *The Washington Post* charging the Caucus with supporting violence. That evening I ran into him at an event in the Library of Congress, and I said, "Con, what happened to your dramatic vow never to attack us?"

He replied with a sheepish smile, "Orders from the Captain." I was never sure whom he meant. The strange thing about Donlon is that years earlier, while I was still in Boston, and he was head of the Anglo-Irish Division of the Department of Foreign Affairs, he called me from the home of a mutual friend in New York City. He told me there was no interest in a united Ireland by anyone in the Irish government. And that if "ÓBrádaigh and O'Connell were to take over in the morning," he would be working for them (ÓBrádaigh was then President of Sinn Féin and O'Connell the most visible IRA leader in Ireland).

As Ambassador, Donlon disgusted Irish-Americans by his silence about British violence and human rights violations. He seemed only concerned about IRA violence, and he had a particular animus for me. One former member of an important Fianna Fáil national organization amazed me by suggesting that one of Donlon's problems with me could be explained by the "spoiled priest" syndrome, i.e. that Donlon had been studying for the priesthood but left the seminary. Therefore, according to the former Fianna Fáil apparatchik, when Donlon arrived in Washington, he was really incensed to find a priest (me) saying, "Don't listen to the Irish Embassy, listen to the Irish National Caucus instead."

But whatever explained Donlon's problems, he seemed to be obsessed with destroying the Irish National Caucus. So much so that we launched a campaign to have him recalled as Ambassador, and it almost worked, too. This is how it came about.

The veteran Donegal politician, Neil Blaney, TD, and MEP, was on a speaking tour for the Irish National Caucus. He was in our office on December 7, 1979, when Charlie Haughey called him with the dramatic news that he, Haughey, had just been elected Taoiseach. Before hanging up the phone, Blaney said, "Fr. Sean McManus is right beside me. Why don't you say hello?" There was silence. I knew very well Haughey would not speak to me. Then Blaney hung up and said Haughey could not speak then, but that he said he would call back. *"Yeah, right,"* I skeptically thought to myself.

But, nonetheless, it did represent the possibility of an improvement. Taoiseach Jack Lynch was gone. Blaney was now in a position to influence Haughey, at least to some degree. Maybe he could convince Haughey to issue a new policy directive to the Irish Embassy, like stating that British injustice was the enemy, not Irish-Americans.

Blaney became convinced Donlon had to go after we told him about how Donlon had sabotaged an effort to free the Birmingham Six.

A month earlier, November 1979, the Caucus had brought Fr. Raymond Murray from Armagh to Washington to help promote our campaign to free the Birmingham Six. We brought him along to meet our dear friend, the late Congressman Hamilton Fish (R- NY) whom I held in great affection and esteem. Ham, as he was known, was the great-grandson of U.S. Secretary of State Hamilton Fish who, having slapped the Fenians on the wrists for one of their invasions of Canada, urged that they be released. On August 16, 1870, Secretary Fish wrote to President Grant: "I always supposed that you would deem it wise to release the prisoners convicted of participation in the Fenian raid. Purely political prisoners are the worst kind of birds to keep caged."[7]

I always kidded Congressman Fish that the reason he was so good on the Irish issue was that he had to do penance "for his great-grandfather locking up the Fenians in the first place." I remember thinking it was a special symbolic moment when—in Fish's office, right in front of his great-grandfather's photo—I introduced my colleague Bob Bateman to the congressman. Bob is the great-grandnephew of the famed Fenian, Captain Timothy Deasy, who was rescued from the Fenian prison-van in Manchester, England (1867) and who—according to Bob—also participated in one of the Fenian invasions of Canada, as had 'Bob's great grandfather.

Anyway, one of the results of bringing Fr. Murray to meet Ham Fish was that the congressman promised to try and get the law faculty of some prestigious university to examine the entire case of the miscarriage of justice that the Birmingham Six represented.

Donlon Moves Against Birmingham Six

Fish, an officer in the American Consulate in Dublin in the 1950s, being a very diplomatic man, met with Donlon at the Irish Embassy to inform him of his plans. Donlon went berserk. Fish told me that he had never been talked to in such a disrespectful fashion. Donlon followed up the meeting with a letter on November 6, 1979:

> Dear Mr. Fish,
>
> In view of our recent conversations and correspondence, I thought it might be useful to let you have the attached recent reports from *The Irish Times*.
>
> The report dated October 27 describes a recent interest of yours in the Birmingham bombings case as "the fruit of the work of Fr. Raymond Murray of Armagh ..." In the report of October 22, Fr. Murray is criticized by the

leading elected representatives of both sections of the divided Northern Ireland community..."⁸

The two "elected representatives" were Gerry Fitt and Martin Smyth, the head of the Orange Order, who was not then an MP.

So, here was the Irish Ambassador in Washington using the head of the Orange Order to discredit a Catholic priest of the caliber of Fr. Murray, all with a view to stopping the campaign to free the Birmingham Six! Neil Blaney was outraged and embarrassed that, in his name and in the name of the Irish people, Donlon would dare pull that stuff. He began to privately urge the new Haughey government to replace Donlon. Haughey agreed, but Donlon rallied Tip O'Neill, Teddy Kennedy and other important Americans to intervene on his behalf (not what one would expect from an ambassador). Haughey backed off. *The Washington Post* reported that "Irish Prime Minister Charles Haughey decided today to keep Sean Donlon as Ireland's ambassador in Washington after being warned that replacing him would harm relations between Haughey's seven-month-old government and leading Irish-American politicians. Haughey was told that he would upset Sens. Edward M. Kennedy (D-MA) and Patrick Moynihan (D- NY), House Speaker Thomas P. O'Neill (D-MA) and New York Gov. Hugh Carey if he removed Donlon in response to complaints about him from the Washington-based militant Irish nationalist lobby, the Irish National Caucus, and its ally in Congress, Rep. Mario Biaggi (D-NY), according to well-informed sources."⁹

Later, Brian Lenihan, Minister for Foreign Affairs, told us on the phone, "Maybe we will have another stab at Donlon and send him to Tehran" (which was then in the midst of the American hostages crisis).

But even when Donlon was eventually replaced in 1981, it did not really change the bad attitude of the Irish Embassy. That only changed with the beginning of the Irish peace process and the IRA ceasefire of August 31, 1994.

In November 1985, Donlon's opposition to the campaign to free the Birmingham Six resurfaced in the Irish newspapers. *The Irish Press* reported: In yesterday's *Sunday Press*, Mr. Donlon said any action he had taken had been on the instructions of the Irish government. But last night, the then Foreign Minister, Mr. O'Kennedy, to whom the diplomat was answerable, rejected the claim ... Mr. O'Kennedy said ... he did not give Mr. Donlon any authority to write."[10]

As I had expected, Haughey himself would go on to condemn the Irish National Caucus on July 27, 1980. But he did so under threat from FitzGerald: "A threat to end the bipartisan policy on Northern Ireland is contained in a letter which will be sent from the Fine Gael leader, Dr. Garret FitzGerald, to the Taoiseach today calling on Mr. Haughey to spell out his attitude to IRA front organizations in the United States."[11] And FitzGerald, eager to claim the credit for the condemnation, released a copy of the letter he had sent to Haughey on July 21, demanding such condemnation:

> You will have seen that John Hume, Frank Cluskey and myself speaking independently ... urged on the 9th July, that you clarify at once your Government's position with respect specifically to Congressman Biaggi, and to organizations such as Northern Aid and Irish National Caucus ... Failure to re-state in unambiguous terms the position of three successive governments on this matter can only confuse the issue in the United States, as may be seen by the statement on RTÉ news program last week by the Rev. Sean McManus, speaking on behalf of the Irish National Caucus, that he presumed that they were "right in thinking that there is a difference between the policies of Mr. Haughey and Mr. Lynch—it is our general impression and hope that Mr. Haughey's policies will be quite different ..."[12]

In his autobiography, FitzGerald crows, "My letter achieved its purpose... the Taoiseach provided belatedly the necessary clear repudiation... The Caucus' leader, Sean McManus, responded that the Taoiseach's statement was a response to "threats and blackmail from me," and that I had "once again dictated policy to Mr. Haughey"—a statement that I did not feel it necessary to deny."[13]

But here it must be noted, as FitzGerald makes clear, that John Hume was in full collusion with the Irish government's policy of marginalization of any group that wanted the British embarrassed and pressured. Hume would later go on to do great work on the peace process, but for too long, he, in effect, gave the British a pass, as will be seen when I give the history of the MacBride Principles.

Donlon was the first person who ever refused to shake my hand. The second and only other person ever to do so, was Donlon's master, Garret FitzGerald. It happened this way: on August 2, 1979, the State Department announced it had suspended the sale of US weapons to the RUC. (This was one of our greatest victories and I will explain it in a moment.) I was back in Belfast at the time, so naturally, the media was very interested in what I had to say about the arms ban. As a consequence, I was constantly in the news. When my press work was over, I noticed that Garret FitzGerald, now no longer in government, was due to give a lecture at the Corrymeela Reconciliation Centre on the north Antrim coast. I decided to attend. And so did, it appeared, the entire Supreme Council of the UDA, including Andy Tyrie, Glenn Barr, etc. FitzGerald spoke eloquently about the need for both parts of Ireland to come together (albeit not in a united Ireland) in mutual understanding and forgiveness. During the question-and-answer period, he warmly addressed the UDA leaders by their first names, clearly making a great play for the UDA. Now, remember, at that very time, the UDA, with the cooperation of the British government and security forces, were slaughtering hundreds of innocent Catholics. After the speech, FitzGerald, his wife, and a core group went into a private room. The Rev. Ray Davey, founder of the center, then came and invited me to join the "inner circle."

FITZGERALD REFUSES TO SHAKE MY HAND

When I entered the room, the group was sitting in a semi-circle, facing the entrance, with FitzGerald and his wife sitting in the middle. The

Rev. Davey announced, "This is Fr. Sean McManus, president of the Irish National Caucus." Of course, all of them knew me anyway, even though I was not in my clerical collar but in a suit and tie. As I approached the semi-circle to the right, they started to stand, and I shook their hands. Out of the corner of my eye, I noticed FitzGerald was still sitting down with his eyes resolutely fixed on the floor. *This is going to be interesting*, I thought, suspecting what was going to happen. I pleasantly shook the hands of all the polite Ulster folk, as I approached FitzGerald. When in front of him, I held out my hand and said, "I enjoyed your lecture, Dr. FitzGerald." Like a clocking hen, he fluttered in his seat. I kept my hand extended; it seemed like forever. He finally hissed, "Please go away; you are creating a disturbance." I calmly responded that the Rev. Davey had invited me. Davey was standing by my side, and he nodded in assent.

I finally moved on, skipping over Mrs. FitzGerald, to shake the hand of Glenn Barr who was sitting next to her. With a smile, I expansively said, "Maybe you guys are right, after all, Glenn, that there are two nations in Ireland." He laughed loudly. (The UDA at the time were advocating an independent Northern Ireland based on the alleged premise that Northerners and Southerners were two distinct peoples.)

So, FitzGerald refused to shake my hand even though I had shaken the hands of ex-Black and Tans, B Specials, RUC, British soldiers, and leaders of every Protestant paramilitary group. But FitzGerald, after hypocritically talking about reconciliation, refused to shake my hand!

Of course, FitzGerald, apart from his long antipathy for me, was seething in particular about our success in stopping the sale of US weapons to the RUC, and about all the publicity the media was giving me. Because, you see, the obvious issue it raised was why did the Caucus have to do it? Why had the Dublin government not done it?

RUC Gun Ban

But it was not just the likes of FitzGerald who resented the Caucus victory. *The Irish Times* clearly had a problem with it. I spoke to a young male and female reporter in the Belfast office of *The Irish Times*. The male reporter, whom I had never met before, could barely hide his hostility. He pompously told me that his sources in Washington told him that the Caucus had nothing to do with the ban. The female reporter did not say much, and I sensed her negative attitude was, perhaps, because I am a priest. (One also develops a radar for that type of prejudice, too.) Months later, *U.S. News and World Report* would write: "High among the concern of the Irish National Caucus is human rights in Northern Ireland. When members protested the issuance of a license to ship machine guns and magnum pistols to the Ulster police, the shipment ceased."[14] And on May 28, 1980, *The New York Times* ran an editorial, "What's a Boycott Between Friends?" Referring to the RUC ban, it said: "What should have been a routine transaction aroused the opposition of the Irish National Caucus, whose leader, the Rev. Sean McManus, has been an open supporter—and occasional critic—of the Provisional wing of the Irish Republican Army. The Caucus has its ardent partisans in Congress, and House Speaker O'Neill was moved to oppose granting an export license for guns. ..."[15]

I duly sent both articles to the male *Irish Times* reporter in Belfast with a letter suggesting that he might want to reconsider his position. I also sent copies to Douglas Gageby, then Editor of *The Irish Times*, and to Sean Cronin, the Washington correspondent. I never heard back from the reporter in Belfast. Cronin emphatically denied that he was that reporter's alleged "source." Later a well-established reporter from another newspaper told me that *The Irish Times* liked to indulge in the conceit that it was not only the paper of record but that it also shaped and influenced national events—and that it had to give its stamp of approval before a person was considered a "player."

The Washington Post would also refute the pompous young man from *The Irish Times* when it wrote, "British officials believe the Caucus and Biaggi's Ad Hoc committee are responsible for influencing the Carter administration to hold up the sale of American-made guns to the police in Northern Ireland ..."[16]

But the Rev. Paisley had no doubt who was responsible. He said it was an insult, but said that clearly it was seen as a triumph for the Irish

National Caucus in America and the Ad Hoc Congressional Committee for Irish Affairs, led by Congressman Mario Biaggi.[17]

Notice in that *New York Times* editorial it says that Speaker O'Neill was "moved." It uses more parliamentary language than Ken Harnett of *The Boston Globe*, but it amounts to the same thing: O'Neill was bounced into taking that position because we made the pressure irresistible. Tip did not want to take that position, but he had to. Why do I say that? Because O'Neill, and indeed Teddy Kennedy, only took anti-British positions when forced to because the Dublin government had pressured them into silence: criticize the British, and you will be seen to be pro-IRA and anti- Irish government.

Perfect proof that the Irish government did not want the RUC to be blacklisted by the United States is that when we got dozens of Members of Congress to co-sign Congressman Mario Biaggi's letter of protest to the State Department, Matthew Nimetz, Counselor, replied in a letter, defending the weapons sale to the RUC: "The Royal Ulster Constabulary is the legally constituted police force in Northern Ireland. ..." He then plays his trump card: "In this connection, I would note that Irish Foreign Minister O'Kennedy, in a May 31 foreign policy speech to the Dail, pledged the continued cooperation of the Irish police and army with the Royal Ulster Constabulary in the fight against violence in Northern Ireland."[18]

Who do you think provided Mr. Nimetz with that speech? Do you think he just happened to have it in his hip pocket? Congressman Biaggi responded to that *New York Times* editorial. As a matter of respect, I quote The Great Man at length:

> "It was my amendment to the fiscal 1980 Department of State appropriations bill which led to the decision by the State Department to suspend further sales or shipments of United States arms to the RUC pending a full review of our policy.

My initial reason for raising this issue in Congress was the incomparability of the sale of arms to the RUC and our foreign policy philosophy—respect for human rights. Section 502 (b) of the Foreign Assistance Act of 1961 bars the sale or export of any U.S. arms to nations or organizations that engage in persistent patterns of human rights violations ... Finally, the leadership provided by the Irish National Caucus on the issue of suspending arms shipments is fully consistent with their role as the leading Irish-American organization working for peace, justice and human rights for Ireland."[19]

Caucus' Growing Influence

It was clear to all by now that the Irish National Caucus was beginning to have significant influence in changing American foreign policy on Northern Ireland—despite the opposition of both the British and Irish Embassies.

The secret of our success was in hammering away on the theme of the single standard: America must apply a single standard, not a double standard, to human rights in Northern Ireland. I zeroed in like a laser beam on all double standards. For example, we had long opposed the policy of refusing visas to Irish Republicans, who wanted to come to the United States to denounce British policy in Northern Ireland, yet the Rev. Ian Paisley was allowed into America. Because he was an MP, I knew it would be all the more difficult to frame the double standard issue. But when the State Department refused a visa to Owen Carron MP, a Fermanagh neighbor of mine, who was elected to fill the seat of martyred Bobby Sands, I struck like lightning. Now I knew we could have Paisley's visa revoked, and we did, on December 21, 1981.

I will let the late David Nyhan of *The Boston Globe* tell the story: "The State Department yesterday revoked the visa of militant Northern Ireland Protestant leader Rev. Ian Paisley, who had planned a visit to the United States next month, because of the 'divisive tone' of his recent speeches. ... The campaign to revoke Paisley's visa was launched Dec. 2 by the Irish National Caucus ... [which] devised a strategy of asking conservative Republicans to lead the fight in Congress, instead of the Irish-Catholic Democrats. ..."[20]

We got 125 Members of the House and 22 senators (including Senator Joe Biden, former US vice president) to co-sign a letter by Congressman Bill Carney (R-NY) and Senator Al D'Amato (R- NY) to Secretary of State Alexander Haig demanding that Paisley be refused entry. And that number did not include Tip O'Neill and Teddy Kennedy who again were forced to take action. When they saw that the two arch-fundamentalists, Senator Strom Thurmond (R-SC) and Senator Jess Helms (R-NC), had signed on, they simply had to get on board. In a previous article, Nyhan pointed out that when O'Neill and Kennedy finally wrote to the Secretary of State, "the letter from the two Massachusetts Democrats followed by several hours a speech on the floor by Rep. William Carney..."[21]

In the lead-up to the visa denial, Paisley kept saying that "priest McManus would never stop me going to America." When he was stopped, he then started blaming Prime Minister Margaret Thatcher and President Ronald Reagan. Of course, it was not lost on him that U.S. Secretary of State Al Haig was Catholic, with a Jesuit brother. Paisley's benefactor, Bob Jones III, attacked Haig as "a monster in human flesh" and publicly prayed that God would "smite him hip and thigh, bone and marrow, heart and lungs."[22]

1981 Hunger Strike

THE WASHINGTON STAR Thursday, April 30, 1981

One-Man Vigil

The Rev. Sean Mc Manus, national director of the Irish National Caucus, Inc., reads scripture yesterday outside the British Embassy Chancery Office o Massachusetts Avenue. He has been fasting and praying on the sidewalk since Friday in sympathy with Bobby Sands and other Irish protest hunger strikers. Mc Manus is from Ireland.

One-Man Vigil

The Rev. Sean McManus, national director of the Irish National Caucus Inc., reads scripture yesterday outside the British Embassy Chancery Office on Massachusetts Avenue. He has been fasting and praying on the sidewalk since Friday in sympathy with Bobby Sands and other Irish protest hunger strikers. McManus is from Ireland.

The year 1981, of course, was the year of the Irish hunger strike. We had been trying to move heaven and earth to get America to put pressure on Margaret Thatcher to grant the hunger strikers' demands. I had asked Congressman Hamilton Fish (R-NY) to work on his good friend Vice President George H. Bush. When Fish called me to tell me that Bush had gotten back to him with a final decision that President Reagan would not intercede, I knew Bobby Sands was going to die. Twelve days before his death I embarked on my own hunger strike right outside the

British Embassy. Because I did not hold any poster, and because I was by myself, I did not have to remain at the mandatory distance of five hundred yards. Prince Charles was staying at the Embassy, and each time he left in the car, he had to drive right past me. I could see him peering out of the darkened car windows—not without empathy, or so I thought. Certainly, he was not glaring with hostility. I stayed on a hunger strike for twelve days, only drinking water, losing twenty-five pounds. When Bobby died, I came off the hunger strike, knowing I had to continue the work.

But I felt disgusted that although two of the most powerful men in the world, President Reagan and Speaker O'Neill, had Irish roots, they did not lift a finger to save Bobby Sands and his nine fellow-patriots who went on to die, "hungering for justice." I could never think the same way again about Reagan and O'Neill. On May 12, Francis Hughes (twenty-four) was the second Irish martyr to die on the 1981 Hunger Strike. Francis is commonly regarded as being one of the most fearless soldiers the IRA ever produced. On May 30, the Irish National Caucus brought his brother, Oliver, from Bellaghy, County Derry, to Washington. Oliver—one of the most dynamic and charismatic speakers I have ever heard—declared in that unique Bellaghy accent: "I came to the United States to give a simple message. My brother, Francis, was not a criminal. He was an Irish patriot."[23] Later we would bring out Mrs. McElwee, the mother of Oliver's first cousin Tom, who would also die on the hunger strike. I marveled at the fortitude of this woman as she went around Capitol Hill speaking to politicians and the media, trying to save the life of her son. I would later attend Tom's funeral and have my heart broken at the sight of his eight beautiful sisters carrying his coffin. I would also attend the funerals of hunger strikers Joe McDonnell, Kevin Lynch and Ciaran Doherty.

CHAPTER 13

The Old Sow that Eats Its Own Farrow

Loyalty is the sister of Justice
Horace[1]

JAMES JOYCE, THROUGH HIS ALTER EGO, Stephen Dedalus, famously quipped, "Ireland is the old sow that eats her farrow."[2] That, of course, could be said of any institution. But maybe it can apply to the IRA with particular force.

The Sunday World carried the headline, with a photograph of President Carter and me, "Provos Fall Out With Caucus Priest" (March 21, 1982). The unsigned article described me as having been "long a painful thorn in the flesh of British Embassy officials in Washington," and reported on the increased attacks by the Republican Movement and Irish Northern Aid on the Caucus: "Changed times indeed, when it's realized that Father McManus probably did more than any single individual to publicize the Provisionals' political aims among influential people in the United States." Its conclusion was that "... the present fallout between the Provisionals and McManus is probably due to the fact that, having built up a powerful Irish-American support lobby in the US, McManus doesn't want it sabotaged by heavy-handed interference...."[3]

That certainly, in part, explained my attitude, but what were the Provisionals' reasons? I always put it down to the age-old fear of Irish leaders (whether Parnell, de Valera, IRA, Dublin government, SDLP, whoever) of the "tail wagging the dog"—that Irish-Americans would end up dictating to Ireland. It was a fear I was always sensitive to. I knew from my study of the history of Irish-American nationalism that the "home group" only fully trusted the Irish-American group to the degree it totally controlled them. I often say (half-jokingly) that that mistrust goes back to December 1866 when the American Fenians deposed James Stephen in New York at gunpoint. Stephens, the "Fenian Chief," had been trying to yet again postpone the Fenian Rising; the Americans wouldn't stand for it anymore, so they took over the Movement in both America and Ireland."[4]

But as the years have passed, and as revelations of British infiltration of the Republican Movement continues to mount, I now begin to wonder who really was behind the attacks on the Irish National Caucus? Now, nothing is as simple as it once seemed. Gerry Adams, then vice-president of Sinn Féin, was the first to launch a personal attack on me. In a question-and-answer interview in *Hibernia Review,* he said: "The [Irish] National Caucus and especially people like Fr. McManus have been using Republicanism as a justification for what they've been involved in. They started off by calling for a United Ireland and now they're into human rights ... I think to a large extent Fr. Sean McManus is an opportunist."[5]

It was Sean Cronin, Washington correspondent for *The Irish Times,* who first alerted me to this article. "If you were an opportunist, you have picked a funny way to opportune," he laughed. Then he went on to point out that the IRA always accused priests for not speaking out because they were scared of the British and that it would damage their career, and now there was I being accused by Adams of speaking out to advance my career!

I had never met Adams, nor spoken with him, but I was struck by the unfairness of his attack. I recognized that it was the beginning of a calculated plan to put the Caucus out of business—just as the British and

Irish Embassies were committed to doing. But I could not miss the irony of Adams thinking there was a contradiction between human rights and national self-determination. It was so reminiscent of de Valera's infamous dismissal of labor and social concerns in 1918 when he said, "Labor must wait."[6]

ATTACKS DON'T DETER ME

Then like clockwork, attacks followed from Irish Northern Aid Committee (Noraid) and their paper, the *Irish People*, which once lionized me. In October 1980, *The Irish People* published an editorial, dictated by the Republican Movement, which declared, "... the Caucus is an anathema to the Republican Movement in Ireland."[7] Notice the exact same term as Jack Lynch used—"anathema." It was as if the attacks were written by the same hand. And, God knows, maybe they were, as it's now known that British agents had penetrated the Republican Movement. We still don't know the full level of penetration of the Dublin Government, but it would be utterly naïve to believe it did not happen. If the Brits could "turn" Republicans with their fierce commitment and discipline, can you imagine what they could do to many of the spineless weaklings in the Dublin establishment of that time?

But I can honestly say the attacks did not really upset me too much. Because I had a clear vision of the absolute need for an Irish lobby on Capitol Hill long before others realized it, I was not going to let anything deter me from my mission—not the British or Irish Embassies, not the IRA or Gerry Adams. Years later, *The Sunday World* would reflect on this: "Political observers in America say he was light years ahead of his time when he set up the Irish National Caucus to fight for justice and rights for nationalists back home in Northern Ireland."[8]

Gerry Adams went on to order a spokesman for Irish Northern Aid and editor of *The Irish People* never to mention me or the Irish National Caucus in the *Irish People*, except to condemn me. In one absurd incident, the New York City comptroller ran an election campaign advertisement in *The Irish People* that mentioned the Caucus, and the editor deleted the name of the Caucus. When the comptroller's office called to demand by what right he had censored a paid advertisement, the editor plaintively pleaded he had no choice as he was under strict orders from Adams.

Years later Adams would tell someone I considered a friend that, "the big mistake Irish-Americans made was to allow Fr. McManus to seize control of the Irish National Caucus."... As if the Caucus had been built up by others, and then I pulled a coup! As if there were a long line waiting to do my job: to move to Capitol Hill with no money, and to work nonstop for no real salary, for over forty years! (It apparently did not occur to my friend that in telling me this he was also revealing that Adams clearly considered him to be in the anti-McManus camp).

Now, in fairness to Adam—for whom I would develop great respect—it could be said that the only thing he knew about what was happening in America was from what he was being told second-hand through Irish Northern Aid or from other Republican leaders who had visited America.

And let me here mention one such visitor.

While I was in Boston, and after the Caucus had formally and constitutionally espoused nonviolence, Belfast Republican Jimmy Drumm came to see me at Mission Church. He had been sent to the United States to make a formal report for the Republican Movement on the state of Irish-American activity vis-a-vis The North. He was accompanied by another Belfast man.

Drumm was very unhappy about my statement on nonviolence that declared the Caucus is opposed to all violence: "Therefore, we are, logically and in the first place, opposed to British violence, the root cause of violence in Ireland." I explained my position, clearly and precisely. And I pointed out that the phrase "no foreign principal"—which we used in all our documents from the very beginning—meant that we could not be directed by any group outside the United States, whether violent or nonviolent.

Sometime later, the sister of the man who accompanied Drumm telephoned me from New York. She told me she had to, "in conscience," tell me something: that when Drumm returned to Ireland, he gave the leadership of the Republican Movement a totally false report on what I had said. He outrageously charged that I was trying to take over the leadership of the Irish Republican Movement in America. After my telling him that the Caucus had to be nonviolent and that we could not have a foreign principal! Now here he is mendaciously reporting to the Army Council of the IRA that I was plotting to be the IRA leader in America. (The only time I ever saw Drumm again was at the funeral of hunger-striker Tom McElwee. He acted as if I were his best friend!)

Now I can well understand that often the Irish Republican Movement had to misinform the public—they are, after all, a secret movement. But how were the interests of the Republican Movement served by that false report? Who benefited? In whose interest did Drumm tell that appalling lie? What was going on here?

The late Jack Mc Kinney, columnist for *The Philadelphia Daily News*, who was sympathetic to the IRA, told me that Drumm, "on behalf of the Army Council asked him not to give any publicity to Fr. McManus." Wouldn't you think the IRA had more to do than to worry about my getting publicity—especially when that publicity was causing huge embarrassment to both the British and Irish Embassies? Shouldn't the IRA have been pleased I was exposing British torture of political prisoners, British shoot-to-kill policy, anti-Catholic discrimination, etc., etc.? How would silencing me help the IRA? It could only help the British. So, again, it must be asked: What exactly was going on here? Did the Army Council actually want me silenced, or was this another outright lie by Drumm?

Over the years as I struggled to keep the Irish National Caucus from being put out of business by the British-Irish Embassies and the IRA, I had assumed that each one was making separate attacks on us. But now, with hindsight and dispassionate objectivity, I must ask: What if the attacks were not indeed separate, but guided all along by the same hand—by British agents inside both the Irish government and the IRA? Wouldn't that make complete sense and be consistent with the modus operandi of the British government?

This is only one of the many things that has surfaced through the writing of this book. Let me give another one.

As was previously mentioned, Neil Blaney, TD and MEP, came on a speaking tour for the Irish National Caucus in December 1979. Shortly before he left Ireland, he was telephoned from New York by a former Donegal neighbor of his. The caller was a woman very active in Irish Northern Aid. She implored him to cancel his trip because it would harm the Irish cause as the Irish National Caucus had gone down the wrong road. Neil, of course, told her to get lost. Now, for years I had assumed that Ruairí Ó Brádaigh had put her up to making that call, and maybe he did. But now I am forced to wonder, as nothing is as simple as it once seemed: What if the lady was making the call on behalf of someone else? Who? Well, who stood to be most embarrassed by the Blaney visit? The Irish Embassy, of course. Blaney was a powerful politician, bitterly opposed to what he saw as Dublin's quisling-like policy on The North.

His visit would cause severe discomfort to Sean Donlon, the Irish Ambassador... Cui bono (Who benefits)? Who would most benefit from Blaney's cancellation—Irish Northern Aid or the Dublin government? What was going on here?

It was not the first time I had witnessed surprising collaboration between the Dublin government and Irish Republicans (if in fact, they were Republicans).

I became very conscious of the "pincer movement" of the Dublin government: To IRA folk, they would present me as not Republican enough; to anti-IRA folk, they would brand me as IRA. And if that did not cover the spectrum, to Irish-Americans who were scared of getting involved, they would imply I was CIA. To right-wing Catholics, they would present me as a "rogue priest" (as former Irish foreign minister, Peter Barry, liked to do); and to left-wing Catholics, they would argue that I was a fundamentalist cleric.

Many Irish Northern Aid members were privately disgusted by the unfair attacks on me and would secretly call me to assure me they did not approve. They would admit to me that the IRA had sent orders that

Irish Northern Aid was to infiltrate, disrupt and destroy Caucus chapters throughout the country—just as the British and Irish Embassies were trying to do.

The head of Irish Northern Aid, Michael Flannery, was especially resentful of the Irish National Caucus. Because he was an old IRA man, and because he lived to be a great age, Flannery had a certain credibility. And he let everyone know he went to Mass every morning. But he could be a mendacious old knave. He put me in mind of Cardinal Spellman of New York (May 4, 1889—December 2, 1967), of whom it was said that he would tell any lie for the good of the Church. But in Flannery's case, he would tell any lie for the good of the IRA, only as long as the IRA agreed with him. He would tell members of Irish Northern Aid, and even journalists, that I had built "a mansion on the shores of Lough Erne with all the money I collected that should have gone to Irish Northern Aid." I sent a message to him that if he wanted to know when my parents' humble home had been roofed (that is, changed from a thatched house to a slated one), all he had to do was ask the chairman and vice chairman of Sinn Féin in Fermanagh, who were both neighbors of ours and they would tell him it was in the 1960s, long before I came to America.

Flannery would also tell people that I had to be a front for the CIA because our office on Capitol Hill "was so big." (Indeed, I only learned in June 2019 that Sean Garland, a well-known Stickie—the Markist faction which split with the Provisional IRA in 1969—who died in December 2018—in recent years, also, had been telling people that I was a CIA agent. ... So, Garland, who despised Flannery and his association with the Provos agreed with Flannery that I was a CIA agent. Who had the power, influence, and resources to systematically disseminate such disinformation? Does "divide and conquer" ring a bell?)

Many Noraid leaders would tell me that they had received specific instructions from the Republican Movement to oppose and obstruct the Caucus in every way possible. One Irish-born woman told me in 2010 that, much to her regret, she had believed the lies the Republican Movement/Noraid had spread about me. One absolute whopper of a lie was that I "owned a yacht." That was told to her by a "person in authority, and one that was respected."⁹ However, some claim this woman herself was one of the main persons Irish Republicans used to spread disinformation about me, as she was one of the Irish Northern Aid leaders in the Washington area. They say she was the one who invented the absurd story about the yacht. Indeed, only a short time after our telephone conversation—during which she pretended to be really friendly and supportive—I discovered she was still trying to undermine me. Even though I never had a cross word with her in my life! I have never been able to understand such two-facedness. This person has not lifted a finger for the Irish cause in almost twenty years, but she has time to still oppose me. Whose agenda is at work here? And to think I was the one who first introduced her to Ruairí ÓBrádaigh!

I always feel there is something tragic about people who are supposed to be working for a just cause but who don't hesitate to tell malicious and malevolent lies. What does that say about their commitment to justice?

To some of the Noraiders I would give a fool's pardon. Many of them were the salt of the earth—fine, decent Irish-Americans with an admirable dedication to Irish justice. But they naïvely thought that if the IRA wanted the Caucus out of business, they had a patriotic duty to oppose us. Later on, of course, they would come to be deeply embarrassed. Over the years, I have had dozens of calls or conversations that began with, "Now, Fr. Sean, I am very embarrassed I opposed the Caucus ..."

However, I was not willing to give a fool's pardon to those who were trying to sabotage us on behalf of the Irish, British, or American governments.

Agents, Provocateurs, and "Useful Idiots"

Professor Joseph Thompson would later reveal in his book that, "... the U.S. government singled out the INC for special surveillance."[10] I was fully aware there was a multilayered campaign to put us out of business. And it was often difficult to know which entity was behind it—though it made no difference to me since they all had the same goal: to destroy the Caucus.

For example, there was a very determined effort to infiltrate the Washington local chapter of the Irish National Caucus, and to use it to oppose the national office. I moved rapidly and disaffiliated the chapter. The leader of the attempted coup then disappeared like snow off a ditch—clear proof that he was up to no good. If he had been committed to working for Irish justice, why did he not continue working in some other capacity? Clearly, his only function was to disrupt the Caucus. When he was thwarted in that, he had no longer any interest in working for the cause of Ireland. That, for me, is always a dead giveaway.

In Detroit, I had taken an Irish-born man "in from the cold" and put him in a leadership position in a local chapter—the late Dan O'Kennedy whom I am naming for the first time in this Third Edition. (This was before Noraid had started to oppose us.) He had been previously isolated in that city, the Irish born local priest and Noraid leaders warned me he could not be trusted. Indeed, Tyrone- born Eoin McNamee, IRA Chief of Staff in 1942, called me in Boston from Chicago and urged me to get rid of him because he was too close to the Dublin government. I refused, but I should have listened to Eoin. Many years later that individual let it slip that an official from the Irish Consulate for that region had visited him with the proposal that the Irish government would back the Irish National Caucus "if they dumped McManus." The same individual was involved with a new Irish grouping in the 1980s. The leader of this new grouping came to see me in my office. (And here, I name him, also, for the first time: He was Jim Delaney, leader, or should I say "front-man for the Irish Unity Conference.) He said he would offer the Caucus two hundred thousand dollars a year if we came under his umbrella. I asked him what I would have to do for such kindness. "Do as I tell you," was his arrogant response. I told him that he had not the slightest idea of who I was, and what I was about if he thought he could silence me with money: "All sorts of people in Church and State have been trying to silence me for years. Do you really think you can?" Then, when I discovered that he had been driven to the Caucus office by the Irish Embassy's car (which was parked around the block with the driver waiting), I knew I had to keep him at a firm distance. Later, I was in the bank of the Irish National Caucus and mentioned to one of the managers that a big-talking Texan was bragging what he could do with all his great wealth for justice and peace in Ireland. The manager really surprised me by saying he would run a credit check on the Texan. Sometime later, the manager told me that the credit check had revealed that Delaney was not wealthy at all. So, where was the alleged "big money" coming from? **(See Appendix E)**.

Years later, my old friend, the late Matt Hannon, would reveal something that would validate all my suspicions. For a while, Matt and I had become alienated because the Irish Embassy had told him all sorts of lies about me. Later on, when he realized he had been deceived by the Embassy and by the IRA and its supporters, he sought to be reconciled with me. I gladly welcomed him back. He then proceeded to tell me that shortly after the visitor to my office attempted to buy me off, a top Irish Embassy official telephoned him, urging him to go to a very important meeting in Chicago, which that same visitor was organizing. "Why is it so important?" asked Matt. The official responded that the meeting was going to get rid of McManus, and the new grouping was going to take over from the Caucus and would be backed by the Dublin government.

Before the Chicago conference, there had been a lot of pressure on me to attend. I had a lot of calls from individuals who had no real history of involvement in the Irish cause, all stressing how important it was for me to attend. I knew something was up, so I had stayed away. Again, my Kinawley instincts had served me well. Also, at the actual conference, Dan O'Kennedy—told people from Boston (not realizing they were friends of mine) that, "the Irish National Caucus would be out of business in six weeks."

Once the Irish Embassy—under the direction of the awful Taoiseach Garret FitzGerald (1982—1987)—had, in effect, set up the Irish American Unity Conference in 1983 to sabotage the Irish National Caucus, another peculiar development took place. The IRA and Sinn Fein instructed their American followers to support the new group. What sort of sense does that make? Imagine the Irish Republican Movement endorsing a Garret FitzGerald front-group! What was really going on here?

No wonder I said earlier that it almost appeared as if the attacks on the Irish National Caucus (by the London and Dublin governments and by elements in the Irish Republican Movement) were directed by the same hand.

I know that it is easy to become a bit paranoid in this area, yet it would be hopelessly naïve not to realize that this is how the British government has manipulated Irish affairs for a very long time. As American history professor Michael Connolly says, "Nearly every Irish political group throughout history has split into factions, thus worsening their chances of success. This tendency, together with a highly effective network of British spies and paid informers, usually doomed these insurrections ... ."[11] So, just who was pulling the strings, both in Ireland and America, in the coordinated attacks on the Irish National Caucus? Why were the attacks so systematic and intense? What were we doing that merited such opposition?

(For a good example of British penetration of Irish groups see Appendix E.)

This is all the more relevant now that it is known that the late exposed British agent, Denis Donaldson, a key Sinn Fein operator, had been dispatched to New York to oversee the Irish Northern Aid Committee. Who made that decision? What was his mission? Why was his role in America brushed under the carpet? I never went public with any of this at the time because there are only so many fronts one can fight on at once. But I also knew that if all these people were going to defeat me, they would have to rise very early indeed and be prepared to fight for a very long time. I also knew that the rank and file of the new grouping had no idea what was going on and that over time the Irish Embassy could not control them. So, I just got on with my work, all the more convinced I was on the right tracks as so many were trying to sabotage me.

Mr. Deceitful

Then there is the peculiar case of a person I will call "Mr. Deceitful," an Irish-American who has kept up an over forty-year campaign against me.

I first met him in the seventies when I stayed in the Albany region of New York State in the home of the late Joe Dooly, assistant attorney general for the State of New York.

Joe was an ardent Irish-American who died far too young. He warned me to watch my back with Mr. Deceitful. I replied that he seemed nice enough. "Until you turn your back and then he will stab you," responded Joe.

That was the only time I actually had a conversation in person with Mr. Deceitful, and I made sure I would keep him at a distance from then on—apart from some telephone conversations. Even though I never had a cross word with him, his one obsession appears to have been to destroy me. He once urged a journalist for a top British newspaper to contact my Provincial in London and demand to know why he was allowing, "Fr. McManus to be involved in politics on Capitol Hill." He then threatened that the next time he himself was in London (he has English connections), he would go to visit my Provincial and make the same demand. All this from a guy who at the same time was condemning clergy for not speaking out about Northern Ireland!

Mr. Deceitful kept hopping from one Irish-American organization to another, but his one consistent theme was "McManus must be stopped." He never, of course, had the guts to say anything to my face—only behind my back or using his position within one of the Irish organizations to attack me.

He would go to absurd lengths. In 2001, a Florida State senator introduced a bill that would repeal the MacBride Principles legislation, which was passed in 1988. I branded the bill as anti-Catholic, wrote to all the Florida State senators and effectively raised the issue in the Florida media. We killed the bill almost immediately. State senators, Protestants, and Catholics, telephoned me to urgently assure me that they were no way associated with the "anti-Catholic Bill." Meanwhile, the individual—who sometimes used AOH as a cover—was lobbying members of the AOH to dissociate themselves from my campaign.

In another example, he went to see Seán MacBride in Dublin to get him to change the MacBride Principles to accommodate the Ford Motor Company, against whom the Caucus had a very effective boycott for their refusal to sign MacBride. I telephoned Seán MacBride to warn him about the impending visit, and he replied, "Do not worry, good Father. People like that have been coming to see me all my life to get me to change my principles and they never succeeded."[12]

Mr. Deceitful's modus operandi was (and still is) to be publicly very anti-British, while secretly opposing any campaign that would expose British injustice. He rants and raves in print against the British, while trying to undermine those most effective against the British. For example, in the seventies, he was insistent that I would condemn Irish Northern Aid. I never would. Lo and behold, he then somehow ends up involved with them. In the nineties, for the first time in over twenty years, I called the office of Irish Northern Aid to speak to the late Belfast Republican, Joe Cahill. I was astonished that Mr. Deceitful answered the phone. Later, of course, it emerged that the infamous British agent, Denis Donaldson, had been placed in that office. So, what was going on here?

Mr. Deceitful's hand inevitably surfaced against our campaign to expose the inherent anti-Catholic sectarianism and discrimination of the British Constitution, because of the Act of Settlement, 1701—as will be explained later.

In 2007, Mr. Deceitful emailed key people trying to sabotage my campaign, bitterly complaining: "Last month it was how Americans should be objecting to the sixteenth century Act of Settlement. I guess under the belief that it has something to do with the conflict in Ireland. It is quite possibly the most idiotic thing for Americans to be lobbying for."

In other words, British state-sponsored discrimination has nothing to do with discrimination in Northern Ireland. The classic British position: "Sorry old chap, the problems in Northern Ireland has nothing to do with us."

When other Irish organizations complained about his peculiar activity, he justified it with: "The response was as much an attempt to separate us [AOH] from ... McManus and to distinguish us from the Sinn Fein 'AMEN' crowd in America." That from a guy who publicly presents himself as a Sinn Fein supporter. How has he gotten away with such deceitfulness for so long?

And predictably, Mr. Deceitful would continually keep trying to spread the lie that I was not, in fact, a priest, or a priest no longer. But when he was challenged on his cowardly and deceitful lie, he backed off adapting a new tack. So, for example, he sent this email to an East-Coast attorney who has done a lot of good work for human rights in Northern Ireland: "Not sure what e-mail you are talking about. First, McManus may or may not be a priest, but my point was don't we have greater need for priests than to sit in Washington issuing fatuous press releases in his delusional world that anyone cares what he thinks ... I still think he should be serving in a mission in Darfur or better still Afghanistan."

The attorney, an honorable and authentic man, replied: "No, [FIRST NAME] I do not see what you mean. But I do see an ugly and childish and envious streak in you. And I suggest that it is offensive to use Darfur and Afghanistan in your denigration of Fr. Sean. You should make better use of your time. Please don't send me any more of the hogwash." (emails. November 7 and 8, 2007).

Mr. Deceitful had manipulated one southern Irish-born AOH leader to a really ridiculous degree. He would draft absurd letters that the AOH leader would send to me, making extraordinary demands. In one case, demanding that I send him a copy of "every letter/memo" I had ever sent to Members of Congress. I replied that the entire Library of Congress could not contain all those letters.

For years I had regarded that as ridiculous nonsense. But what if there is another explanation—one that never even occurred to me until I started doing the research for this book? Demanding a copy of all my letters to Congress may seem, on the face of it, ridiculous. But what if it were an intelligence-gathering attempt? Wouldn't the British Embassy have loved to see all those letters?

Leaders of both the AOH and Irish Northern Aid have told me that they, too, found Mr. Deceitful to be deceitful. One key leader in the MacBride campaign (whom Mr. Deceitful likes to cultivate) emailed me on May 10, 2002, regarding Mr. Deceitful's obsession: "I find it incredible that personal animosity toward one individual can so distort someone's political judgment. It's like he's Captain Ahab to your Moby Dick. Does he have to be for everything you're against, and vice versa?"

Of course, it is much too simple and naive to see the issue as just as a matter of "personal animosity." As explained, I never really knew Mr. Deceitful, so that cannot rationally explain his sustained campaign against me. His "obsession" only makes sense when seen as his being appointed to fulfill his master's wishes.

Even as recent as July 2012, Mr. Deceitful was still at it. One person who had figured out Mr. Deceitful's identity chastised him for his deceitfulness, contrasting it with my "charity" in not outing him by name. Mr. Deceitful snarled back in an email: "McManus never did anything out of charity in his life." For all my faults, even the most bitter Orangeman would not say that about me—not even Maggie Thatcher, Garret FitzGerald, or Rev. Ian Paisley at his former and most vicious anti-Catholic worst. The person replied to Mr. Deceitful: "Very interesting. You make no attempt to challenge, not to mention refute, anything the Father actually writes about you. You just make more petty and mean accusations... You are just the type of venial, cowardly Irishman history has taught us to deplore." ... And that serves very nicely as the last word on Mr. Deceitful.

ROGUE AOH MAN

And then there is the case of another prominent "former AOH leader," a close associate of Mr. Deceitful. He began by working closely with us, but then "they" (whoever they are) got to him. I knew he had turned when he telephoned to tell me he was going to open an office on Capitol Hill.

When I asked him why, he replied, "To steal your thunder." Not to struggle for justice, not to promote the Cause, but to compete against me! How sad is that? Of course, I knew that if that were his sole motivation, then nothing would come of it, and nothing did. But it spoke volumes about him. In 1989, the Irish National Caucus was leading a very strong campaign in Pennsylvania to get the MacBride Principles passed by the State Legislature. The INC leader in Scranton, the late John Breheny, had done magnificent work. He had got the local Scranton bishop and the Governor of Pennsylvania to support the Principles. The chairman of the Senate Finance Committee, State Senator Gibson Armstrong (R-Lancaster) had bottled up the MacBride Bill in his committee, and we were having a hard time getting it out. Lancaster was heavily Amish, very conservative, with hardly any Irish connections. John and I went to see his staffers and convinced them to hold a hearing on the MacBride Bill.

Shortly after our meeting, I had a call in my office from one of the staffers expressing alarm because he had had visitors who demanded I should be taken off the witness list, i.e., the list of people who were scheduled to testify at the hearing. I told him he should not be surprised as I had told him up front that both the British and Irish Embassies were very hostile to me. "But Fr. McManus," this non-Catholic staffer said, "it was not the embassies but someone we thought supported the Irish cause." And he named the former prominent AOH leader. I almost fell off my chair.

John Breheny almost cried when I told him. John was an ardent student of Irish history with a particular horror of the traitor. "This is treason," John exclaimed. "The man is a traitor to Ireland and the AOH."

The AOH in Pennsylvania went on to eloquently repudiate the rogue AOH member by electing me Grand Marshal of the Harrisburg Saint Patrick's Day Parade for March 1990. Neil McGinley, prominent AOH leader and general chairman of the parade, said: "We chose Fr. McManus to acknowledge the leadership of the Irish National Caucus on the MacBride Principles nationally and specifically in the State of Pennsylvania ... Having him Grand Marshal will effectively demonstrate that we want the MacBride Principles passed in Pennsylvania, to which end, we have dedicated the Parade."[14]

And so, it came to pass. The MacBride Principles were passed and signed into law by Governor Robert Casey (D-PA). "The stain of 'treason' had been erased, and the noble John Breheny could sleep again at night." (In 2007, one of Governor Casey's sons, Bob, became a US Senator for Pennsylvania and he would write to me: "It is with great pride and honor that I ... join the esteemed Irish National Caucus. Your organization's commitment to advancing the cause of peace, justice and equality among the Irish people have long inspired the support of the Casey family.")

However, the rogue AOH member would just not quit. On March 10, 1993, there was a public hearing on the MacBride Principles Bill before the Baltimore City Council. The bill had mistakenly been crafted as a disinvestment bill, but we had lined up the complete support of the city council to have it changed and brought into conformity with our national MacBride campaign. Bill Hughes was my key ally. A fervent Irishman and an all-round justice campaigner, Bill was one of the first Irishmen I met when I had arrived in Baltimore in 1972. And by a very nice coincidence, the person who introduced the bill, council member Perry Sfikas, represented my old parish of Sacred Heart of Jesus. The president of the city council, Mary Pat Clarke, would write to me: "It is our family's honor to be counted among your Irish-American supporters. Best wishes for a Brit-free Ireland."[15]

Well before the Hearing, I discovered that the rogue AOH man was still lobbying against me and trying to ensure that the bill would remain a disinvestment bill. Therefore, I telephoned the then National President of the AOH, George Clough, in St. Louis, Missouri. I urged him to write a letter to all members of the Baltimore City Council counteracting his rogue member. On February 11, 1993, George wrote to the city council: "The MacBride campaign, from its inception, has never called for divestment or disinvestment. I would urge you on behalf of our entire membership, and, in particular, our members in Baltimore and Maryland, to make certain that the legislation in its final form reflects this quite clearly. It would be counter-productive at this time if the campaign were seen as calling for disinvestment or for divestment."

When the Rogue AOH man he was informed of Clough's letter, he responded: "It doesn't matter what Clough thinks. He's in Missouri, and I am in Maryland. And furthermore, I used to be the leader of the AOH." However, despite his arrogant response, I thought he would now back off. He did not.

At the Hearing, he was the very last witness, and the first words out of his mouth were, "I am here to oppose Fr. McManus." Then in an incoherent rant, he proceeded to say that the MacBride Principles had failed, there was no point in getting American companies to sign the Principles, and the only effective thing was to get American companies out of Northern Ireland. I quickly squashed his nonsense. Maryland Attorney General, Joe Curran, backed me up, as did his son-in-law, city council member Martin O'Malley, future governor of Maryland—a most ardent Irishman, and a possible future U.S. president.

This AOH member's outburst played right into the hands of the British government—intentionally or otherwise. But he was routed, and the day was saved for MacBride.

At first, I was not going to mention any of this petty nonsense, but it is necessary for the authenticity of the narrative. While it would be nice to think that in struggling for a just and noble cause, one would only have to face the oppressor, it would be naïve and unrealistic. Sadly, one also has to watch one's back from some of one's own people—or those who would present themselves as your "own." I have not named some of these people, as I feel I must show them more charity than they showed me. Moreover, their names are insignificant and can be left out without weakening the historical record—but their actions and agendas had to be recorded.

The words my father said to my brother Patrick when he announced he was going "on the run" back on December 10, 1956, have always echoed down the years: "You will not be halfway out the lane until the police know."

I used to think that informers and agents were few and far between. But over the years I came to realize that they were, in fact, heavy on the ground. The governments had the ground well and truly covered—in both Ireland and America.

I knew I could not do anything about that, but I was determined they would never gain control of my work. And the only way they could stop me was by killing me.

For a long time, I tended to dismiss some of the nasty opposition I received as petty jealousy and stupidity. However, reviewing files that cover forty-seven years and doing intense research can change perspective. One can dispassionately and objectively follow where the evidence leads. I am now ineluctably forced to see that much of that opposition was neither petty nor personal but official and institutionalized. It was not random or ad hoc but carefully choreographed and directed. And, surely, that should not surprise any knowledgeable person.

One striking feature of it has been that none of the individuals concerned ever confronted me to my face and said, "I disagree with a, b, and c." That I could accept and respect. Furthermore, there is another criterion one must use in retrospectively analyzing the evidence. I can understand individuals holding a grudge for many years if one had a fight with them or insulted their family. But how would those persons hold a grudge for forty years if you never had a fight or a disagreement with them—nor even any contact with them? How could they hold a grudge, if they cannot point to one bad thing they personally experienced from me?

So, grudges or "the Irish fighting each other again" cannot be conveniently trotted out here to explain things away. It was not about "a failure to communicate." It was about intelligence operations of the British government. And, gentle reader, you would be very naïve, indeed, to think such intelligence operations were confined to the Six Counties!

The sad thing is that many genuine Irish-Americans who thought they were opposing me on behalf of the IRA were, in fact, unknowingly following the agenda of the London-Dublin governments. How ironic is that?

But enough of informers, agents and "useful idiots"—those being used by the British without even knowing it—and front-organizations for the London and Dublin governments **(again, see Appendix E)**. For every scoundrel, back-stabber, and charlatan, there were thousands upon thousands of honest, decent, patriotic Irish-Americans. Those are the people who made my work possible. And despite all the attacks on me, from the right and the left—from Garret FitzGerald to Gerry Adams - the *Times* of London had to concede: "The most influential group of all is the Irish National Caucus ... From an office on Capitol Hill in Washington, a few yards from the heart of the U.S. government, Father Sean McManus, leader of the Caucus, can sit at his computer terminal and summon up the names of 50,000 supporters

Fr. McManus with Senator Edward Kennedy. Washington, D.C. 1980.

Fr. McManus with ardent Irish advocate Congressman Richie Neal (D-MA). Washington, D.C.2009.

Fr. McManus testifying before the Ad Hoc Congressional Committee. 1979.

Fr. McManus testifying at Congressional Hearing on MacBride Principles. Washington, D.C. 1995.

Fr. McManus with Congressman Hamilton Fish (R-NY). Washington, D.C. 1977.

Fr. McManus with Congressman Chris Smith (R-NJ). 2000.

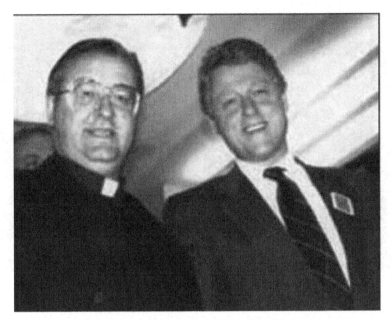

*Fr. McManus with presidential candidate Bill Clinton.
New York, 1992.*

*Fr. McManus with Vice President Al Gore and Congressman
Walsh (center).Washington, DC, 2000.*

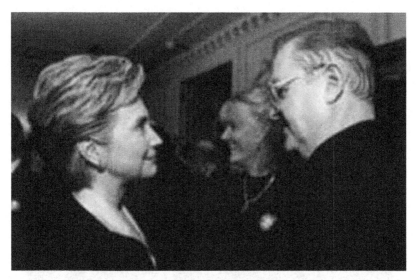

Fr. McManus with Hillary Clinton, secretary of state. Saint Patrick's Day. White House 2009.

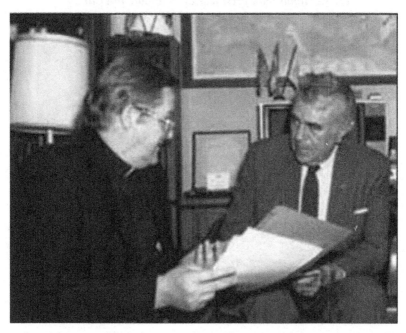

Fr. McManus with Congressman Ben Gilman, who would later Chair the House Committee on Foreign Affairs. Washington, DC. 1989.

Fr. McManus with Richard Harris and Ann Turkel. Baltimore, MD. 1974.

Fr. McManus with Muhammed Ali. Washington, D.C., 1998.

*Fr. McManus with Gerry Adams and John Hume.
New York, Feb. 1994.*

*Fr. McManus with Speaker Gingrich. St. Patrick's Day,
Washington, DC. 1995.*

Fr. McManus with Speaker Nancy Pelosi. Washington, DC. 2008.

Fr. McManus with Ballymurphy Massacre Committee on Capitol Hill. (L-R): Alice Harper, Fr. McManus, Briege Voyle, John Teggart. 2010.

Soon to be president of Ireland, Michael D. Higgins congratulates Fr. McManus. on his Memoirs, as journalist Vincent Browne and artist Bobby Ballagh look on. Dublin, 2011.

Michael D. Higgins, now President of Ireland promotes Fr. McManus' Memoirs. Dublin Castle book launch. Apr.5, 2011.

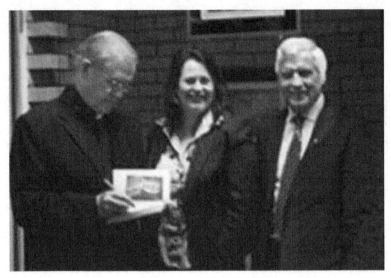

Fr. McManus with Michelle Gildernew, Sinn Fein MP for Fermanagh,/S. Tyrone and the intrepid Donal Donnelly. Enniskillen, 2011.

Fr. McManus with Sinn Fein leader Martin McGuinness, MP, Deputy First Minister of Northern Ireland. Washington, D.C. 2012.

Fr. McManus with DUP Leader Arlene Foster. Washington 2019.

Geraldine Finucane and Fr. McManus. Washington, DC. 2019.

Fr. McManus with Michelle O'Neill, Sinn Fein Vice President and Northern leader. Washington, D.C. 2018.

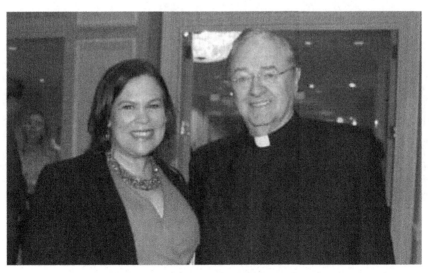

Fr. McManus with Mary Lou McDonald, President, Sinn Fein. Washington, DC. 2019.

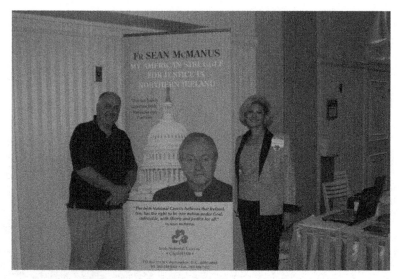

Ray O'Hanlon, The Irish Echo editor and Barbara Flaherty, prime promoter of book. New York, 2011.

Sean with Barbara Flaherty, and her Grandchildren: Joey, Adam, and Sarah. Maryland. 2011.

Sean and Brendan Gabriel Corkery (Barbara's grandson). Brendan's password for entering the INC office is "God save Ireland." Washington, DC, 2019. Photo by Barbara Flaherty.

Barbara is the Executive Vice President for the Irish National Caucus, and a judge and the USA corporate manager for the World Peace Prize.

Barbara holds a Bachelor of Science Degree in Secondary Education and a Master of Science in Curriculum and Instruction. She taught in the Prince George's County, Maryland School System, and in 2005, she received the "Outstanding Educator" Award.

In 2013, The World Peace Prize Council honored her with the "Roving Ambassador for Peace" Award.

Currently, she is a member of the Ladies Ancient Order of Hibernians, Division 9 and is the Recording Secretary for the Irish American Club of Washington, D. C.

A Washington, DC resident, she has three children.

CHAPTER 14

Capitol Hill Struggle

If there is no struggle, there is no progress.
Frederick Douglass[1]

As indicated previously, our presence on Capitol Hill really rocked the boat. However, there is no doubt that without that presence, the issue would have been horribly neglected. Noted journalist and commentator Vincent Browne in August 1979 stated in the Irish media, "The growing U.S. interest in the Northern Ireland issue is traceable almost entirely to the efforts of the Irish National Caucus."[2]

Our job was to get the US Congress involved in Northern Ireland—the aim of the British and Irish Embassies was, in effect, to block that involvement. I know Irish Embassy officials at the time would publicly deny that. Indeed, Sean Donlon would later claim that he was responsible for creating congressional pressure on the British. And I know the Irish government (like the Vatican) can pull out a document to prove it always supported or opposed something. Sean Donlon and Irish Embassy officials had tried to persuade Members of Congress that there was no role for Congress in Northern Ireland. In his authoritative book *American Policy and Northern Ireland: A Saga of Peacebuilding*, Professor Joseph E. Thompson states it well: "The British Government and the Congressional leadership stopped laughing ... when the Ad Hoc Congressional Committee membership went over the 100-member mark."[3] Thompson further explains: "Despite being ignored by the leadership ... the Ad Hoc Congressional Committee joined with the INC to successfully make the Northern Irish question a public issue."[4] And then, very revealingly, he states what I always knew but which the Irish media would never acknowledge: "To counterbalance the growing impact of the Ad Hoc Congressional Committee, Michael Lillis of the Irish Embassy masterminded Tip O'Neill's trip to Ireland in April 1979. This visit was to muster the Irish-American leaders behind the John Hume–Sean Donlon—Michael Lillis approach toward moderate nationalism."[5]

I would add this, however, so that the perspective is not lost: it is not as if the Irish National Caucus was advocating "immoderate" nationalism. And this is where Professor Thompson tends to fall prey to Irish Embassy propaganda. We never asked Congress to support the IRA or anything radical or revolutionary. Indeed, the reason we were so effective was because our demands were reasonable: ending torture, human rights violations, unfair trials, anti-Catholic discrimination, unfair visa policy towards Irish Republicans, etc.—everything the American Constitution stood for. And we had an official policy of nonviolence to which we adhered totally.

So why did the Irish Embassy oppose us so bitterly? Because they did not want the British exposed, which, in turn, would expose the shameless, cowardly record and policy of the Dublin government on Northern Ireland.

Throughout his book, Professor Thompson refers to us as, the "Republican Irish National Caucus." Well, we are certainly not monarchist, but I have never said the INC is Republican. Indeed, I have always refused to use labels like that, and I've always stressed that the Irish National Caucus has no foreign principal that is, it does not support any group or party in Ireland, North or South, nor do we take orders from there.

So, when Thompson says the Irish Embassy was for "moderate nationalism" and we were "Republican," he is echoing the Irish Embassy spin—unconsciously, I'm sure, as he is a professionally objective political scientist.

Again, let me stress, there was not one thing the Caucus was lobbying for that the Irish Embassy should have properly and legitimately opposed. I fully understand that governments and people in power have to be diplomatic and do a lot of stuff in private. And that's OK. But the Irish Embassy has absolutely no right to attack Irish-Americans for speaking out—has no business attacking Americans, period. And certainly, no business spying on them or interfering with their constitutional right of petitioning their government.

Irish-Americans, like all Americans, have a right, even a duty, to demand that the United States apply a single, not a double, standard in its foreign policy. And why should Irish- Americans not have demanded that their Congress denounce British violations of human rights in Northern Ireland? Why should the Irish Embassy seek to muzzle Irish-Americans and the US Congress?

I know the Irish Embassy—remember here we are speaking of the 1970s and 1980s—welcomed American pressure, discreet and private, if it enhanced their own status (and the status quo), but just as surely they did not want a Catholic priest from County Fermanagh kicking the hell (nonviolently, of course) out of the British government all over Capitol Hill and across the United States. Seriously, could anybody in Ireland at that time dispute this?

Again, Professor Thompson provides suitable context: "As the republican INC and the Ad Hoc Congressional Committee grew in strength, so too did Dublin's commitment to lobby in support of Irish constitutional nationalism and Irish-American leaders in Congress."[6]

However, by this time, it was clear to the Irish Embassy that it could not make us go away. Furthermore, its sterile policy of telling Members of Congress that they had no role to play was clearly in shambles. We now had one hundred thirty members signed up. Taoiseach Jack Lynch's frontal attack on the Ad Hoc Congressional Committee had spectacularly failed, as previously explained.

FRIENDS OF IRELAND

What could the Irish Embassy do to save face, and also take the heat off the British that we were so very effectively applying? ... Drum roll, please ... Enter the Friends of Ireland! Yes, indeed, the Irish National Caucus not only initiated the Ad Hoc Congressional Committee for Irish Affairs—the Friends of Ireland also came into existence as a direct reaction to our forming the Ad Hoc Committee.

The Friends of Ireland was launched on Saint Patrick's Day, 1981 by Tip O'Neill, Teddy Kennedy, Senator Patrick Moynihan, etc. As my good friend Congressman Gilman told me at the time, "It was a place for Tip to hang his hat." Desmond Rush would write in *The Irish Independent* that Speaker O'Neill's office had told him that its purpose was to put the Ad Hoc Committee out of business, and it would happen in six weeks.

"That's what Jack Lynch thought," I told Rush. I then called Kirk O'Donnell, one of O'Neill's top people. O'Donnell would not deny Rush's story. Former British MP, Kevin McNamara, in his book, *The MacBride Principles: Irish-America Strikes Back* (more of that later), says: "The Ad Hoc Congressional Committee was proving so successful that the SDLP supporters ... encouraged by the Irish Embassy established the Friends of Ireland ... The Embassy was alarmed by the activities and influence of the Ad Hoc Committee on the Hill and its closeness to the INC."[7] And even more tellingly, Mc Namara goes on to say that Werner Brandt, a key aide to future Speaker Tom Foley, would later authoritatively state that "The Friends of Ireland was formed to prevent Northern Ireland becoming 'an irritant' in Anglo-Irish-U.S. relations."[8] And there you have it, folks: the less than noble origins of the Friends of Ireland. However, I was careful not to condemn them, feeling that in time they could do good. Our aim was to have a strong Irish presence on Capitol Hill. And now there were two Congressional committees, where a short time ago there was none.

Congressmen Mario Biaggi, Ben Gilman, and Hamilton Fish asked me to come over to meet with them regarding the formation of the Friends of Ireland. I urged them to immediately join and told them we would be urging all members of the Ad Hoc Congressional Committee to join. I knew that although Tip and Teddy would toe the safe Dublin line, there was no way large numbers of congressmen would be content with a "do nothing" policy. They were being pressured by their constituents to speak out against British violations of human rights, and there would be no use in their just saying "We can't do anything, but Tip and Teddy are engaging in private diplomacy with the Dublin government." That was no platform to run on. So many of them became just as outspoken as the members of the Ad Hoc Congressional Committee.

In time, our strategy would bear great fruit. When the Democrats lost power, and the Republicans took over in 1995, Congressman Jimmy Walsh from Syracuse, NY, took over as chairman of the Friends of Ireland. He was an ardent Fenian, a good friend, and a strong member of the Ad Hoc Congressional Committee. He would go on, in effect, to merge the two Committees together—making the Friends of Ireland just as strong on the issue. (And by this time, the Irish Embassy had eased off from trying to demonize me.) When the Democrats came back into power in 2007, Congressman Ritchie Neal (D-MA) became the chairman—a most dedicated Irishman who had long been a member of the Ad Hoc Congressional Committee, and whom we listed on our letterhead as a Congressional Friend, as we did Congressman Walsh until he retired from Congress in 2009. And in 2019, Congressman Neal became Chairman again.

Congressional Friends of Irish National Caucus

I should explain here that in 1982, we began the practice of listing on our letterhead the names of the senators and representatives who had become "Friends of the Irish National Caucus"—those who sent us a signed written statement confirming their support of our "nonviolent work for justice and peace in Ireland." The list had to be updated every two years because of the elections for the House of Representatives. And the list got so long that we had to put the names on both the front and the back of our stationery. Democrats, Republicans, Conservatives and Liberals wanted their names to be proudly displayed—from

Congressman Barney Frank (D-MA), commonly seen as the most liberal, to Senator Strom Thurmond (R-SC), commonly seen as the most conservative (which made the Irish Embassy look a bit daft in trying to brand us as radical revolutionaries with old Strom on board!)

Since 1982, we have had scores and scores of Members of Congress, House and Senate, sign up as Congressional Friends of the Irish National Caucus. Now, in 2019, some of them have become Chairs of key House Committees. For example, Eliot L. Engel (D-NY) is the Chairman of the Committee on Foreign Affairs; Nita M. Lowey (D-NY) is the Chairwoman of Committee on Appropriations; Richard E. Neal (D-MA) is the Chairman of Ways and Means Committee; Jerrold Nadler (D-NY) is the Chairman of the Committee on The Judiciary; Elijah E. Cummings (D-MD) is the Chairman of the Committee on Oversight and Reform, and Alcee L. Hastings(D-FL) is the Chairman of the Commission on Security and Cooperation in Europe (U.S. Helsinki Commission); Jim McGovern (D–MA) is the Chairman of the House Rules Committee; and Ted Deutch (D–FL) is the Chairman of the House Ethics Committee.

I should add a note of interest here about the development of the Friends of Ireland. Congressman Brian Donnelly (1979–1993) was elected with the help of many of our supporters in Boston and pledged to them that I would be one of the first people he would meet with when he came to Washington. He kept his promise. I went to see him in his office, and the very first words out of his mouth were, "Father, I want to be briefed by you before I hear the bullshit from the Irish Embassy"— exactly his words. Brian would go on to attend our functions in Boston. He would, however, become a protégé of the future Speaker Foley, and one of the first chairmen of the Friends of Ireland. He always remained friendly and did good work on increasing the number of Irish visas.[9] However, when Joe Kennedy came to Congress (1987–1999), the first thing he told me when I met with him was that I "should keep him involved with the issues with an edge, as Brian Donnelly had all the soft issues." And I knew I could count on this eldest son of the revered Bobby Kennedy to do the "heavy lifting." I was sorry Joe left Congress as I felt, in time, he could have become president. He had guts and charisma in abundance.

Bobby's Son and Grandson

Fr. McManus, Congress man Joe Kennedy II, Derek Warfield and Bob Bateman (back). Washington, DC. 1987.

And I was delighted and excited when his son, Joe III, became a Member of Congress in 2013 for the 4th District of Massachusetts—the Congressional seat from which Barney Frank retired. I was even more excited when I later learned of Joe's Fermanagh's connections: JFK's and Bobby Kennedy's mother, Rose Fitzgerald Kennedy, was the granddaughter of Rosanna Cox, who was born circa 1835 in Tonymore, in the parish of Knockninny, the next parish to Kinawley.

On February 8, 2018, I wrote to Joe III and told him from now on, the Kennedys had to talk more about the girls of Fermanagh and less about the boys of Wexford. "The Boys of Wexford" was JFK's favorite Irish song, and probably Bobby's too.

(For more details, see Appendix F.)

More About "The Girls of Fermanagh" and less about "The Boys of Wexford."

Fermanagh-born Fr. Sean McManus with Fermanagh-descendant Congressman Joe Kennedy III (D-MA).

STRUGGLE FOR CONGRESSIONAL HEARINGS

One of the mandatory ways for a human rights lobby to frame its issue on Capitol Hill is through Congressional hearings. Nothing happens in Congress without the appropriate committee (Appropriations, Judiciary, Foreign Affairs, etc.). Obviously, the Committee for our concerns was Foreign Affairs. And the way to get real action by a committee is to have it hold a hearing, at which experts and concerned citizens are called to testify—like the hearing we arranged back in 1973 at which my brother Frank testified.

So, with crusading zeal, we set out to have another Hearing on human rights in Northern Ireland. But this time it would not be so easy. In1973, we had snuck in under the radar, so to speak. We had pulled off the Hearing before our opponents (all those who did not want the British embarrassed) could block it. After that, I knew there would be all-out opposition to further Hearings.

On Ash Wednesday 1979, I was concelebrating Mass in Saint Peter's, which is on the same side of Capitol Hill as the House of Representatives. Hence, Catholic congressmen/women tend to go there (whereas Catholic senators tend to go to Saint Joseph's, on the Senate side of Capitol Hill). I "gave the ashes" to Tip: dipping my thumb into previously blessed ashes, I made the sign of the cross on his forehead, saying, "Remember, man, thou art dust, and to dust thou shalt return." I did the same for Congressman Clement J. Zablocki (D–WI), the Polish-American Chairman of the House Foreign Affairs Committee from 1977 to 1983. After the Mass, I cornered Chairman Zablocki on the steps of St. Peter's. "You've got to do the right thing, Mr. Chairman. You should not block our hearings on Northern Ireland," I said. He grasped me by the arm—looked over his shoulder to make sure Tip was out of hearing range—and pleadingly said, "Fr. Sean, I want to, but Tip won't let me." He then assured me that as a good Catholic he was deeply sympathetic to the plight of Catholics in Northern Ireland. "But Tip won't let me," he said again, ever so plaintively. I was sure he was telling me the truth.

I went back into the empty church and knelt for a long time to compose myself, and to pray for the grace to forgive Tip. (My head was pounding; here was a Polish American willing to hold hearings, and an Irish-American was blocking him). But while I was prepared to forgive Tip, I was not prepared to give up my struggle for justice. I had come to adopt a motto as my spiritual compass: "Fight like hell for justice, but always forgive like Heaven." As I knelt there, my mind went back to kneeling in the other St. Peter's in Rome when Bishop Drury blessed me. And, again, I experienced the same tranquility and the same determination to fight on—because the doing of justice is, indeed, the primary expectation of God, and blessed are those who hunger and thirst for justice. (Matt. 5:6).

Tip, A Lost Cause

There had to be something about Ash Wednesday and my relationship with Tip. The previous time I had a meeting with him was the year before on Ash Wednesday, 1978. I was still in Boston at the time, and I had been trying for a long time to arrange a meeting with him. He had become Speaker in January 1977, and, understandably, it was difficult to get a meeting. I had gotten to know the wonderful John McCormack of Boston who was Speaker from 1962 to 1971. By then he was a very old man, having been born in December 1891. He used to take me to the famous Jimmy's Harborside Restaurant for dinner at 4:30 p.m. And he used to love it when I had him invited to Mission Church to join the other priests for dinner. Speaker McCormack had taken Tip under his wing when he came to Congress, and Tip felt very indebted to him. Anyway, I told Speaker McCormack I was having difficulty in getting a meeting with Tip. He took care of it right away, and on Ash Wednesday, February 8, 1978, I brought a group of INC leaders into Tip's office. Tip greeted me with great charm and friendliness. As I introduced each of the others, Tip very openly refused to shake the hands of one, a judge from Pittsburgh (I later found out it was because Tip considered the judge to have been part of a group that had sent him thirty pieces of silver—Judas' price for selling out).

Tip immediately began the meeting from behind his very imposing desk: "Fr. Sean, what is all this spying about?" he asked most sternly. I was dumbstruck and said I had no idea what he was referring to. He said, "Before this meeting, the Irish Embassy called me to express concern and was able to tell me the names of the entire delegation. Did you give them the names of these people?"

I told him I certainly had not. (Dan O'Kennedy was in the group.)

"That's what I mean about spying," he said.

I briefed Tip on the situation and urged him to speak out; nobody expected him to support the IRA, but his silence could give the impression that he was condoning British oppression.

He shot back, "There's a long history of anti-English bigotry in my family." Tip then told me that Desmond O'Malley TD, of Fianna Fáil, had been in to see him recently and had told him that both main parties in the Irish Republic, Fine Gael and Fianna Fáil, supported the Sunningdale Agreement.[10] I just happened to have in my briefcase a copy of an article by Vincent Browne in *The Sunday Independent* that said the exact opposite: "The government would not reiterate the Sunningdale declaration on the status of Northern Ireland, according to the Minister for Foreign Affairs, Michael O'Kennedy ... 'That declaration is merely part of the negative British guarantee to help the Unionists ...'"[11] As I read out the article, Tip got visibly angry at what he was hearing. He said he would demand an explanation of the Irish Embassy.

He then told me that the Irish Embassy kept insisting I was a front for terrorism. I told him exactly where I stood. Then he demanded: "I want you to write a letter to me, in your own hand, stating that you are not involved in violence, and I will keep it here in my drawer [and he pulled out the top drawer on the right of his desk to demonstrate], and when anyone tells me you are a terrorist, I will show them it." I promised him I would, and as we were leaving, he said, "Don't forget your ashes, Father." Two days later, on February 10, I wrote him a three-page letter—not in my own hand, as he wouldn't be able to read it! But I spelled out exactly where I stood.

Sometime later, I went to see Ari Weiss in the Speaker's office. Ari was Tip's top policy adviser, and then only twenty-five. Kirk O'Donnell, then thirty-two, was the general counsel and chief political strategist. Ari was considered one of the most brilliant people on The Hill, and I had great regard for him. He was a straight shooter: "A strict orthodox Jew who won't ride in a car on Saturday [he] walked 22 miles in a torrential downpour to attend the Speaker's son's wedding."[12] I always felt I would get total directness from Ari, whereas not from Kirk who would dance and weave. He tended towards the elitist approach on Ireland. Furthermore, because he was Irish-American, he was more susceptible to pressure from the Irish Embassy. Ari told me that Tip was very impressed with the honesty and openness of my letter and that he completely believed me. Ari himself tried to get to the bottom of the Irish Embassy's accusations, and he called well-known journalist Jimmy Breslin to ask his opinion. Breslin told him that "there was likely more truth on the priest's side." But then Ari added that for as long as the Irish Embassy was insisting I was an IRA agent, the Speaker felt he could not continue to meet me—even if John Mc Cormack called him again.

Now back again to Ash Wednesday 1979, and to what Chairman Zablocki had told me about Tip not letting him hold hearings.

Tip's Cover-Up

Of course, I was already well aware of Tip's conniving with the British and Irish governments. We had gotten the famed Jack Anderson column—nationally syndicated and carried in nearly 1,000 papers—to expose it three times within one year, 1977/1978.

> (1) "Speaker Thomas (Tip) O'Neill, the big beloved boss of the House, is as Irish as anyone who ever kissed the Blarney stone. But he quietly squashed a congressional hearing on alleged British outrages against the Irish ...To dig up atrocities, the speaker pleaded, would only inflame the already emotional issue. It would be an 'inappropriate' time to stir up trouble over Irish rights, he said."[13]

> (2) "Under pressure from two foreign governments, President Carter is betraying a campaign promise to speak out against human rights violation committed by British authorities in Northern Ireland. He made the pledge to ... [the Irish National Caucus] in Pittsburgh

six days before the 1976 election, in exchange for their endorsement. Shortly after Carter took office ... [the Irish National Caucus] supplied the White House with ten documented cases of alleged torture perpetrated by British security forces against suspected IRA members or sympathizers ... A move to air the charges on Capitol Hill is being thwarted by House Speaker Tip O'Neill at the behest of the Irish government ... An aide told us that the Speaker, a Carter confidant, was told by prominent members of the Irish government that an investigation would be counterproductive. In Dublin's view, the Irish National Caucus is pro-I.R.A., and a congressional hearing would signal U.S. support of the terrorist IRA gunmen."[14]

(3) "Human rights violations, reported to us by a number of reliable sources, have put Northern Ireland on an unenviable par with some of the most barbarous regimes of communist commissars or tinhorn Latin American dictators. The British are trampling on the rights of Irish citizens in a manner reminiscent of Oliver Cromwell's iron-fisted rule more than three centuries ago ... An Ad Hoc Committee of 119 members has been formed in Congress. But the committee's attempts to publicize the outrages being committed in Northern Ireland, along with the efforts of the Irish National Caucus, have been blocked by House Speaker Tip O'Neill and other congressional leaders who are reluctant to offend our British ally."[15]

What's wrong with that picture? A Mormon journalist, of Swedish-Danish descent (considered one of the fathers of modern investigative journalism) forced to outrage at an Irish- Catholic Speaker of the House covering up British atrocities against Catholics in Northern Ireland. How profoundly sad is that!

But now—after all these years and many months of dispassionately reviewing the historical record—I am, again, forced to wonder about something which in the early years would never have crossed my mind. Why would Tip O'Neill, who was so concerned about his place in history, go so far out on a limb to protect British interests? He had to know that in years to come (i.e., 2019) nobody would dare try to defend his blocking and, in later years as Speaker, his banning of Congressional Hearings on human rights in Northern Ireland. It was indefensible, absurd and corrupt. What possible, conceivable pressure was he under? What would force him to so undemocratically corrupt the Congressional process? What hold had the British on him?

British-Irish Government Cover-Up

Despite all this, the Dublin government was not too eager, at the time, to admit its role. However, Professor Thompson in his previously mentioned book (published in 2001) tells us that "the Irish and British ambassadors to the United States, John Molloy, and Sir Peter Ramsbotham, respectively, made a joint request to Speaker Albert [1971–1977] not to hold any official hearings on Northern Ireland." Professor Thompson explains he elicited this information in a personal interview with Garret FitzGerald in 1999. Thompson then says: "Speaker Albert did not hold any official Hearings on Northern Ireland, but to combat the growing influence of the INC in Congress, he followed Congressman O'Neill and Senator Kennedy's advice and requested that the Congressional Research Service (CRS) of the Library of Congress produce the report Developments in Northern Ireland 1968–1976." Professor Thompson continues with keen observation:

"The introduction to the 1976 CRS report spread the blame for Northern Ireland's increased violence among several parties. The Nixon and Ford administrations were admonished for not offering to facilitate a solution to the crisis. The administrations were accused of hiding behind the pernicious policy of realism, which allowed the party inflicting the injury to decide if an outside party should come in and expose the injured party's grievances. Kissinger knew that Britain would never ask the United States to assist in UK domestic affairs.... The same excuse for inaction in Northern Ireland was used by the United Nations (UN) when it was confronted by the INC request for an investigation into British violations of Irish human rights. U.N. Secretary-General, U Thant, said that he was waiting for the United Kingdom to ask for U.N. assistance, implying that this request would publicize Britain's ineptitude to control its domestic violence."[16]

As I rewrite this 2019 Edition, and as I go back over the record, I must confess to feeling that old righteous Kinawley anger stirring up within me. Can any lover of justice blame me? Can any Irish person worth his/her salt defend this outrageous cover-up? The cover-up was cynical, calculated, and cowardly. And the ever-compliant establishment media went along with it (with a few honorable exceptions). Shame, shame, shame on all responsible. Tip sold his Irish soul to England, prodded on by gombeen men in Ireland, whom Irish history will never forgive.

In an October 1986 interview with Niall O'Dowd, a well-known commentator on Northern Ireland, Tip said, referring to Irish activity in Congress: "It all started with Father McManus. When he came over here, we were all sympathetic to him. Then he started to bring over some of the terrorists from Ireland, and we didn't agree with their philosophy and basically their means to the end, which we didn't like. So, we broke away and started our own group, a more stable one."[17]

The British and Irish Embassy had done their cover-up job well. O'Neill would trot out the nonsense that the reason he opposed a Congressional hearing on Northern Ireland was because it would provide a platform for the IRA. Yet he knew perfectly well that for years the IRA and members of Sinn Féin were denied visas to enter the US. Furthermore, even if they had been able to enter, they just could not turn up and testify because Tip had the power to veto the witness list. So, his excuses were dishonest and corrupt. Tip and the Irish government were covering up for the oppression, torture, and state-assassinations of the British government. Tip was betraying not only his homeland but the United States Congress and all it's supposed to stand for. It is a disgraceful episode in American history.

TIP WAS NOT JUST OPPOSED TO HEARINGS

My problem with Tip was that he was not just opposed to Congressional hearings on Northern Ireland. After he had been "re-educated" by the British and Irish Embassies, he refused to show any interest in individual human rights violations—the Birmingham Six, the Guildford Four, etc. (The same, sadly, can be said about Teddy Kennedy. This is particularly ironic in the case of the Guildford Four, as one of them, Paul Hill would eventually marry Bobby Kennedy's daughter Courtney).

Tip turned a blind eye to torture and showed no interest in combating anti-Catholic discrimination. It is as if the little people did not count—the victims of London's oppression and Dublin's negligence—despite Tip's image as champion of the working class. Nothing seemed to matter but "the big picture," whatever that is. All that mattered was that Tip would, to use that famous phrase of Werner Brandt, "prevent Northern Ireland becoming 'an irritant' in Anglo-Irish-US relations." Of course, he would occasionally raise a question about British practice, and in private he might nudge them, but always within the Brandt parameters. It is the typical elitist approach—again, despite Tip's image to the contrary. He may have been a working-class guy from Boston, but like so many Irish before him, when it came to Her Majesty's government, Tip would doff his hat and become ever so "respectable and diplomatic." And, in the meantime, Irish- Americans were supposed to sit down and shut up. Oh, sure, let them talk about every issue under the sun, except their own homeland—that had to be left to the quiet diplomacy Tip himself, Teddy Kennedy, and the Dublin government. And it must be said, John Hume went along with all this betrayal, and was used as a foil to defend it—until he abandoned the FitzGerald policy of trying to marginalize those totally opposed to British policy and embarked on the true path of the Irish Peace Process. I also recognize Teddy Kennedy went on to do very important work in the Irish Peace Process, and I salute him for that. Tip and I would also clash over US contributions to International Fund for Ireland (IFI), which was formed to support the Anglo-Irish Agreement of 1985.[18]

There was considerable concern about the Agreement, especially because FitzGerald had a dismal and obsequious record on the Agreement. FitzGerald—revealing his true intent—promoted the Agreement as a way to marginalize those who were totally opposed to England's rule in The North. The words of T.S. Elliott immediately come to mind here: "The last temptation is the greatest treason: to do the right deed for the wrong reason.[19]

Anyway, we were determined that any US money for the IFI would have conditions attached. On January 14, 1986, I wrote to every member of the House Foreign Affairs Committee (twenty-four Democrats and thir-teen Republicans) saying: "The Irish-American community is deeply concerned that U.S. Foreign Aid to support the Anglo-Irish Agreement could in effect serve to bolster up British oppression and injustice in Northern Ireland or subsidize anti-Catholic discrimination. That is why we urge: (1) Foreign Aid should not be used by the British Government for military or security purposes or for the gathering of intelligence; (2) Foreign Aid should be tied to the MacBride Principles; (3) Foreign Aid should be tied to the human rights provisions of the Foreign Assistance."

When the Foreign Affairs Subcommittee on Europe and the Middle-East held its Hearing on Wednesday, March 5, 1986, Tip made a point of testifying in person . Although he did shake my hand, his look said, "I am going to blow you out of the water." And he certainly tried. "I believe," he thundered, "that Congress should make the aid subject to standard conditions for assistance and not make it contingent on a long list of politic conditions. We need to express our unqualified support for the Accord [Agreement], not our doubts about it."

BEATING TIP AT HIS OWN GAME

However, we won the day. I had lobbied the Subcommittee so thoroughly that they were prepared to stand up to the Speaker. Congressman Lee Hamilton (D-ID) actually held up my letter, read out our conditions, one by one, and—looking directly at me—said all of them had been met and that should satisfy those who had concerns. It was a remarkable achievement, and of course, the British and Irish media played it down. However, an excellent reporter for the Union Leader Manchester, New Hampshire, Tom Gorey would report: "The House Foreign Affairs Committee approved Reagan's aid proposal on Thursday, after attaching certain conditions that McManus had lobbied for and were inserted by Rep. Ben Gilman (R-NY). Gilman's—provisions restate an existing ban on the use of US economic aid for military or security purposes and insist that the aid be distributed according to the principles of equality of opportunity" and that it promote "human rights." (As we shall see later, Gilman and I would finally succeed in getting the actual MacBride Principles tied to the International Fund for Ireland in 1998, when the Principles became part of US law.)

Gorey's article then continues:

> "McManus said O'Neill 'wanted to come in and personally crush the campaign to add conditions. And yet, we won this one ... We took him on—toe to toe—and we won. McManus branded O'Neill's testimony to the subcommittee as 'vintage British propaganda.' His presentation was exactly how the British government presents the Northern Ireland problem ... Namely, that the British government is not at fault for maintaining an unjust, sectarian, oppressive system (in Ulster) in which violence is inevitable. But the problem in Northern Ireland is the inability of the two tribes—Catholic and Protestant—to get along with each other. There wasn't one condemnation of British violence—military or institutional. There was only a condemnation of IRA violence. [20]

That is fine journalism by Tom Gorey. He captured the story perfectly, and accurately reported my long-standing grievance with typical elitist misrepresentation of the Northern Ireland problem.

By this stage, I'd had it with Tip. I was always fond of him—he was a hard man not to like—but I could no longer excuse his action. And it was not a matter of his being totally controlled by the Dublin government because when it suited him, he could take a strong line. Remember in Chapter 12, when Tip thought Taoiseach Charlie Haughey was going to take a stronger anti-British line and remove Sean Donlon as ambassador, Tip very "undiplomatically" and, some have argued, very improperly intervened and made Haughey back off. Garret FitzGerald would claim that by removing Donlon, Haughey was siding with IRA supporters in America. Nonsense. Who would expect the Irish Embassy, for goodness sake, to be pro-IRA? Haughey did not want the Embassy to be pro-British, but apparently Tip did.

In celebrating that his protégé, Donlon, had been spared, Garett FitzGerald would write: "Our American policy was back on course... thanks to the intervention of Tip O'Neill."[21] That policy being, of course, that the Irish Embassy would continue to shield the British government from really serious Washington pressure. No self-respecting country should have tolerated the Lynch, Cosgrave or FitzGerald governments. Their spineless policy ensured that Catholics in the North would continue to suffer needlessly, and that, in fact, the IRA would thereby increase, not decrease.

Finally, regarding Tip's public record on Northern Ireland, he may have argued that he was doing all sorts of good things privately, but one cannot judge a public figure by his private, secret negotiations. Furthermore, what politician runs on a platform of secret negotiations? What politician can get away with saying, "You don't know what I'm doing, and I can't tell you, but trust me anyway"? That certainly was not his policy on all the other issues he felt strongly about. On those—South Africa, El Salvador, etc.—he was vehemently outspoken, But on Northern Ireland, he had to be "diplomatic" and ever so careful in criticizing Her Majesty's government. Unqualified condemnations were only for the IRA. That was the double standard and dishonesty that would drive me up the wall. I just could not take it, and never could. It is what forced me to get involved in the first place back in England, and it kept me going all these years.

Now I recognize that Tip occasionally did apply some pressure, and the British reacted out of all proportion. One could argue that the British disproportionate reaction was their way of making sure that Tip would back off and not apply real pressure. I favor the latter argument.

Nobody wanted Tip and President Reagan to "nuke" London, send in the marines, or apply sanctions. But can you imagine what real pressure could have accomplished? Sadly, the two most powerful Irish-Americans in the world did not have the guts to do it—and the Irish governments at the time did not want them to do it. So, we had to wait for President Bill Clinton; God bless his southern Baptist heart.

Speaker Tom Foley

The International Fund for Ireland (IFI) would also be the arena for another joust with one of Tip's successors, Congressman Tom Foley (June 6, 1989, to January 3, 1995) from Washington State. (Tip was Speaker from January 4, 1977–January 3, 1987, and Jim Wright from Texas replaced him from June 6, 1987– June 6, 1989).

By this time there was growing concern about the performance of the IFI. Most of the funds were simply adhering to the systematic pattern of discrimination in Northern Ireland—going to the Unionist/Protestant areas. The Second Annual Report on the IFI revealed, for example, that West and North Belfast and Derry received less than 6 percent of the 1988 budget: ".... The bulk of the money went to a variety of projects which had had no relation to northern violence: funding for hotels, tourist amenities, a skydiving club, golf courses and a $1.9 million gift of a fishing vessel to the British government ..."[22]

I had been inundating the Foreign Affairs Committee with documentation and creating a lot of noise. I convinced Chairman Lee Hamilton that my concerns should be aired at a Hearing and that he should allow other Irish-American groups to testify, too. Gerry Coleman, an Irish-American from New Jersey, would represent eight Irish-American organizations, including Irish Northern Aid. I would speak for the Irish National Caucus.

On April 26, 1989, the Subcommittee for Europe and the Middle East held its Hearing. In strode Tom Foley (Speaker-in-waiting) who proceeded to launch an attack, which clearly took the subcommittee members by surprise: "We don't usually ask criminal organizations to come before the committee and recommend how to improve the law."[23] Sean Cronin of *The Irish Times* recorded that when asked to whom he was referring, Foley said, "Mr. Coleman has chosen to appear before you for Irish Northern Aid, the registered agent for the IRA ... Mr. Coleman ... looked startled."[24]

Then I would be given a blast, but I wasn't a bit startled as I was well used to holding my own with Members of Congress. Significantly, Foley did not claim I was IRA. The worst he could come up with was that I "was on record of opposing the Anglo-Irish Agreement." Then, clearly thinking he had the knock-out punch, pronounced: "Father McManus has referred to Tip O'Neill, President Reagan, Pat Moynihan, and Teddy Kennedy as lapsed Irishmen. Well, if that's a lapsed Irishman, I want to be included." *Come on Foley*, I thought, *is that all you've got?* My good friend Congressman Gary Ackerman (D-NY), a Jewish American, asked Foley what it meant to be a "lapsed Irishman." "It means that you do not agree with Father McManus," was his reply.[25] First time I knew Foley had a sense of humor.

STRUGGLE AGAINST EXTRADITION TREATY

Another major battle we fought on Capitol Hill, this time in the Senate, was against the Supplemental Extradition Treaty agreed between the British and the State Department in the summer of 1985. It proposed to remove the historic and venerable "political exception" to extradition giving Britain the privilege of being the only country in the world without a political exception clause in its treaty with the United States, which meant that no Irish person who was wanted for a violent crime–and had escaped to America—could plead in a US court that his or her offense was political. The British had hoped the treaty would go through quietly, especially because of a recent Beirut hijacking. British Prime Minister Margaret Thatcher would also link to the Treaty her support for President Reagan's bombing of Libya on April 15, 1986.

However, the treaty had to be ratified by two-thirds of the Senate. And I was determined to battle it for all my worth. I formulated three basic arguments, which became the accepted platform of all opposed to the treaty: (1) it legitimized British rule in Northern Ireland; (2) it took away authority from the US courts, which historically and properly adjudicated such cases; and (3) it surrendered an Irish person to a corrupt system of British law.

Although this treaty was a terrible development, I pointed out to Irish-Americans all across the country that it provided us with the chance to bring our cause right into the U.S. Senate (to the Senate Committee on Foreign Affairs)—an opportunity that rarely arises. We had to make the most of it. I extensively briefed the Minority Staff, i.e., the staff that worked for the Senate Democrats, whose ranking member was Joe Biden (who became vice president in January 2009). We put out a press release saying:

> It was a delight to hear Senator Biden right in the middle of the most prestigious Committee state: "But I think this Extradition Treaty is an opportunity to do what we have been unable to do so far. There is an incredible reluctance on the part of this government to criticize one of our closest allies for what I believe to be an absolutely outrageous position which they have continued to maintain with regard to Northern Ireland, and an unwillingness on the part of the present government to do anything constructive about it, that is, the British government. So, I want to make clear to you that I am going to do all that

I can do to hold this up as long as I can to make the case."[26]

You know you have done your job when you hear your own words being repeated back virtually word for word in a US Senate Hearing. The press gave our struggle considerable coverage. Even the British press was relatively fair with us this time. "Britain and Irish in battle on Capitol Hill," said the *Observer*, while displaying a photograph of the British ambassador to Washington, Sir Oliver Wright, with whom I had clashed many times. The reporter, the well-respected Simon Hoggart, explained: "The British government and the powerful Irish republican lobby are squaring up this week for their greatest fight ... Father Sean McManus is an affable and persuasive man who operates from an elegant office a few hundred yards from the Capitol ... [He] has sent a direct mail package to 250,000 people. The [outside] envelope says urgent: "The British are coming, the British are coming"—so cunningly associating their cause with the American Revolution."[27]

The Washington Post, national weekly edition, not usually a fan of those opposing Jolly Old England, was so taken with my direct mail package that it published a photograph of the outside envelope, with its entire graphics. In a lengthy article, it proceeded to explain: "Inside the direct mail package the letter began: 'The British are indeed coming, this time into the United States Senate, and it's here we must meet and beat them.'"[28]

Even the brilliant curmudgeon Christopher Hitchens—who would go on to say bad things about God and Mother Teresa—did not badmouth me:

> The master of these revels, in publicity terms, is Father Sean McManus, a burly, plausible charmer whose Irish National Caucus has taken center stage. In the years since the Redemptorist order found him too much of a handful to retain in Britain, the good Father has made himself expert in congressional lobbying techniques ...

I spent a long and, to be perfectly frank, rather enjoyable afternoon with Father McManus in his Capitol Hill office. He knew that I wanted him to come clean about the Provisionals, and it became clear that he hadn't been raised as a clerical apologist for nothing ... Did he regard the Irish government (which through its embassy is lobbying for the extradition treaty) as the legitimate government of Ireland? A knowing smile: "Do the Dublin government recognize Sir Oliver Wright as the legitimate representative and envoy of Fermanagh and West Belfast? If they do, they admit they represent only part of the Irish people."[29]

I knew I had a massive task, but I was committed. *The Sunday Times* revealed just how committed: "The powerful Irish lobby is... working hard to kill the treaty. For example, Father Sean McManus ... has even canceled his annual summer holiday in Ireland."[30] Now that's commitment—giving up a chance to go back to Kinawley!

Our first task was to block speedy ratification, which we did. *The Boston Globe* reported, "The committee originally intended to hold one hearing last July 25. But opposition quickly developed chiefly under the auspices of the Irish National Caucus."[31] "Caucus blocks anti-IRA move: Irish group's pressure works on US Senate," was how Niall O'Dowd's article in *The Sunday Press* heralded the story. "The US Senate has balked at quick ratification of the proposed new extradition treaty ... following a major lobbying effort by Irish-American groups headed by the Irish National Caucus ... According to a spokesman for Sen. Richard Lugar, head of the Senate Foreign Relations Committee, pressure from Irish and concerned civil rights groups played a major role in the postponement."[32] Margaret Thatcher lashed out: "The British Prime Minister, Mrs. Thatcher, yesterday criticized the delays, through 'a very effective Irish lobby' in the US Congress, that have prevented the introduction of extradition for people accused of IRA activities."[33]

But despite our gallant effort, we did not win this one—but we were not beaten either. Although the "political exception" was rescinded, we, nonetheless, succeeded in getting some important conditions attached. Noted journalist Karen Tumulty who covered Congress for the *Los Angeles Times* for fourteen years and would later join *Time* Magazine—assessed it this way:

"A compromise ... essentially allowed both sides to declare victory. Included in the compromise is a provision that permits a judge to deny extradition if he determines the accused could not get a fair trial because of "race, religion, nationality, or political opinions."

Additional language in the accompanying report, not part of the treaty itself, would allow US judges handling extradition cases to consider whether the British court system is fair. The language was added to answer criticism of the non-jury, single-judge courts, called Diplock courts, that are used to try IRA defendants.

As I said, we were not beaten either. And I think it may have been a pyrrhic victory for the British. An indication of this is that the British did not try to extradite Joe Doherty—who had been in prison for years in New York—under the terms of the new treaty. He was deported but not extradited.

I should note here that we not only briefed the Democrats on the Senate Foreign Relations Committee but also the Republicans, as was always our bipartisan approach. Senator, a Mormon from Utah, whom we got to know quite well, became a strong opponent of the treaty. This deeply conservative man became an ardent supporter of Irish justice. Indeed, at that time, he was very critical of Teddy Kennedy's weak response. We proudly listed him on our letterhead as a Congressional Friend of the Irish National Caucus for many years. But in 1991, I sent out a very large, direct mail package in an attempt to stop Margaret Thatcher from getting the Presidential Medal of Freedom, and from being invited to speak at the Republican National Convention in 1992. As you can imagine, I told the truth about Thatcher's racist and anti-Irish Catholic record. Senator Hatch wrote demanding I take his name off our letterhead because of the "... offensive and intolerable language that was directed at Mrs. Thatcher ..."

I responded in kind. "You shall, indeed, be removed because anyone who is prepared to condone and cover-up Margaret Thatcher's record of anti-Catholic bigotry and oppression in Northern Ireland has no right to be on our stationery."[34]

It was the end of a beautiful relationship. I never met with him again. But, still, he was a fine man, and I will always be grateful for what he did to oppose British violations of human rights—when some Irish-American Congressional leaders were too scared to take a stand.

STRUGGLE AGAINST ACT OF SETTLEMENT 1701

I must not neglect to mention one other campaign, which like so many others had not been attempted until the Caucus came along: repealing the anti-Catholic sections in The Act of Settlement, 1701.

The Act of Settlement is an integral part of the unwritten and uncodified British constitution. It determines succession to the Throne of England, and is, therefore, a fundamental constitutional statute, indeed, the very foundation stone of the Royal Family. It contains provisions that decree a Catholic cannot succeed to the English Throne, and that if the monarch becomes a Catholic, or marries a Catholic, he/she forfeits the throne and "the people are absolved from their allegiance." (The ban on the Monarch marrying a Catholic was repealed in October 2011).

Imagine had there been a provision in the US Constitution forbidding an African-American becoming president or forbidding the president to marry a black person—think how that would have stoked the flames of racism and white supremacy.

While this statute may mean little to the average British man in the street, it has always been of the utmost importance to Protestant/Unionist/Orange extremists in Northern Ireland. It provides the ideological and philosophical underpinnings for their bigotry and sectarianism. For, you see, the spurious but deadly logic goes, if a Catholic by law can't get the top job, then Catholics are inferior to Protestants, and therefore, it's OK to discriminate against them.

But don't first blame extreme Orangemen—they did not create the Act of Settlement. Put the blame where it belongs: on the British monarchy and parliament—and on the Church of England and the British establishment for going along with this inherently sectarian Constitution. (The Constitution is also sexist and discriminates against women: if there is no direct male heir, a royal princess can succeed to the throne, but a younger brother takes precedence over an elder sister.)

It was a source of satisfaction to me that at long last the sectarian, anti-Catholic and undemocratic Act of Settlement, 1701, was getting a public airing. For thirty years I had been "a voice crying in the wilderness" when I raised this issue. It astonished me that some Irish-Americans and indeed many Catholics in Northern Ireland failed to see that there was a causal connection between an anti-Catholic Constitution and anti-Catholic behavior by those extreme Orangemen who saw themselves as loyal upholders of the British constitution.

But now, in great measure due to the consciousness-raising done by the Irish National Caucus, there is a growing awareness in Britain and Ireland that those bigoted and sectarian provisions must be repealed.

One of the first Irish-Americans to appreciate the importance of exposing the sectarian Act of Settlement was a bright young attorney, Larry Downes, who was a leader of the Brehon Law Society in New York. Years later Larry, as Chairman of the Friends of Sinn Fein, would go on to raise millions of dollars for Sinn Fein. Few have shown more commitment to The Cause than he.

SOLIDARITY: PICKETING FOR JUSTICE AT BRITISH EMBASSY, WASHINGTON, DC.

Martin Luther King, III and Fr. MManus protesting outside the British Embassy. Saint Patrick's Day, 1988.

Fr. McManus welcomes the late, famed Labor leader Cesar Chavez to 1988 Saint Patrick's Day picket at the British Embassy, Washington, D.C.

Fr. Sean shakes hands with Representative John Lewis (D-GA) at 1988 Saint Patrick's Day picket at the British Embassy, Washington, D.C.

Fr. McManus with Congressman Joe Kennedy II (D-MA) at 1988 Saint Patrick's Day picket at the British Embassy, Washington, DC.

CHAPTER 15

The MacBride Principles: Genesis and History

An Army of Principles Will Penetrate Where an Army of Soldiers Cannot
Thomas Paine[1]

I WANT TO SET OUT HERE FOR THE HISTORICAL record how the Irish National Caucus initiated, proposed, and launched the MacBride Principles. This is all the more important since there have been some attempts at revisionism. I will have to give an abundance of quotes from the press and other sources to document the clear and incontestable role of the Irish National Caucus. And the issue here is not the drafting of individual Principles, which are not particularly unique but generally modeled on the Sullivan Principles[2] and other such principles.

But first a statement of what the Principles are: the MacBride Principles—consisting of nine fair employment principles—are a corporate code of conduct for U.S. companies doing business in Northern Ireland and have become the Congressional standard for all U.S. aid to, or economic dealings with, Northern Ireland.

The Principles do not call for quotas, reverse discrimination, divestment (the withdrawal of US companies from Northern Ireland) or disinvestment (the withdrawal of funds now invested in firms with operations in Northern Ireland). The Caucus positively encourages non-discriminatory US investment in Northern Ireland. The MacBride campaign is conducted on a three-fold level:

1. Federal: the MacBride Principles became the law of the U.S. in October 1998.

   The US House and Senate passed the MacBride Principles—as part of the Omnibus Appropriations Act for Fiscal Year 1999—and President Clinton signed them into law. The MacBride law mandates that recipients of U.S. contributions to the International Fund for Ireland (IFI) must be in compliance with the MacBride Principles. (The U.S. has been contributing about $19.6 million per year since 1986 to the IFI.)

2. State and cities: millions of dollars in State and city pension and retirement funds are invested in American corporations doing business in Northern Ireland. The MacBride campaign lobbies to have legislation passed to direct these funds to be invested, in the future, only in companies that endorse the Principles (again, note, not divestment or disinvestment). This is the first step. The second step—once the MacBride Principles investment law has been passed—is to get a contract compliance law passed.

3. Shareholder Resolutions: the Campaign works to have shareholders pass resolutions endorsing the Principles.

The MacBride Principles did not suddenly appear from the sky like the Ten Commandments. They were the result of many years of hard and unrelenting work by the Irish National Caucus. The Principles were "conceived" in August 1979; "born" in June 1983; and "christened" in November 1984.

THE MACBRIDE PRINCIPLES CONCEIVED

One of the first objectives of the newly opened office of the Irish National Caucus was to "stop United States dollars subsidizing anti-Catholic discrimination in Northern Ireland." To have impact on foreign policy, you have to find the foreign policy nexus—that which connects Northern Ireland and the United States. The obvious "nexus" was the United States companies doing business in Northern Ireland. These companies could also be the "fulcrum" through which we could exercise leverage to oppose discrimination in Northern Ireland.

So, these companies had to be held accountable to American legislators and investors. In July 1979, Congressman Ben Gilman (R-NY), a member of the House Committee on Foreign Affairs, and a member of the Subcommittee on International Economic Policy and Trade, commissioned the Irish National Caucus to conduct an investigation of the U.S. companies in Northern Ireland. We traveled to Northern Ireland at the end of July 1979, and the *Sunday News* announced our mission:

CAUCUS IN JOBS BLACKLIST MOVE:
AMERICANS PROBE WORKERS' RELIGIONS

American firms with production plants in Ulster are to be asked for a religious breakdown of local workers in a move to tighten up on United States equal opportunity laws. And some companies located in "sensitive" areas of the Province which do not have balanced Protestant-Catholic worker ratios could have a black mark against them in a report to an influential Congressman in Washington.

Later this week leading members of the Irish National Caucus from the federal capital will be touring Northern Ireland, knocking on the doors of American firms for details of their employment registers.

The most significant of the credentials the team will present is a letter from New York Republican Congressman Ben Gilman, who sits on an international trade subcommittee with powerful controls on US corporations operating overseas.

Fr. Sean McManus said the letter from Congressman Gilman gave their visit to American firms in the North a semi-official status. He added that the INC delegation would almost certainly be visiting the Ford-owned Autolite components factory at Finaghy and the management of the new DeLorean car assembly plant.[3]

The Irish Times said:

> While in Northern Ireland the members of the Caucus will visit some American-owned companies to ascertain whether any discriminatory employment practices operate. The investigation is being carried out at the request of Congressman Benjamin Gilman, who is a member of the House Committee on Foreign Affairs and the Subcommittee on International Economic Policy and Trade. U.S. corporations, which are found not to reflect American respect for and protection of equal opportunities for all, could face withdrawal of tax concessions and trading licenses.
>
> One of the Caucus' recent achievements concerns the suspension of U.S. arms sales to the RUC, pending an investigation into the human rights situation in the north. They are also speaking of their determination to make Ireland an issue in the coming Presidential campaign.[4]

The Irish Press carried the story this way:

> [Leaders of the Caucus] are in Ireland at present to investigate the behavior of American firms in the North. They are undertaking this mission on behalf of Congressman Benjamin A. Gilman, who is a member of the Congress Committee on Foreign Affairs and the Subcommittee on International Economic Policy and Trade.
>
> This committee controls overseas aid, and if American firms locating outside the country are found to be discriminating against anyone on the basis of race, creed or color, their US tax concessions may be cut off.[5]

The *Belfast Telegraph* said:

> The Irish National Caucus is investigating alleged discrimination at Goodyear's Craigavon factory. The Caucus has asked for a breakdown of religious affiliations of the 1,400 people employed at the Silverwood plant.
>
> Goodyear was one of many firms which signed the Fair Employment Declaration ... Prominent members of the Caucus are involved in the investigation—including Fr.Sean McManus.[6]

We made contact with most of the US companies and asked them to submit a detailed breakdown of the religious composition of their workforce (in doing so we were years ahead of the British government's Fair Employment Laws, which did not make this demand until 1989).

SEAN MACBRIDE, INC LIAISON GROUP

But the launching of the investigation into U.S. companies in Northern Ireland was not the only important initiative the Caucus took on its August mission to Ireland. There was another equally important initiative that would be full of significance, symbolism, and solidarity for the MacBride Principles later on. The Caucus established, in Dublin, the Irish National Caucus Liaison Group, chaired by Dr. Seán MacBride himself. The inaugural meeting was held in Seán's home, Roebuck House. *The Irish Times* reported:

> Mr. Seán MacBride, the Nobel Prize, and Lenin Peace Prize winner, has become chairman of a new group in Ireland which aims to put forward the views of the Irish National Caucus, a United-States-based organization.

Mr. Michael Mullen, general secretary of the Irish Transport and General Workers' Union, is another member of the new group.

The Rev. Sean McManus, a leader of the Irish National Caucus, said last night in Dublin that the new group in Dublin would be called Irish National Caucus Associates. It would be based in the Republic and, besides Mr. MacBride, it would include Mr. Mullen and Mr. Kevin Boland, a former Fianna Fáil Minister.

The initial meeting, which was attended by 20 people, was held on Thursday, and another one would be held later this month.[7]

Back in the US, the *Irish World* told Irish-Americans of this initiative in the following way:

"Sean MacBride, recipient of both the Nobel Peace Prize and Lenin Peace Prize, has announced his agreement to act as chairman of a new organization in the Republic of Ireland which aims to act as a liaison between the US–based Irish National Caucus and the people of Ireland

"The idea of our organization," MacBride said, "is to get across to the Irish public the truth about the United States organization and to emphasize the significance of the Irish-American dimension. The success of the Irish National Caucus was seen in the US State Department policy review on supplying arms to the RUC." MacBride added that, in his opinion, the work of the I.N.C. had been somewhat misrepresented by a number of individuals in Ireland and that it is his hope that the work of the new organization will present a clearer picture of Caucus activities. "The Irish National Caucus is not a "front" for any group in Ireland. It is undoubtedly the most effective and widely-respected Irish-American Organization in the States, and we hope to contribute to its goal of a just and lasting peace in the North of Ireland."[8]

It should be obvious to all that in these two Caucus initiatives (investigation of U.S. companies in Northern Ireland and Seán MacBride becoming Chairman of our Liaison Group in the Republic of Ireland) were sown the seeds of the MacBride Principles. Since he had left the Dáil in 1958, Seán MacBride had established a policy of not belonging to any party or group dealing specifically with Northern Ireland. But he broke this policy to identify with the Irish National Caucus. He was attracted to the Irish National Caucus for the following reasons:

(1) It is nonviolent.
(2) It has no foreign principal—that is, it is neither controlled nor directed by any, party, or government in Ireland.
(3) It did not send funds to Ireland.

Seán MacBride particularly admired the Caucus' focus on stopping U.S. dollars subsidizing anti-Catholic discrimination in Northern Ireland. Paddy Harte, TD for Donegal, launched an appalling personal attack in the press on MacBride, calling him senile and other abusive things. (Harte never apologized for his attack.) The other Donegal TD, the late Neil Blaney, congratulated MacBride, joined the Liaison Group and announced he was going to the U.S. to speak for the Irish National Caucus. Neil had a life-long record of concern for the North of Ireland. Paddy Harte would later become the founder of Irish-American Partnership that was launched by Taoiseach Garret FitzGerald in 1984.

We decided that a good way to "frame the issue" of US dollars subsidizing anti-Catholic discrimination in Northern Ireland would be to have the Ad Hoc Committee for Irish Affairs, which we had initiated, hold a Hearing, and bring Fr. Brian Brady over from Belfast to testify about the hiring practices of US companies in Northern Ireland. The Hearing took place on July 22, 1981. It was the first time ever that discrimination by US companies in Northern Ireland was raised in the United States Congress.

After the Ad Hoc Congressional Hearing, the Irish National Caucus planned to have our principle, that United States dollars should not subsidize anti-Catholic discrimination in Northern Ireland, enshrined into law. We worked assiduously on this. In 1983, we succeeded at last in having a Bill introduced into Congress, HR 3465: "Requiring United States persons who conduct business or control enterprises in Northern Ireland to comply with certain fair employment principles." It was modeled on the Sullivan Principles and became known as the "Ottinger Bill," after its chief sponsor, Congressman Dick Ottinger (D- NY). Although the Bill did not pass, it was of singular importance because it perfectly framed our issue. We now had in place all the essential elements of what we would later call the MacBride Principles:

> (1) The ongoing investigation of the United States companies in Northern Ireland.
>
> (2) The high-profile involvement of Seán MacBride in our campaign.
>
> (3) A set of fair employment principles for those companies to serve as a corporate code of conduct.

The very first lobbyists against the Ottinger Bill were the Irish Embassy in Washington, DC, and John Hume. I issued the following press release:

Irish Embassy Cover-up on Anti-Catholic Discrimination
Washington, D.C., November 4, 1983

> The Irish National Caucus has reacted with anger to attempts by the Irish Embassy to sabotage legislation in Congress that would outlaw discrimination by American companies in Northern Ireland.

The Caucus claims that it has been told by a number of Congressional offices that the Irish Embassy is advising them not to sponsor the Bill of Congressman Richard L. Ottinger (D-NY). One office reported in amazement to the Caucus that the Irish Embassy is saying that the Ottinger Bill would actually increase unemployment in Northern Ireland.

Fr. Sean McManus, National Director, said: "The Irish Embassy is quite simply conspiring with the British Embassy to cover up anti-Catholic Discrimination in Northern Ireland. I call upon the Opposition Parties and Independents in the Dail to demand that this disgraceful sellout of the Catholics in Northern Ireland cease."

When Congressman Ottinger first introduced the Bill, Irish Embassy officials told him that they approved of it. Then John Hume and [the Rev.Ian] Paisley came to Washington. John Hume was quoted in the *Washington Times*, September 20, 1983, as saying, "There are twenty seven US plants in N.I., and I have not heard one complaint about discrimination practices. We have a fair employment bill that makes discrimination illegal." That is an extraordinary thing for John Hume to say. Paisley has leaned on John Hume, and the British government has leaned on the Irish government to oppose the Ottinger legislation. How can Garret FitzGerald possibly explain to the people of Ireland that it would be bad for the US Congress to make it illegal for U.S. companies in N.I. to discriminate?

The greatest weapon the British have for oppressing Catholics in Northern Ireland is the Irish Embassy in Washington.

Whenever the Irish National Caucus succeeds in raising the Irish issue, the British always make the Irish Embassy jump to defend British interests," concluded Fr. McManus.[9]

Niall O'Dowd—who would later become the publisher of the *Irish Voice* newspaper and *Irish America* magazine in New York—would report from San Francisco:

> The revelation that the Irish Embassy was actively campaigning against the Bill came yesterday from the offices of Congresswoman Barbara Boxer (D-CA) who confirmed that in separate meetings representatives from both the Irish and British governments had asked her to oppose the Bill ... In response to Fr. McManus' criticism, Michael Collins [later the Irish Ambassador in Washington], the Irish Government's press and information officer in the United States, stated that the embassy had "taken a long and detailed look at all aspects of the Ottinger Bill and that they foresee problems with it. We believe that this Bill could have a counter-productive effect."[10]

THE MACBRIDE PRINCIPLES BORN

The Ottinger Bill contained, in essence, the principles we would later call the MacBride Principles. That is why we say that the MacBride Principles were born in 1983. To promote the Ottinger Bill, the Irish National Caucus sponsored a visit to Northern Ireland by Congressman Ottinger in 1983. We hosted the Congressman's appearances at meetings and press conferences in Belfast. The visit received considerable press coverage in the Irish and British media. Bob Blancato, the staff director of the Ad Hoc Congressional Committee for Irish Affairs, was also part of the delegation, representing the Chairman of the Committee, Congressman Mario Biaggi (D-NY).

We could tell we were on to something very important by the way the press reacted. The *Daily Telegraph*, under the heading "Americans in Ulster Maelstrom," said:

"Mr. Ottinger's mission is regarded with far more suspicion in the Protestant camp. At the moment, he is steering legislation through Congress to force American companies investing in Northern Ireland to employ more Roman Catholics.

In June, he introduced a Bill called the Northern Ireland Fair Employment Practices Act, which would require American firms with branches or other enterprises in Ulster to desegregate employees of different religions and eliminate religious discrimination in jobs.

The spotlight is being put on Short Brothers, the Belfast planemakers, who are bidding to sell aircraft to the United States Air Force. The contract would mean an extra six hundred jobs ... Advising the Congressman, and helping him in the talks, was Fr. Sean McManus, the Washington-based Redemptorist priest ordained in England and now a scourge of the British government. The lime-and-soda-drinking cleric is not liked by British diplomats in the American capital, where he leads the Irish National Caucus, a lobbying group aimed at influencing American foreign policy with the target of Irish unity, freedom, and peace."[11]

The *News Letter* screamed the headline, "Anti-British to the Hilt," and said:

"The leading light in the delegation, Fr. Sean McManus, is a well-known republican sympathizer who rarely disguises his anti-British stance ... this fiery advocate of Irish republicanism did his utmost to embarrass British diplomats in Washington with a brief hunger strike outside the Embassy in support of Bobby Sands' death fast.

He was instrumental in persuading the Carter administration to impose an embargo on American gun sales to the RUC in Belfast. And his latest campaign aimed at undermining the attempt by Shorts to secure a multi-million-pound order to sell its SD-330 Sherpa freighters to the United States Air Force.

It was back in 1979 that Fr. McManus told reporters: "The British thought they were getting rid of me in 1972 when they had me packed off to America. Little did they know I would be far more vocal on Capitol Hill."[12]

The *Daily Express*, August 18, 1983, however, really outdid itself. It devoted an editorial to our visit:

> Sean McManus, a rancid bigot, loosely described as a "priest," is campaigning to stop a £33 million order from the United States Air Force going to Shorts, the Belfast plane-makers.
>
> McManus—born in Northern Ireland but now in Washington heading an anti-British group—alleges there is discrimination against Catholics at Shorts: though the firm denies it.
>
> Doubtless, he is delirious at the calls from other pipsqueak Irish-American politicians urging President Reagan to appoint a special envoy to Northern Ireland.
>
> Indeed, he probably has a hand in the setting up of the "Irish-American Presidential Committee" to push the issue of a unified Ireland into the 1984 presidential campaign."[13]

SHORTS

While in Belfast, we took the occasion to pursue the other very hot issue—the question of the United States Air Force doing business with

Short Brothers (Shorts had a notorious record of anti-Catholic discrimination). The Caucus had been raising this issue for quite some time. This was really one of our pivotal campaigns because it dramatically raised the whole issue of US dollars subsidizing anti-Catholic discrimination in Northern Ireland. We met with Short's executives at the office of the Fair Employment Agency. Again, this meeting received considerable press coverage. Our Shorts campaign would eventually lead to Congressman Joe Kennedy (D-MA) getting an Amendment passed (1988, 1989, and 1990) in Congress to the US Defense bill. The Amendment required Shorts to submit an annual statistical report to the Defense Department on its subcontracting and recruiting practices.

At the meeting, I remember the Shorts' spokesman—with barely concealed hostility—telling me, "Shorts does not have to give any explanations to the Irish National Caucus or anybody in America." How their tune has changed. That same spokesperson would later have to go, cap in hand, to meet with the then comptroller of New York City, Elizabeth Holtzman, to assure her that Shorts was making attempts to hire more Catholics..

The Empire Strikes Back

Just before one main press conference was due to take place, Fr. Brian Brady called and told us that a high-ranking Catholic Church official in Belfast had asked him to ask us to meet with someone who had a special interest in the Shorts issue. We agreed.

The person arrived and asked to meet with us behind a big curtain in the room where the press conference would take place in the Europa Hotel in Belfast. He did not want to be seen by the press. His name was James Eccles, a former Head of the Knights of Columbanus (a lay Catholic organization in Ireland. It is quite powerful and very "respectable.") Eccles' pitch was that the Knights had done a lot of investigation into anti-Catholic discrimination in Northern Ireland. We asked him to provide us with the results of the alleged investigation. He was completely taken aback. We knew the guy had an angle, to say the least. He said he agreed that Shorts was guilty of very bad discrimination, but ... "But," I cut in, "you still think they should get the contract with the US Air Force?" Eccles said yes. He then promised if Shorts got the contract, the Knights would put pressure on them to end discrimination. We politely told him that we would keep up the pressure on Shorts, and showed him the door (or rather, the curtain).

While he was giving us this unbelievably disingenuous pitch, I couldn't help remembering that it was the Catholic Bishop of Belfast, Cahal Daly, who was among the very first to voice public opposition to our campaign against Shorts. There is a morning radio program in Northern Ireland called *Thought for the Day* on BBC Ulster. Bishop Daly instructed Fr. Gerry Patton—the media person for the diocese—to use the program to attack our campaign. Patton deplored the fact that there was a campaign in the US to oppose Shorts getting an Air Force contract and wanted to make sure the people realized that the priest (myself) who was leading it had no connection with the Diocese of Down and Connor.

Mr. Eccles, about a year later, sent us an unsigned note identifying himself as the person who had met with us prior to the press conference and he wanted us to know that we had been right about Shorts—that they had only made promises to get the contract with the US Air Force, and then it was business as usual.

The same Mr. Eccles would surface again in the US as the main lobbyist against the MacBride Principles—assuring legislators that discrimination was a thing of the past, that the MacBride Principles would only hurt Catholics, etc. Eccles traveled all across the US with the same message.

At one MacBride Hearing in Nebraska, on March 13, 1989, one of Eccles' prize statements was: "I was knighted by the Pope, and I'm very close to the workings of the Catholic Church in Ireland." I hung my head in shame and thought to myself, *Once again the Catholic Church is being used for British interests in Ireland.*

I had many reports that while lobbying in the US against the MacBride Principles, Mr. Eccles allegedly gave the impression that he was doing so with the blessing of the late Cardinal Tomás O'Fiaich, Archbishop of Armagh and Catholic Primate of Ireland. I made a statement in *The Irish Times* that I would be very surprised and deeply disappointed if Cardinal O'Fiaich were allowing his name to be used by the British government's anti-MacBride campaign in the US. The next day, I received a Mailgram stating, "No one authorized to use my name in any way to oppose MacBride Principles. Northern Catholic Bishops have never made any statement on the MacBride Principles."[14] It was signed: Cardinal O'Fiaich, Ara Coeli, Armagh.

Mr. Eccles would later spread the word in *The Sunday News* that he was not paid for his anti-MacBride work: "... Mr. Eccles' son Jim said: 'My father does speak out against the MacBride Principles because he firmly believes that they will do more harm than good. But he has never received money for it, not even traveling expenses ... He visits America frequently. While he is there, he makes his views known on the MacBride Principles ... He sees it as an extension of the charity work he has been heavily engaged in for nearly 30 years.' "[15]

But former British MP Kevin Mc Namara in his book on the MacBride Principles would reveal—having had access to British government documents—that Eccles, "was expensive. He was employed for a maximum of sixty days a year at £220 per day plus expenses, and was in receipt of an annual retainer.'[16] Mr. Eccles was also a member of the board of the Fair Employment Agency (FEA) from 1985 to the autumn of 1989 when the Agency was replaced by the Fair Employment Commission (FEC). In May 1990, the FEC issued a report charging that the motor trade in which Mr. Eccles worked had a very serious imbalance—that Catholics were seriously under-represented. Indeed, the FEC said that the actual company for which Eccles worked—A. S. Baird Ltd—was only 18 percent Catholic. The FEC 1991 figures are 67 Protestants (73.6 percent); 24 Catholics (26.4 percent); 34 "unknowns"; in all, a total of 125 employees.

What did Mr. Eccles say in response to this very embarrassing exposure? He alleged he "had not come across any pattern of discrimination during his years in the trade. I was too busy trying to earn an honest pound."[17] Indeed.

AER LINGUS COVER-UP

By the way, the other very interesting "champion" that sprang to the defense of Shorts was Aer Lingus. One of our members had written to them complaining that they were using Shorts 330 aircraft. The chief executive officer of Aer Lingus, David M. Kennedy, wrote back on June 23, 1983, saying, "We are satisfied there is no religious discrimination in recruitment or employment practices of Shorts." At that time, Short's percentage of Catholics was less than 5 percent out of a workforce of 6,300.[18]

I was outraged and issued the following press statement: "I simply cannot believe that any responsible spokesperson for Aer Lingus—not to mention the chief executive—would make such an extraordinary statement. There is simply no other way to put it: This is a blatant cover-up. Whenever the British government is in trouble, it seems it can always get some gombeen man to do its dirty work. Mr. Kennedy is but the latest example in this dismal tradition."[18]

Aer Lingus is semi-state owned, and it is unlikely Mr. Kennedy would have made that statement without the explicit approval of the Irish government. Garret FitzGerald was Taoiseach at the time.

On May 3, 1983, I sent a letter to all 535 Members of the United States House of Representatives and Senate, outlining the case against Shorts. The following week (May 10, 1983), the British Ambassador, Oliver Wright, sent letters to all the same people—with a glossy brochure, specifically written by Shorts to refute our charges of discrimination. Two black-and-white photos were enclosed with the brochure: one of Garret FitzGerald standing beside a Shorts' aircraft, and one of the heads of Aer Lingus receiving a Shorts' aircraft.

DUBLIN GOVERNMENT COVER-UP

But the plot thickens. In 1983, James Shannon was a Democratic congressman from Massachusetts. He was very close to the Irish Embassy in Washington, DC, and would not make a move on the Irish issue without the blessing of the Embassy. One of our members—a constituent of his—wrote to the Congressman asking him to support the Caucus' campaign of opposing Shorts getting a U.S. Air Force contract. This was his response:

> The Irish Government recently reviewed the situation at Short Brothers in Belfast. It noted historical patterns of clear discrimination, and also noted recent efforts to correct that situation, including: the appointment of a Catholic personnel director, active recruitment in Catholic schools and in the Catholic press, and agreeing with the Fair Employment Agency to set up an affirmative action program. It also noted that the prevailing opinion in both communities in the North was that the proper approach is to eliminate discriminatory hiring practices, and then to promote foreign investment and employment. The Irish Government recently contracted with Short Brothers for the production of aircraft for the national airline, Aer Lingus. This is the best evidence that progress is being made in correcting historical patterns of injustice.[19]

So, there you have it. The first opponents of our campaign to stop the U.S. subsidizing anti-Catholic discrimination were John Hume, the Catholic Bishop of Belfast, the Knights of Columbanus, Aer Lingus, and the Irish government. And you thought the British government ruled only through the Protestants of Northern Ireland! It would seem that the Irish Embassy was a wholly owned subsidiary of the British government. The architects of the Embassy's policy were Garret FitzGerald, Sean Donlon, Michael Lillis—and John Hume.

Who could blame me for my utter disgust at the Dublin government of that time? And, examining all this again in 2019 makes me no less disgusted. It was disgraceful and appalling.

THE MERCURIAL MR. DEVLIN

It is also interesting to note here that on our visit to Ireland in 1979, we met with the late Paddy Devlin, former Social Democratic and Labour Party (SDLP) leader. He was very excited about our idea of making an impact on discrimination through the leverage of American companies. He kept saying he could not believe that he himself had not thought of this idea and that nobody in the North even knew which ones were the American companies.

The next time I saw Paddy Devlin was in the US at a State Hearing testifying against the Principles. He became one of the team of Catholics the British government (through its Department of Economic Development) recruited. Devlin would write later in his column in *The Sunday World*: "My personal view of the Principles is that they will undermine our efforts to eliminate discrimination, deflect US investment away and cause the withdrawal of US companies by putting them into conflict with our labor laws."[20] The following year he said, "The MacBride Principles are a sham. It is time we identified the primary issue of the hidden agenda that is the disestablishment of Northern Ireland society."[21]

WATERSHED

The Caucus/Ottinger visit to Northern Ireland served as a watershed in our campaign. After this, a number of elected officials contacted us, wishing to become associated with our campaign. Chief among these were: New York City Comptroller Harrison J. Goldin, Councilman Sal Albanese of the New York City Council, New York State Assemblyman John Dearie, New York State Senator John Flynn, and Massachusetts State Senate President Bill Bulger.

The Caucus saw the need not only to involve United States legislators but also institutional investors in our campaign. As New York City comptroller, Mr. Goldin was one of the custodians of millions of dollars of New York City funds invested in a number of United States companies doing business in Northern Ireland. We eagerly welcomed him into our campaign. We worked with his office on issuing a new set of principles.

For me, there could be no question as to the person after whom we should name these principles: Seán MacBride.

MacBride Principles Christened

But let me go back a bit. I first met Seán MacBride in New York City in the spring of 1976 when he was the guest speaker at an AOH function. At the time I was the Deputy National Chaplain of the AOH, and as such, I was seated at the head table, next to Seán. I was amazed and humbled he took such an interest in me and the work of the Irish National Caucus. I was used to the "great and the good" in Ireland not wanting to know me, which I took as a badge of honor.

The next time I saw Seán was at the American AOH Convention in Killarney, June 27–29, 1978. When he spoke, he went out of his way to commend me and the work of the Irish National Caucus. A journalist commented to me that it was significant that he had done so, given the open hostility of the Dublin government to me. I kept in touch with Seán, and as explained earlier, in July 1979, I asked him to head up the INC Liaison Group in Dublin.

Then I invited Seán to be the guest speaker at the Fifth Annual Testimonial Dinner Dance of the Irish National Caucus on December 10, 1982, in New York City, attended by close to a thousand guests. The following morning, I picked him up at his hotel to bring him to speak to the Caucus chapter in Huntington, New York. "Did it [the dinner dance] end peaceably?" he smilingly inquired in his still partial-French accent. I asked him why he put the question. "Well, in my day, Irish-American events sometimes ended in a fight," he replied.

Later on, I dropped him off at the airport. As we sat for a moment, before he left the car, I was deeply conscious of the history he represented and felt in some inchoate way that I needed to do something to honor his family history. In truth, he was the only person in whose presence I felt overawed, indeed, a bit intimidated. I asked him if we ever came up with something—a document, proclamation something—if he would lend his name to it. Without hesitation, he consented.

So, when the time came, I talked to Seán MacBride on the phone a number of times about naming the Principles after him. On October 18, 1984, I formally wrote him, proposing and enclosing, the Principles.

On Monday, November 5, 1984, the Irish National Caucus announced the launching of the MacBride Principles. Thus, the Principles were "christened."

Our press release carried the heading, "Caucus' New Plan to Combat Discrimination" and went on to say: "The Irish National Caucus today announced a major new initiative to combat employment discrimination in Northern Ireland ... The Caucus has endorsed a set of Equal Opportunity Affirmative Action Principles for Northern Ireland that have been sponsored by Seán MacBride ... 'This approach,' said Fr. Sean McManus, '... is the way for Americans to deal with anti-Catholic discrimination.' "

The Irish Echo (New York) captured the historic moment accurately with the headline: "Caucus Proposes New Initiative to Stop Discrimination in Northern Ireland."[22] The *Sunday Tribune* reported: "The nine-point employment code, which was drawn up by the Washington-based Irish National Caucus (I.N.C.) is sponsored by Seán MacBride S.C., leading Northern Ireland trade unionist Inez Mc Cormack and Northern surgeon Senator John Robb and Father Brian Brady."[23] That was the very first occasion the MacBride Principles were mentioned by name in the Irish or American media.

Thus, a historic initiative was conceived, born, and christened.

We wanted to mention Comptroller Goldin's name in our announcement, but at that stage, he was not prepared to associate his name with the Principles. In fact, he backed out at the last moment, after I had told Seán MacBride that he would join us in the announcement. The first New York politician, in fact, to publicly associate himself with the MacBride Principles was City Councilmember Sal Albanese (D-BayRidge). I had been advising Goldin to associate himself publicly with the MacBride Principles, otherwise, other New York politicians would beat him to the punch. But he thought it was just a tactic to stampede him into supporting the Principles earlier than he wanted to.

Caucus Launches MacBride Campaign

The moment Councilmember Albanese read *The Irish Echo*'s report on the launching of the MacBride Principles, he contacted the Irish National Caucus with a view to introducing a Bill in the New York City Council. He and the Caucus worked on the drafting, and on December 19, 1984, a Bill was introduced: #878. This was to be the very first MacBride Bill in the U S.

And so, the MacBride campaign had formally begun. The *New York Daily News* reported: "City Councilman Sal Albanese (D-Bay Ridge) will appear at City Hall tomorrow in a rally with Rev. Sean McManus, National Director of the Irish National Caucus, to seek support for the bill."[24] *The Irish Echo* announced: "Fr. Sean McManus, national director of the Irish National Caucus, will hold a press conference with Councilman Albanese at City Hall on Jan. 3 at 10:30 am calling on Irish groups to support Intro. No. 878."[25] The *Chief Leader* said: "The Irish National Caucus has chosen New York City to be the first where pension fund investments will be used to increase pressure for equal rights for Catholics in Northern Ireland ..."[26] The *Catholic New York* newspaper said: "Father McManus was present at City Hall recently to speak in favor of the [Albanese] legislation ... Father McManus said that proposed legislation is 'eminently reasonable ... One of the most effective ways for us to combat the situation is to get the investors involved and make them aware they are supporting anti-Catholic discrimination,' he told *Catholic New York*."[27]

The Sunday Times of London: "The [MacBride] campaign is being run by the Irish National Caucus... The move, inspired by Father Sean McManus, who has been consistently opposed to British policy, is particularly well timed. For even if the law is never passed, it provides an opportunity to link, however, tenuously, the issues of South Africa and Northern Ireland. The MacBride Principles also call for the same kind of affirmative action programs for Catholics which American companies already use in the employment of women and blacks in the USA."[28] This was the very first mention of the Principles in the English press.

In an interview with Niall O'Dowd in *The Irish Press* Comptroller Goldin said: "Moreover, having reviewed the MacBride Principles, I endorse this initiative."[29] (Notice: he speaks about "having reviewed," not having originated the Principles. It was only later that people associated with the Comptroller made the retroactive claim that he had "initiated or launched" the Principles.)

But in New York papers, Comptroller Goldin, unfortunately, came out very publicly against the Bill. The *New York Daily News*, under the headline "Koch & Goldin Oppose Ulster Investment Ban," said:

> Mayor Koch and City Controller Harrison Goldin expressed opposition yesterday to a City bill that would prohibit city Pension fund investments in the U.S. owned businesses that discriminate against Northern Ireland. Their reaction came after the Rev. Sean McManus, National Director of the Irish National Caucus Inc., a Northern Irish Catholic lobbying group based in Washington, appeared at City Hall to urge passage of the bill. The measure, sponsored by Councilman Sal Albanese (D-Brooklyn) [*sic*], is awaiting a hearing in the Council's economic development committee... Goldin said the Council Bill was premature.[30]

A leading column in *The Irish Echo* stated:

> Mayor Koch and City Comptroller Harrison Goldin are opposed to such tough measures on the grounds that the British have an official policy that is against discrimination, and the situation in Belfast is very different from South Africa where the government has an official policy of discrimination.
>
> The "unofficial" nature of discrimination in Northern Ireland notwithstanding, it is still a fact that Catholics do

not have equal opportunity in the North, and that New York City officials have every right to be concerned about it ...

It is for this reason Councilman Albanese should be encouraged ... and that Mr. Koch and Mr. Goldin—who I am sure are acting in good faith—should be asked to take another look at their position. Mr. Koch has the strong support of the majority of the Irish community in New York, and I am sure he would like to maintain that support.[31]

The New York Times reported: "The Council measure is opposed by Mayor Koch, who sits on the boards of the four largest pension funds for city workers, and City Comptroller Harrison J. Goldin, the custodian for all five funds in the system and a trustee of the four largest funds."[32]

At this stage—and for a good while later—Goldin was opposed to legislation on the Principles. He felt that shareholder resolutions would have sufficient leverage, and his office did not want anything to overshadow his role. His office fought Albanese's office on this, so much so that Albanese and I had to call a meeting in New York City to push the need for legislation. About four hundred Irish-Americans attended the meeting. I spoke very forcefully about the need for legislation—not just shareholder resolutions. Even at that meeting, Goldin's office opposed the idea of legislation. But the mood of the meeting was clearly in our favor, and soon afterward, Goldin's office withdrew their opposition to legislation. That meeting was a key building block in the long construction of the MacBride campaign.

At the meeting, Pat Doherty, Goldin's aide, was visibly shaken by the anger towards Goldin. Time and time again, I witnessed people say to him, "There has to be a law. There has to be a law," the adopted refrain of the Albanese–Caucus supporters. Indeed, I had to run interference several times to ask them to leave Pat alone. Goldin soon realized, however, that he had made a terrible mistake. The train was leaving the station, and he was not on board! He was in a position to play a key role in our campaign, but his public opposition to the New York City legislation had hurt him badly.

Comptroller Goldin had lost the high ground. How could he reclaim it? The Caucus wanted Goldin to be prominently involved, because as the custodian of millions of dollars, he represented the vitally important role of investors in the MacBride campaign.

Caucus-Golden Visit

There is a well-known technique whereby American politicians stake claim to an interest in Irish issues—the highly publicized visit to Ireland. There is nothing wrong with this. Presidents Kennedy and Reagan did it; why shouldn't a non-Irish-American also do it? So, Comptroller Goldin needed to visit Ireland. But how to go about it? Who would sponsor the visit? Who would set it up? And very importantly, who would have the resources to pay for it? The answer—the Irish National Caucus. That the Caucus attached great importance to the role Goldin could play is seen in the fact that it was prepared to spend so much money on the trip.

Furthermore, the Caucus had already "covered" the legislative dimension of the MacBride Principles—we now needed to "cover" the investment dimension. The *New York Daily News* would give the Caucus–Goldin visit prominent coverage: "A U.S. based Irish lobbying group paid up to $12,000 so City Comptroller Harrison Goldin could visit Ireland—with his family and aide—to look into complaints of economic discrimination against Catholics in Northern Ireland ... A spokesman for the comptroller said it was official city business."[33]

The aide was Pat Doherty, who would go on to feature prominently in the MacBride campaign and become a good friend. Some Irish-American groups shortsightedly criticized the Irish National Caucus for "wasting money." But when they finally understood the significance of the Caucus strategy, they were very eager to associate themselves with the MacBride campaign. The Goldin visit received heavy coverage in the British and Irish media, thereby helping to establish the MacBride

Principles firmly in the public mind. It was on this trip that Goldin met Seán MacBride for the first time—eight months after the Irish National Caucus had launched the MacBride Principles.

The Caucus arranged meetings with Charlie Haughey, the Fair Employment Agency, John Hume and various U.S. companies. It was ironic that the British government attempted to make great play out of the fact that Sinn Féin was the only political party in Northern Ireland to support the MacBride Principles. However, when Sinn Féin met with the Goldin group in Belfast, they expressed strong opposition to the Principles, saying they were not radical enough—that they were "akin to President Reagan's constructive engagement with [apartheid] South Africa." However, the real reason for their opposition was because the Principles were launched by the Irish National Caucus. (Sinn Féin opposed the Irish National Caucus because it is nonviolent and because the Caucus does not allow itself to be controlled from Ireland.) But later, when Sinn Féin saw that the Principles were driving the British government up the wall, they reversed their position and began to express public support for them.

In the United States, the trip was also given considerable press coverage. *The New York Times, The New York Daily News* and *The New York Post* all devoted editorials to it. For example, *The New York Daily News* editorial said: "How did Goldin get involved with the so-called MacBride Principles? Although named for an aging Irish Nobel laureate Seán MacBride, they were actually drawn up in the U.S. by the Irish National Caucus. The Caucus organized and paid for Goldin's trip—at a cost of about $12,000."[34]

The New York Times editorial said: "A lofty but misguided proposition for opposing discrimination against Catholics in Northern Ireland has reared its head in Congress, three state legislatures and the New York City Council. Based on what is called the "MacBride Principles" ... The principal sponsor is the Irish National Caucus, a Washington lobby intent on getting Americans to pressure Britain to withdraw from Northern Ireland ... Comptroller Harrison Goldin, just back from Northern Ireland, is pressuring pension funds to act on their own."[35]

MacBride Becomes State Law

At our urging, our good friend State Senator Billy Bulger used his influence to have Massachusetts become the first State to pass the MacBride Principles. I launched the Massachusetts campaign in Springfield with a speech before the John Boyle O'Reilly Club—a very appropriate place—in February 1985. *The Sunday Republican* reported: "US dollars mustn't subsidize anti-Catholic discrimination in Northern Ireland... the Caucus is asking American firms to adopt the MacBride Principles... 'American businesses can have a profound effect, [Fr. McManus] said, "You're talking about millions of dollars ... We're not calling for disinvestment. We are not trying to end American investment in Northern Ireland," he said.[37]

We worked closely with State Representative Tom Gallagher (D-18th Suffolk District). On October 1, 1985, he wrote to me: "I expect the Massachusetts House will shortly take up legislation applying the MacBride Principles to state pension fund investment. I believe the measure will reach the Governor's desk this session and will make Massachusetts the first state to apply MacBride to its investments. I look forward to working with you in the future."[38]

The Massachusetts MacBride Bill was signed into law by Governor Michael Dukakis on November 21, 1985. It was the first MacBride law in America. Dukakis still supported the MacBride Principles as a presidential candidate in 1988 (despite the strong lobbying of John Hume). While I was still based in Boston, Governor Dukakis invited me to his office on Saint Patrick's Day 1978 to present me with a proclamation he was issuing at our request, "Human Rights for Ireland Day." (That, of course, caused Irish Consul Carmel Heaney further fury.)

New York Assemblyman John Dearie and New York State Senator John Flynn initiated Bills on the MacBride Principles.

Soon afterward, in May 1986, New York became the second State to pass the MacBride Principles. In 1992, New York State became the first State to pass a MacBride Principles Contract Compliance Bill.

The Irish National Caucus then initiated Congressional legislation on the MacBride Principles (the Fish-D'Amato Bll, introduced on

October 1, 1986), just as we had done on the seminal Ottinger Bill in 1983. And, as they say, the rest is history. Virtually all Irish-American organizations, the AFL-CIO, many religious groups (Catholics and Protestants) rallied behind the MacBride Principles, making them the most powerful American campaign on Northern Ireland since its creation in 1920.

MacBride's Death

After Seán MacBride's death on January 15, 1988, his son Tiernan—with typical MacBride generosity wrote to me: "On behalf of the late Seán MacBride, I would like to thank you most sincerely for traveling to Dublin to attend his funeral. He will never be forgotten while the Principles drawn up by the Irish National Caucus are named after him."[39]

And on June 28, 1993, Caitriona Lawlor in Dublin wrote the following letter to Ken Bertsch, Investor Responsibility Research Center:

> I understand that you are preparing an updated version of "The MacBride Principles and US companies in Northern Ireland" ... During the years 1976 to 1988, I worked as Personal Assistant to Seán MacBride and witnessed the attention he paid to the causes in which he believed, in days when such causes were neither popular nor profitable. It amused me, therefore, to see the reference contained on p. 60 of the current edition, "Doherty and McManus dispute exactly who should take credit for the idea of a fair employment code for recruiting Seán MacBride as Sponsor." My understanding always was that the fair employment initiative for Northern Ireland lay squarely with Father Sean McManus and the Irish National Caucus in Washington, and it was to great advantage when the Comptroller of New York City, Harrison Goldin, and his office took up the cudgels. Indeed, Father McManus was adamant even in the initial

stages of preparation, that MacBride should be involved and should lend his name to the Principles, based loosely on the Sullivan Principles for South Africa.

This is a very slight correction, but I feel in the interests of historical accuracy, due credit for initiating the code and recruiting Seán MacBride, should be given to Father McManus and the Irish National Caucus, and I hope you will feel able to do so ..."[40]

In 2009, former British MP Kevin Mc Namara released his book, *The MacBride Principles: Irish-America Fights Back*. In it he makes the remarkable statement about me: "What is not comprehensible is why he [McManus] should seek to exclude the important role played by Comptroller Goldin's office in the run-up to the launch, particularly as he takes great pains to credit him for his support once he came on board in 1985."[41] Of course, McNamara partly refutes his own accusation by pointing out that Goldin only came on board in 1985, whereas we had launched the Principles in November 1984. However, it is patently absurd to claim I tried to exclude Goldin when I went to great pains, and expense, to dig him out of the hole he had dug for himself.

Things admittedly became messy when Pat Doherty improperly made an issue of the drafting of the MacBride Principles. That was not expected, as staffers are not supposed to claim pride of authorship when assigned a project. And I have never known one to do so except for Pat. These were the MacBride Principles, not anybody else's. Just as, "Ask not what your country can do for you ..." is JFK's speech, not anybody else's.

That is also why I found it extraordinary when McNamara criticized me for saying the drafting of the Principles never concerned me too much: "This was a surprising statement to make."[42] There was nothing surprising about it. I was never too concerned about the drafting of the principles contained in the Ottinger Bill, the Fish–D'Amato Bill, or the Gilman legislation that became Federal Law in 1998. Nor did their staff make an issue of it.

But what had really forced me to go public and set the record straight was Doherty's bizarre version of events as reported by the iconic journalist, Mary Holland in *The Irish Times* in 1987: "Mr. Doherty researched the problem and drew up a set of guidelines for American companies ... Through Irish-American contacts, he then approached Seán MacBride and asked him to sponsor them."[43] Now that's chutzpah for you! Pat did not even really know who Seán MacBride was until I named the Principles after him as Pat himself admitted to me at the time. Mary Holland was very upset when she realized she had got the story wrong. She apologized profoundly, writing in a personal letter to me: "I am really sorry that ... I misrepresented the genesis of the MacBride Principles ... I'm sure you'll understand that I was told the story as I recounted it."[44]

The historical reality is that the Principles only became the powerful force they did when they became the MacBride Principles. And the Principles would never have gotten off the ground with such a bang had they not been launched by the Irish National Caucus, which did all the initial publicity—framing the issue, briefing the media, educating the public, and lining up political support. As McNamara states, Goldin only "came on board in 1985."[45]

However, apart from the corrections forced on me here, I am the first to acknowledge the vital importance of Pat's contribution. In 2008, *The Irish Echo* asked me to rate his work. This is what I said: "Pat has played a key role in the campaign to stop U.S. dollars subsidizing anti-Catholic discrimination in Northern Ireland ... He is one of the most effective Irish-American campaigners since the time of the Fenians in 1858."[46]

Pat just needs to be reminded occasionally that it was the Irish National Caucus that took him and Goldin to Ireland—not the other way around; and that we dug them out of the hole they had dug for themselves politically, launching Pat onto an excellent Irish-American adventure.

CHAPTER 16

Anti-MacBride Campaign

The Irish National Caucus have never seemed to us to have the interests of the people of Northern Ireland genuinely at heart.
British Embassy, Washington[1]

THE IRISH NATIONAL CAUCUS LAUNCHED the campaign for MacBride Principles. The British government launched the campaign against the MacBride Principles. The battle lines were as clearly drawn as that. For Irish-Americans, the moral clarity of the campaign could not be more luminous.

The extraordinarily arrogant quote above is from N. E. Sheinwald, who in 1985 was First Secretary of the British Embassy and from 2007–2012 British Ambassador to Washington. He wrote it in a letter in March 1985 to my good friend Tom Donahue, then Secretary-Treasurer of the giant labor organization, AFL-CIO. It strikingly personifies the imperial attitude. He is concerned about the people of the North and I, a Fermanagh man, am not! Talk about the hubris of Empire! He then goes on to lecture Donahue: "As always with this sort of thing, it is important to look not only at the words used but at the people and the organizations promoting the initiative and the commentary they themselves provide on the text. It is, in my view, instructive that the Irish National Caucus is playing a prominent part in promulgating the MacBride Principles."

But then, in the best imperial fashion and in the favorite British technique, Mr. Sheinwald conscripts the Dublin government by stressing: "The leader of the Irish Labour Party and Deputy Prime Minister, Dick Spring, said in January that the INC campaign may be designed at depriving the people of Northern Ireland of much-needed investment rather than any concern about discrimination." Well, thank you, Mr. Sheinwald and Mr. Spring. Your opposition made us all the more determined to win—all across the United States and in the US Congress, making the MacBride campaign one of the most successful Irish-American initiatives ever. Had those gentlemen supported me, I would have been examining my conscience.

Of course, neither Sheinwald nor Spring was calling the shots. That was the job of the secretary of state for Northern Ireland, Douglas Hurd. On February 11, 1985, he laid down the marching orders: "We continue to brief US companies and U.S. opinion to oppose the INC campaign..."[2]—Now there's a perfect example of British government understatement and euphemism. When that government says it will "brief to oppose"—look out. What it really means is that it will vilify, demonize and resort to every dirty trick in the book. It means "crush the INC by any means necessary."

I can well understand some individuals in Northern Ireland being naturally opposed to the MacBride Principles, and I can respect their opinion. But there was nothing spontaneous about the campaign in the U.S. against the MacBride Principles. Someone in Northern Ireland did not wake up one morning and say to himself or herself: "There's a Hearing on the MacBride Principles in Nebraska or Texas or Washington, DC. I'll get dressed, slip over and give my opinion."

Big Money

The anti-MacBride campaign was highly controlled, highly financed, and fiercely fought by the British government, the Dublin government and, sadly, by John Hume. The agencies the British government used to fight the campaign were the Department of Economic Development (DED) and the Fair Employment Agency (FEA) (now the Fair Employment Commission (FEC) of Northern Ireland). The late Bob Cooper, former head of the FEA and later head of the FEC was dispatched to lobby against the MacBride Principles in California and Pennsylvania. How could Irish-Americans, therefore, have had confidence in the FEC? In the United States, the campaign was coordinated by the British Embassy—the largest embassy in Washington. The Embassy hired the top lobbyists, attorneys, and public relations professionals.

I remember, during the MacBride campaign in Maine, meeting one of the top lobbyists, Severin M. Beliveau. He told us that the British Embassy called and asked to come and see him. He had no idea what it was about. They came to his office, told him they wanted to hire him to block the MacBride Principles from becoming law in Maine, and offered him big money. "Sorry, gentlemen," he said, "but my grandmother from Enniskillen would turn in her grave if I were to work for you." (As he was telling me this, he had no idea where I came from, until I shouted, "Up Fermanagh".)

But not all lobbyists were so principled—even ones with Irish names. In fact, the British Embassy at the beginning always tried to recruit Irish-American lobbyists. For example, one very well-established law firm in Washington is O'Connor and Hannan, a big Democratic law and lobbying firm. Their home base is in Minnesota. The embassy hired them to lobby against the MacBride Principles in Minnesota. When they were asked, "How could you?" O'Connor replied, "Their money is green, also." Irish-Americans in Washington and Minnesota were disgusted. But the embassy succeeded in getting an Irish-American lobbyist to work for them in Maine: John Doyle of Doyle & Nelson in Augusta.

Another anecdote about a lobbyist hired by the British Embassy is worth recounting. Someone—just for the fun of it—told the lobbyist that other lobbyists were being paid far more than he was and urged him to demand more money. He did, and the embassy gave it "without batting an eyelid."

So clearly, money was no problem when it came to defeating the MacBride Principles. On their admission, the British government spent millions of dollars to battle the MacBride Principles. A senior official in the Department of Economic Development (DED) said, referring to myself, "We did not take him very seriously at first but the MacBride Principles have caused serious problems and cost millions to try and counteract."[3]

Isn't it too bad they didn't spend those millions of dollars creating fair employment in Northern Ireland?

THE MACBRIDE HEARING

I wish everyone in Ireland could have attended a MacBride Hearing. (To get the MacBride Principles passed into law in a particular state or city, the legislature has first to hold a hearing, taking witness from experts or concerned citizens.) The Hearing Room was typically packed with enthusiastic Irish-Americans and other supporters. The British Embassy officials were there with one, two, sometimes three or four "castle-Catholics" whom they had flown from Northern Ireland. Yes, it was nearly always Catholics whom they recruited. I guess they thought it was the clever thing to do.

The first thing those Catholics said when they testified was, "I'm a Catholic, and the MacBride Principles will only hurt the Catholics of Northern Ireland."

Legislators—especially African Americans—saw right through that attempted subterfuge. At the MacBride Hearing in Washington, DC, January 30, 1992, it was a delightful sight to watch the Chairman of the Committee, and the author of our MacBride Bill, Councilmember John Ray, systematically shred the arguments of Sean Neeson, a leader of the Alliance Party, and a Catholic from Northern Ireland. Ray told him that he was not surprised (i.e., not fooled) that a Catholic should come before his Committee to argue against MacBride because he had seen blacks from South Africa come to Washington to argue that US pressure could only hurt blacks in South Africa. Ray might not know all the history of Ireland, but as a proud African American, he understood discrimination. In fact, I have never met a politically aware African American who does not intuitively know that Catholics are oppressed in Northern Ireland. At the DC Hearing, I knew I had the game won when a friend of mine, African American Fr. Ray East, marched into the Hearing Room with about a dozen determined and formidable black women parishioners. Chairman Ray stopped the hearing and invited them all up to the front. Can you imagine the suppressed groans of Neeson's handlers from the British Embassy? It had to be a very chastening experience for the British government to see themselves being beaten time after time in the MacBride campaign. (And, I confess, it warmed the cockles of my Kinawley heart. I took huge joy and consolation in it.) The constant defeats created much pressure, which sometimes showed itself. For example, at a Hearing on MacBride in Minnesota, after the vote was taken and we had won handsomely. I turned to shake someone's hand in congratulations. As I turned, I saw a woman glare at me with unconcealed venom. I thought to myself, "My goodness, what's the matter with her?" I immediately asked someone who she was and was told that she was the British consul from Chicago. On the way out of the Hearing Room, I happened to be walking right behind the same person. She slammed the door right in my face. So much for the British stiff upper lip.

One advantage, from the MacBride point of view, of the British government's practice of bringing out mostly Catholics to testify, was that it did not frame the issue in sectarian terms as it would if the people they brought out been Protestants. Then the press would be reporting that the Protestants and Catholics were clashing at hearings. But since it was, in general, only Catholics who came out, the issue was framed as Irish-Americans against the British government. In the early days of the MacBride Campaign, I had stated publicly in the press that it was very interesting to watch the "body language" in the MacBride Hearing Room: "Large numbers of enthusiastic Irish-Americans looking forward to inflicting another defeat on the ancestral enemy of their homeland. They take over the room ... And sitting at the back, looking very forlorn, are the few Catholics from Northern Ireland, along with their handlers from the British Embassy. Well, after I had said that, I noticed that at the next Hearing the anti-MacBride forces occupied the front- row seats!"

Of course, there was another reason why the British recruited Catholics to testify against the MacBride Principles—they did not want to give Protestants a platform to attack the Anglo-Irish Accord. Thus, for many reasons, the British government was very badly snookered by the MacBride campaign. If they did not oppose the MacBride Principles, they lost by default. But, on the other hand, in opposing the Principles, they alienated a lot of legislators. These legislators got very annoyed when they saw the British government coming into their state and city to oppose their legislation. But, by the same token, the legislators got a kick out of the British opposition. It showed them that their legislation was having an impact—that it was "tweaking the lion's tail."

PROCESS AS IMPORTANT AS PRODUCT

Why was the British government so opposed to the MacBride Principles? Well, the simple answer is that the discriminator always has to oppose a campaign against discrimination—whether it is South Africa, South America, the United States, or Northern Ireland.

But it is important to understand that when it comes to the MacBride Principles, the "process" is as important as the "product." The product is, of course, getting the Principles passed into law, with all their implications, both politically and economically. But consider what is involved in the "process."

For a MacBride campaign to begin in a state or city, legislators have to be "recruited" to introduce the legislation. They have to become familiar with the issue; their colleagues have to be lobbied; supporters have to be activated to make MacBride an issue. And then there has to be a Hearing (which often lasts for hours).

When, without the MacBride Principles, would state and city legislators ever have focused on the Northern Ireland issue? The answer is never. And that was a huge reason why the British government feared the MacBride campaign because it powerfully and nonviolently exposed—in a responsible and important setting (the Hearing Room)—the malicious record of British rule in Northern Ireland. Even though the Hearing was about discrimination in Northern Ireland, inevitably, and very properly, all the other British government abuses of human rights got an airing—and I made sure they did. And that profoundly embarrassed the British government.

There is another thing that really frustrated the British government: knowing that time, for a change, was on our side. If we failed to get MacBride passed in a particular city or state, we would be back next year or the year after—more determined, better organized, and more experienced. And the harder they fought us, the better we liked it. Therefore, the British government was in a no-win situation.

The basic strategy of the British government was to use Catholics (and, of course, the Dublin government and John Hume) for their propaganda in the United States. That, of course, is nothing new. It is as old as British policy in Ireland. Uneducated and politically unaware Catholics can be excused for being used in such a manner. But what can one say about politically sophisticated Catholics? Surely, granting the reality of the anti-MacBride campaign, such Catholics could not argue that they just made statements in a vacuum, not knowing that their statements would be used by the British government. The two Catholics whose names were most used (apart from the Dublin government) in British government propaganda were John Hume of Derry and the late Bishop Cahal Daly of Belfast, later Cardinal of Armagh.

JOHN HUME

On December 10, 1982, International Human Rights Day, Seán MacBride spoke at the Caucus Testimonial Dinner in New York. The following day, I traveled with him by car from Manhattan to Huntington, New York. I was asking Seán all sorts of questions about international affairs. I finally asked him if John Hume and Garret FitzGerald had ever consulted him about the problem in the North of Ireland. Seán gave me a very emphatic "no." I asked him what he thought the reason was. "Because they know I'm implacably opposed to Partition" was Seán's equally emphatic answer. Significantly, neither Hume nor FitzGerald attended Seán's funeral in Dublin in 1988.

Hume was in a very strong position as leader of the Social Democratic and Labour Party of Northern Ireland (SDLP) and a member both of the British Parliament (MP) and of the European Parliament (MEP). He was committed to the Anglo-Irish Agreement of 1985, of which he was a key architect along with Garret FitzGerald. The quid pro quo for that agreement was "thou shall not criticize the British government." (In fact, Hume had long since stopped criticizing that government.) All problems could and must now be solved within the context of that Agreement. The MacBride Principles were outside the Agreement, and outside Hume's control and imprimatur, thus beyond the pale for John Hume. So much for his alleged awareness of the importance of the American dimension.

Hume was to be one of the first and potentially most deadly opponents of the MacBride Principles. Without a doubt, he blunted to a small degree the cutting edge of the MacBride Campaign. But in the process, he came out the worse—because the campaign was not significantly weakened by him. But he was weakened. His credibility and judgment were put into question. It is probably one of the few times John Hume has been wrong-footed in America.

His opposition to the MacBride Principles did not make sense to Americans—even to many of his own supporters and admirers. The Principles were, after all, what Americans would expect Hume to be for: a modern, progressive, enlightened way to address discrimination in this global economy. We must be responsible investors.

In *The Boston Sunday Globe* of March 8, 1987, Hume had a half-page interview, with a photograph, under the headline, "Ulster Leader Assails American Supporters of MacBride Plan." And assail he did. "Those responsible for the campaign just don't know the damage they're doing. Discrimination against Catholics in Ulster had to be attacked on the ground, not in America," Hume said—missing the whole point of the MacBride Principles.[4]

The huge—and obviously orchestrated—interview was followed up three days later, March 11, 1987, by an editorial. In an appalling example of parroting British government propaganda, the editorial said, "Unless this long-term economic decline can be reversed, the only way the MacBride Principles could get jobs for the unemployed Catholics is if Protestant workers were fired." And then it continued with incredible fatuity: "If new investment arrives, pressure from the Catholic community, and from the Irish and British governments working together through the Hillsborough Agreement [Anglo-Irish Agreement] will see to it that jobs are fairly apportioned."[5] Yet everyone knew that the only pressure on the British government on the issue of discrimination was the MacBride campaign.

There is simply no way of avoiding it: Hume allowed himself to be used by the British government in their anti-MacBride campaign. He was, however, smart enough not to get his hands dirty. He never put himself through the indignity of testifying against the MacBride Principles. Hume was not prepared to be on the losing side at a Hearing. But the British government used Hume's name as the main weapon in their arsenal, quoting him liberally in their anti-MacBride discrimination material. And when both the previous governors of California vetoed the MacBride Bill, they quoted John Hume to justify their veto.

The following month *The Boston Globe* ran an interview with Seán MacBride under the headline "Ex-IRA Leader Fights for Jobs" (even though MacBride had left the IRA in 1936). "When asked to respond to Hume's statement, 'Fairness will prevail but first get companies to invest,' MacBride replied, 'That's wishful thinking on his part. Ideological baggage. Without pressure, there is no reason to believe Catholics would be hired ...'"

Seán MacBride then proceeded to give his ultimate assessment of John Hume. "Hume," he said, "has become an apologist for British rule in Northern Ireland," and "is in a position of defending the existing system in Northern Ireland."[6]

Hume's anti-MacBride campaign (in conjunction with that of the British and Dublin governments) did ensure that its main target,

Senator Teddy Kennedy, would fall into line. Teddy never supported the MacBride Principles. But great credit must be given to former Mayor Ray Flynn of Boston, later Ambassador to the Vatican, for resisting Hume's pressure. Flynn has been a fearless and effective advocate of the MacBride Principles. Credit must also be given to former Congressman Joe Kennedy II. He stood firm on his election pledge and supported the MacBride Principles—as did the vast majority of the Massachusetts Congressional Delegation.

CARDINAL CATHAL DALY

Another prominent Catholic from Northern Ireland who was perceived to have joined the British Government anti-MacBride campaign was Bishop Cahal Daly, later Cardinal Daly, Archbishop of Armagh and Primate of Ireland.

In November 1989, as the Bishop of Down and Connor (the diocese that includes Belfast) Cahal Daly came to the United States in what was widely perceived to be, at least in part, an escalation of the British government's campaign against the MacBride Principles. We were in the middle of fighting a very tough battle to get the Principles passed in the state of Pennsylvania. I got calls that one key supporter of the Principles was contacted to see if he would meet Bishop Daly so that the Bishop could show him the error of his ways.

Bishop Daly proceeded to confirm suspicions by an interview he gave to *The Boston Globe*, November 25, 1989, with James L. Franklin, who was a very experienced writer, having been the Religion writer for that newspaper since 1976:

> The Catholic bishop of Belfast yesterday opposed the adoption of the United States of measures to reduce job discrimination against Catholics ... He was reacting to a recent adoption by Boston and several states of the MacBride Principles. Such legislation is more likely to discourage companies from investing in Northern

Ireland, said the bishop. "I feel great hesitation about any program that unilaterally insists on fairness without concerning itself at the same time with increased employment opportunities particularly by American investment," he said. Instead, he urged support for legislation recently adopted by the British government.[7]

I was very upset, and issued the following statement: "It is not the first time in Irish history that the English government was able to use an Irish bishop."[8]

This is the same Bishop Daly who, in 1983, had ordered the radio attack on our campaign against Shorts.

From the mid–1940s to the mid–1960s, Cahal Daly taught Moral Philosophy at Queen's University of Belfast—then a bastion of anti-Catholic discrimination. In all these years, he never opened his mouth against discrimination. What if Rev. Martin Luther King, Jr. had taught for twenty years in a discriminatory university, and never spoke in protest? Would he have any credibility as a spokesman on justice and peace? The first maxim of nonviolent resistance to injustice is that you can only teach it by example. You cannot turn a blind eye to injustice all your life, and then expect people to listen to you lecture them on how to respond to injustice.

When it was known that Cardinal Daly and three leaders of the main Protestant Churches in Northern Ireland were coming to the United States in February 1993, some feared that it was another anti-MacBride attempt. I felt it would not be—but only because President Clinton was on record for supporting the Principles. I felt that Irish Church leaders—who are very establishmentarian and somewhat obsessed by "respectability"—would now "cut their cloth to suit the fashion of the times," and not publicly denounce the MacBride Principles, which is what happened.

When Cardinal Daly and the other Church leaders were questioned in New York, *The Irish Echo* of February 12, 1993, quoted Daly as saying,

"We are not opposed to the MacBride Principles here or at home."[9] Quite a backing-off from what he told *The Boston Globe* in 1989.

However, there seems to have been some dissembling going on in Cardinal Daly's response, as an American bishop would unwittingly expose. In August 1993, Bishop Michael F. McAuliffe STD, Bishop of Jefferson City, Missouri, wrote to John Carr, secretary of the Department of Social Development and World Peace of the US Catholic Conference: "The Cardinal indicated there were some others that could very well be added as part of those Principles … ."[10] Bishop McAuliffe, along with Bishop Anthony O'Connell of Knoxville, Tennessee had visited the Cardinal in Ireland during July. (O'Connell later had to resign because of a sex abuse scandal.) It was on that visit, according to Bishop McAuliffe, that the Cardinal had stated that he wanted to see the changes in the Mac Principles.

Mr. Carr's office, as we shall see, had been very much involved in the controversy over a proposal to hold a conference on the MacBride Principles in Washington in the Fall of 1993. He had also been denying any attempt by the Catholic Church leaders either in Ireland or the United States to change the MacBride Principles.

And how had Bishop McAuliffe "unwittingly" exposed Cardinal Daly? Well—again through the grace of God—he had mailed his Carr-letter to me instead.

Ah, and some say there is no God!

I was used to people sending us copies of letters they have written to someone else. So, I thought this was a case of some bishop sending me a copy of a letter he had written to the Catholic Conference. I had sent a copy of the letter I had written to John Carr to every bishop in the US. It was only when I had reread Bishop McAuliffe's letter that I realized it was not a copy, but rather that the bishop had addressed the letter to John Carr at the address of the Irish National Caucus.

So, doesn't providence work in a strange way? Here was a letter he clearly did not want me to see, but yet he had addressed it to my office. So that there would be no further delay with the letter, I very obligingly faxed it on to John Carr and faxed off my own letter to the good bishop explaining his error.

I had never heard Bishops McAuliffe or O'Connell ever open their mouths about anti-Catholic discrimination in Northern Ireland. Yet they had the bloody nerve to interfere in the MacBride campaign. Did that happen accidentally? You bet it didn't. Someone had to recruit them. The question is who?

A final note on Daly. In 1979, after we had stopped American guns going to the RUC, and when the Caucus group was in Ireland, we met with the late Fr. Denis Faul. He had just come from a meeting with Daly, who was still Bishop of Ardagh and Clonmacnoise. Denis suggested that the Caucus should meet with Daly. I was not too interested, but out of respect for Denis, I agreed and asked him to set it up. Denis got back to me with Daly's response: "It would not be good for the Church for me to meet with the Irish National Caucus." Not good for the Church? But it was OK for Irish Bishops to rotate priests, from parish to parish, who abused kids! That's the classic "Bishop's speak"—the spiritual narcissism and arrogance that has caved in the institutional church structures in Ireland.

I think it is pathetic that Ireland was inflicted with a Cardinal like Cathal Daly and a Taoiseach like Garret FitzGerald. Both of them personified what was wrong with church and state.

US CATHOLIC CONFERENCE AND MODERATOR DUNLOP

The US Catholic Conference (of Bishops) is in part the social arm of the Catholic Hierarchy. Its large headquarters in Washington has many departments—one of which is the Office of International Justice and Peace. This is the department, of course, that would deal with the Northern Ireland issue (on the rare occasions it had a mind to). Sadly, it had the same "establishment-elitist" attitude of all entrenched bureaucracies. On January 6, 1978, I met with that office. Afterward, I said, "It was just like being at the British Embassy. The Office of Justice and Peace has become the ecclesiastical arm of British propaganda."[11] As if to prove my point, the then Advisor on European Affairs—Edward Doherty, a layman, and British to his fingertips—wrote in a letter: "It is the Provos who are mainly responsible for the violence in Northern Ireland and this is recognized by every careful and impartial observer ... after due consultation with the Irish bishops, and in recognition of the efforts being made by the governments and church bodies directly concerned, we [the U.S. Catholic Conference] had concluded that there is no appropriate basis for public intervention in the problems of Northern Ireland, either by this conference, or any branch of the United States government ..."[12]

Thank God Bill Clinton was a Protestant because had he been guided by that godless and immoral teaching of the Catholic Conference, he would never have intervened.

Do you think for one moment that the Office of International Justice and Peace would have released that document without first checking with the Irish Embassy? Indeed, you can be certain that the Irish Embassy approved (indeed, may have drafted) every word. To me—though the Irish Embassy would have denied it—it is the clearest and most frank expression of Irish Embassy policy of that time: "no appropriate basis for public intervention ... by this conference or any branch of the United States Government"... And it shows clearly what we were up against.

As explained earlier, in August 1979 the Irish National Caucus led a successful campaign to have a ban put on the sale of U.S. weapons to the RUC. Well, later on, in January 1981, Archbishop Hickey of Washington and Bishop Thomas Kelly, Secretary General of the US Catholic Conference, visited the White House to urge President Reagan to continue the ban on military aid to El Salvador.

I wrote to them, begging them also to urge President Reagan to continue the ban on the sale of US weapons to the RUC. Archbishop Hickey responded to me saying, "... Bishop Kelly and I will be in touch with our counterparts in Northern Ireland to seek their advice in this vexing question. Our intervention will depend on their response." And Bishop Kelly replied "... We have known of your position [on the RUC] for some time ... In the case of El Salvador, we have been encouraged to take what action we have taken by the local hierarchy. We have not, at this time, received such encouragement from the Irish hierarchy on the subject you have brought to our attention ..."[13]

By now you get my drift—dealing with these people was like dealing with the British Embassy. So you can imagine my surprise when I discovered, at the height of the MacBride campaign, a plot from these same folk to muscle in on our work—having never lifted a finger to help. Why would they do that? To enhance MacBride? The very opposite: to sabotage and neutralize it. Here's what happened.

Through a stroke of good fortune in May 1993, a letter from the Presbyterian moderator, Rev. Dr. John Dunlop of Belfast, came into my possession. It made the astonishing revelation: "I have been advised that the Presbyterian Church USA and the United States Catholic Conference are prepared to convene a conference on fair employment and investment. I believe that such a conference, which would include a discussion about MacBride would be very helpful. Maybe an improved version of the MacBride Principles could command widespread support ... maybe even the name could be changed or modified to indicate that improvements have been made and at the same time move it from its explicitly partisan association ..."[14]

And, six days later, Josiah Beeman, chair of the Northern Ireland Working Group of Presbyterian Church in the United States said in a letter (announcing the conference) that one purpose of the conference would be to raise "support for the MacBride Principles or a modified version of them that would eliminate contentious issues among supporters of fair employment."[15]

Well, you can imagine I was not going to take this lying down. I released a blistering press release:

> Is this the latest assault by the English Government against the MacBride Principles? These Church groups have never lifted a finger to support the MacBride Principles; indeed, they either passively or actively opposed the Principles. Now they are going to have a

conference about the MacBride Principles, with a view to changing the name and contents of the Principles.

Well, with all due respect, I think they have a bloody nerve and a colossal arrogance. Let me make it perfectly clear that no Church leader (Catholic or Protestant) or anybody else in Ireland or the United States has the right or authority to change one syllable—not one jot or tittle—of the MacBride Principles.

If these Church groups have had their conscience pricked by the effective MacBride campaign and at long last want to oppose English Government discrimination in Northern Ireland, then I would welcome that. But surely a little bit of repentance—at least one *mea culpa*—would be in order from these Church people who, either passively or actively opposed the MacBride principles," McManus argued. "But instead of a *mea culpa*, they arrogantly call a conference to change the MacBride Principles—the one effective campaign against anti-Catholic discrimination in Northern Ireland."

I then did one of my massive mailings. The outside envelope carried the eye-catching warning: "Don't let the English government use the Catholic Church against the MacBride Principles." I included a pre-written postcard the recipients could mail to their own Bishops. And I also wrote a very strong letter to each bishop in the US: "It is beyond doubt that the English government has often succeeded in using Church leaders in Ireland for its own oppressive purposes. It would be an enormous scandal if that tradition were transported across the Atlantic and that the Catholic Conference would become the latest tool of the English government."[16]

Well, it scared the hell out of them, so to speak. You have never seen such scampering in all your life. The bishops became truly alarmed and immediately disassociated themselves from any anti-MacBride implication. All talk of a conference was dropped, even denied it had ever been planned. And in its place, the four main Churches in Ireland and their counterparts in the U.S. issued "A Call For Fair Employment and Investment in Northern Ireland." Not only that but they were forced to actually endorse the MacBride Principles: "Many Americans support the MacBride Principles, as amplified, as a good faith, nonviolent means to promote fair employment. We urge that any support of these amplified principles, which offer positive values and focus on fair employment, be joined with continued support for strong fair employment measures and an active commitment to investment and job creation ..."[17]

It was a remarkable turnaround. What started out as a covert and cynical effort to sabotage the MacBride Principles ended up as a ringing endorsement of them, by entities that, to say the least, were never too keen on them.

THE IRISH GOVERNMENT

The Irish Embassy in Washington was one of the very first to oppose the MacBride Principles. The Consul in New York actively lobbied against the MacBride Principles in Albany, New York, in 1986, much to the righteous anger of Paul O'Dwyer, the famed Mayo lawyer in New York.

Taoiseach Garret FitzGerald spelled out his attitude in a speech in Boston on May 3, 1985: "There is, however, a campaign underway which aims at discouraging American investment in Northern Ireland ... Those who pursue this campaign should know that they are inflicting injustice on both communities ... One can only wonder whether some of those who press for disinvestment do so as part of a calculated strategy which has as its goal the further weakening of the already strained Northern

Ireland economy so that terrorism may have greater opportunities to flourish."[18]

I understandably condemned FitzGerald. He knew full well that the very first thing the Irish National Caucus said when it launched the MacBride Principles was that "they [the Principles] do not call for reverse discrimination, quotas or disinvestment." This mischievous statement by FitzGerald was used with abandon by the British government in the United States.

But here, again, Kevin McNamara puts a peculiar spin on my reaction to FitzGerald. In his book, he writes: "FitzGerald is reported as saying that 'new evidence' had caused him to drop the passage from his speech ... The Irish Consul-General in New York specifically informed the Comptroller of the decision to omit the passage. This did not prevent McManus from declaring it to be: 'The Big Lie. Vintage FitzGerald smear tactics. England has no better Friend than FitzGerald.' It might be argued that these comments were 'vintage' McManus; to attribute to a political opponent words that he had not used, particularly when the lack of their use could be portrayed as a victory for McManus' own campaign."[19]

McNamara is ridiculous when he says that because FitzGerald did not use that passage when he spoke, it did not matter. Nonsense. That passage had been widely disseminated in the media. Did FitzGerald ever officially withdraw it and apologize for it? FitzGerald, in effect, accused me (the Irish in Boston were very familiar with me and would have seen me as the main leader of the MacBride campaign) of "inflicting injustice on both communities ... so that terrorism may ... flourish." And yet, Mc Namara reshapes this to make FitzGerald the victim, and me the culprit. And he does that repeatedly in his book. Each time I stand up for MacBride, he sides with the governments and the establishment and tries to make me the villain (as we shall see later regarding my letter to Taoiseach Charles Haughey).

Finally, on this, I remember the late, very just and honorable Kevin Boland, former TD and Minister, telling me that he was always shocked by the common tactic of government officials not saying at actual meetings what their press statements claimed.

However, imagine this delicious irony. Just eleven short years later, Taoiseach John Bruton in Washington was presented with a plaque "commemorating the inclusion of strong support in the Republican Party platform for the MacBride Fair Employment Principles." The presentation was done by presidential candidate Senator Bob Dole on behalf of the entire GOP (the "Grand Old Party," i.e., the Republican Party) leadership. According to a RNC (Republican National Committee) news release, "Prime Minister Bruton thanked Mr. Dole and Republicans in Congress for ... the inclusion and endorsement of the MacBride Principles in their platform."[20] I was so elated I had to call my brother Frankie in Ireland, as he would be able to fully appreciate the incredible irony.

CHARLIE HAUGHEY

I believe the most effective thing Charlie Haughey did regarding Northern Ireland was his reversal of FitzGerald's policy on the MacBride Principles. In an address to the Dáil on April 7, 1986, Haughey said:

> I want to avail of this opportunity to state that I fully endorse the MacBride Principles. I welcome the efforts and initiative of concerned Americans who wish to see something done about the chronic discriminatory patterns in employment in Northern Ireland.
>
> The regrettable position is that fourteen years after the imposition of direct rule in Northern Ireland, the situation in most sectors of employment is as bad as it ever was. The purpose of the MacBride Principles is to ensure that if there is to be American investment, if there are to be American orders, the firms concerned will have to act fairly and in a non-discriminatory fashion in regard to employment.

When Haughey became Taoiseach, his government's position was that there was nothing "objectionable" to MacBride. However, it took a long time for Haughey's policy to be implemented by the Irish Embassy. On Seán MacBride's last trip to the United States, in April 1987, he spoke at the Eire Society dinner in Boston. He was accompanied by his son, Tiernan. The Irish Ambassador, Pádraic McKernan, also attended the dinner, quite openly advising people that the MacBride Principles were a bad idea and that they should follow John Hume's lead. Seán MacBride took the issue up with Haughey, writing to him on April 29, 1987: "... there is a general feeling among our leading supporters that our diplomatic and consular staff in the U.S. are using their influence to oppose the adoption of the MacBride Principles."[21] When Tiernan MacBride returned to Dublin, he complained to Haughey's people. They promised to force McKernan to comply with Haughey's position, but it took a long time for that to happen.

Indeed, on February 11, 1988, I was forced to write this letter to Mr. Haughey—the very first time I ever thought it was worth writing to an Irish Taoiseach.

> Dear Mr. Haughey,
>
> Through the initiative of the Irish National Caucus, legislation on the MacBride Principles (Bill 7-394) has been introduced in the City Council of the District of Columbia.
>
> You are on record as stating that you are not opposed to the MacBride Principles, and that you have not instructed any Irish gvernment official in the United States to campaign against them.
>
> Because the Irish Embassy is in Washington, DC, it will be particularly of interest to the Irish National Caucus to see if the Irish Embassy officials will campaign against

the DC legislation on the MacBride Principles. We will be monitoring their activity very carefully.

We certainly hope that the Irish Embassy officials will not interfere with the D.C. legislation. Indeed, we will regard this as a test case.

Both before and after you were elected Taoiseach, Irish government officials in the United States have actively campaigned against the MacBride Principles.

For example, on one of Sean MacBride's last visits to the U.S. to speak to the Eire Society (April 29, 1987), you were Taoiseach. The Irish Ambassador (then and now) Mr. Padraic McKernan let it be known in conversation at the Eire society event that he was opposed to the MacBride Principles. One person told me that Mr. McKernan vehemently expressed his opposition and declared his support of John Hume's position on the MacBride Principles.

Now that the great and illustrious Sean MacBride is dead, the Irish National Caucus is more determined than ever to promote the MacBride Principles in the United States. We see this as the most fitting memorial.

While he lived, there were many attempts to discredit the MacBride Principles by trying to discredit him.

And, I am ashamed to say, there is reason to suspect that this smear campaign was—in part—orchestrated by the Irish Embassy and Mr. John Hume M.P. S.D.L.P. The first shots in this anti-MacBride campaign were fired by US

Senator Daniel Patrick Moynihan (D-N.Y.)—who takes his cue on Irish matters from the Irish Embassy—when he spoke to a breakfast meeting of Irish-Americans and Irish-American labor leaders in Washington DC at the Sheraton-Carlton Hotel on May 7, 1985. When I challenged Senator Moynihan that he was misrepresenting the MacBride Principles, he retorted: "You tell your readers that MacBride was the Nobel Peace Prize Winner. Tell them he was, also, the Lenin Peace Prize Winner, and you don't get that for nothing."

It was a shocking and deliberate smear.

In follow-up conversations with his office, Senator Moynihan refused to retract his smear.

In August 1987, a Member of Congress visited Ireland on a fact-finding mission. He met with Mr. Seamus Mallon, M.P. S.D.L.P. Mr. Mallon told him that he had no real trouble with the MacBride Principles. His trouble was that Sean MacBride had been given and had accepted the Lenin Peace Prize. The attempted smear again.

A few weeks before Sean MacBride died, elected representatives from the State of Maine visited Ireland. They met with Mr. John Hume, M.P.D.L.P. He told them that Sean MacBride had been senile for years, and that he was being exploited by the MacBride Principles. "He's an old man whom they prop up to say what they want him to say," said Mr. Hume.

I think you will agree that this is an outrageous pattern of vilification of one of Ireland's most illustrious sons. Coupled with the scurrilous British press commentaries on Sean MacBride's death, it represents a deliberately orchestrated campaign.

Padraig Pearse predicted that an Irish patriot can be more powerful in death than in life. We are confident this will apply to Sean MacBride. He was deeply committed to and deeply interested in the progress of the MacBride Principles.

The Irish National Caucus is now more than ever dedicated to the MacBride Principles. It is our earnest hope that you will immediately instruct all your officials in the United States to stop opposing the MacBride principles.

Thank you for your attention.
Sincerely,
Fr. Sean McManus

McNamara Distorts My Letter

Kevin Mc Namara again chooses to attack me for this letter in his book: "An intemperate letter from Fr. McManus to Haughey, included the old accusation that before and after Haughey's election [to his third term as Taoiseach, 1987 to 1992], 'Irish government officials in the United States have actively campaigned against the MacBride Principles.'"[22] It was not an "old accusation" but another example of the embassy's opposition to MacBride. Then he—very usefully, indeed, and much to the credit of his research—makes public for the first time Ambassador McKernan's response as contained in the DFAMP (Department of Foreign Affairs. MacBride Papers) undated cable: "Although one can readily dismiss Fr. McManus's lurid assertions, at the same time there is a serious and unscrupulous intent behind them ... This is to try to intimidate Irish officials in the United States ... it is an attempt to intimidate the government. You have observed the minatory note struck in the letter when Fr. McManus says that the Caucus will be monitoring the activities of the embassy." McNamara blithely continues: "The day to day work of the embassy continued: monitoring the progress of the MacBride campaign..."[23] So it was perfectly OK for the embassy to monitor the MacBride campaign, but it was intimidatory and minatory for me to monitor theirs?

Yet, McNamara does not describe the ambassador's letter as intemperate, and he seems merrily oblivious to his own double standard, not to mention the Ambassador's. This is such a pity because Kevin McNamara has had a great record on Ireland, and it is truly puzzling that he can't seem to help himself: the "Brit-speak" holds him captive. For example, when I refer to Seán MacBride's past, I call it heroic and noble—to McNamara it is "tempestuous."[24] It is as if he had his computer programmed to automatically enter a negative adjective before MacBride's name and mine.

What should have really upset the ambassador was Senator Moynihan's attack on Seán MacBride. If Moynihan had accused a former British, Israeli or French foreign minister of being a Soviet agent or mole, their respective embassies would have created uproar. There was not one word of protest from the Irish Embassy. What does that reveal? After the meeting, I confronted Moynihan, demanded an apology, and told him that he had slandered a great man. He refused to apologize and walked off in a petulant huff. I refused to have any dealings with Moynihan's office from then on. By the way, this is how Moynihan histrionically ended his speech: "If the Soviets increase their subsidy to the Provisional IRA, think Lebanon."

The Irish Embassy's possible role in slandering Seán MacBride—and in their refusal to repudiate it—was similar to their role in blocking the Caucus' campaign to free the Birmingham Six. It was only in 1991, when Dermot Gallagher became ambassador, that I noticed a change of attitude. Since that time, I have had nothing but respect for the Irish ambassadors to Washington. I often wonder who really calls the shots in all these events—civil servants or Irish Taoisigh.

Senator Moynihan

In case the fanatical anti-MacBride role of Senator Daniel Patrick Moynihan (D-NY) is missed (buried as it is in the above letter to Charlie Haughey) let me expand on it. One writer said Moynihan left Hell's Kitchen in New York City, joined the Navy, and came back a British Dandy. That may give some insight into his conflicted attitude to his "Irishness," if one can call it that.

Here's what happened when he addressed the Labor and Irish National Caucus breakfast, mentioned in my letter.

While Moynihan was speaking to the audience, he picked up an Irish National Caucus newsletter on the MacBride Principles, referred by name to the Irish National Caucus, and charged that the MacBride campaign was a sinister attempt to destabilize Northern Ireland by causing disinvestment. Now, I've always made sure never to interrupt a public speaker, but this time I felt I simply had a moral obligation to object to a barefaced lie. So, in a loud, controlled voice, I said, "That's not true, Senator."

He stopped, glowered at me, gestured towards me and said, "What is the truth?"

I responded, "Well, you are not the first person to famously ask that question, Senator" (referring, of course, to Pontius Pilate question to Jesus, John:18:38). I then asked him to read out the paragraph at the bottom of the middle column of our Newsletter. He read aloud: "We are not calling for disinvestment."

Realizing he was disproving his own allegations, he became really angry and roared at me, "You tell people that Sean MacBride got the Nobel Peace Prize, but you don't tell them that he also got the Lenin Peace Prize," adding with all his famous dramatic emphases "and you don't get that for nothing."

We had always, of course, stated that MacBride was the only person to have received the Noble Peace Prize (1974); Lenin Peace Prize (1977); and American Medal of Justice (1978)—the year after he received the Lenin Peace Prize!

When I got back to the Caucus office on Capitol Hill, I telephoned Sean MacBride in Dublin to tell him about Moynihan's outrageous, irresponsible and venomous smear. Sean expressed surprise and told me that when he was appointed UN Commissioner for Namibia (December 18, 1973–January 1, 1977), Moynihan, then US Ambassador to the UN, profusely praised his appointment.

Later, one of Moynihan's staffer came to see me as he was concerned about blowback to the Senator's appalling charge.

I told the staffer that not even Maggie Thatcher believed that the Provisional IRA was funded by the Soviets—that, after all, was one of the reasons why the "Provisionals" split from the "Officials" because the latter were seen to be Marxists. The Staffer agreed but said the Senator had convinced himself of this and there was no talking him out of it. And that from the "smartest man in the US Senate"—and one that had served as Vice-Chairman of the Senate Intelligence Committee.

God help us all! What pathology was at play there?

Yet, when it suited him, Moynihan, could play the Irish card.

When he had previously heard the Irish National Caucus was doing one of its massive mailings, polling Members of Congress on their Irish position, Moynihan made sure that he would be recorded as being in favor of a United Ireland—just like so many politicians in Southern Ireland would have to say they had an "aspiration" for unity.

Years later, during the Irish Peace Process, Taoiseach John Bruton—whom I had come to see as a decent man—brought back Sean Donlon as a special adviser. Moynihan told elected officials he was delighted because he said, "Donlon would know how to deal with those bastards." Did he mean the British government which had conducted a campaign of torture and state-assassinations? Did he mean some of the bigoted, extreme Orangemen who had colluded with the British government in the assassination of hundreds of innocent Catholics? Of course not. He meant and spelled it out, Sinn Fein—Gerry Adams and Martin McGuinness.

In 2010, Public Affairs published *"Daniel Patrick Moynihan: A Portrait in Letters of an American Visionary."*[25] The letters reveal that for the New York Saint Patrick's Day Parade in 1983, Senator Patrick Moynihan felt he had to wear a bullet-proof vest in case the IRA would shoot him because he had criticized the choice of Mike Flannery as Grand Marshal for the year's parade.

In a 1988 letter to Cardinal O'Connor of New York, Moynihan wrote that because of his anti-IRA stand: "I, for one, am now required to march in body armor, which takes some of the spring out of one's step."

And after the 1993 attack on the World Trade Center, the book further reveals, Moynihan wrote to Mayor Dinkins—a strong supporter of our MacBride Principles—that he feared that the IRA on "some deranged impulse" would bomb a New York site!

Some visionary he. Is it any wonder that I used the word "fanatical" to describe his attitude to the struggle for justice and peace in Ireland. How could such a knowledgeable, learned man be so out of touch? But, then, consider all the brilliant British statesmen who were stupid when it came to Ireland.

Moynihan may have been brilliant and fascinating, but as an Irishman, he was a disgrace—no empathy, no solidarity, no compassion. A British Dandy who couldn't care less about suffering in Ireland. Jimmy Breslin famously christened him Gypo Nolan after the pathetic informer in the Liam O' Flaherty play.

TEDDY KENNEDY

I always knew that Teddy Kennedy—with his good heart and right instincts—had to be most uncomfortable with being forced by John Hume and the Dublin government into a position of not supporting the MacBride Principles. And sure, enough, Mc Namara's book comes up with the evidence.

McNamara—in one of his most important revelations—explains:

> The campaign outside Washington was being carefully watched by those on Capitol Hill, who felt that their position locally might be being undermined by the activities of the INC and the Ad Hoc Congressional Committee. Burke of the Irish Embassy reported a conversation that

he had with a senior member of Senator Kennedy's office concerning the possibility of Kennedy introducing a bill into the Senate incorporating the MacBride Principles. The purpose was to pre-empt Representative Biaggi in the House or Senator De Concini in the Senate, both of whom were associated with the INC and were thinking about introducing similar legislation. Burke cautioned against this course of action ... it would be perceived as a victory for the Ad Hoc ... and the INC. Burke's advocacy was successful. The idea of a Kennedy bill was quietly dropped."[26]

So, there you have it: it was all about stopping the Irish National Caucus, and the Irish Embassy would use Kennedy—or any means necessary—to accomplish that.

But I was determined the Irish Embassy would not stop us. And no matter what the British Embassy tried, I was certainly not going to let them beat us, even though they had transferred, as Mc Namara's book reveals, "[Andrew] Henderson from the British consulate in New York to the embassy in Washington, to operate on a full-time basis to counteract the MacBride campaign;" and even though the secretary of state for Northern Ireland, Sir Patrick Mayhew, approved that "Mr. Hume should be approached as a potential ally."[27]

I had earlier exposed that the British Embassy had brought in an MI5 agent to try and defeat us: "[President] Clinton was informed by a White House staffer that Father McManus had discovered ... a British intelligence MI5 agent used his embassy job to direct a campaign specifically against the MacBride Principles."[28]

I was not going to allow anyone to stop MacBride from becoming US law—not even Bill Clinton, to whom I felt so deeply grateful for his magnificent work on the Irish peace process, and whom I see as Thomas Jefferson and Elvis Presley all rolled into one.

CHAPTER 17

Forcing Clinton to Sign MacBride

The time is always right to do the right thing.
Martin Luther King, Jr.

PRESIDENTIAL CANDIDATE BILL CLINTON made his pledge to support the MacBride Principles at the Irish-American Presidential Forum in New York City on April 5, 1992: "I like the Principles very much, I think they are a good thing, and if I were President, I would ask all state governments to take a look at adopting them. There's always that argument [that the Principles discourage investment] with this kind of thing, but I don't buy it. I see the MacBride Principles as a way of helping investment because it would help stabilize the Troubles."

After Clinton spoke, I told a group of Irish reporters at the Forum that one of the most important effects of Clinton's promise would be to ensure that the new Irish Government did not revert to a position of opposing the MacBride Principles. Charlie Haughey had just ceased being Taoiseach, and I was concerned that his successor would revert to the position of the previous Irish government under Garret FitzGerald.

Because of my direct experience with how FitzGerald had tried to sabotage Jimmy Carter's first pledge to the Irish National Caucus back on October 27, 1976, in Pittsburgh, I was especially concerned at how the new Taoiseach, Albert Reynolds, would react to Clinton's interest in the Irish issue. Reynolds welcomed Clinton's interest. And I knew it was the beginning of a new day. Because had Reynolds rebuffed Clinton, the way FitzGerald had rebuffed Carter, there would not have been an Irish Peace Process.

Surely there would now be plain sailing for MacBride? Well, in Washington, one learns there is no such thing. I had been pushing for a federal/congressional bill on the MacBride Principles for some years now. In 1987 Congressman Fish (R–NY)—whom Irish Ambassador Sean Donlon had so disrespected over the Birmingham Six case—had introduced a Bill in the House (H.R. 725) and Senator Al D'Amato (R–NY) had introduced it in the Senate.[1]

But Congressman Lee Hamilton, Chairman of the House Subcommittee on Europe and the Middle East, would not schedule a Hearing. He even told me there was not much interest in the bill, despite the fact we had signed up almost a hundred co-sponsors.[2]

But it was not just Congressman Hamilton who was opposing us. Let me switch you back here to Kevin Mc Namara's book on the MacBride Principles. You saw earlier how the Irish Ambassador at that time, Pádraic McKernan, had responded to my letter to Taoiseach Haughey. Well, in the same undated cable reply (which was his response to a letter of February 11, 1988, from the Department of Foreign Affairs (DFA) in Dublin), McKernan denied that the Irish Embassy was still conspiring against the MacBride Principles: "... Irish government officials have not campaigned and are not campaigning against the MacBride Principles."[3]

Here again, Mc Namara reveals vital information hitherto unknown. (He had been given "unfettered access" to the files of the Irish government and Irish Embassy on the MacBride campaign.[4]) He reveals the Fish–D'Amato Bill was, indeed, of concern to the Irish Embassy: "The Ambassador, Pádraic McKernan, wrote a private and confidential letter to Noel Dorr, the Secretary of the DFA, in which he conveyed the alleged concerns expressed by the Friends of Ireland and Tom Foley, the Majority Leader in the House of Representatives, at what they perceived as the shift in policy contained in Haughey's interview. They were concerned that two bills languishing in committee, Fish's in the House and D'Amato's in the Senate, might now emerge. Both bills were very divisive."[4]

So, here we go again! Were the Friends of Ireland really concerned or was it Ambassador McKernan? I had been well familiar with that tactic: the Irish Embassy would first wind up Members of Congress and then report to the Irish government that Members of Congress were "very concerned."

Lobbying Clinton on the National Mall

For years I have been doing my early morning, one-hour walk on the National Mall (the stunning, almost two-mile-long park that stretches from the Capitol Building to the Lincoln Memorial). On the morning of June 18, 1993, I was on the return stretch of my walk, facing the Capitol, plodding along and silently saying my Rosary. I heard an unmistakable voice shout hello to someone on the Mall. I turn around, and there comes President Clinton, in shorts and a baseball cap, running at a pretty good clip, with a large retinue behind him, huffing and puffing. Now while my walk on the Mall is sacred time, how often does one get a chance to lobby the President of the United States?

"Bill," I shouted, "don't forget your Irish promises."

He turned his head towards me as he kept going and said, "Don't worry."

I then shouted as he sped away, "Keep supporting the MacBride Principles." He put his hand above his head and waved affirmatively. I continued saying the Fourth Joyful Mystery of the Holy Rosary, which the Baptist President had interrupted.

Later that day, Mayor Flynn of Boston telephoned me. "A good job of lobbying the President on the MacBride Principles, Fr. Sean," he said. "How did you know that?" I asked. "The President called me and said, 'You know that Irish priest friend of yours? Well, he lobbied me on the Mall about the MacBride Principles.'" Clearly, according to Flynn, the President got a real kick out of it.

However, nice as that was, we were still not getting any real congressional progress on the MacBride Principles. Nor would we, until the Democrats lost the House and Senate and Republicans took over in January 1995. Isn't that an extraordinary thing to say—especially when people in Ireland mostly associate the Irish issue with Catholic Democrats?

CHAIRMAN GILMAN

For me, the Republican takeover meant one thing: the great Ben Gilman would be Chairman of the Foreign Affairs Committee (which would then be called the International Relations Committee). And, not just a subcommittee but the full committee. It was a perfect—although ironic—confluence of events. Bill Clinton in the White House, and Ben Gilman in the Chair of the House International Relations Committee.

With Ben as Chairman, I was now able to do in two minutes what I had not been able to do in twenty years. Immediately, Ben told me I would get two Hearings: one on the MacBride Principles and one on acceptable policing in Northern Ireland. My two top issues, just like that.

While two Irish Catholic Speakers—Tip O'Neill and Tom Foley—were in power, human rights Hearings on Northern Ireland were banned. Yet, when Newt Gingrich became Speaker, Hearings were allowed. It took a Protestant Speaker (Newt later became Catholic) and a Jewish Chairman to end the Congressional cover-up of British oppression of Catholics in Northern Ireland. For all time, that has to be a powerful ecumenical message for Irish-American Catholics. Their Church was silent, famous Irish Catholics were silent, even complicit. A Protestant and a Jew stood up to the British—broke the ban—and had Hearings.

With Ben Gilman becoming Chairman, Congressman Chris Smith of New Jersey became Chairman of the Human Rights Subcommittee and of the Helsinki Commission (Organization on Security and Cooperation in Europe). As of 2019, he had held seventeen Hearings on Northern Ireland, the Pat Finucane case, and other human rights issues.

Chris is the quintessential good guy—dedicated, courageous, and committed to human rights everywhere.

Ben told me to get him a list of witnesses for a MacBride Hearing, and told me to gird for battle because, although he could schedule a hearing, I had to get the committee members to vote for the MacBride Principles.

But first, we had to have a Congressional Reception to celebrate Ben becoming Chairman. On January 26, 1995, the Irish National Caucus hosted an evening reception in Ben's new fiefdom—the huge and impressive House International Relations Committee Hearing Room. Forty Members of Congress and about two hundred local Irish-Americans attended. And in a sign of how completely things had changed for both Ben and me, the new Chairman of the Friends of Ireland, Congressman Jimmy Walsh, attended and expressed total solidarity with the Irish National Caucus and the Ad Hoc Congressional Committee for Irish Affairs. Chairman Gilman lavishly praised my work, which he said had been unfairly condemned by both the Irish and British governments, and by some big names in Congress "who should have known better." Then he officially announced that he was going to give "Fr. McManus his long-sought prize: a Hearing on the MacBride Principles."[5]

CONGRESSIONAL HEARING ON MACBRIDE

And so, it came to pass. On March 15, 1995, I had my long-sought-for hearing. This despite the fact that the U.S. Ambassador to Ireland, Jean Kennedy Smith, had telephoned from Dublin to urgently beseech Chairman Gilman to call off the hearing.

The hearing would consider linking the MacBride Principles to the International Fund for Ireland (IFI).

Congressman Payne, the first speaker after Chairman Gilman's introduction, quickly set the scene: "As an African American, I and eight other Members of the Congressional Black Caucus who are Congressional Friends of the Irish National Caucus can easily identify with the Catholic minority [in Northern Ireland] ... The MacBride

Principles were modeled after the Sullivan Principles ... In the campaign for a free South Africa, we received a lot of help from Irish-Americans. For example, Fr. Sean McManus, president of the Irish National Caucus, was the first white Catholic priest to go to jail overnight for protesting outside the South African Embassy."[6]

After that opening salvo, it was almost all downhill for the British government. The Clinton administration attempted to bail them out. Assistant Secretary of State for European and Canadian Affairs, Richard Holbroke, speaking on behalf of President Clinton and responding to questions later submitted by committee members, said: "While we support the MacBride Principles, the Administration sees no reason to promote additional legislation in the Congress. Federal enactment of the MacBride Principles would add reporting requirements on US companies investing and operating in Northern Ireland. To put the Principles into specific legislation could have an inhibiting effect on the investment goals we seek."

Assistant Secretary of State for Legislative Affairs, Wendy R. Sherman, testified on behalf of the Clinton Administration at another hearing on May 15, 1995:

> We support and strongly prefer Mr. Hamilton's version of this. We believe that the amendment that Mr. Hamilton is offering [i.e., to delete mandatory linking of the MacBride Principles to the IFI] offers a constructive way forward to advance objectives that we all share. **As Mr. Hamilton has appropriately pointed out, senior levels of the Irish government have told Administration officials that linkage of the basic MacBride Principles to IFI funding will be controversial and could disrupt the White House Conference, which is aimed at increasing economic activity toward the disadvantaged and discriminated in Ireland.**

As was mentioned, all the parties, Ambassador Jean Kennedy Smith and Ambassador Crowe both do not support the mandatory linkage through the IFI. We think it is quite important to advance the objectives and goals, but do not think it should be mandatory.

Certainly, the President absolutely, positively embraces the MacBride Principles completely, as does Mr. Hamilton's amendment. The only difference is whether it should or shall be mandatory. And I don't think anyone for a minute would think Ambassador Jean Kennedy Smith does not endorse and completely embrace the MacBride Principles or Ambassador Crowe or this Administration.

Chairman Gilman dismissed all that malarkey with: "Saying one supports the MacBride Principles without implementing them is like saying one supports the Ten Commandments as long as I don't have to implement them." He also dispensed with that old canard, beloved by the establishment and administrations, that although the idea was good, "the time was not right." Quoting Martin Luther King Jr., he told the Clinton Administration, "It is always the right time to do the right thing."

Notice the words of Ms. Sherman that I place in emphases. They show that even then the Irish Embassy still opposed the MacBride Principles—seven long years after I wrote to Taoiseach Haughey, complaining about the Irish Embassy's obstructionism. Those words make nonsense out of Kevin McNamara's charge that I had raised "an old accusation."

We Win 32 to 8

Throughout the Hearing—whenever possible—I was grabbing every Member of the Committee urging them to vote for MacBride.

Remember, just six months previously, Congressman Hamilton was the all-powerful Chairman who had been resisting me for years, trying to tell me there was no support for the MacBride Principles in the committee. However, later that day when the committee voted on the Hamilton amendment, we beat him by thirty-two votes to eight. It was a sweet victory. All the members of the Democratic Minority panel in deference to Hamilton, now Ranking Member, prefaced their remarks with something like, "As much as I respect Mr. Hamilton, etc. ... I cannot support his amendment." When it came his turn, the usually unflappable Hamilton was visibly annoyed:

"I could do with less respect and more support," he huffed at the Democrats. "I know what has happened here. The Irish National Caucus did its work on this committee."

Later during the Hearing, I went up to Chairman Gilman (while Hamilton still sat on his left). "You have just been handed your diploma in lobbying," said Gilman—referring to Hamilton's bellyaching.

By the way, the committee vote revealed an insight into how the "establishment" Irish media operates. When the results were announced, I glanced over at a reporter for a paper in Ireland. He could not hide his disappointment and displeasure at my victory.

Staffers on the committee had long regarded him as a "spy for the Irish Embassy." At the end of the Hearing, I stood near him to test if he would ask me for a comment—as was surely warranted because I had pulled off an extraordinary victory, which any good, objective reporter would acknowledge. I waited and waited. Not a thing. He never looked at me. There was no way, of course, I was going to let him off with his self-censorship. So, I strode over to him, as he was about to depart, and said: "[First name], aren't you going to ask me for a comment?"

He shuffled around, tried to look professional and sighed reluctantly, "OK. What do you want to say?"

If, for example, someone favored by the Dublin government had pulled off a 32-8 victory, the Dublin media would have hailed it as an outstanding achievement.

One, therefore, simply cannot understand The Troubles if one does not realize the complicity of the Irish media. Large sections of this media acted as if they were departments of the Dublin government. They bear huge responsibility and shame for their complicity.

On February 28, 1996, Ms. Sherman wrote as follows to Members of the House and Senate conference, giving the "Administration's Position on Provisions in HR 1561": "The Administration opposes this provision ... Requiring compliance with the 'principles of economic justice,' as defined in this provision would place an undue burden on small business and community development organizations ... We propose that all reference to the 'principles of economic justice' be deleted."

On April 11, 1996, Tony Lake, assistant to the president for national security affairs, wrote to me. "Thank you for your letter about the legislation linking the MacBride Principles of fair employment to the funding for the International Fund for Ireland ... The President does not believe it would be useful to place conditions on the funding we provide to the International Fund for Ireland ..."

On April 12, 1996, President Clinton vetoed HR 1561.

Standing Up to President Clinton

I got eleven major Irish-American groups to co-sign a letter that I sent to President Clinton on April 19, 1996: "Because of our great gratitude for your crucial support of the Irish peace process, we've been reluctant to say anything up to now. But you cannot expect us to be silent as you continue to oppose one of our very top legislative issues. It is ironic that Senator Dole, the entire Republican leadership and the Republican National Committee are all supporting Congressional legislation on the MacBride Principles and you are opposing it. The peace process in Ireland cannot be separated from non-discrimination ... We are totally committed to both."

The letter was signed by the following organizations (in alphabetical order):

John Finucane, President, American Ireland Education Fund
Kathleen Holmes, Chairwoman, American Irish Congress
Edward J. Wallace, National President, Ancient Order of Hibernians
Larry Downes, Chairman, Brehon Law Society
Mike Moroney, Secretary, Clan na Gael
John D. Worral, President, Federation of Irish-American Societies of the Delaware Valley
James V. Mullin, Coordinator, Irish-Action Coalition
Fr. Sean McManus, President, Irish National Caucus
Paul Doris, Chairman, Irish Northern Aid Committee
Edmund Lynch, Chairman, Lawyers Alliance for Justice in Ireland
Jean Forest, U.S. Coordinator, Voice of the Innocent

(Of the principal activist groups on the North, the Irish-American Unity Conference was the only organization that refused to sign on.)

The letter from the Irish-American leaders caused considerable attention and put considerable pressure on President Clinton in the middle of an election.

Because of my deep gratitude for President Clinton's role in the Irish peace process, initiating that letter was one of the most difficult decisions I have ever made. I did not want to do it, yet I knew it would be a dereliction of duty not to. Behind the scenes, I had privately talked to White House officials and other key players in an effort to get the administration to stop opposing the MacBride legislation. But I met with no success, and so I was reluctantly forced to go public. Some Irish-Americans condemned me for criticizing President Clinton. Maybe they did so because they lacked political self-confidence, or maybe it was because they did not have the experience of sitting for hours at Hearings and listening to Clinton administration officials opposing the MacBride legislation. Journalist Jimmy Breslin called to curse me out. In a tirade loaded with the F-word, he berated me. "Clinton is the only president who has ever done so much for Ireland," he screamed.

"Don't you think I know that, Jimmy?" I replied. "Didn't I stress that in our statement." Uttering a few more expletives, he hung up on me.

But because I had stood up to President Clinton on principle (pun intended), I was later able to stand up for him with credibility. During his impeachment difficulty, I wrote to every member of the House and Senate, telling them "Let those without sin, cast the first stone." Jimmy Breslin went on to write the most outrageous stuff against Clinton.

But whatever their reasons for opposing my standing up to Clinton, those Irish-Americans were ignoring a fundamental principle in political campaigning: When a political leader does the right thing on your issue, you praise him; when he does the wrong thing on your issue, you call him on it.

Just look at what the President's two most loyal constituencies—African Americans and the Labor Movement—do. When the President goes against them on basic issues, they do not hesitate to criticize him publicly.

Indeed, when one very prominent labor leader chastised me on the phone for criticizing President Clinton, I pointed to how Labor criticized him over NAFTA. He objected by saying, "But that was about jobs for our people." I replied, "And what do you think the MacBride Principles are about, but jobs for our people?" He had no answer to that.

There is another hard political reality in all of this. How could I go back to Members of Congress and campaign again for the MacBride Principles if I let the President roll us over without a murmur of protest? How could I expect Members of Congress—both Republican and Democrat—to fight for the MacBride Principles if I was not prepared to fight for them? By my silence, I would be taking a dive and jeopardizing the integrity of the MacBride campaign.

Here again, Kevin McNamara's book on the MacBride Principles shows an inability to appreciate the dynamics of American politics. He asserts that my standing up to President Clinton "... was probably the most significant political error that he [McManus] had made ... he shot himself in the foot." McNamara was clearly misled, again, by Pat Doherty, whom he quotes as saying that I should not have stood up to Clinton, "despite this one difference" (i.e., Clinton's opposition to the MacBride Principles becoming U.S. law). However, "this one difference" would have in principle invalidated the entire MacBride campaign. If one accepted Clinton's argument against the Federal MacBride Bill, then one would have to accept the same argument against all state and city bills. Pat had absolutely no role in lobbying Congress on the Federal MacBride Bill. Indeed, his position—in effect, that I should have rolled over and sold out the Federal MacBride Bill—shows that he was not committed to Federal legislation—just as he was not at first committed to state and city legislation, as I've previously documented.

Despite his claim that I had shot myself in the foot, McNamara proceeds to prove that my strategy was very effective and successful. He writes:

> "The administration was caught unaware by the size of the storm ... There was no one better to orchestrate such an uproar than McManus ... The strength of McManus' attack ... forced the administration to consider making a gesture to placate the pro-MacBride Democrats ... The truth of the matter is that the President did not wish to go to Chicago ... without attempting to achieve a reconciliation with the MacBride campaign ... In an attempt to quell the controversy ... James Lyons (the U.S. observer to the IFI) wrote [to *The Irish Echo*, May 22, 1997] '... whether or not Congress sees fit to incorporate the principles ... in legislation, the Clinton administration and I ... will continue to see that these principles remain fully implemented in the International Fund for Ireland ... .'"

Then McNamara adds the clincher of all clinchers, delighting this Kinawleyman's heart: "Officials in the DED privately acknowledged that the UK government had lost the battle on MacBride. The UK Embassy in Washington immediately recognized that the Lyons letter was likely to encourage McManus to press for legislation."[7]

In further evidence that our strategy was right, on August 24, 1996, President Clinton—in a move widely regarded as an attempt to defuse the MacBride controversy—issued a directive to the United States representative for the International Fund for Ireland, James Lyons:

> In the 1996 Foreign Affairs Authorization Act (HR 1561) as passed by Congress, Section 1615 stated that U.S. contributions to the Fund "should be used in a manner that effectively increases employment opportunities in communities with rates of unemployment higher than the local or urban average of unemployment in Northern Ireland. In addition, such contributions should be used to benefit individuals or entities which employ practices consistent with the principles of economic justice' as defined by the Act."
>
> I vetoed HR 1561 for reasons entirely unrelated to the language in Section 1615. I am committed to equal opportunity and fair employment as necessary foundations for a just, peaceful, and prosperous future for all the people of both jurisdictions in Ireland. I, therefore, ask you, in discharging your duties under the Anglo-Irish Agreement Support Act of 1986, to ensure that the intent of Section 1651 of HR 1561 is carried out to the greatest extent possible."

Ray O'Hanlon of *The Irish Echo*—the most professionally objective journalist I've ever known—summed it up this way, "Against the backdrop of the Democratic National Convention in Chicago, President Clinton has moved to mend damaged fences with Irish-American backers of the MacBride Principles."[8] The Irish National Caucus put out a press release: "Caucus Welcomes President Back to MacBride Fold."[9] Remember, all this was happening in August 1996, with the Presidential elections scheduled for November 5, between President Clinton and Senator Bob Dole (R-KS).

REPUBLICAN AND DEMOCRATIC PARTIES ENDORSE MACBRIDE

On August 9, the Republican Party at their National Convention included support for the MacBride Principles in their party platform language. And on August 27, the Democratic National Convention also included the MacBride Principles in their platform. *The Irish Times* observed: "The reference to the MacBride Principles could be seen as a mild criticism of British rule in Northern Ireland, but it is also intended to mollify ... the Irish National Caucus."[10]

As I told Kevin McNamara in my review of his book, "For results like that, I would have shot myself in both feet".[11]

Let's take a moment to reflect on what had been achieved to date.

We had routed the powerful enemies of the MacBride Principles. Against all odds—the British government, the Irish government, John Hume, Tip O'Neill, Teddy Kennedy, etc.,—we had taken the MacBride Principles from a simple press release on November 5, 1984, all across the United States, into the White House, to being endorsed by both the Democratic and Republican parties. By any criterion, it was a stunning achievement. And it was done by the so-called "little people," the ordinary decent Irish-Americans, without big power or big money. Now, surely, we would get the Federal MacBride Bill passed into law?

But things were not as rosy as they appeared. Because, after the 1996 election, the Clinton administration would again unbelievably oppose the MacBride Principles being attached to the International Fund for Ireland.

In 1997, Congressman Ben Gilman (R-NY) again attached the same MacBride language to the Foreign Policy Reform Act (HR 1486). On Wednesday, April 30, 1997, HR 1486 was in Markup (when Committee Members can make amendments). I spoke with Rep. Lee Hamilton, former House International Relations Committee (HIRC) Chairman, at his seat in the Committee Room and asked him if he was still opposed to the MacBride legislation. He emphatically said he was. I asked him what form his opposition would take. He said he wasn't sure yet. He then asked me if the language was the same as last year. I told him it was. Then he said, "You know that it will never become law." I asked why. "Because the president is opposed to it," he replied, with great emphasis.

I then lobbied the other Democrats on the Committee and expressed concern that Hamilton was still opposing the MacBride legislation. Next, I spoke to Barbara Larkin, assistant secretary of state for legislative affairs, in the committee room. She confirmed the administration's continued opposition to linking the MacBride Principles to the IFI in the legislation. Later that day, I called Steve Kashkett, at the Irish desk of the State Department. He said the president's letter to Lyons did not represent a softening of the president's opposition to legislation linking the MacBride Principles to the IFI. I told him that Mary Ann Peterson, director for European affairs at the White House, was supposed to have said that President Clinton was no longer opposed to linking MacBride to the IFI. He expressed surprise and disbelief at that and told me he would check it out and call me back.

On Thursday, May 1, 1997, the Markup continued. I spoke to Barbara Larkin in the Committee Room. She said, "This is the man (me) who knows all about Ireland," and introduced me to Michael Klosson, her assistant for legislative affairs. He told me that the Administration was opposed to legislation linking MacBride to the IFI for a two-fold reason: because the British Fair Employment laws made MacBride unnecessary; and because MacBride would place onerous burdens on recipients of the Fund.

On Friday, May 2, 1997, at 4:40 p.m., Steve Kashkett called me back and told me he could find no indication that the President had changed his position, or that Mary Anne Peterson had ever said the President was no longer opposed to Congressional legislation linking the MaBride Principles to the IFI. The President, he said, was opposed to Congressional legislation linking MacBride to the IFI for the reasons stated last year. Those reasons still stand, and that is the position of President Clinton, Kashkett emphasized. However, despite Clinton's opposition, the House passed HR 1486 on March 27, 1998.

MacBride Becomes US Law

Because the MacBride language was not contained in the Senate version of the Bill, the House and Senate conference had to reconcile the two versions, (and not, of course, only onMacBride).

The reconciled bill—now called the Omnibus Appropriations and Authorization Bill—was passed by the House on Tuesday evening, October 20, 1998, and by the Senate on Wednesday morning, October 21, 1998. Because the Omnibus Appropriations and Authorization Bill had bi-partisan support—and because the Administration wanted it—President Clinton signed it into law. He did not have the option of removing the MacBride section. It was either accept the whole bill or veto the whole bill.

Although the administration was adamantly opposed to the MacBride Principles being linked to the International Fund for Ireland, the administration was forced to accept that link—and so were the British Embassy and the Irish Embassy.

Congressman Gilman took to the floor of the House of Representatives and declared: "I want to make a special note regarding Father Sean McManus. No one has fought harder against discrimination in Northern Ireland. Father Sean single-handedly brought the MacBride fair employment principles to ... enactment."

Thus, because of the determined leadership of Congressman Ben Gilman, Chairman of the House International Relations Committee, and the Irish National Caucus, the MacBride Principles became US law.

There is no other victory to match it in the history of Irish-American nationalism. John Devoy (1842–1928) would have been proud of us, and I dedicated this victory to him. His grave lies close to Seán MacBride's grave in Glasnevin Cemetery, Dublin. Each year I kneel and say an "Ave" there at the graves of my two Irish heroes—while remembering my Jewish-American hero, the late great Ben Gilman (December 6, 1922-December 17, 2016). **(Please go to Appendix I to see photograph of my kneeling in prayer at John Devoy's grave).**

MARY MCALEESE, FUTURE IRISH PRESIDENT, ON MAC BRIDE PRINCIPLES

"One evening in 1988, Mary was at dinner in Queen's University with a group of people who were celebrating the introduction of equality legislation in Northern Ireland. Roy Wallace, who was a pro-vice chancellor of Queen's at the time, was the host, and apart from Mary and a couple of civil servants, most of the other guests were member of the Alliance Party. There was a lot of congratulatory talk at the dinner, people complimenting each other on the work they had done to achieve parity of opportunity in the workplace for Catholics and Protestants in Northern Ireland. Mary put the question to the assembled guests: how significant was the work of Sean MacBride, particularly his MacBride Principles, in preparing the way for the passing of the legislation that had been enacted in Westminster earlier that day? The senior civil servant, Sir David Fell, a man respected by all present, took it upon himself to answer the question: "If it were not for the MacBride Principles, and the ameliorating influence they had on the British government, this legislation would not be in place today"...p. 153

*The footnote states, "As given by Mary McAleese from memory".

The Road From Ardoyne: The Making of a President, by Ray MacManais, Brandon Press, Dingle.Co. Kerry Ireland. 2004

25th Anniversary of MacBride Principles

Fr. McManus was the keynote speaker for the 25th Anniversary of the MacBride Principles at New York City Hall on December 8, 2009. His address—which has been described as "In effect, a panegyric to Jewish-Americans"—is given below in full.

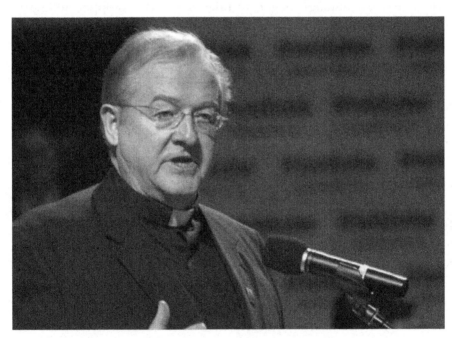

Fr. Sean McManus speaking in New York City Hall on 25th. Anniversary of MacBride Principles. December 8, 2009: "In effect, a panegyric to Jewish-Americans."

In 1795, Thomas Paine wrote: *"An Army of Principles Will Penetrate Where an Army of Soldiers Cannot"* (Agrarian Justice. Pamphlet was written in 1795, published in 1797).

I think that perfectly applies to the MacBride Principles.

The Principles penetrated the previously UNPENETRATABLE bastion of anti-Catholic discrimination—the Northern Ireland State.

In the early years of our campaign, our opponents used to tell us to mind our own business—they clearly did not subscribe to Martin Luther King's dictum: "Injustice anywhere is an affront to justice everywhere." But when our campaign began to take effect, they stopped telling us to mind our own business—because when Americans make sure that US dollars are not subsidizing anti-Catholic discrimination in Northern Ireland, they **ARE** minding their own business.

It is generally accepted that Martin Luther King's movement would not have succeeded without Jewish-American support. And the MacBride Principles would not have succeeded without Jewish-American support.

Just look at the record:

In July 1979, Congressman Ben Gilman (R-NY commissioned the Irish National Caucus to conduct an investigation of the U.S. companies in Northern Ireland.

We then planned to have our principle, "United States dollars should not subsidize anti-Catholic discrimination in Northern Ireland," enshrined into law. In 1983, Congressman Dick Ottinger introduced Bill HR 3465: "Requiring United States persons who conduct business or control enterprises in Northern Ireland to comply with certain fair employment principles." We had, of course, modeled the Ottinger Bill on the Sullivan Principles.

Our activity got a lot of attention and soon many State, and City officials who wanted to join our campaign contacted us: most notably, New York City Comptroller Harrison J. Goldin and Council Member Sal Albanese (who introduced the very first MacBride Bill in the entire United States).

Comptroller Goldin went on to provide magnificent support and economic muscle for the MacBride Principles until he left office in 1989. His successors, Liz Holtzman (1990—1993) and Alan Hevesi (1994–2001), continued to provide indispensable support for the MacBride Principles.

My dear friend, Congressman Ben Gilman, Chairman of the House International Relations Committee, championed our campaign in the Congress and the MacBride Principles (despite very powerful opposition) became US law in 1998.

So, you can easily see the importance of Jewish-American support.

Since 2002, Comptroller Thompson has provided magnificent leadership on the MacBride Principles. And here, again, is something that has touched me deeply: the support of African-Americans, who know a thing or two about discrimination. Along with Comptroller Thompson, the other names that immediately come to mind are Congressman Charlie Rangel of New York, one of our very earliest supporters, and Congressman Don Payne of New Jersey.

I have already mentioned Sal Albanese and the key role he played in our campaign. But one cannot mention American activity on behalf of Ireland without mentioning that other great Italian, Congressman Mario Biaggi, who for many years was our key ally in Congress.

Isn't it very striking? The elected officials who led the campaign to end anti-Catholic discrimination in Northern Ireland were not

Irish-Americans, but Jewish-Americans, African-Americans, Italian-Americans, Hispanic-Americans and others!

To me, that is the great moral lesson of the MacBride Campaign.

God bless America and God save Ireland.

In Praise of Father McManus

Fr. McManus and Congressman Gilman at Speaker's Saint Patrick's Day Lunch 2010.

By
Congressman Ben Gilman, former Chairman,
House International Relations Committee
February 2003

As I retire from Congress, I want to pay tribute to Father Sean McManus, the President of the Irish National Caucus.

For 30 years as a Member of Congress, I have been privileged to work for many good and noble causes around the world. None has given me more pleasure than my work for equality, justice, and peace in Ireland.

Throughout my 30 years of congressional work, Father McManus has been constantly by my side—encouraging, guiding and giving invaluable advice from his unsurpassed knowledge of the Irish issue. No one has done more than Father McManus to keep the US Congress on track regarding justice and peace in Ireland. Indeed, I believe historians will record that no one since John Devoy (1842–1928) has done more to organize American pressure for justice in Ireland. (The only difference being that Father McManus—in keeping with his priestly calling—is committed to nonviolence).

During the past 30 years, the fingerprints of Father McManus are over every piece of Congressional action on Ireland: from the formation of the Ad Hoc Congressional Committee For Irish Affairs in 1977 (which in turn sparked the formation of the Friends of Ireland in 1981) to Congressional Hearings on Northern Ireland, once banned until I became Chairman of the International Relations Committee in 1995; from individual human rights cases, like the Birmingham Six and Guildford Four to the political assassinations cases of Pat Finucane and Rose Mary Nelson; from the Hunger Strikes of Bobby Sands and his nine colleagues to the general mistreatment of political prisoners; from individual cases of anti-Catholic discrimination to the full, frontal and triumphal campaign of the MacBride Principles; from stopping the sale of U.S. weapons to the RUC to putting human rights conditions on US dealings with the Northern Ireland police.

Summarily, Father McManus' doctrine "that the United States must not subsidize anti-Catholic discrimination in Northern Ireland" has now become US law and policy. Accordingly, it has been my honor and privilege to have given Congressional shape to Father McManus' dream for his beloved Ireland.

CHAPTER 18

"A Protestant Boy" on Capitol Hill

May the Lord in His mercy be kind to Belfast.
Maurice Craig

Raymond Mc Cord and Fr. McManus, 2009.

I ARRIVED IN AMERICA ON OCTOBER 2, 1972. And in one year and one week, I had arranged my first Congressional Hearing on October 10, 1973—at which my brother Frank and Ruairí Ó Brádaigh, President of Sinn Féin testified. Who would have thought then that thirty-six years later

I would organize a Congressional Hearing for a hardy "Protestant boy" from Belfast?

In Northern Ireland parlance, "a Protestant boy" not to a child but to an adult, a hardy defender of the Unionist/ Protestant cause. The folk song "The Protestant Boys." gives the flavor:

> The Protestant Boys are loyal and true
> Stout hearted in battle and stout handed too
> The Protestant Boys are true to the last
> And faithful and peaceful when danger has passed
> And Oh! they bear
> And proudly wear
> The colors that floated o'er many a fray
> Where cannons were flashing
> And sabers were clashing
> The Protestant Boys still carried the day ...

On October 22, 2009, before the same House Human Rights Subcommittee, I facilitated a hearing for Raymond McCord, Sr.—a staunch Unionist/Protestant, though never a paramilitary. I had been deeply touched by the compelling narrative of his heroic struggle to get justice for his son, Raymond Jr., murdered in 1997 near Belfast.

Because young Raymond's killers were part of a Protestant paramilitary group—and because some were police informers and British agents—the killers were protected, and their crime covered up by the Northern Ireland police and the British government.

Raymond, Sr. embarked on a long quest for justice. His persistence persuaded Police Ombudsman Nuala O'Loan to launch an investigation that essentially vindicated his charges. Her report, *"Operation Ballast,"* was published in 2007. Still, despite that, nobody was arrested for the murder. Raymond then felt his only hope lay in the Irish National Caucus and the US Congress.

I brought Raymond to Capitol Hill from May 3-15, 2009. We did a political blitz of Capitol Hill or, as one observer put it, "the priest and the Protestant took the Halls of Congress by storm." I introduced Raymond to many members, especially Congressman Don Payne (D-NJ), Congressman Joe Crowley (D-NY), one of the co-chairmen of the Ad Hoc Congressional Committee for Irish Affairs, and Congressman Ritchie Neal, Chairman of the Friends of Ireland—all of whom treated Raymond with great respect and kindness. Then I brought him along to meet the Chairman of the Human Rights Subcommittee, Congressman Bill Delahunt (D-MA).

I began by saying: "Bill, for over thirty years I have been telling the Congress about how the British government covered up the murder of Catholics in Northern Ireland. But today I bring you a staunch Protestant from Belfast to tell you how the British government has covered up the murder of his son." I then sat back and let Raymond do the talking. Within fifteen minutes, Congressman Delahunt promised a Hearing.

Raymond could not believe it. That hardy boy—considered to have been one of the toughest street fighters in Belfast for the past forty years—was deeply moved by Delahunt's compassion and solidarity.

We took time out to meet with the Northern Ireland Bureau, which treated Raymond very nicely. But because justice and policing had not been devolved back to Northern Ireland, the Bureau could not deal with Raymond's case. They did, however, arrange for him to meet with the duly accredited spokesman at the British Embassy, Nic Hailey. Because of my own particular history with that embassy, I excused myself from the meeting. However, I did drop Raymond off outside the embassy.

McCord at British Embassy

I sat and watched him walk towards the massive building (the biggest embassy in Washington, with over six hundred employees) all by himself. A small man, with a slight limp that day—his knee was acting up. I watched as others passed him on the footpath, thinking how they would not have any idea of who he was ... and the huge mistake any young hood would have made trying to mug this hardy Protestant boy. I felt an overpowering sense of sadness as I watched Raymond enter the embassy. I reflected on my own two past visits to the embassy, on the arrests, and the nights in prison and thought how different it was for Raymond... I was an Irish Catholic rebel, he a staunch Protestant Unionist. For me, the British Embassy was the symbol of institutionalized violence, injustice, and bigotry in Northern Ireland. But for Raymond, entering the British Embassy had to be a vastly different experience. It was his embassy; his flag, the Union Jack, flew outside it; and his government operated it. Yet, there he was, going in alone, to charge his embassy with participating in the cover-up of the murder of his beloved Protestant and Unionist son.

I drove off, ruefully pondering how the British government had used and abused the Protestants and Catholics of Northern Ireland. And, yet, I waited with optimism for Raymond's report when he came back. Because he had not just walked in from the street, but had his visit arranged by the Northern Ireland Bureau, and because we were so well into the peace process, I was expecting the British Embassy to give Raymond some sort of satisfaction and comfort (the word "closure" is over-used, and besides, for the bereaved, there is no such thing). "Well, how did it go?" I asked Raymond the moment he walked back into the Caucus office. "Useless, a waste of time," was his answer. I was really disappointed and said so. "That's because you don't know the British government as well as I do, Sean," said Raymond.

What is wrong with that picture? I, a Kinawley man, disappointed that the British were not more generous, and Raymond, a staunch Ulster Protestant telling me I was naïve. Raymond then issued a statement:

> I was low-keyed and respectful, but Mr. Hailey never answered one question. He never even tried, maintaining almost virtual silence throughout the hour meeting. And when he did speak, it was to ask: "Whom are you meeting on Capitol Hill? Do you think you are having any impact, and when are you going home?" See here, I am an Ulsterman, a British citizen. The British Government and the Northern Ireland police colluded in the brutal murder of my son, Raymond Jr. I am given a fantastic

reception on Capitol Hill. Then I go to my own embassy in Washington, and I get nothing, absolutely nothing. Hailey's treatment of me is exactly what I get from his colleagues in the Northern Ireland Office in Belfast ... My treatment at the British Embassy illustrates and vindicates the need for my visit to Capitol Hill. It confirms my conviction that Congressional pressure in my son's case is my only hope ..."[2]

MCCORD HEARING

But Raymond would have the last word. On October 22, 2009, he had his Congressional hearing before the House Human Rights Subcommittee—and he gave the fight of his life. There was a stunned, somber atmosphere as he recounted his son's murder, the collusion, and the cover-up. And I knew that from then on, I would never have any difficulty convincing the Congress that the British can do bad things in Ireland.

But I was also deeply sad at how difficult it had to be for Mrs. McCord, young Raymond's mother, who had to listen to the retelling of the slaughter of her son. Raymond, Sr. somehow got through it all, with his voice breaking only once. Indeed, not only did he get through it—but also, very importantly, he kept to his allotted time. At Hearings, the oral testimony is five minutes (to allow for other speakers and for question-and-answer time) with the written testimony—submitted for the record—being much longer. It is generally acceptable that the oral testimony can actually go a bit over five minutes, but witnesses abuse the privilege and courtesy of the Congress if they go over seven minutes. Raymond—a rough and ready working-class man—spoke for six and a half minutes—further earning the respect of the Subcommittee.

Since that time, Raymond has kept up his remarkable struggle for justice—relentlessly, vigorously, and with incredible courage. Needless to say, he continues to have the support of the Irish National Caucus and wide support in the US Congress and among Irish-Americans.

Raymond's latest initiative is to take a civil action in the High Court against seven individuals whom he blames for being connected with the murder of his son.

In 2018, Raymond was appointed to the International-Interfaith Board of the World Peace Prize (explained in the next chapter), representing Ireland and Britain. Founder and World Leader, the late Rev. Dr. Han Min Su, said: "Mc Cord has demonstrated what one person can accomplish through dedication to justice and peace. He has been honored by being invited to testify before the United States Congress, where he has received strong support, and where his views are regularly disseminated. And now, he honors the World Peace Prize Awarding Council by joining us in our mission of world peace."

Raymond McCord, Jr.

CHAPTER 19
World Peace Prize

"Today, one could say ... peace is the fruit of solidarity."
Pope John Paul II

IN 2013, I WAS SURPRISED TO BE CONTACTED by Rev. Dr. Han Min Su, World Leader and Founder of the World Peace Prize in Seoul, South Korea. He told me he was very impressed by my almost fifty years of work for justice and peace in Ireland, and that he was calling for my help. He wanted Barbara and me to represent the World Peace Prize in Washington and pleaded with us to come to Seoul for a very formal Induction Ceremony as Judges into the World Peace Prize Awarding Council (WPPAC). I was touched by the good Presbyterian heart of this peace visionary and agreed to help him in his most worthy mission of World Peace. After all, it was a seamless extension of our work with the Irish National Caucus and its sister organization, the Irish Peace Foundation.

Here is the story so far.

Rev. Dr. Han Min Su

World Leader and Master Planner.
World Leader and Master Planner, the late Rev. Dr. Han Min Su, founded the World Peace Prize in Seoul, Republic of Korea, in 1989. Dr. Han was a Presbyterian Minister.

Dr. Han's vision was one of world peace and harmony.

Dr. Han has devoted his life to this great mission—knowing, as President Kennedy did, "that here on earth God's work must truly be our own." *(Inaugural Address of President John F. Kennedy. January 20, 1961).*

The World Peace Prize Awarding Council (WPPAC), which is headquartered in Seoul with an office in Washington, D.C, was established to select the recipients of the World Peace Prize.

The International and Interfaith Board is composed of representatives of all the major worldwide religions: Judaism, Islam, Hinduism, Buddhism, Confucianism, Catholicism, Protestantism, Orthodox, and Zoroastrianism.

Fr. Sean McManus, President of the Capitol Hill-based Irish National Caucus, and Barbara Flaherty, Executive Vice President, were awarded with the World Peace Prize of Roving Ambassador for Peace and inducted as WPPAC Judges at a Ceremony in Seoul in 2013.

Fr. McManus was then selected as the Chief Judge of WPPAC.

Fr. McManus explained: "When we joined the World Peace Prize Awarding Council in 2013, we set out to accomplish TWO OBJECTIVES:

The FIRST OBJECTIVE was this: to assert the fundamental truth and basic principle, that peace is the fruit of justice—that working for peace means, in fact, working for social justice. Without justice, there is no love. No Faith. No equality. No fairness. No decency. Without justice, there is no love of God, and, certainly, no love of neighbor.

And our SECOND OBJECTIVE was this: to firmly place the American Labor Movement in the category of those who, in fact, work for peace because the Labor Movement works for justice for working men and women.

If you look at America and ask the question: What group since the late 1800s has consistently worked for justice for the working men and women of America, what group comes to mind? What group has stood for equality, for solidarity, for "a just pay for a just day's work"?

Labor Leaders who spend their entire lives working in solidarity for justice for working men and women are, indeed, working for peace—not only nationally but also globally. Hence, Labor leaders are eminently qualified to be candidates for the World Peace Prize of 'Roving Ambassador for Peace.'

Of course, a memorable quote by Pope John Paul II, from one of his great Encyclicals helped us to make the case. Reflecting on the maxim "peace is the fruit of justice," the Pope declared: "Today, one could say, with the same exactness and the same power of biblical inspiration (cf. Isaiah 32:17; James 3:18) ... peace is the fruit of solidarity"—Encyclical, "Solicitude for social concerns ." 39. 1988.

Hence, Labor leaders are eminently qualified to be candidates for the World Peace Prize of Roving Ambassador for Peace. And to further affirm this principle, in 2018, the WPPAC created a secondary prize: World Peace Prize for Labor Leadership. Our Peace Prizes encourage members of the Labor Movement to positively think of themselves as not just fighters for justice, but as peace builders as well. Our World Peace Prize for Labor Leadership, in particular, makes the connection between Labor and peace. I believe this gives an important dimension to Labor's self-understanding, self-image, and self-identity.

I urge Labor leaders to proudly claim this identity, to embrace it, and to promote it among the AFL-CIO. It is a powerful way to advance Labor and promote solidarity."

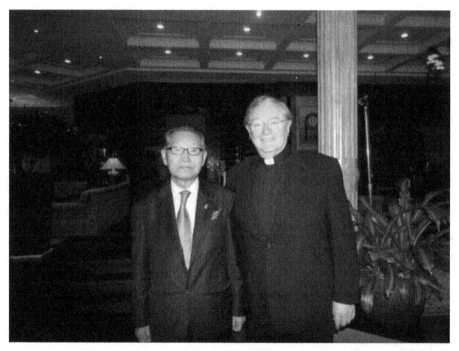

Dr. Han Min Su and Fr. Sean McManus in Seoul, 2013

Fr. Sean McManus, Barbara Flaherty, President Richard. L. Trumka. June 19, 2018.

President Richard L. Trumka was the inaugural recipient of the two World Peace Prizes: "Roving Ambassador for Peace" and "World Peace Prize for Labor Leadership"—thereby wonderfully launching the Prize within the AFL-CIO and throughout the entire American Labor Movement. He declared:

"I want to thank Barbara Flaherty, Fr. McManus and the World Peace Prize Awarding Council for recognizing the nexus between Organized Labor and peace. Too many times in the past we were not looked at as being part of the peace process. So, I really appreciate the World Peace Prize Awarding Council recognizing the connection between fighting for social justice and peace."

—President Richard L. Trumka, AFL-CIO in his acceptance address on receiving the World Peace Prize for Labor Leadership at AFL-CIO Headquarters in Washington, DC. June 19, 2018. (To review President Trumka's acceptance speech, go to vimeo.com/275953504).

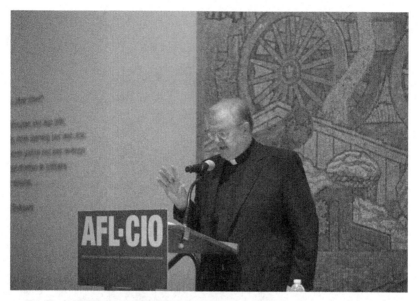

Fr. Sean McManus, Chief Judge, World Peace Prize Awarding Council and President of the Irish National Caucus, speaking at AFL-CIO Headquarters on the occasion of President Richard Trumka receiving the Roving Ambassador for Peace Prize. February 3, 2016.

Barbara Flaherty, Fr. McManus, President Trumka, Princess Nakamaru and Dr. Chai Ho Kim at AFL-CIO Headquarters. February 3, 2016.

Barbara Flaherty, Chairperson, closes the World Peace Prize Award Ceremony at AFL-CIO Headquarters. Feb. 3, 2016.

Induction Ceremony, Seoul, South Korea, 2013. Dr. Han is at the podium.

Fr. Sean McManus speaking at Induction Ceremony, Seoul, South Korea, 2013.

Barbara Flaherty speaks at Induction Ceremony, Seoul, South Korea, 2013.

Induction Ceremony, Seoul, South Korea, 2013.

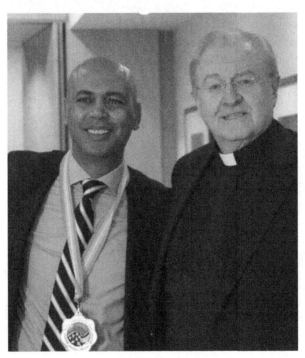

Tefere Gebre, Executive Vice President, AFL-CIO, received Roving Ambassador for Peace. Washington, DC. Dec. 5, 2017.

Liz Shuler, Secretary-Treasurer of AFL-CIO; Elizabeth Powell, Secretary-Treasurer of APWU; Esther Lopez, International Secretary-Treasurer of UFCW, recipients of the World Peace Prize for Labor Leadership. Feb. 5, 2019.

Barbara Flaherty, Roving Ambassador for Peace Monserrat Garibay, Secretary-Treasurer, Texas State AFL-CIO, and Fr. McManus. Austin. February 18, 2019.

And the mission continues with may more presentations to be made to worthy men and women of the American Labor Movement.
(Please see Appendix J for a list of judges and officers).

CHAPTER 20

IRISH AMERICAN PEACE PRIZE ANNOUNCED

First of its kind

CAPITOL HILL. Wednesday, October 23, 2018—A new Peace Prize has been launched from Washington, DC to honor and recognize individuals who have struggled for Irish justice over the past 50 years.

It is not primarily focused on public figures, the rich or the famous, but rather on "the real people" who spent many years in the background struggling to get America and Irish-Americans to stand up for justice in Northern Ireland/The North.

The "Irish American Peace Prize" is being launched by the Capitol Hill-based Irish National Caucus. The Prize consists of a beautiful plaque with an imprint of Irish National Caucus famous logo: the Dove of Peace super-imposed on the Shamrock. The citation declares:

Presented to [NAME]:

For dedcation to the founding principle of the Irish National Caucus:

"Ireland, too, has the right to be One Nation under God, indivisible, with liberty and justice for all."

Irish National Caucus president/founder Fr. Sean McManus explained: "We believe this Prize was needed to bring balance, truth and a sense of realism to the whole history of the past 50 years. And, I felt—as one of the persons who has been longest involved in the struggle (and still living!)—that I had a duty to launch the Irish American Peace Prize in order to honor real people who have been ignored: individuals who bore the heat of the day, who were not 'sunshine patriots,' and who were not afraid to take a stand when it was not fashionable or easy. The reality is that many Irish-Americans were too scared or disinterested to take a stand, and some just emerged when it was easy and had no cost... As is always the way, and as the history of Ireland amply illustrates. So far, the common reaction of those to whom I've spoken is: 'It's about time such a Prize was given.'"

Fr. McManus continued: "Anyone who did not struggle for justice, confronting British Government oppression in Northern Ireland does not deserve this Prize because to me, the only way to work for peace is to struggle against injustice. There is only one government in charge of Northern Ireland, and that is the British government, and that is where the buck stops. To ignore that fundamental fact is to cover up government injustice and to become complicit in that injustice. The Irish American Peace Prize will not cover up or be complicit.

The Irish American Peace Prize places justice at the heart and center of peace because, as the maxim states, peace is, indeed, the fruit of justice. Or, as Pope John Paul II added—in his reflection on that maxim—"peace is the fruit of solidarity" (Encyclical:Sollicitudo rei socialis: "Solicitude for social concerns") 1988. The Irish American Peace Prize is all about justice and solidarity, about opposing State-sponsored racism, sectarianism, and inequality in Northern Ireland, and about unity and peace."

Fr. McManus concluded: "We had considered such a Peace Prize for a long while. However, the idea crystallized and became more compelling through my work as Chief Judge of the World Peace Prize. In this work, we have presented the World Peace Prize to a number of Labor Leaders in the United States, and we will be traveling across the country to present the same Prize, so it seemed a very natural moment to institute the Irish American Peace Prize. I was, also, increasingly conscious if I waited much longer, some of these great, dedicated and humble individuals would be no longer with us. The names of the winners of the Irish American Peace Prize will be announced at the upcoming World Peace Prize events in different cities across the United States beginning in November."

To date, the recipients of the Irish American Peace Prize are Dick Stanton, IL.; George McLaughlin, RI; Neil Conway, OH; Tommy Clifford, MA., Shawn Sidway, FL; Mattie Reilly, NY; and Robert J. Bateman, NY.

Shawn Sidway, FL, is pictured with Fr. McManus receiving the Prize in front of the hallowed Rayburn House Office Building on Capitol Hill where he has done effective lobbying for equality, justice, and peace.

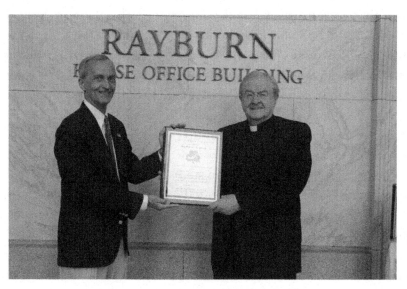

Shawn Sidway and Fr. McManus. 2019.

CHAPTER 21

Changing My Sky, Not My Soul

"Caelum non animum mutant qui trans mare current."
(*They change their sky but not their soul who cross the ocean.*)
Horace

ON NOVEMBER 19, 2011, I held a launch of the Irish edition of this book at the Maine Irish Heritage Center. I was very impressed by what those fine people are doing.

They have preserved the "historic landmark that was formerly St. Dominic's Church, a hub of early Irish community in Maine." They kindly presented me with a copy of the book *They Change Their Sky: The Irish in Maine*.[1] I am indebted to this excellent collection of essays for the Horace quote, for which in turn that book credits Thomas Cahill's *How The Irish Saved Civilization*.[2] Cahill says the Horace quote is, "a good maxim for all exiles, and in this context, a reminder of the constancy of the Irish personality."[3] (Daniel O'Connell, The Liberator, liked to use the Irish version of that proverb: "They change the climate, not their hearts, who leave their native shores."[4])

However, while crossing the Atlantic doesn't, and shouldn't, change one's soul, it does for sure change one's perspective—and not just geographically.

I am very conscious that I have changed my perspective. Growing up Catholic, and then being a member of a religious order, I was always acutely aware of the "common good"—of the importance of community, and that the individual is not autonomous and separate from society.

But living in America has also taught me the importance of individual freedom and the right to privacy. That was not always appreciated in Britain and Ireland, where State and Church were too intrusive. And, of course, in England, there is no separation between Church and State—the ultimate source of anti-Catholic sectarianism and bigotry, mandating that a Catholic cannot be Monarch.

I am consequently very grateful to America for giving me this perspective.

At the Speaker's Saint Patrick's Day Lunch, 2010, I was speaking to Congressman Russ Carnahan (D-MO) who had recently succeeded Congressman Bill Delahunt (D-MA) as the Chairman of the House Human Rights Sub Committee. I urged him to hold a Hearing. He said he would love to. I told him there was a group of human rights people from Ireland in Washington at that moment with whom he should meet. He immediately called his office, changed his appointments for the following day, and asked me to bring the group to his office in the morning. I brought along the Northern Ireland Human Rights Consortium, represented by a number of young, very competent human rights activists, one of whom was Aideen Gilmore, Deputy Director, Committee for the Administration of Justice, along with Jane Winter of British Irish Rights Watch. I secured a commitment from Congressman Carnahan that, indeed, he would hold a Hearing.

On September 16, 2010, Chairman Carnahan held the Hearing. Aideen Gilmore was one of the witnesses along with John Finucane, Pat's youngest son.

Then in December 2010, Rita O'Hare, Sinn Fein Representative to the United States, brought the Ballymurphy Massacre Committee to see me, seeking a Congressional Hearing on the British Army Massacre in 1971. I promised I would do all in my power to help.

In January 2011, the Republicans took over power in the House of Representatives. Thus, Congressman Carnahan lost the chairmanship of the House Human Rights Subcommittee. However, his successor could not have been more perfect: the admirable Congressman Chris Smith (R-NJ), a veteran holder of Congressional Hearings on injustices in Northern Ireland. He would also assure Chairmanship of The Helsinki Commission, which could also hold Hearings.

I worked closely with Congressman Smith's excellent staff, earnestly promoting the cause of the Ballymurphy Massacre Committee. On March 16, 2011, Congressman Smith held his thirteenth Northern Ireland Hearing. John Teggart, Chairman of the Ballymurphy Massacre Committee, gave excellent and very moving testimony. The eleven murdered victims of the British Army Massacre—including John's own father—would have been proud of his performance. And I was honored and humbled to have been able to help these noble Belfast families. **(See Appendix K on the film Ballymurphy Precedence.)**

Ciaran McAirt testified on the McGurk Bar bombing.[5]

In 2012, we focused on getting Mark Thompson, Relatives for Justice, Belfast, to testify. Oddly enough, Mark had never testified before Congress even though he has spent many years "in the trenches" doing very important work in exposing collusion and other forms of England's dirty war.

Again, we worked closely with Congressman Smith's excellent staff. And on March 21, 2012, the intrepid Congressman Smith held his fourteenth Hearing, with Mark Thompson being a witness—along with Mrs. Finucane, Christopher Stanley, British- Irish Watch, Dr. Patricia Lundy, University of Ulster and Brian Gormley, Director, Committee on the Administration of Justice.

So ... in 2009, 2010, 2011 and 2012—And right through to 2018—we have had Congressional Hearings on Human Rights in Northern Ireland. Tip O' Neill—who corruptly used his power to collude with the British government and ban Human Rights Hearings on Northern Ireland—must be turning in his grave. And, please God, we will continue to have Congressional Hearings—because at the end of the day, the only thing the British Government fears is opinion on Capitol Hill.

The writing of this book was a wonderful experience, and so was its launching and promotion. The first edition of this book was published by Collins Press, Cork. We launched it on April 5, 2011, in Dublin Castle—formerly, and ironically, the center of British administration for the whole island of Ireland. When I walked into the Castle, the first person who bounded up to shake my hand was Raymond Mc Cord: "We used to own this place, Sean," he chortled.

My brother Frank quipped, "No wonder the Brits held on to it for so long" (referring to its splendor and magnificence).

I was truly taken aback that three hundred guests showed up for the book launch. Frankie and the organizing committee—one of whom was my cousin, John McKay—had done a superb job. A key member of the committee was Donal Donnelly, who previously had his own book launch in Dublin Castle for his "Prisoner 1080"—a wonderful account of his famous escape from Crumlin Road Jail, Belfast, in 1960. Donal had been, like my brother Patrick, in the 1956 IRA campaign. Indeed, there were a number of 1956 veterans at the book launch, and I was proud to see them all. Tom Cooper, Irish National Congress, provided key support.

The two speakers at the event were Bobby Ballagh, the famous artist and ardent Irishman, and Vincent Browne, the noted Dublin journalist and broadcaster. Browne, whose job is to give everyone a hard time, conceded: "[Fr. McManus] stood out against powerful forces in a fight for justice and fairness. I didn't always agree with the causes he supported, but I admired his persistence, his courage, his relentlessness. And admiration that one person, almost alone, could make such impact on public policy in the United States."

During the proceedings, the Collins Press photographer assembled different people outside in the Castle yard to be photographed with me. The process seemed to last forever, and I found it hard to keep smiling all the time. At one point, as I turned round to my right, from shaking some well-wisher's hand, I noticed that the photographer had placed a small grey-haired man in position to be photographed with me. I immediately recognized him. I loudly asked: "Was this man dragooned into the photo?" He replied, shaking my hand, "Not at all, Father. I am proud to be here. Congratulations on your Memoirs."

It was the eminent Michael D. Higgins, whose sense of social justice and independence of mind I had always admired. He was running for president of Ireland and would be elected on October 27, 2011 ... And there he stood proudly holding my book for the cameras. He stayed for the entire event, listening to the speeches with great interest.

I was especially pleased and honored that my old friend and fervent Irish patriot Derek Warfield and his Young Wolfe Tones performed for the event.

Next, I had the book launch in Belfast, which was sponsored by Mairtin O'Muilleoir, publisher of *The Irish Echo* and hosted by Mark Thompson and Clara Reilly, Relatives for Justice.

Then it was onto Bellaghy, where Oliver Hughes hosted me at the Wolfe Tone's GAA. Deputy First Minister, Martin McGuinness, had planned to attend the book launch in Bellaghy, but at the last minute, he had to cancel. However, he graciously telephoned me before the event to apologize.

Next, it was back to my home turf. My brother Frankie and his organizing committee assembled a large crowd at the Enniskillen Library. The well-known Peter Quinn, former president of the GAA, was the speaker. I was honored that Michelle Gildernew, MP for Fermanagh and S. Tyrone, attended the book launch, and spoke warmly and supportively.

I was deeply touched by the enthusiasm and support at all three book launches in Ireland. It was a wonderful experience.

Then it was back to Washington. We had the Capitol Hill book launch on May 1, 2011. The indefatigable Barbara Flaherty ran the show and since then has been the prime promoter of my book—demonstrating remarkable devotion to the success of the project. She has played a key, and central role in all the book launches: Boston, New York City; the Ladies and Men's AOH New York State Convention, Pearl River, NY; Woodlawn, Bronx, NY; Philadelphia, PA; Seattle, WA; Portland, ME; Cleveland, OH; Greensboro, NC; Greenville, SC; and New York City.

Barbara, who had become Executive Vice President of the Irish National Caucus, generously remarksed "Working on the project is a labor of love. It is a truly joyful experience." Indeed, she maintains the book will be made into a movie!

Over the years, I had to cut back on speaking around the country, so the book tour has given me an opportunity to see a lot of people I had not seen in a long time, as well as meeting new faces. It was heartening to see that Irish-Americans are still as nice as I discovered them to be when I first came to America in 1972, and that they still care deeply about justice and peace in Ireland. I am so proud of them.

I am particularly grateful to the Ladies AOH and the AOH for all their support. They very graciously and generously provided me with a platform all across the U.S. to promote my book. Mary Hogan, former National Secretary and National President of the LAOH, became a most enthusiastic promoter of my book. She has done excellent work in spreading the word. Mary says: "Fr. McManus' book is a blessing to the LAOH. It is educational and inspiring—and full of spiritual insights into how working for justice is at the heart of the Gospel and the teaching of the Catholic Church."

Dan Dennehy, National Chairman of the AOH Immigration Committee, is also a key leader. He has shown impressive commitment to Irish immigrants in general, and especially to the case of "the Deportees"—those who fell through the cracks of the Clinton initiative that gave permanent status to those who had to flee Ireland to escape from The Troubles. Malachy McAllister and Matt Morrison are two of the better-known cases.

Another key player on immigration issues is Mayo-born Ciaran Staunton with whom I'm proud to work. Ciaran, a brother-in-law of publisher Niall O'Dowd, played a vital role with Niall in facilitating Sinn Fein's dramatic and successful entrance onto the American scene.

Owen Rodgers, a proud native of County Tyrone, has been a strong, dependable ally for many years. He specializes in providing forums for important Irish issues and has twice hosted my book-launches in New York City.

I am very gratified by the American response to the previous Editions of this book. I trust Irish-Americans will find this Third Edition enlightening and helpful. I have been particularly struck by the number of people who have told me they have read my book twice—some even three or five times. That has to be pleasing to any author. Perhaps the most fulsome praise of all came from the late great Bill Flynn, Chairman Emeritus, Mutual of America and Chairman, National Committee on American Foreign Policy. He telephoned to tell me he was profoundly moved by reading my book, saying, "Your book's authenticity is its crowning glory."

Forty-seven years ago, I came to America. I based my work on three principles:

1. A Catholic principle, spelled out in official Church teaching: "Action on behalf of justice ... [is] a constitutive dimension to the preaching of the Gospel ..." (Justice in the World. Synod of Bishops. 1971).

2. An American principle: Respect for international human rights is an integral part of American foreign policy.

3. An Irish National Caucus principle: US dollars should not subsidize anti-Catholic discrimination in Northern Ireland (the genesis of the MacBride Principles). **(For a useful summary read my "Trilogy of Articles" and "The Best Kept Secret of the Catholic Church" from the Irish Echo in Appendix G).**

These principles are still valid. And, the work must continue, especially because of Brexit, which is a large part of our work.

I wrote this book—over and above the reasons already given—to provide Irish-Americans with a tool to replenish, reinvigorate and recharge the Irish cause in America—to be, in effect, a handbook for all authentic Irish-American activists.. I hope I have succeeded because we still have a long way to go, and it is imperative that we keep America involved in standing up for justice and peace in Ireland. That remains the key and is now as important as ever. And I pledge that the Irish National

Caucus will stay the course…until Ireland, too, has the right to be One Nation under God, indivisible, with liberty and justice for all.

I believe now more than ever before the words of Fr. Haring, previously quoted: "If strength and resolve to become witnesses to justice, peace and nonviolence do not flow from our Eucharistic celebrations, then we must fearfully and sadly conclude that far too many priestly and lay Christian vocations are not sufficiently authentic."

I have stressed throughout this book that struggling for justice is at the very heart of the Judeo-Christian faith. To me, it is also the essence of being authentically Irish.

Thus, I was honored and blessed to celebrate in Kinawley in August 2018 my faith and my calling on the occasion of my 50th. Anniversary of my Ordination. **(Please see my sermon and extended family photo in Appendix H).**

Epilogue

Rem tene, verba sequentur
Cato the Elder[1]

As I've said, writing this book—and updating the different Editions, including this Third Edition of 2019—has been quite an experience: joyful, sorrowful, exciting, frustrating. But above all, it has been liberating to get all that stuff out of my head and onto paper. I knew I would not be content until I did so.

Furthermore, I was very aware if I did not write this book, with all its editions nobody would—indeed, nobody could. Nobody—and certainly no Catholic priest—ever moved to Capitol Hill to lobby the U.S. Congress full-time and for as long as I have, with one mission: to maximize American pressure on the British government to end injustice in Northern Ireland and to create unity, justice, and peace in Ireland.

Of course, one disadvantage of going through—again and again—almost forty-seven years of files is that it raises a lot of ghosts, and inevitably rakes up old issues one had put to rest, to a great extent....But as Lincoln said, we cannot escape history. In retelling the story, and revisiting the evidence in cold print, I could feel the old righteous Kinawley anger bubbling up again—especially, it must be confessed, at the Dublin government and the likes of Jack Lynch, Garret FitzGerald, and their protégés in Ireland and in the Irish Embassy in Washington, DC.

I should point out one thing here. For much of this book, I have referred to the "Dublin" government. However, because of my respect for the way Taoiseach Albert Reynolds bravely supported the peace process—as did Bertie Ahern—and in deference to the person and office of President Mary McAleese and President Michael D. Higgins—I no longer use that terminology. Instead, I use the term, Irish government. As a Northerner, I was deeply encouraged when Mary McAleese became the Irish president. I saw it as a critical and integral part of the peace process. I have been proud of the way she has reached out to Northerners, especially the Unionists/Loyalists/Protestants.

And, now, since the Irish Embassy and consulates have ceased their campaigns to vilify and demonize me—in order to cover up British injustice—I have no longer reason to be angry at them. Indeed, I am now able to appreciate the important work they do in support of the peace process. I am grateful that there are no more Sean Donlons, Michael Lillises, Carmel Heaneys, or others trying to block my work.

I had considered editing out "the old anger" (in previous editions and in this 2019 Edition) but decided that would be unrealistic and unhistorical. Anger at injustice was an integral part, an ever-present-dynamic of The Troubles—at least for those who were troubled by injustice. Furthermore, one cannot understand The Troubles if one does not understand the anger of Catholics at how they were treated by the British government, and how they were abandoned by the Irish government, with all the resulting feeling of powerlessness that entailed. (That is why I greatly welcomed current Taoiseach Leo Varadkar's promise that the Irish government would never again abandon the Nationalist/Republicans/Catholics in The North. And I was proud to shake his hand at the 2019 Irish Embassy's Saint Patrick's Day reception. Of course, the fact that his family in India was part of the resistance to the British Empire was an added bonus!)

Now, of course, anger can lead to very bad things—spite, revenge, and murder. That is why I use the term "righteous anger." My online dictionary says: "Righteous is similar in meaning to virtuous but also implies freedom from guilt or blame (i.e., righteous anger)." St. Thomas Aquinas tells us that anger used for revenge is bad, but good when used to "maintain justice."[2] God himself showed righteous anger at injustice. He told Moses, "I have observed the misery of my people; I have heard their cry on account of their taskmasters. Indeed, I know their sufferings, and I have come down to deliver them. (Exodus 3:7). God also tells us in Exodus that if we practice injustice, His "anger will be aroused." (22:23). The Hebrew prophets and Jesus Himself showed righteous anger. The Black Freedom Struggle in the United States would never have succeeded had Martin Luther King, Jr. not blazed with righteous anger at injustice. But when did Irish bishops (with a few exceptions) show sustained righteous anger at British injustice? I, long ago, came to the conviction that my righteous anger could only be channeled through nonviolence. But (and this is something apparently often forgotten) "nonviolence" is only short for "nonviolent resistance." Many of the reports on the death of the late Cardinal Daly mentioned he was "committed to nonviolence." Well, whatever the cardinal was committed to, it certainly was not nonviolence. Unless you resist, you are not practicing nonviolence. If you close your eyes to injustice and violence—as so many churchmen do—you are not being nonviolent: you are being cowardly, lazy and indifferent to human suffering. Instead of "staying out of politics" you are being complicit in the worst politics of all—political collaboration in oppression and injustice.

I have told my story. It is not the full story, and it is certainly not the only story: many dedicated people in America were doing a lot of work of which I was not even aware, but they must give their own account. I feel it is a blessing from the Lord to have been able to do what I've done. Others might have done it better, but they did not do it, so I had to do it the best I could. In my haste to get the job done, I may have rubbed some people the wrong way, and for that I am sorry. But I always tried to treat people with kindness and respect.

Since I started writing this book, my large family has again been visited by death—but equally by the sure hope of eternal life. My lovely sister Celia in Enniskillen died from cancer on November 24, 2008, at the age of seventy-seven, and my indomitable brother Thomas, in Cornwall on the Hudson, New York, died on May 16, 2009, at the age of seventy-six, after a long battle with Alzheimer's. And since I started writing this

2019 Edition, my sister Mary Kate, who had been living in Clonliff and was the eldest in the family, died on February 5, 2019, at age 92.

I am hopeful for the future of Ireland—the whole island of Ireland. Even though, I think, we have still a long way to go. I believe "the Union" will die on the vine. And Brexit has hastened that. The only way the Union can be saved is if the IRA came back into business. One of the great Irish ironies! But it is an irony I hope that patriotic young Irish men and women take heed of: no Irish person need be killed—or kill—for full Irish freedom.

There is one thing. however, that really concerns me about the present process: the digging-in of MI5. Instead of disengaging, they are building a massive infrastructure in Northern Ireland.

Their withdrawal would, in one sense, be more important than that of the British Army (which, of course, is still there). The British Army has always been just the crude symbol of British rule in Ireland. How often were there pitched battles between the British Army and the IRA in the past fifty years?

British control of Ireland has always essentially been a policing and intelligence operation. I believe acceptable policing will eventually be achieved. But even with the best of good faith, the police will have absolutely no control over MI5. And that shadowy organization can so easily manipulate the still deeply entrenched anti-Catholic sectarianism in The North.

However, I want to finish this book on an appreciative note. I am deeply grateful to former British Prime Minister, Tony Blair. He is the only British prime minister of whom I could ever think kindly. And God rest Mo Mowlam. She, more than anyone else, symbolized the sea change that was going to take place in Britain's attitude toward Ireland. When she saw me at an event in Washington, she came right over and said, "You're the MacBride Principles priest," and hugged me. Being hugged by a British minister was definitely a new experience for me. And, of course, like all Irish-Americans, I will always be grateful to Bill and Hillary Clinton. Without them, there would not have been an Irish peace process. And I salute the leadership of Gerry Adams and the late

Martin McGuinness. They pulled off the impossible. God bless them both.

From the bottom of my heart, I am grateful to all those dedicated and generous Irish-Americans who made my work possible. I could not have done a thing without them. They are the salt of the earth. Nor could I have done anything without some magnificent Members of Congress. I was always particularly moved by help from members who were not Irish or Catholic. The entire Jewish American Congressional delegation over the past forty-seven years has been superb. There are too many members to mention by name, but here are some of them: Lester Wolff (D-NY) 1965-1973; the already mentioned Dick Ottinger; Nita Lowey (D-NY); Elliott Engel (D-NY); Gary Ackerman (D-NY) former vice-chairman of the House Foreign Affairs Committee; Senator Chuck Schumer (D-NY); and, of course, the great Ben Gilman.

The late Don Payne (D-NJ), as I kept telling him, had been to Northern Ireland more often than I had. That African-American Baptist lent the moral authority—and the insight—of Martin Luther King, Jr. to the Irish cause.

It gives me great ecumenical joy when Protestant Irish-American Members of Congress stand up for justice and peace in Ireland. Carolyn Maloney (D-NY) is a Presbyterian and a fervent Irish woman. As a member of New York City Council, she strongly backed the MacBride Principles and takes great pride in having played a key role in naming a street after Joe Doherty when he was imprisoned in New York.

The other ethnic group that has featured very significantly in my work are the Italian Americans. I have already mentioned Mario Biaggi, who, despite massive opposition, stayed the course and backed me all the way. Former Speaker Nancy Pelosi is also Italian American. When she became Speaker, she did not follow Democrat Tip O'Neill's disgraceful ban on human rights hearings on Northern Ireland. Speaker Pelosi—when she was Speaker the first time—always invited me to her Saint Patrick's Day Lunch—as, indeed, did Speaker Newt Gingrich (R-GA) and Speaker Denny Hastert (R-IL).

But I have to pay tribute to another great Italian lady—not a Member of Congress, but my valued and trusted colleague in the Irish National Caucus—Barbara Flaherty. Barbara was first introduced to the Irish community in 1968 by her late husband, Martin, who was born and reared in Galway. Once—when I was singing the praises of Kinawley—he shot back: "The only good thing that ever came out of Kinawley was the road to Galway." He was a committed Irish patriot. After his death, Barbara wanted, in his honor, to devote more time to the Irish cause. Since then, she has played a key role in the Irish National Caucus—and in the production of this book. I can never adequately thank her for her help and counsel, and the friendship of her wonderful family.

Finally, let me conclude with a profession of faith, so to speak. After all these years, I still believe that God is the mystery at the center of all reality; that Jesus Christ is the Person at the center of all human history; that the Holy Spirit gathers us all into the Body of Christ—the Church, which is the Sacrament of Christ on earth. Throughout my long struggle, I have—despite my faults and failures—been sustained by faith and prayer and nourished by the Word of God and the Eucharist—the Bread of Life and the Cup of Eternal Salvation.

God bless America and God save Ireland.

APPENDIX A
The Carn Lintel
by Patrick Maguire

(Thoughts on a visit to Carn with American cousins. August 20, 2002)

Tired and hungry fields, receding, as the gorse reclaims its space,
Our ancestral tracks have vanished, footprints faded beyond trace.
Vengeful bramble, angry briar, that for long were held at bay,
Boldly colonize the meadow where my mother trampled hay.

Where the spud proliferated, with the cabbage and the corn,
Greedy rushes are competing with the thistle and the thorn.
And the path up to the bogland purple heather now conceals
Where, in sunshine, neighbours ambled with their donkeys and their creels.

Scalloped thatch has long since fallen on this little house that's died.
Still the naked walls are standing ... sadly ... strangely dignified.
Now the chimney lies in rubble, choking up the cold fireplace,
And a rusty crook's protruding from the ruins of the brace.

Nettles, tall as were my uncles, stretch up from the strewn floor
And yet, the stubborn lintel sullenly protects the door.
Persevering through the decades, resolutely standing fast,
Tireless, it maintains the portal; guards this entrance to our past.

Fr. Sean McManus

Underneath its rugged toughness life was played across the years.
Here were scenes of hope and heartache; joy and laughter; anguished tears.
Here were cameos enacted in a drama of the strife
Of a family for survival - in the tragedy of life.

O'er this threshold, worn and weathered, once a girl was borne, with pride,
By a young man—my grandfather—celebrating his new bride.
Was that moment lost, I wonder; had it gone beyond recall,
When, by hand, my sister led him, in his dotage, lest he'd fall?

In the years intervening, sons and daughters travelled through;
Maggie, Celia, Katie, Alice, Terence, James, Pat, Felix, Hugh.
From beneath this guardian lintel, each first looked upon the world.
Back through here they ran for refuge, as their early lives unfurled.

Hence they went as carefree youngsters; off to school… to church… to dance;
Later, forth to work and marriage, and to fight a war in France.
Here the ceilidhers were greeted, welcome of a winter's night.
(Others came, though uninvited, black and tanned, at dawn's first light.)

Round this doorway neighbors huddled; men came in, with voices low,
Muttered, "Sorry for your trouble", on an August evening, long ago.
So the family decremented, till but one was left to cope,
With the cross of aged parents and the withering of hope.

Then the long and lonely winters, in the turf and tilley light;
One alone where there'd been many, in the cold and silent night.
Till the solitude and shadows sapped, at last, the will to try
And the fire was raked forever and the house was left to die.

Now, some forty years later, ruined; derelict; and yet
There remains a sense of life here; this is not a place of death.
What has pulled us here together, some who've never met before?
What has drawn us from the distance back to this, our common core?

Are there threads we are unaware of; bonds we do not comprehend?
Links that cross the generations and our simple thoughts transcend?
Is there something here of others; those who left long, long ago?
Susan, Catherine and Bessie; Jemmy, Terry, Hugh and Joe?

Underneath this granite lintel they too passed in younger days;
Travelled tracks that are no longer; moved along those mountain ways.
Here they loved and laughed together, whispered secrets, hopes and fears,
In the days before New Zealand; long before the Boston years.

Yes, the golden thatch has perished; stones, once white, are hushed and grey.
Now the stacks of weeds and briars stand instead of turf and hay.
While we have spread across the world, nature has regained its space
But, beneath this, here we have yet a sense of place.

APPENDIX B

Lloyd George and Churchill: Racist and Anti-Catholic Creators of Northern Ireland

Lloyd George (1863-1945) was Prime Minister from 1916-1922. He like all the British leaders of this period was a vicious, virulent anti-Catholic bigot. He is on record of declaring he hated all Catholic priests. Imagine if an American president in the past one hundred years was on record of stating he hated all Black pastors. Imagine the message, the dog-whistle, that would have sent to all African-Americans—and, equally, to all White racists.

This was the bigot who would go on to set up the sectarian state of Northern Ireland, along with Winston Churchill, a racist imperialist and also virulently anti-Catholic. For example, Churchill wrote: "Superstitious faith in nations rarely promotes their industry…[Catholicism] … checks our growth and saps our strength [impeding] the improvement of the British breed …"

In 1911, Churchill wrote in a letter to his wife: "The Catholic Church has ruined every country in which it has been supreme. … In 1961, Churchill's biographer son—without any sense of embarrassment or shame—published that letter under the very revealing title of "The

364

Curse of Catholicism." Imagine if an American president referred to the "curse of Judaism" or the "curse of Blacks."

On December 23, 1920, the Government of Ireland Act would partition Ireland—the artificial State of Northern Ireland would come into existence in 1921. But the word "partition" doesn't quite capture the reality, implying that the country was divided into co-equal parts: North and South. In reality, six Counties in the northeast were torn away from Ireland, which is composed of thirty-two counties—and torn, too, from the province of Ulster, which is composed of Nine Counties, not six counties.

Why were County Donegal (the most northern County in Ireland), County Cavan and County Monaghan not included in "Northern Ireland"? Well—while some may be reluctant to state it—the plain, historical truth is this: had these three Counties been included, there would be too many Catholics in the new, artificial State of Northern Ireland for the British government and the Unionists to control in what was designed to be an anti-Catholic state.

In 1920, the Unionist/Protestant leader and founder of the State of Northern Ireland, Edward Carson, MP bluntly stated in the British Parliament the reality of these statistics:

> "The figures will at once show where the difficulty comes in. We have to refer in these matters to Protestants and Catholics—we should only be making the very greatest camouflage of argument if we did not treat them in that way—because these are really the burning question over there. The inclusion of these six counties would bring in under the jurisdiction of the north of Ireland parliament 820,000 protestants out of 890,000 in the whole province [counting Donegal, Cavan, and Monaghan]. On the other hand, while you would leave out 70,000 who are in these three counties [Donegal, Cavan, and Monaghan], you would bring in from these three counties into the northern province, an additional 260,000

Roman Catholics." (Edward Carson. Westminster. May 18, 1920).

The Dublin-born Carson and the northern Unionists felt free to set up their sectarian, anti-Catholic state because they knew that all the top British leaders were deeply and venomously anti-Catholic: Robert Cecil, "Bloody" Balfour, Asquith, Lloyd George, Churchill, Bonar Law—imperialists, bigots and racists, every one of them. Even worse, that irrational religious bigotry was condoned and enshrined in the top law of England: the Act of Settlement, 1701—the foundation stone of the Royal Family—that forbids a Catholic from inheriting the English Throne. (That would be like having a provision in the US Constitution forbidding a Black person from being president).So, ultimately, it is the unwritten, uncodified British constitution that provides the foundation for sectarian, anti-Catholic bigotry in Northern Ireland—the extreme Orangemen were just being loyal to the anti-Catholic bigotry and sectarianism of the British un-written and un-codified constitution.

APPENDIX C

FR. MCMANUS, ENOCH POWELL AND THE REDEMPTORIST INFORMER

Capitol Hill. Thursday, March 19, 2015—Everyone connected with Northern Ireland has become conscious of Informers. They seem to have been everywhere: in the IRA, Sinn Fein, the Loyalists/Unionists, the political parties, North and South, the Dublin Government, etc.

However, Fr. Sean McManus—president of the Capitol Hill-based Irish National Caucus—has become aware of maybe the most unlikely informer of them all: a Redemptorist priest who once lived in the same monastery as Fr. McManus in England: the late Fr. Douglas (Duggie) Brice, CSsR, who died in1989.

Fr. McManus takes up the extraordinary story: "I received a Google Alert informing me that I was mentioned in a book on Enoch Powell. My first reaction was that it was a mistake. I surely would not appear, I thought, in a book about that old racist Englishman who was ranting and raving about blocking all immigration into Britain, while I was still based there. When Powell's racism became unfashionable even for the Tories, he fled to a safe haven for bigotry—Northern Ireland, where Unionists/Protestants proudly elected him as MP (1974–79).

But Google had made no mistake. I was, indeed, the Sean McManus mentioned in the book on Powell. The only thing more surprising than being mentioned in the book was the reason."

The book in question is *ENOCH POWELL AND THE MAKING OF POSTCOLONIAL BRITAIN* by Camilla Schofield. Cambridge University Press. 2013. Page 306-307.

In May 1971, there was a national Census in Britain and Northern Ireland. Many Catholics in The North, including many priests and teachers, refused to comply with the Census, as a protest against the corruption of the judicial system and the wholesale violation of civil rights. Fr. McManus, deciding to take a lone stand in Britain, refused to comply with the Census as a gesture of solidarity.

Fr. McManus was based in Liverpool at the time, at the Redemptorist Monastery. The local Catholic newspaper, Catholic Pictorial, ran a rather melodramatic story, "Why I, a Priest, Will Risks Prison." (But at least the newspaper had the courage to run it).

The book on Powell picks up the narrative:

"Much like his rejection of the civilizing principles of the Commonwealth and Trevor Huddleston's Christian socialist activism against apartheid in South Africa—on Ulster, Powell continually criticized the translation of Christian teaching into radical political practice. In the early 1970s, a Catholic priest from Liverpool—a city with a large Irish community—started keeping Powell regularly informed of radical Irish priests' activities in the United Kingdom. Their correspondence began when the priest sent Powell a newspaper cutting from the Catholic Pictorial entitled, "Why I, a Priest, Will Risk Prison," which included an interview with a young, radical priest named Father Sean McManus.

Powell's informer wrote to Powell in the accompanying letter, "This man Sean McManus has all the qualities of skillfulness that go to make an outstanding troublemaker, and there are many of his kind about."

Powell quickly replied. The interview had touched a nerve: when asked [by Catholic Pictorial], 'Does the division of Ireland, in your opinion then, contravene Christian rights?' McManus had answered, 'Very definitely. The basic right of any country is to freedom and independence. It is a grave act of immorality that any country should be artificially divided, like Ireland, against the vast majority of the people.'

To this Powell wrote Brice, "I was particularly struck by the expression, used in one of the questions, 'Christian rights.' The more one reflects upon it, the more profound and significant is the contradiction in terms."

Over the next two years, Powell's informer would continue to send information to Powell regarding radicalism in Britain's Irish Catholic community. "Let me make it perfectly clear," he told Powell, "an Irish Catholic clergyman would not think twice about giving active material assistance to the IRA. I have lived with the IRA for years."

In 1972, less than a month after Bloody Sunday, Powell's informer wrote:

> "The Hatred of these men is implacable, and as they do not appreciate being allowed to come to England and permitted to live here, I think -- with I am sure, a lot of others—that the 'ever open door' for which this country is well known, should now be closed, and that trouble-makers should either be sent home or issued with Passports ... At the moment they are like fleas in the mattress."

Powell forwarded the priest's reports to a Detective Inspector Waller and, by 1973, the priest had become a police informant.

Footnote number 208 on page 306 identifies Fr. Brice as the informer: "Why I a Priest, Will Risk Prison," Catholic Pictorial, no date; Douglas Brice, Letter to Powell, July 25, 1971, 'Immigration Cases open at Feb. 1974,' SRO D4490/4.

Fr. McManus said: "If anyone had told me 40 years ago that a fellow Redemptorist would be an Informer, I just would not have believed it. And look how the author, Camilla Schofield describes me—'a radical young priest.' For just refusing to comply with the Census? Hell, I hadn't even gotten started! But it does show clearly how much the Irish in Britain were supposed to keep their heads down. One could speak about anything in Britain—except one thing: British Government oppression of Catholics in Northern Ireland. That was the one remaining taboo, and it applied with a vengeance to young Irish priests."

It also illustrates that if the Brits could get an old Redemptorist priest like Fr. Brice, who was then in his 70s, to become an informer, then whom could they not turn into informers—especially over a forty years-span of The Troubles?"

Fr. McManus concluded: "The Census protest led to my being transferred to Scotland because of the commotion caused in Liverpool... and eventually to my being 'transported' (to use the old word for Irish 'troublemakers' being shipped off into exile to Van Diemen's Land/ Tasmania) to the United States on October 2, 1972. I knew that Catholic MPs in England put pressure on the Cardinal of England, Cardinal Heenan (1905—1975) who put pressure on Fr. Charles (Charlie) Shepherd, the Provincial of the London Province of Redemptorists. But I never knew that the old racist, anti-Irish, Enoch Powell had a role in trying to silence me about British Government injustice in Northern Ireland.

But thank you, Enoch, thank you Duggie, thank you, Charlie, I was exiled to the one place on earth where I could do the most good for Irish justice—the good old US of A. God works in mysterious ways!

APPENDIX D
Telegram Protesting Fr. McManus' Invitation to White House

CONFIDENTIAL

FM WASHINGTON 190112Z APR
TO PRIORITY F C O
TELEGRAM NUMBER 1538 OF 19 APRIL.
INFO DUBLIN, NIO BELFAST, NIO LONDON, BIS NEW YORK.

IRISH NATIONAL CAUCUS: MEETING WITH PRESIDENT CARTER.

1. I AM GRATEFUL TO THE DEPARTMENT FOR ALERTING ME TO THE REPORT IN THE IRISH PRESS OF 11 APRIL THAT FATHER SEAN MCMANUS, NATIONAL DIRECTOR OF THE IRISH NATIONAL CAUCUS, WAS TO MEET PRESIDENT CARTER AT THE WHITE HOUSE THAT DAY AS ONE OF 150 REPRESENTATIVES OF QUOTE ETHNIC AND FRATERNAL ORGANISATIONS UNQUOTE INVITED TO A BRIEFING ON INTERNATIONAL AFFAIRS.

2. WE IMMEDIATELY TOOK THE MATTER UP WITH THE STATE DEPARTMENT, FIRST AT DEPARTMENTAL LEVEL AND SUBSEQUENTLY WITH VEST, MAKING IT CLEAR THAT WE WERE SERIOUSLY CONCERNED THAT MCMANUS, A SELF-CONFESSED SUPPORTER OF THE PIRA, SHOULD BE INVITED TO THE WHITE HOUSE AND GIVEN THE OPPORTUNITY TO CLAIM OFFICIAL RECOGNITION FOR THE AIMS OF HIS ORGANISATION. VEST, WHO SAID THAT THE STATE DEPARTMENT HAD NOT KNOWN OF THE INVITATION UNTIL WE RAISED IT WITH THEM, UNDERTOOK TO ENSURE THAT BRZEZINSKI, WHO WAS TO ADDRESS THE GROUP AFTER THEIR INITIAL MEETING WITH THE PRESIDENT, WAS ADEQUATELY BRIEFED, BUT SAID HE COULD DO NOTHING TO HAVE THE INVITATION RESCINDED AT THAT LATE STAGE.

3. MCMANUS DID ATTEND THE WHITE HOUSE MEETING (THE FIRST TIME HE HAS MET THE PRESIDENT SINCE CARTER'S UNFORTUNATE REMARKS ON NORTHERN IRELAND DURING THE 1976 ELECTION CAMPAIGN). LIKE OTHERS PRESENT, HE WAS PHOTOGRAPHED WITH THE PRESIDENT AND SUBSEQUENTLY RAISED THE QUESTION OF HUMAN RIGHTS IN NORTHERN IRELAND WITH BRZEZINSKI. BRZEZINSKI TOLD MCMANUS THAT THE BRITISH AND US AUTHORITIES HAD THE SAME VIEW OF TERRORISM BUT, FROM ANOTHER ACCOUNT WE HAVE RECEIVED, IT SEEMS THAT BRZEZINSKI MAY HAVE BEEN RATHER MORE EQUIVOCAL. I UNDERSTAND THE IRISH TIMES CARRIES A REPORT BEARING OUT THIS SECOND VIEW.

CONFIDENTIAL /4.

4. IT IS INTOLERABLE THAT THE PRESIDENT OF THE UNITED STATES SHOULD INVITE TO THE WHITE HOUSE THE REPRESENTATIVE OF AN ORGANISATION WHICH SUPPORTS THE PROVISIONAL IRA AND WHICH IS OVERTLY HOSTILE TO THE BRITISH GOVERNMENT. THE IRISH AMBASSADOR, WHO WAS AWAY AT THE TIME, ALSO TAKES A VERY SERIOUS VIEW, AND INTENDS TO COMPLAIN.

5. WHEN I SAW BRZEZINSKI TODAY I PROTESTED STRONGLY TO HIM ABOUT WHAT HAD HAPPENED. HE SAID HE DID NOT KNOW WHO FATHER MCMANUS WAS, NOR THAT HE HAD BEEN AT THE WHITE HOUSE BRIEFING. WHEN I TOLD HIM ABOUT THE LINKS BETWEEN THE IRISH NATIONAL CAUCUS AND THE SUPPLY OF ARMS TO THE IRA AND THAT IT WAS AS BAD FOR MCMANUS TO BE RECEIVED AT THE WHITE HOUSE AS IT WOULD BE IF THE BRITISH PRIME MINISTER RECEIVED ONE OF THE IRANIAN TERRORISTS AT NUMBER 10, BRZEZINSKI ENTIRELY AGREED. SOMEONE ELSE MUST HAVE DONE THE INVITING. HE WOULD SEND A NOTE ABOUT IT. I ASKED HIM IF HE COULD GIVE ME AN ASSURANCE THAT MCMANUS WOULD NOT BE INVITED TO THE WHITE HOUSE AGAIN. HE SAID HE COULD DO SO THREE YEARS OUT OF FOUR, BUT I WOULD UNDERSTAND THE POLITICS INVOLVED. I SAID THAT IT WAS MORE THAN POLITICS. IT WAS INTOLERABLE FOR THE PRESIDENT TO BE ENTERTAINING A TERRORIST OF THIS KIND. BRZEZINSKI AGAIN SAID THAT HE ENTIRELY AGREED.

HENDERSON

FILES
RID
NAD
OID
WED
MAED
NEWS.D
SEC.D
PUSD
PS
PS/LPS
PS/MR HURD
PS/MR RIDLEY

PS/MR BLAKER
PS/PUS
SIR.D.MAITLAND
SIR.A.ACLAND
CHIEF CLERK
MR FIGG
MR BULLARD
MR FERGUSSON
LORD N.G.LENNOX
MISS BROWN

ADDITIONAL DIST:
NORTHERN IRELAND

CONFIDENTIAL

Telegram reveals British fury over McManus invite.

Ray O'Hanlon, *The Irish Echo.* October 14, 2014.

Fr. McManus and President Jimmy Carter at the April 11, 1980, gathering in the White House.

He has campaigned for fair employment and human rights in Northern Ireland and beyond; he has penned books, non-fiction and fiction; and now he is on a committee that chooses winners of an international peace prize.

But Fr. Sean McManus was viewed by London as being little more than a terrorist during his early years as founder and president of the Washington, D.C.-based Irish National Caucus.

This is confirmed by the contents of a "confidential" telegram dating back to 1980 and written by a top British diplomat.

Dated April 21, 1980, the telegram was written by then British ambassador to the United States, the late Sir Nicholas Henderson.

The telegram was disseminated to "Dublin, Belfast and British Information, New York."

A handwritten "Prime Minister" on the document would appear to indicate that it was also sent to then British Prime Minister Margaret Thatcher.

The two-page typed telegram, a copy of which was recently obtained by the INC, complains that the Fermanagh-born Fr. McManus had been invited to the White House on April 11 to meet with President Jimmy Carter.

The INC was present at the meeting, featuring representatives of about 150 fraternal and ethnic organizations and which included an address on international affairs by President Carter's National Security Advisor, Zbigniew Brzezinski.

Ambassador Henderson outlines in the communication that he had attempted to have McManus blocked from attending the meeting.

He states that upon learning that Fr. McManus was invited, the matter had been "immediately" taken up with the U.S. State Department, first at department level and subsequently with a high-ranking official at State.

Henderson wrote that he had made it clear that the British embassy and government were "seriously concerned" that McManus, "a self-confessed supporter" of the PIRA (Provisional IRA) should be invited to the White House "and given the opportunity to claim official recognition for the aims of his organization."

Henderson wrote that the contacted official had said that the State Department had not known of the invitation until "we raised it with them."

The official had undertaken to ensure that Brzezinski "was adequately briefed," but Henderson added that the official had said that he could do nothing to have the invitation rescinded at that late stage.

Henderson went on to say that McManus did attend the White House meeting while stating, in parentheses, "the first time he has met the president since Carter's unfortunate remarks on Northern Ireland during the 1976 election campaign."

Henderson continued: "Like others present, he was photographed with the president and subsequently raised the question of human rights in Northern Ireland with Brzezinski."

Brzezinski told McManus that the British and US authorities had the same view of terrorism but, from another account, we have received, it seems that Brzezinski may have been rather more equivocal."

Henderson states that "it is intolerable that the President of the United States should invite to the White House, a representative of an organization which supports the Provisional IRA and which is overtly hostile to the British Government. The Irish Ambassador, who was away at the time, also takes a very serious view, and intends to complain."

Ambassador Henderson subsequently met with Mr. Brzezinski, and in the encounter, he had "protested most strongly to him about what had happened."

Henderson wrote that Brzezinski replied that he did not know who Father McManus was, nor that he had been at the White House briefing.

"When I told him about the links between the Irish National Caucus and the supply of arms to the IRA and that it was as bad for McManus to be received at the White House as it would be if the British Prime Minister received one of the Iranian terrorists at Number 10, Brzezinski entirely agreed.

Someone else must have done the inviting. He would send a note about it.

"I asked him if he could give me an assurance that McManus would not be invited to the White House again. He said he could do that three years out of four, but I would understand the politics involved. I said it was more than politics. It was intolerable for the President to be entertaining a terrorist of this kind. Brzezinski again said that he entirely agreed."

Thirty-three years on, Fr. McManus said that if it was true that a man could be judged by the enemies he made, then he was proud to be seen as an enemy at the time by Ambassador Henderson.

"Isn't it ironic that at the very same time the IRA and Sinn Féin were also attacking me, and trying to put the Irish National Caucus out of business," he said.

Fr. McManus   *Zbigniew Brzezinski*

APPENDIX E

British Penetration of Irish-American Groups

CAPITOL HILL. September 8, 2016—Recently released British/ Northern Ireland Office (NIO) State Papers have caused considerable interest and have given further insight into how the British Embassy spied on Irish-Americans.

The Papers were released by the Public Record Office of Northern Ireland (PRONI), and cover the period 1980 to 1989. The Papers were released under the "30/20 rule"—the phased release of official documents that were previously secret for 30 years but are to be released after 20 years. (Google PRONI CAIN for the released Papers).

As always, such released Papers are of intense interest to historians, the media and all those concerned about the history of The Troubles in Northern Ireland. Not, of course, that the full truth is ever revealed by the British Government.

Fr. Sean McManus—President of the Capitol Hill-based Irish National Caucus—whose life-long work always features in such Papers, said: "This time the Papers are of particular interest for a two-fold reason: (1) they reveal how deeply worried the British Government was about our MacBride Principles campaign (which they accurately state is 'largely instigated by the Irish National Caucus'; and (2) the Papers reveal how the British Embassy penetrated and spied on Irish-American organizations.

One of the released papers, titled "Irish American Unity Conference [IAUC]," consists of a report dated October 10, 1985, by the British Embassy to the Head of the Civil Service in Northern Ireland, Ken Bloomfield. (Yes, the same Mr. Bloomfield, whom another released State Paper exposed as outrageously stating that the Catholics in West Belfast are "alienated from normal civilized behavior"). The Paper gives a Report on the IAUC meeting in Philadelphia, August 23-25, 1985, and explains how one of the IAUC Members, Steve Ryan, monitoring the meeting was spying for the British Embassy. The Report lists a number of those present at the meeting, several members of Irish Northern Aid, and others, including Bob Linnon who would become the president of the IAUC (1987-1995), and a Ms. Patricia O'Hagan, Chairperson of the New York IAUC.

The Report exposes, "the IAUC's ... intense rivalry with Fr. Sean McManus and the Irish National Caucus," and that "... the meeting revealed a deep hatred of Father Sean McManus among the IAUC elite." The Report states Ms. O'Hagan, "declared she 'hated' McManus."

When asked to comment, Fr. McManus said: "I have a life-long policy of not responding to personal attacks. But I have to make an exception in this case as it is not really a personal attack, but one gloried in and recorded by the British Embassy. It is sad and pathetic that at the height of the MacBride Principles campaign—which I initiated with Sean Mc Bride's personal consent and which I launched on November 5, 1984—that the Brits could report that another Irish organization was spending its time in attacking me. How absurd and traitorous is that!

Fr. McManus explained: "However, I do not take all that stuff personally. My "feelings" are not hurt because on the Irish issue I don't do feelings. I do analysis and discernment: because of my life-long experience and background, I can figure out from whence come the constant, systematic attempts to sabotage my work. And it has ALWAYS come, one way or another, from the British Embassy, and, at least in the early years, from the Irish Embassy. Thus, it has always been. For example, I follow a rule of thumb, which is also a good religious principle: if one never had a personal confrontation or had personally offended a person, then an attack from such a person can never be "personal." Something else is always behind it. In all my 47 years in America, and in all my Irish activity, I've never had a personal fight or a nasty confrontation with any person on the Irish issue. And even though I have received hundreds of thousands of letters, phone-calls and emails, not one person has ever outlined to me what they disagreed with in my work. And that is because no genuine Irish person could reasonably oppose the main pillars of my life's work on Irish justice. However, any time anyone contacted me to make individual suggestions as to how I could do my work better, I always listened with great respect and attention. And I will always be eternally grateful for the huge and splendid individual and collective support I've received over all these years."

Fr. McManus continued: "Regarding Ms. O'Hagan: I had never heard of her, and I've no idea who she is. Therefore, I know her attack was not personal. She was—willingly or unknowingly—used by one of the aforementioned Embassies. It also must not be forgotten that Denis Donaldson, a British Agent was later in the late '90s placed in charge of the Irish Northern Aid Office in New York City. So, for a crucial period, a British Agent was telling members of Irish Northern Aid and other Irish organizations what to believe and what to do. In fairness, it could be said Michael Flannery was probably too old to be held responsible, but the younger New York City Irish Northern Aid leaders and spokespersons, and those in charge of the Irish People newspaper, must surely accept some responsibility and blame [Furthermore, who took Donaldson's place? The Brits are unlikely to change a spy without replacing him/her with another spy.—Added in July 2019.] I know if I had placed a British Agent in charge of the office of the Irish National Caucus, I would never hear the end of it, nor should I."

Fr. McManus concluded: "However, in all of this pathetic stuff, the central issue is: By what right and under what law is the British Embassy—or, indeed, the Irish Embassy—entitled to spy on Americans who are exercising their Constitutional rights?

Memo to the file on British Penetration of Irish-American Groups
[The Irish American Unity Conference has failed to publicly disassociate itself from the actions of its member British spy Steve Ryan or to repudiate and condemn the shocking words of its New York leader Patricia O'Hagan. Surely, that should be an easy thing to do? And just as Fr. McManus had a duty to expose the collusion of a fellow Redemptorist with the racist Enoch Powell (Appendix C), he likewise had a duty to expose how the British government penetrated Irish-American organizations. That's what real leaders do. And it is why Fr. McManus has retained the support and admiration of all authentic Irish-Americans for his almost 50-year struggle for Irish justice. **Memo to INC file by Barbara Flaherty.**]

Fr. McManus added for the historical record: "Some leaders of the Unity Conference had, as I had counted on, appeared to exorcize the baleful influence of its real founder and puppeteer—Garret FitzGerald (aided by Sean Donlon)—but now it seems the ghost of the awful FitzGerald is reappearing. Kathy Kelly, a top leader of the Irish America Unity Conference—whom we always saw as a friend and colleague in the struggle—referred to me as an "one man show" (April 19, 2018) with the clear intent to demean and diminish Barbara's huge role—the biggest and most high profile of any woman in any Irish-American organization in one hundred years. Not much sisterly solidarity there.

Peter Kissel—while to my face always effusively praised my work—was secretly writing behind my back to his members that my measured, precise and occasional critiques of the pathology of past and current British government-sponsored anti-Catholicism in Northern Ireland were objectionable to him: "Sean McManus' continued harping on it being Catholics vs. the world drives me nuts—it's counterproductive to progress." (April 1, 2017). It is, of course, a malicious, stupid lie that I see the issue as Catholics versus the world. It is appalling that Peter Kissel would be so deceitful, and so profoundly ignorant of both Irish and British history? To be unaware that England used both racism (anti-Irish hatred) and sectarianism (anti-Catholicism, after the English Reformation) in its conquest of Ireland and its creation and maintenance of Northern Ireland since 1920 is inexcusable and shameful.

NOTE: Neither Kelly nor Kissel use the title "Father," just "McManus," as in the long anti-Catholic and Orange tradition. Even Paisley near the end called him Father McManus. In 47 years in the U.S., Fr. McManus never initiated an attack, not to mention a back-stabbing, on another Irish organization.

APPENDIX F

Fr. Sean McManus Makes Pilgrimage to Fermanagh Ancestral Home of Great-Grandmother of JFK as part of celebrating his 50th Anniversary of Ordination

Fr. McManus outside ancestral home of Rosanna Cox-Fitzgerald, Toneymore West, Co. Fermanagh.

CAPITOL HILL. Sunday, August 19, 2018—It's well known that Fr. Sean McManus, President of the Capitol Hill-based Irish National Caucus, is very proud of his native County Fermanagh—one of the Six Counties of Northern Ireland, still under England's control.

Well, Fr. McManus is even more proud of Fermanagh since it has been established that the great-grandmother of President Kennedy, Rosanna Cox-Fitzgerald (c.1835-1879), was born in Fermanagh—and in the next parish to Fr. McManus' own parish of Kinawley. Indeed, Rosanna's father was from the parish of Kinawley. Rosanna apparently emigrated to America in her late teens or early twenties.

Fr. McManus explains: "The historic parish of Kinawley has essentially been in existence since the Sixth Century. It is now divided by the damn Border, its other part being in County Cavan. The neighboring parish to Kinawley is the parish of Knockninney, and it is in that parish that Rosanna Cox was born."

Fr. McManus continued:" On Saturday, August 4, I celebrated the 50th Anniversary of my Ordination in St. Naile's Church, Kinawley (actual date of my Ordination was September 1, 1968). The Curate of Knockninney, Fr. Ultan Mc Goohan, was one of the six priests who concelebrated Mass with me, and a few days later he took me 'on pilgrimage' to the ancestral home of Rosanna.

Fr. McGoohan, who has a degree in history, has recently done groundbreaking work in bringing to light this neglected lineage of the Kennedy family. We have heard a lot about 'The Boys of Wexford,' and, now, it's due time to hear about 'The Girls of Fermanagh.' I am sure the younger generations of the Kennedys will want to pay due homage to the neglected distaff side (female side) of family. Such neglect, of course, was common in older days. But now, I am hoping the younger Kennedys will see it as a matter of historical justice, as well as due and equal respect to Rosanna Cox-Fitzgerald, to right the family record of this extraordinary Irish-American family."

Fr. Ultan McGoohan and Fr. McManus on "pilgrimage" to ancestral home of Rosanna Cox -Fitzgerald

Fr. McGoohan in his key article, "The Fermanagh roots of John F. Kennedy" (February 28, 2018), explains how the Fermanagh connection had been lost for so long:" In summary, I am proposing that there has been a mistake. Rosanna Cox was not a Cavan woman, but a Fermanagh woman. We know her father was Philip Cox and there is a baptism registered to Philip Cox and Mary McGauran/McGovern in Kinawley parish. We know she gave her home address as Tonymore, Tomregan, Co. Cavan. Tonymore is in the civil parish of Tomregan, the home address given at the Kennedy Center in the United States and in Dunganstown, as the birthplace of Rosanna. As we now know, Tomregan was a civil parish, but Tonymore is in the Catholic ecclesiastical parish of Knockninny. At the time Tomregan was probably still being used as a postal address by the residents of Tonymore. We can claim her as a Fermanagh woman, with Kinawley and Knockninny roots and to be even more parochial, we might call her a Teemore woman! "

APPENDIX G
FR. MCMANUS' TRILOGY OF ARTICLES ON NORTHERN IRELAND AND ON CATHOLIC SOCIAL TEACHING.

The IrishEcho

OLDEST IRISH AMERICAN NEWSPAPER IN USA, ESTABLISHED IN 1928

Don't mention anti-Catholicism in the North

Fr. Sean McManus. OpEd. Irish Echo. New York City. May 31-June 6, 2017.

Thanks to The Irish People newspaper (now discontinued) being digitalized, one can read this:

"Father Sean McManus in giving the Benediction said: 'We pray for an Ireland free and independent, where the little man, the man of no property, the ordinary guy, can walk tall without having to depend on political patronage.... An Ireland where all power, whether political, ecclesiastical, military or economic will always be used for the good of the people.

'We pray, in particular, that once [England's diversive rule] has been banished, we will have a Country of harmony and reconciliation. An Ireland where religion will never again be used as a political device. An Ireland where the Catholic man from the Falls Road can go and have a pint of Guinness with his Protestant pal from the Shankill Road. . . An Ireland where the young Protestant woman from the Shankill Road can date the young Catholic man from the Falls Road.

'We pray above all for the little children of Ireland that one day they will soon be able to share the same playground, the same classroom, the same school, and, yes, one day the same Church to worship the same God that died for both.'"(Second Annual Irish Northern Aid Dinner, New York City. January 18, 1974.) The Irish People Newspaper. Page 9. January 26, 1974.

That brought back a lot of memories.

It also bears witness that this Fermanagh man has always had a deep ecumenical theology and has been animated by a non-sectarian vision for his homeland, or as Wolfe Tone put it, the desire to "substitute the common name of Irishman, in place of the denominations of Protestant, Catholic, and Dissenter."

When I first came to America, on October 2, 1972, I saw it as my duty to counteract England's Big Lie: that there was a "Religious War" in Northern Ireland (the Six Counties of Ireland that England was still holding onto).

But being from Fermanagh, I knew it would be silly and woefully non-historical to ignore that, in fact, England had (since The English Reformation, as distinct from the German Reformation) used anti-Catholicism as a major weapon in its conquest of Ireland.

Before the English Reformation (1169 to 1536), very Catholic England oppressed very Catholic Ireland without using the weapon of anti-Catholicism.

Some silly Irish Americans, however, felt that to deny that there was a religious war in Northern Ireland they had to avoid condemning anti-Catholic discrimination. That stupid idea was spread by the Stickies (the Official Republican Movement, as distinct from the Provisional Republican Movement. (It was also spread by the British embassy, naturally).

In the early 80s, I launched a campaign to expose the constitutional foundation of anti-Catholicism in Ireland: The Act of Settlement, 1701- the foundation stone of the Royal Family.

This act still today forbids a Catholic from being the monarch. It's like having a provision in the U.S. Constitution barring a black person from being president.

I always point out that the Orangemen did not enact the Act of Settlement. Thus, state-sponsored sectarianism and anti-Catholic bigotry are enshrined in the unwritten, non-codified British constitution.

One person—believing in the Stickie nonsense and the British big lie—tried to oppose my campaign: "[McManus claims] Americans should be objecting to the Act of Settlement, under the belief it has something to do with the conflict in Ireland. It is quite possibly the most idiotic thing for Americans to be lobbying for."

How convenient. Absolving the British monarchy and parliament from any connection with "the conflict in Ireland."

Fortunately, nobody listened to that egregious nonsense.

However, the big lie is hard to keep down. It has popped up recently.

Another person—the spiritual heir, perhaps, to the former person—took to the internet to decry my analysis of the root causes of Anti-Catholicism in Northern Ireland, and how the Protestants are not to be ultimately blamed but the British constitution: "Sean McManus' continued harping on it being Catholics vs. the world drives me nuts—it's counterproductive to progress."

A bit like trying to dismiss African American opposition to anti-black bigotry as being counterproductive to progress. God save us from such progress, and from such egregious misunderstanding!

Furthermore, isn't the phrase "Catholics against the world" a very strange formulation for someone proclaiming his concern for justice in Northern Ireland? It almost betrays an animus for all Catholics in the world, period.

But isn't it a bit ironic that this Fermanagh man has to listen to lectures from people who apparently have a very superficial understanding of the real nature of England's rule in Ireland?

Indeed, especially ironic, given the quoted benediction at the beginning of this article over 43 years ago about my vision for the relationship between northern Protestants and Catholics.

Not to mention that for this year, the 500th anniversary of Luther's Reformation, I have made many statements rejoicing in the theological agreement between the Catholic Church and the Lutheran World Federation on the Doctrine of Justification—the one issue that more than anything else sparked the Reformation; and welcoming, also, the fact that the Anglican/Episcopalian Church and the World Methodist Council have endorsed the Agreement on Justification.

The Root Cause of anti-Catholicism in North

Fr. Sean McManus, OpEd. Irish Echo. New York City. July 12 -19, 2017

A state's constitution is the fundamental set of principles by which the state is to be governed.

It is, therefore, of foundational importance and superior to all other laws of the state, as in the case of the written U.S. Constitution and Bill of Rights.

Can you imagine how awful it would be if there were a discriminatory law still within the Constitution?

Imagine, for example, if there were a provision prohibiting a black person being president of the United States.

Imagine how that would have powerfully condoned and promoted white racism, bigotry, and contempt in the 1950s and 1960s in, say, Mississippi.

And suppose presidents and members of Congress had ignored that foundational provision and merely expressed concern about some individual Jim Crow laws in Mississippi.

Would they have gotten away with it? Would the rest of the world have ignored that Pontius Pilate hand washing act?

How come, then, that the British constitution and "the Queen/King in Parliament"—have gotten away with constitutionally enshrined discrimination and sectarianism?

Since 1701—316 years, for goodness sake—until this very moment, and ongoing, there is at the heart of the British constitution a law prohibiting a Catholic being king or queen of England.

The Act of Settlement of 1701 is an integral part of the unwritten, uncodified British constitution which consists of, according to University College London, "an accumulation of various statutes, conventions, judicial decisions, and treaties which collectively can be referred to as the British Constitution."

The 1701 Act of Settlement determines succession to the Crown of England, and is, therefore, a fundamental constitutional statute.

Indeed, it is the very foundation stone of the royal family.

The Act of Settlement contains provisions that decree only a Protestant can succeed to the British throne and that if the monarch becomes a Catholic, or marries a Catholic, he/she forfeits the throne and "the people are absolved from their allegiance."

The ban on marrying a Catholic was repealed in February 2013 by the Succession to the Crown Act.

However minimalistic that change may have been to the ordinary Englishman in the street, how do you think the extreme Orangeman would react to any proposed change in this Anti-Catholic law?

The Belfast Telegraph gives the answer: "Members of the Protestant Orange Order [led by Jeffrey Donaldson MP, DUP] have descended on Downing Street to oppose the lifting of a ban on those in line to the throne from marrying a Catholic." (Orangemen at No. 10 over Catholic ban." Saturday, November 12, 2011).

The Succession to the Crown Act also removed the outdated sexist rule that allowed a woman in the line of succession to be superseded by a younger brother.

Thus, Queen Elizabeth II would not, in fact, have become queen in 1952 had she had a younger brother.

In effect and consequence, the ban on a Catholic being king or queen would be like having a provision in the U.S. Constitution prohibiting a black person being president of the United States—irrespective of the historical reasons for the Act of Settlement, 1701 (and there are always historical reasons, anyway, for all sorts of sectarianism/racism, two sides of the same coin).

Certainly, pointing out that the queen is also head of the Church of England is no valid excuse, and should cut no ice with Americans who know, and are proud of the fact that the Founding Fathers insisted on separation of church and state, this being enshrined in the First Amendment to the United States Constitution: "Congress shall make no law respecting an establishment of religion, or prohibiting the free exercise thereof..."

The Act of Settlement may mean little to the ordinary Englishman in the street, but it does, indeed, mean a whole lot to extreme Unionists/Loyalist/Protestants in Northern Ireland.

Time and time again, unionist leaders in Northern Ireland have pointed out that their allegiance is not just to the British Crown but, rather, to "Protestant succession to the British Crown."

This is like American white supremacists saying their allegiance would only be to the U.S. Constitution if it guaranteed their supremacy while ensuring that blacks were deemed inferior.

Why am I one of the few people in America who, for over 40 years, has raised the state-sponsored anti-Catholicism of the 1701 Act of Settlement?

How can constitutional bigotry and discrimination be conveniently ignored? And to be clear: anti-Catholicism is not about theological disagreement with Catholicism, but rather a socio-political system and mind-set determined to keep Catholics down.

Just as anti-Semitism is not a theological disagreement, but rather an organized system of hostility towards people of the Jewish faith or heritage.

Of course, it is easy for some people to criticize the extreme anti-Catholicism of the Orange Order and the thuggery of associated Protestant paramilitaries.

But it was not the Orangemen who enacted the anti-Catholic Act of Settlement.

To quote the University College of London again: "It has been suggested that the British Constitution can be summed up in eight words: What the Queen [Monarch] in Parliament enacts is law. This means that Parliament, using the power of the Crown, enacts law which no other body can challenge."

And that's where the buck stops.

In significant measure, orange bigotry and anti-Catholicism is but a logical, inevitable outworking of the 1701 Act of Settlement, which must be seen as an utter disgrace to modern-day England.

For as long as it is in place, extreme fundamentalist Orangeman will see it as their patriotic duty to endorse and implement this Act, which means refusing to accept Catholics as equals, because the British constitution does not accept Catholics as equals.

[Northern Ireland as "The Beloved Community"]

A homage to 'The Beloved Community.'
(The text of the article is given below in Word. The entire article, including photos, is available by clicking this link:
http://pages.cdn.pagesuite.com/0/4/04f3c5a7-e309-4fa1-b93b-fc7a790cc978/page.pdf
Fr. Sean McManus. OpEd. Irish Echo. New York City. July 26-August 1. 2017

In the words of the motto of the Irish National Caucus, I believe "Ireland, too, has the right to be one nation under God, indivisible, with liberty and justice for all."

In the meantime, I also believe the Good Friday Agreement is the proper way forward. And that, in effect, means seeing Northern Ireland as "The Beloved Community." (Not too difficult for this Fermanagh-native to do).

The term, "The Beloved Community" was first devised at the beginning of the 20TH Century by the important American philosopher-theologian Josiah Royce (1855–1916). But it was Blessed Martin Luther King, Jr. who made the term famous, investing it with a deeper and wider meaning. The King Center explains:

"For Dr. King, The Beloved Community was not a lofty utopian goal to be confused with the rapturous image of the Peaceable Kingdom, in which lions and lambs coexist in idyllic harmony. Rather, The Beloved Community was for him a realistic, achievable goal that could be attained by a critical mass of people committed to and trained in the philosophy and methods of nonviolence.

Dr. King's Beloved Community is a global vision, in which all people can share in the wealth of the earth. In the Beloved Community, poverty, hunger, and homelessness will not be tolerated because international standards of human decency will not allow it. Racism and all forms of discrimination, bigotry, and prejudice will be replaced by an all-inclusive spirit of sisterhood and brotherhood."

This—for the time being, pending the common-sense and inevitable reunification of Ireland—is the Northern Ireland that the Irish National Caucus has worked for since its inception on February 6, 1974, and for which it opened the very first Irish office on Capitol Hill on International Human Rights Day, December 10, 1978.

Now, only the utterly naïve and those totally lacking in a knowledge of Irish history, not to mention British history, would think that this means one does not expose on-going injustice, human rights violations and anti-Catholic discrimination and bigotry in Northern Ireland. (Or perhaps the applicable phrase here is "useful idiots"—useful, that is, to the British Government).

Certainly, Blessed Martin Luther King, Jr. did not believe such nonsense. Even in one of his most famous speeches—and the most conciliatory—"I Have a Dream" (1963), he pulls no punches, but speaks truth to power: "I have a dream that one day even the state of Mississippi, a state sweltering with the heat of injustice, sweltering with the heat of oppression, will be transformed into an oasis of freedom and justice. ... I have a dream that one day, down in Alabama, with its vicious racists, with its governor having his lips dripping with the words of "interposition" and "nullification"—one day right there in Alabama little black boys and black girls will be able to join hands with little white boys and white girls as sisters and brothers."

Yet, a misguided few in the United States have begun to criticize me for continuing to point out that—in the words of our Animated Internet Video (http://www.irishnationalcaucus.org)

—"There is still deep-rooted Anti-Catholic bigotry in Northern Ireland. A significant section of the Unionist/Protestant community resents sharing power with Catholics (Nationalists and Republicans) because they have never accepted Catholics as equals."

One person charged I was "too Catholic"; and at the same time, another person accused me of not being Catholic enough because I issued a statement supporting Michele Gildernew in her successful campaign to become MP again for Fermanagh/South Tyrone.

The first person opined my emphasizing that Anti-Catholicism was enshrined in the British constitution—and, consequently, not ultimately the fault of the Protestants of The North—was "counterproductive to progress."

No wonder the 1972 lyrics of "Stuck in the Middle With You" came to my Fermanagh mind, "Clowns to the left of me, jokers to the right."

Wouldn't you think those two Irish-Americans would think twice before they would try to lecture me about Fermanagh and about the history of anti-Catholicism in The North? That, as we say in Fermanagh, takes some chutzpah. Both should have remembered the Fermanagh adage: "Don't try to tell your Granny how to try the ducks."

Furthermore, the strange, inexplicable attempt to deny/invalidate the entire basis for our MacBride Principles campaign, and its operating motto: "American dollars must not subsidize anti-Catholic discrimination in Northern Ireland." ... So now we are being told the MacBride Principles—the most successful Irish-American campaign for Irish justice since 1921—was "counterproductive to progress." God help us all

Now back to The Beloved Community. I want to give The King Center the last word:

"In a July 13, 1966, article in Christian Century Magazine, Dr. King affirmed the ultimate goal inherent in the quest for The Beloved Community: 'I do not think of political power as an end. Neither do I think of economic power as an end. They are ingredients in the objective that we seek in life. And I think that end of that objective is a truly brotherly society, the creation of The Beloved Community.'" That is what I want to see in all of Ireland, north, south, east and west.

This is the final of three OpEds penned in recent weeks for this page by Fr. Sean McManus, founder and president of the Washington, D.C.-based Irish National Caucus.

Catholic Social Teaching

"The Best kept secret of the Catholic Church."

A version of this article was published in the Irish Echo, December 19-25, 2018

By Fr. Sean McManus

On International Human Rights Day, December 10, 1978, I embarked on a Special Ministry of Justice and Peace and opened the Capitol Hill office of the Irish National Caucus.

Ecclesiastically, it was the first of its kind, and also the first and only Irish office ever opened on Capitol Hill to lobby for justice and peace in Ireland (and, of course by that term, I mean all of Ireland, particularly The North/Northern Ireland).

As a Catholic priest, my work had to be based not only on secular understanding of human rights, justice, and peace but also on Catholic Social Teaching. I was conscious, therefore, that I had a double struggle ahead of me: (1) explaining the basics of England's injustice in Northern Ireland/The North: and (2) reminding Irish-Americans that "working for justice" is not only the patriotic thing to do, but it is also an essential part of the Catholic faith .

Irish-Americans needed such reminding about their faith because—as the expression has it—"Catholic Social Teaching is the best-kept secret of the Catholic Church," (and that expression was coined not by Church opponents but by American Church leaders themselves).

Never applied it to Ireland

I also knew that even those very knowledgeable of Catholic Social Teaching—like many priests, nuns, Bishops, and theological experts—never somehow applied it to Ireland: to Latin America, South Africa, etc., yes, but never to Ireland. Just like in secular America, many leading experts and politicians never applied fundamental American foreign policy principles to Ireland: like national self-determination, respect for human rights, non-discrimination, etc., etc. It appeared there was a conspiracy of silence between Church and State regarding England's injustice in Ireland.

So, I felt it was my duty to challenge this silence by holding both Congress and the Catholic Church to their own their own beliefs on human rights, equality, justice, and peace—even if it offended Jolly Old England. And, I had to try to do this while the British Embassy—and, shamefully, the Irish Embassy of those days—were systematically and falsely spreading the word that the Irish National Caucus was a front for the IRA.

So, what then is the Church's best-kept secret? Its essence is articulated in the document issued by the World Synod of Catholic Bishops, Rome, 1971, "Justice in the World": "... Action on behalf of justice [is] a constitutive dimension of the preaching of the Gospel...and of the Church's mission for the redemption of the human race and its liberation from every oppressive situation."

The word "constitutive "means: that without which something will not stand... So, without justice, the Gospel of Jesus Christ, the New Testament, and the Catholic Church DO NOT STAND.

Inspiration for my Special Ministry

This profound and prophetic declaration provided me with the inspiration and theological/canonical grounds for my full-time Special Ministry—for which I thank God every day.

"Justice in the World" makes it clear that we are here on this earth to worship God, preach the Gospel in word and deed, and build up God's kingdom on earth—in truth, justice, love/solidarity, and freedom. State-sponsored—to use a modern term—racism/sectarianism, the flip side of the same coin, are the historic twin evils of the world. It is upon these twin evils that the British Empire was built, including, of course, the long genocidal and ethnic cleansing conquest of the entire island of Ireland, England's very first oppressed colony. Racism/sectarianism were also the foundation stone of Northern Ireland in 1920: in this context, racism equals anti-Irish, and sectarianism equals anti-Catholicism.

Now, that the context has been set, let me continue with the overview of Catholic Social Teaching.

Modern Catholic Social Teaching, of course, began long before 1971. This Teaching is considered to be the corpus of Catholic social teaching contained in official Papal and hierarchical documents, commencing in 1891 with Rerum Novarum ("The condition of Labor ") by Pope Leo XIII, right up to the present time.

"Social justice" has been mainly a religious concept in that it emerged from religious circles. It covers the just and fair relation of the individual to society.

Social justice, therefore, requires the mutual obligation of individual and society. The Encyclopedia of Catholicism explains: "The individual has an obligation to contribute to society through participation, and society has the obligation to order its institutions so that such participation is possible. The primary form of social injustice is the exclusion or marginalization of persons from participation in the life of the society." (page 727).

The actual term, "social justice" was first coined by a Jesuit priest, Luigi Taparelli d'Azeglio, in 1843. It was first mentioned in Papal Teaching by Pope Pius XI in his Encyclical, Quadragesimo Anno (1931), issued to commemorate the 40th anniversary of the previously mentioned landmark Encyclical, "Rerum Novarum" by Pope Leo XIII. (Full disclosure here: I have issues with this great Pope because the British Government got him to condemn the Irish Plan of Campaign, 1886-1891—a campaign of boycott and refusal to pay rent to absentee and rack-rent brutal landlords. The Pope had no damn business condemning that struggle for justice).

SOLIDARITY

Later other papal documents would introduce another key term of Catholic Social Teaching "solidarity." Catholic thinkers adopted this term from European labor unions to distinguish Catholic social theory from the then modern theories of extreme liberal/unbridled capitalism on the one hand, and materialistic communism on the other hand. Both were seen by the Church to be disconnected from God and from God's law.

Pope John Paul II, of course, would make the term solidarity a most prominent principle of Catholic Social Teaching. For example, in his great 1981 Encyclical, Laborem exercens ("On Human Work") he mentions solidarity ten times—no doubt, thereby, sending his blessing to the Solidarity movement in his native Poland.

In his 1988 Encyclical, Sollicitudo rei socialis ("Solicitude for social concerns") the Pope referring to the maxim "peace is the fruit of justice," says: "Today, one could say, with the same exactness and the same power of biblical inspiration (cf. Isaiah 32:17; James 3:18), peace is the fruit of solidarity."

And in 2009 Pope Benedict XVI in his encyclical Caritas in Veritate (Charity in Truth) uses the term solidarity an amazing 40 times.

(Solidarity is also, of course, the lifeblood and driving force of the AFL-CIO, with which I am honored to be associated—in my earlier work on the MacBride Principles and now as Chief Judge of the World Peace Prize Awarding Council. Current President of the AFL-CIO, the great Richard L. Trumka, ardently believes that peace is the fruit of solidarity, nationally and globally, and that is why we honored him with the World Peace Prize).

In, Sollicitudo rei socialis ("Solicitude for social concerns"), Pope John Paul also introduces the striking and meaningful concept of social "structures of sin." This means we not only have to repent of personal sin, but also oppose, preach and campaign against, structures of sin/injustice/unfairness in society. Furthermore, this is the first Papal Encyclical to dedicate the Catholic Church to a "preferential option for the poor."

Until Pope John XXIII and Vatican II (1962-65), Catholic Social Teaching was mainly based on natural law rather than on scripture. (However, that had the benefit of being able to communicate with people of no faith and of all faiths). But, of course, the origins of this teaching were always Scriptural, based on the Hebrew prophets who announced God's special love for the poor and oppressed—and based especially on the words and actions of Jesus Christ, who identified Himself completely with "the least of our brothers and sisters"—not with the rich, the famous and the powerful.

Pope John moved the Church's social teaching away from a rigid interpretation of natural law to "a reading of the sign of the times" making it more Scripturally based. This highlighted the point that Biblical justice is not cold-hearted legal justice, but a matter of the heart that heeds the cry of the poor—as personified by Jesus Christ. Pope Paul VI in his pivotal Encyclical would further powerfully place social justice teaching at the very heart of the Gospel (thereby endorsing the document, Justice in the World). He declared: "As the main point and the very center of his Good News, Christ proclaims salvation; this is the great gift of God, which is liberation from everything that oppresses people, particularly liberation from sin and the Evil One..." (Evangelii Nuntiandi, par. 9, December 8, 1975). And, now today, thanks be to God, the Catholic Church powerfully and clearly teaches:" Action on behalf of justice [is] a constitutive dimension of the preaching of the Gospel..."

APPENDIX H

Fr. Sean McManus
50th Anniversary Sermon

Kinawley Church. Saturday, Aug. 4, 2018

God bless Kinawley.

I want to thank all of you—Fr. McMorrow, the parish council, the Choir, the Altar Servers, all the priests at the Altar, and all of you here—for giving me the opportunity to celebrate the 50th Anniversary of Ordination at this Mass in Kinawley.

The first thing the Catholic Church teaches about the priesthood is this: all the Baptized share in the priesthood of Jesus Christ. It is called the "priesthood of the faithful."

And it is because of this priesthood that the ministerial/hierarchical priesthood—the priesthood of all the priests here at the altar—is possible.

Like the other Sacraments, the Sacrament of Ordination has a particular mission: it is a call to serve the faithful and all God's people; it is a mission of service; it is a Sacrament of service.

Pope Francis says this: "It is true that God has made His entire holy people a royal priesthood in Christ. Nevertheless, our great Priest Himself, Jesus Christ, chose certain disciples to carry out publicly in His name, and on behalf of mankind, a priestly office in the Church. They were elected by the Lord Jesus not to embark on a career, but to undertake this service."

Ordination is a special anointing, a special commission, so that one can proclaim the primary command of God, as powerfully summed up by the Prophet Micah: "Do justice, love mercy and walk humbly with your God." (Micah 6:8).

Jesus himself spelled it out more fully when he said of Himself: "The Spirit of the Lord is upon me because he has anointed me to proclaim good news to the poor. He has sent me to proclaim liberty to the captives and the recovering of sight to the blind, to set at liberty those who are oppressed." (Luke 4:18).

And the Catholic Church teaches: "Action on behalf of justice ... [is] a constitutive dimension of the preaching of the Gospel ... and of the Church's mission for the redemption of the human race and its liberation from every oppressive situation.

The word "constitutive" means "that, without which, something cannot stand."

Simply put: The Catholic Church teaches that without justice, the Gospel of Jesus does not stand, and without its social-justice mission, the Catholic Church does not stand.

Of course, part from this social service aspect of the priesthood, the liturgical/sacramental service of the priesthood is nowhere more evident than when the priest gathers with the faithful for the Celebration of the Eucharist—just as we are doing now, faithful to one of Christ's most sacred and important commands: "Do this in memory of me." And, of course, without prayer—both private and Liturgical—and without the Mass and the other Sacraments, the Gospel of Jesus does not stand, and the Catholic Church cannot stand.

A Catholic celebration—especially one held in the context of The Eucharist/The Mass—always has the same fundamental meaning: celebrating, rejoicing in, and giving thanks for the Gift of Jesus Christ to the world. And for me, this is fundamentally what the 50th Anniversary of my Ordination is about: giving thanks for the Gift of Jesus Christ—without whom there would be no priesthood, whether the Priesthood of the Faithful or the Ministerial Priesthood.

Jesus is the Sacrament from which all other sacraments flow.

Now, all of us probably have a verse from Scripture that sticks in our mind more than others... a verse that is particularly moving for us ... one that resonates down through the years ... that sums it all up for us. I have mine, and it's a verse that after all these years can still raise the hair on the back of my neck, filling me with wonder and amazement: "The Word was made flesh and dwelt among us ..." (John 1:14).

For Christian believers, the most central and profound historical event in the history of humankind is The Incarnation: that moment in history when the Blessed Virgin Mary conceived Jesus Christ by the power of the Holy Spirit. The moment that God broke definitively and fully into human history.

Naturally, this happened not on the First Christmas Day in Bethlehem, but nine months before Christmas Day. For nine months, The Second Person of the Blessed Trinity, God Incarnate, The Savior of the world, Our Most Holy Redeemer, lived in Mary's womb—otherwise "the Word would NOT have been made flesh." The only way Jesus could have been human was to have a Mother—He took his flesh from His mother.

If Jesus had not also been human (as well as Divine), there would—according to God's plan—have been no Salvation, no Redemption, no Death and Resurrection, no Holy Spirit descending on the Church, no eternal life.

The Incarnation, therefore, is the fundamental Christian Mystery—from which all other Christian mysteries flow. The Incarnation not only reveals to us the mystery of God's love and mercy but it also reveals the mystery of our own humanity, bringing to light our very high calling: which is, to build up God's kingdom on earth in justice and solidarity, and to inherit eternal life through Jesus Christ by the power of the Holy Spirit.

Our Faith, therefore, comes down to fully accepting The Incarnation: the gift of Jesus Christ, Son of God and son of Mary.

One advantage of seeing Christianity as a matter of fully accepting the Gift of Jesus Christ to the world is that none of us can claim credit for the gift of Christ. Who could claim the credit for that?... Well, perhaps Our Blessed Lady could.... But we know that She did not claim credit but, instead, sang out her famous prayer, The Magnificat: "My soul magnifies the Lord, and my spirit rejoices in God my Savior." (Luke 46-47). Thus, Mary, the first and perfect Christian, teaches us how to respond to the Incarnation—how to accept the Gift of Jesus Christ—with prayer and action, with joy and gratitude, with faith and trust.

And that is why Our Blessed Lady has such an important role in our lives, especially Catholic lives. I have a saying "If anyone has a problem with Mary, let them take it up with Jesus, and see how far that gets them!"

Can you imagine beginning a conversation with any son or daughter by saying, "I have a problem with your Mother."

So, today, I am, of course, very conscious of my Ordination fifty years ago. But I am also very conscious of my Baptism, right here in this Church 74 years ago. It was here—like many of you—that I was Baptized into the Death and Resurrection of Jesus Christ; here I became a member of The Body of Christ, here I became a member of the Catholic Church, the Sacrament of Christ on earth. Right here in this Church. In St. Patrick's, Killesher, I made my First Communion and received Confirmation.

So, everything I am, my entire Catholic faith, my Catholic identity, and my Catholic ethos, I owe to the parish of Kinawley, to my family and relatives, to my neighbors in Clonliff, and to all the wonderful people of this parish. That is why my heart is never far from Kinawley.

God bless Kinawley. ... And God save Ireland.

Thank you.

Extended family photo in sanctuary of Kinawley Church. 2018. Photo by Mary McElroy.

APPENDIX I

Fr. McManus kneeling in prayer at John Devoy's grave. Glasnevin Cemetery, Dublin. 2008.

APPENDIX J

WORLD PEACE PRIZE AWARDING COUNCIL

Judges and officers

Founder and Master Planner, Korea

Dr. Han Min Su

Chief Judge, USA
Father Sean McManus
Judge, USA, Corporate Manager
Ms. Barbara J. Flaherty
Judge, Canada - Hong Kong
Dr, Shiu Loon
Judge, USA
Dr. Herman Keck Jr.

Judge, Israel
Dr. Hilda Naim
Judge, Egypt
Dr. Mohamed A. Cholkamy
Judge, Philippines
Dr. Carlito S. Puno
Judge, India
Ran Prakasn Saxena
Judge, Australia-South Pacific Region
Hon. Peter Lewis
Judge, Germany
Hon. Karl Prinz
Judge, Ethiopia
Dr. Ephraim Isaac
Judge, Europian Community
Hon. Dr. Shahin Saperstein
Judge, Russia
Gen. Dr. Gennady P. Turmov
Judge, Chinese Community
Dr. Lin Chu Sung
Judge, Japan
Dr. Princess Kaoru Nakamaru
Data-information Officer
Mr. Jung Sang Chul
Evaluation Officer
Mr. Han Sang Yoon
Judge, China
Dr. Daniel Yiu San Poon
Judge, Myanmar
Dr. Khin Shwe
Judge, Russia
Dr. Nikolay Sadovnikov
Judge, UK Anglican Church
Raymond McCord

Data-information Officer
Mr. Jung Sang Chul
Evaluation Officer
Mr. Han Sang Yoon

APPENDIX K

Four key films to be watched by all concerned Irish-Americans and all those who love justice, peace, and solidarity.

The Ballymurphy Precedent: film premieres in Washington.

Distinguished film director Callum Macrae and Fr. Sean McManus

CAPITOL HILL. Monday, June 10, 2019—A packed cinema in Washington DC watched the film **The Ballymurphy Precedent** on Monday evening.

The film, sponsored by the Pulitzer Center—and strongly promoted by the Irish National Caucus—is about the Ballymurphy Massacre, when the British Parachute Regiment slaughtered 11 innocent civilians, including a mother of eight and the local Catholic priest, over a 3-day period in Belfast in August 1971. It was just six months before the same murderous Regiment slaughtered 13 unarmed civilians in Derry on Bloody Sunday—hence the word "precedent." It was a brutal, calculated act of State-terrorism, sadly setting the course for the next 30 years.

The film and its director, Callum Macrae, have been critically acclaimed in both Ireland and Britain. Total Film describes it as: 'An astonishing documentary ....urgent, angry and moral, this is top tier film-making.' The Guardian calls it *'Impressive..shocking....a desperately sad film'*.

Fr. Sean McManus—president of the Capitol Hill-based Irish National Caucus (pictured with director Macrae)—said: "It is an extraordinary film; powerful, moving and beautiful—agonizingly beautiful. Not only beautifully filmed and narrated, but beautifully revealing the dignity, courage, and grace of the innocent victims' families: their heroic determination to find and reveal the truth, without hatred or vengeance.

Director Macrae is a gifted artist, a seeker, and revealer of truth, and a most impressive Scotsman. He also captured the essence of the problem in Northern Ireland: state-sponsored racism, state-sponsored sectarianism, and inevitably the enforcement of those twin evils by brute military violence, as in the Ballymurphy Massacre. If Americans do not understand that England has—Wales and Scotland can hardly be blamed—sponsored racism and sectarianism in Ireland, they do not understand either British or Irish history. A few might think naming these evils is 'counterproductive to progress,' but the Irish National Caucus has long believed that we must speak truth to power, and help all victims find the truth—including my heroic friend, Belfast Protestant victims' campaigner, Raymond McCord. My friend Ciaran MacAirt on Sunday organized a march of several thousand in Belfast, demanding truth for all victims. This is the way forward: demanding and speaking truth, which is not 'counterproductive' to progress but the very foundation of progress, as those of us long involved in the struggle know. Dr. Martin Luther King, Jr. told us, the Beloved Community cannot be built on lies, injustice, and cover-up. And Pope John Paul II reminds us that peace is the fruit of solidarity."

Fr. McManus has had a long association with the Ballymurphy families. On Wednesday, March 16, 2011, he arranged for the Ballymurphy Massacre Committee to testify at a Congressional Hearing before the U.S. Commission on Security and Cooperation in Europe (The Helsinki Commission). He has promoted their cause throughout the U.S. Congress and in his Memoirs: My American Struggle for Justice in Northern Ireland.

END.

No Stone Left Unturned

"Investigative documentary filmmaker Alex Gibney—best known for 2008's Oscar-winning Taxi to the Dark Side, Enron: The Smartest Guys in the Room, and at least a dozen others—turns his sights on the 1994 Loughinisland massacre, a cold case that remains an open wound in the Irish peace process. The families of the victims—who were murdered while watching the World Cup in their local pub—were promised justice, but 20 years later they still didn't know who killed their loved ones. Gibney uncovers a web of secrecy, lies, and corruption that so often results when the powerful insist they are acting for the greater good. The documentary exposes how senior elements of the British State actively colluded with an extra judicial loyalist killer gang, for one of the worst sectarian atrocities of the Troubles. This is the film that the British establishment do not want you to see."

In 2012, the Irish National Caucus was proud to host in Washington the Loughinisland families of the victims, with their dogged attorney, Niall Murphy.

The Irish National Caucus has been briefing Members of Congress for over 40 years about the systematic, institutionalized policy of collusion. It is sad to think that it has taken so long for the truth to finally out.

Also, many years ago, the Irish National Caucus met in Washington with relatives of the Kingmills Massacre. And it now appears the British and the police colluded in the killing of the ten Protestant victims."

Fr. Sean McManus, seated center, with the Loughinisland families. Washington 2012.

IRISH CONGRESSIONAL BRIEFING ON MIAMI SHOWBAND MASSACRE

Distributed to Congress by Irish National Caucus

"My friend Stephen Travers in Ireland would like Members of Congress to see this review of the film The Miami Showband Massacre—the 1975 massacre in Northern Ireland that he and one other member of the Band survived.

Stephen has shown extraordinary courage, with a remarkable determination to expose the ensuing cover-up, and doing it all without bitterness or revenge. He is truly a hero of non-violence, truth, and justice—a man who deserves our solidarity."—Fr. Sean McManus

*The Miami Showband Massacre Directed by Stuart Sender Written by Jeff Zimbalist & Michael Zimbalist *By Chris Jenkins—Source: Green Left Weekly*

https://www.netflix.com/ie/title/80191046

The Miami Showband massacre: A cover-up in plain sight

By Chris Jenkins. Global Rights. Australia. Wednesday, May 8, 2019.

It's a strange thing, scrolling through the options on Netflix and seeing a documentary on the Miami Showband.

For most in Australia and the world, the name is unfamiliar, but for people who lived through or have studied what became known as "The Troubles" in Northern Ireland between the late 1960s and the Good Friday Agreement in 1998, the situation is different.

Here on this global media entertainment platform, amid rom-coms and action movies, is a film detailing how the British government organized, supplied and directed a terrorist group to murder people in six counties in Ireland's north under British occupation. Among their targets was a music group on a country road outside of Banbridge, County Antrim, on July 31, 1975.

The documentary's primary commentator is Steve Travers, bass player for the popular rock band from Dublin in Ireland's south. Travers describes growing up respecting uniforms and believing he would one day join the Beatles. He joined the Miami Showband, widely considered one of Ireland's best groups at the time. His band mates were Des Lee, frontman and saxophonist; lead singer and dreamy heartthrob Fran O'Toole, drummer Ray Millar, guitarist Tony Geraghty and Brian McCoy on trumpet.

The band would cross the island living a life relatively unaffected by the growing outbreaks of violence and resistance in the north.

All such sheltered naivety came to an end, however, when the band drove home to Dublin following a gig in Banbridge on July 30. Early into the drive, they were stopped at what appeared to be a British military checkpoint. There were uniforms and a request to inspect the van from a curt, posh British accent, followed by an explosion and machine gun fire that killed three band members—O'Toole, McCoy and Geraghty. Travers himself was taken to intensive care after Lee ran to the local police station to get help.

The killing of the band members, the first case of a music group being targeted, caused shock across Ireland. As one interviewee put it, "With violence all around, the dance hall was a place where you could get away for a bit. It was therapy for us." Travers describes how he thought at the time that "as a band, as musicians, we were immune to what was going on around us".

Following their recovery in hospital and the funerals for the three killed, the surviving band members tried to put the band back together, but the highly traumatic events of that night would shape the rest of Travers' life: "You go into an event, and come out of that event a completely different person ... the person I was was left back in a field on July 31, 1975."

The explosion was a bomb in the van that detonated prematurely. Two men who died placing it were quickly identified as members of the Ulster Volunteer Force, a unionist paramilitary group. Days later, two more men were arrested, also UVF members and active in the British "Home Guard" Ulster Defense Regiment (UDR). Investigations would discover that all weapons used in the attack had come from army compounds.

The documentary lays out the struggle undertaken primarily by Travers to learn the truth of what happened that night. From a starting point of believing that this was a case of "some bad apples", Travers is confronted with the reality of direct collusion between the UVF and agents of the British Intelligence Service.

Former British intelligence officers Colin Wallace and Fred Holroyd testified that they and their superiors knew that the UVF were committing terrorist acts, but were not permitted to act against them. Many of those involved in the attack had been responsible for four bombs in Dublin and Monaghan the year before, but still were left untouched by the police.

Evidence was found that proves senior police officials warned local UVF leader Robin Jackson (the "Jackal") to "lie low," and provided him with alibis and information related to the police investigation.

According to Margaret Urwin from Justice for the Forgotten, this proves that Jackson was operating as a British agent, stating: "We believe that this and other important information proves that Robin Jackson was an agent. You have somebody who is murdering people at the same time he is being controlled by the state. In my mind, that then makes the state complicit."

On the ongoing dismissal of his testimony that a British officer was present that night, Travers states: "The more evidence I saw, I had to realize that the British government, through its proxy army, they chose us as innocent victims, to murder us in order to achieve their political objective. They wanted the southern government to close the border with the north.

"So they decided, 'Let's frame the most innocent and trusted commuters; people who travelled up and down. And we would have gone down in history as terrorists carrying bombs for the IRA'."

With the mission botched, "It became plain to me that [they were] determined to keep guilt for what happened on this side of the Irish Sea," said Travers. "They clearly wanted to throw anyone from this side, be it the UDR or the police, to the wolves. They didn't want to implicate the British establishment."

During the Prime Ministership of Margaret Thatcher, Wallace and Holroyd wrote to her outlining, in a 32-page dossier, the various illegal activities of the British army and intelligence in the north of Ireland. Soon after, Wallace was sentenced to 10-years' jail on circumstantial evidence on a charge of murder, while Holroyd was committed to a military psychiatric hospital.

Years later, Travers gained access to declassified correspondence from 1987 between the UVF and the Irish government in Dublin, in which the UVF complained that British agency MI5 gave them dodgy bombs and weapons to carry out their work, including the Miami killings. The UVF explosively claimed MI5 had tasked them with assassinating Irish Prime Minister Charlie Haughey.

There, on a single piece of paper, was not only proof that the UVF was responsible and being directed by the British government, but that its Irish counterpart had known for so long and done nothing. It exposed an appalling betrayal of the people and their families, whose lives had been so affected by British state crimes.

No matter what you know of the Miami killings, or the covert activities of Britain or other imperialist powers, The Miami Showband Massacre is still an important, troubling watch. One thing I keep mulling over is that it exists on Netflix at all. The documentary is a damning exposure of the crimes of the British state, crimes that have never been formally acknowledged, let alone acted upon, and yet here is the case sitting on a digital shelf accessible to all as an entertainment option.

But then comes the realization that, rather than unique, the case of the Miami killings is just a particularly dramatic moment in the historical Irish/Irish Catholic experience; a mixture of trauma, indifference and compassion fatigue. People know, people might find it interesting, but the assumption is that no cares enough to do anything about it.

Nonetheless, films like this are important, to teach real people's history and hopefully inform social processes aimed at ensuring such violence and agendas don't play out in the future. Ironic, then, that Netflix is arguably contributing more than either of the current Irish and British establishments.

The growing prospects of a Jeremy Corbyn-led Labor government in Britain gives hope that this historic agenda might change with a dismantling of colonial attitudes and formal recognition given to crimes of the past. Until then, people like Travers will be taking on the whole system in the fight for answers and justice.

Bobby Sands: 66 Days

"Father Sean [McManus] is in the film, of course, and makes an important and memorable contribution."—Director Brendan Byrne.

Fr. McManus said: "I have the honor of being in the critically acclaimed film documentary Bobby Sands: 66 Days [66daysthefilm.com]

It is a powerful, factual and moving explanation as to why Bobby Sands and his nine colleagues sacrificed their lives on hunger strike for justice in 1981.

The film is also a testimony to the work of the Irish National Caucus, since I am the only Irish-American organization leader to appear in the film. I was selected because since February 6, 1974, the Irish National Caucus has led the charge to get the United States Congress to stand up for equality, justice and peace in Northern Ireland. In the film, I explain the American reaction to the 1981 Hunger Strike, and the powerful odds against us in our struggle to expose British Government injustice."

ENDNOTES

INTRODUCTION

1. The four letters—CSsR—that follow a Redemptorist's name represent the Congregation's official Latin name: Congregatio Sanctissimi Redemptoris (The Congregation of the Most Holy Redeemer). They are more popularly known as the Redemptorists: "A society of missionary priests [and Brothers] founded by St. Alphonsus Maria Liguori, 9 Nov. 1732, at Scala, near Amalfi, Italy, for the purpose of laboring among the neglected country people in the neighborhood of Naples. The Redemptorists are essentially and by their specific vocation a missionary society." (Catholic Encyclopedia, www.newadvent.org/cathen/12683a.htm). JMJA stands for Jesus, Mary, Joseph, and Alphonsus. Fr. Shepherd was the Provincial, the superior, with total power, of the London Province of Redemptorists, which was then comprised of England, Scotland, Wales, and a Vice-Province of South Africa. Since that time South Africa has become its own independent Province.

2. "With malice toward none, with charity for all, with firmness in the right as God gives us to see the right, let us strive on to finish the work we are in; to bind up the nation's wounds; to care for him who shall have borne the battle, and for his widow and his orphan—to do all which may achieve and cherish a just and lasting peace, among ourselves, and with all nations." Abraham Lincoln's Second Inaugural address, March 4, 1865.

3. "Action on behalf of justice and participation in the transformation of the world fully appear to us as a constitutive dimension of the preaching of the Gospel, or in other words, of the church's mission for the redemption of the human race and its liberation from every oppressive situation." "Justice in the World." Number 6. Synod of Bishops. Rome, November 30, 1971. www.osjspm.org/majordoc_justicia_in_mundo_offical_test.aspx

4. There was one splendid exception, one American bishop who was not scared to take a stand against Britain's oppression in Ireland: my good friend, the late Bishop Thomas Drury of Corpus Christi, Texas. The late Bishop Mark Hurley of Santa Rosa and the late Cardinal O'Connor of New York were fairly outspoken but were not in the same league as Bishop Drury, a native of Gurteen, County Sligo.

5. Rev. Walter Rauschenbusch, (1861-1918, Rochester), led the Social Gospel: Christian faith is not just about personal conversion and salvation but also about doing justice in this world. In the fifties and sixties. Rev. Martin Luther King, Jr. would give it his own special stamp.

CHAPTER 1: BONNY BANKS OF LOUGH ERNE

1. Saint Naile was a contemporary of Saint Columcille (AD 521–597). He became the second abbot on Devenish Island on Lower Lough Erne, just north of Enniskillen. Devenish is one of the finest monastic sites in Ireland, first established in the sixth century. The site is dominated by a round tower thought to date from the twelfth century (see www.kinawleyparish.com).

2. "The Cladagh River (Irish: An Chlaideach or "washing river" or Swanlinbar River is a moderately large river which forms from a number of small streams rising on the south-eastern slopes of

Cuilcagh Mountain, County Cavan and flows through the village of Swanlinbar, before crossing the border into County Fermanagh and eventually flowing into Upper Lough Erne. It is ultra-oligotrophic upstream before gradually becoming oligotrophic and oligo-mesotrophic through its middle and lower reaches." (www.revolvy.com/topic/River Cladagh (Swanlinbar).

3. The Big Snow of '47 (www.irishidentity.com/extras/weather/stories/snow.htm).

4. Kinawley Parish bulletin, July 29, 1984.

5. Nicholas Christopher Michael Ring (October 12, 1920–March 2, 1979), better known as Christy Ring, was a famous Cork hurler. He is gener- ally regarded as one of the greatest hurlers in the history of the game.

6. Owen F. Cummings. *Eucharistic Doctors: A Theological History*. (Paulist Press New York. 2005), 98.

7. Malachy McCourt. *A Monk Swimming* (1998). (Wheeler Publishing. 1998).

8. Frank McCourt, *Angela's Ashes* (Scribner, New York, 1996). When I told Frank that an elderly lady in Kinawley had read *Angela's Ashes* five times he was so touched he wrote her a lovely letter. Later when I was coming out of Kinawley chapel after saying Mass, there was that wonderful lady, since deceased, waiting to thank me for putting Frank McCourt in touch with her. I asked her if she had told the *Fermanagh Herald* about the letter, but she responded with great dignity: "No, that's between Frank McCourt and me." And then added with obvious pride, "But I will leave it in my will."

Chapter 2: The Day Celia was Married and Patrick Was Killed

1. Patrick McManus. *United Irishman.* August 1958.

2. J. Bowyer Bell, *The Secret Army: the IRA, 1916–1970* (John Day Company, New York, 1970), 309, footnote 14.

3. In 1953, Rocky Marciano defended his world heavyweight title against Jersey Joe Walcott, knocking him out in the first round with his deadly uppercut. The previous year, Marciano had taken the title from Jersey Joe.

Chapter 3: The Call

1. 1. Bayard Rustin (March 17, 1912 – August 24, 1987) was an American civil rights activist and principal organizer of the 1963 March on Washington for Jobs and Freedom. He counseled Martin Luther King, Jr. on the techniques of nonviolent resistance.

Chapter 4: Kinnoull and Hawkstone Years

1. Karl Barth (May 10, 1886 – December 10, 1968) (pronounced "Bart") was an eminent Swiss Reformed theologian, one of the most important Christian thinkers of the twentieth century. Even Pope Pius XII described him as the most important theologian since Thomas Aquinas.

2. Hawkstone Hall is an early eighteenth-century Georgian mansion set in extensive parkland in Shropshire, England. It served the Church for many years as an international center for spiritual renewal, but in 2017 the Redemptorists had to sell it.

3. Richard P. McBrien (ed.), *Encyclopedia of Catholicism* (HarperCollins, New York, 1995), 1,254.

4. Thomas F. O'Meara, O.P., *A Theologian's Journey*, (Paulist Press, NY, 2002), 25.

5. McBrien, *ibid.*, 1,254–1,255.

6. Fergus Kerr, *Twentieth-Century Catholic Theologians* (Blackwell Publishing, Malden, MA., 2007), 4–5.

7. "This decree of condemnation may be found in *Acta Sanctae Sedis* (5th ed., Rome, 1872–1911), V (1911), 389." Fr. William D'Arcy, O.F.M. Conv., *The Fenian Movement in the United States: 1858–1886*. Washington, DC: (The Catholic University of America Press, 1947), 329.

8. From "Flower of Scotland" (1974) by the Scottish folk group, The Corries. It celebrates the victory of the Scots, led by King Robert the Bruce over the King of England, Edward II, at the Battle of Bannockburn, 1314. It has become the unofficial Scottish Anthem for rugby and soccer events.

   > "O flower of Scotland
   > When will we see your like again That fought and died for
   > Your wee bit hill and glen
   > And stood against him Proud Edward's army And sent him homeward Tae think again

9. Seán MacStíofáin. *Memoirs of a Revolutionary* (Edinburgh R. & R. Clark Ltd, 1975).

CHAPTER 5: THE TROUBLES COME BACK TO HAUNT

1. "But just when I thought I was out, they pull me back in." Michael Corleone in *Godfather III* (Mario Puzo and Francis Ford Coppola, 1990).

2. Michael Farrell, *Arming the Protestants: The Formation of the Ulster Special Constabulary and the Royal Ulster Constabulary, 1929–27* (Brandon Books, Kerry, 1983).

3. "Enniskillen Anti-Internment Meeting." Letters to the Editor, *Fermanagh Herald*, Saturday, August 21, 1971.

4. J. M. Synge, *Playboy of the Western World* (J. W. Luce, Boston, 1911).

5. Henry David Thoreau's essay "On the Duty of Civil Disobedience." 1849.

6. "The Devlin made me do it." *The Big Issue*.

7. Letter from Birmingham Jail. April 16, 1963. Penn University, African Studies Center (www.upenn.edu).

CHAPTER 6: BOUND FOR AMERICA

1. Bernard Haring, *Priesthood Imperiled* (Chicago: Triumph Books. 1989), 146–147.

2. Thomas Merton, *Passivity and Abuse of Authority* (New York: The McCall Publishing Company, 1968), 128–133.

3. Raymond Arsenault, *Freedom Riders* (Oxford: Oxford University Press, 2006), 419.

CHAPTER 7: FORMATION OF IRISH NATIONAL CAUCUS

1. Joseph E. Thompson, *American Policy and Northern Ireland: A Saga of Peacebuilding* (Westport: Praeger, 2001), 38.

2. Frank McManus, statement, June 6, 2008.

3. Jack Holland, *The American Connection*.(New York: Viking Penguin, New York, 1987), 117; Two later books repeat Holland's error: Andrew J. Wilson, *Irish-America and the Ulster Conflict 1968–1995* (Washington, DC, The Catholic University of America, 1995), 99; and Joseph E. Thompson, *American Policy and Northern Ireland: A Saga of Peacebuilding* (Westport Praeger, 2001), 51; this latter book seems to confuse the formation of the Irish National Caucus with its later endorsement by many different Irish-American organizations.

4. Jack Keane, telephone interview with the author. May 30, 2008, 7:30 p.m.

CHAPTER 8: CAUCUS BAPTIZED IN BLOOD AT BRITISH EMBASSY

1. "Stickies" and "Pinheads": after the 1969–70 IRA split, which led to the emergence of the Provisional IRA, the Official IRA used a type of Easter Lily with a self-adhesive backing. This led to them being branded as the "Stickies." The Provisionals retained the traditional paper-and-pin Easter lily and thus became known as the "Pinheads," a nickname which has not lasted.

2. Jack is one of the very few in the Washington area from that time who has stayed the course and is still active in the struggle for Irish justice.

3. The following account is largely based on contemporaneous notes I made and on a report I wrote at that time.

4. C. Schoettler, "Embassy Protest Held By An Unlikely Band." *Baltimore Sun*, Apr. 27, 1974.

CHAPTER 9: ALL THE NEWS THAT'S FIT TO PRINT—OR NOT

1. John Organ, "Papacy at the Crossroads." *Sunday Telegraph*, Jan. 4, 1976;

2. Carl Schoettler, "Irish-American Group Aired Issue In Vatican." *Baltimore EveningSun*, Dec. 26, 1975; "Irish Caucus Delegation Well Received," *The National Hibernian Digest*, Jan.– Feb. 1976; "Jackson's Bid to Scoop the Irish," *Irish Post* (London), January 24, 1976.

CHAPTER 10: THE CAUCUS AND JIMMY CARTER

1. Professor Paul Power, "The United States and Northern Ireland: The Carter Initiative and Its Aftermath," (paper. American Committee for Irish Studies, University of Delaware, April 24-26, 1980).

2. "Boston, Where it Began, Salutes the English Queen." *The New York Times*, July 12, 1976

3. Al Stern, telegram. September 8, 1976. INC files.

4. "The Peanut and the Shamrock," the *Guardian*, October 29, 1976.

5. *Boston Globe*, Monday, April 18, 1977.

6. Tim Pat Coogan, *A Memoir*, (Weidenfeld & Nicolson, London, 2008), 198.

7. "Irish Priest Denies Forcing Carter Remark in Talk Here." National Catholic News Service, week of Nov. 17, 1976.

8. Jack Anderson with Les Whitten, "The one about Jimmy & the Irish." *Daily News*, Tuesday, Nov. 16, 1976.

9. Paul O'Dwyer's letter to Jimmy Carter. INC files.

10. Maurice Fitzpatrick, John Hume in America. 61. Irish Academic Press. 2017

11. "President's hearty welcome in Massachusetts shows strength of popular support." *The Times*, March 18, 1977.

12. Stephen Aiello, White House Mailgram from special assistant to the President for Ethnic Affairs, April 2, 1980. INC files.

13. "Fr. McManus Meets Carter in White House," *Fermanagh Herald*, June 14, 1980.

14. Professor Paul Power, "The United States and Northern Ireland: the Carter Initiative and its Aftermath," (paper. American Committee for Irish Studies, University of Delaware, April 24-26, 1980)."

15. Joseph E. Thompson, *American Policy and Northern Ireland: A Saga of Peacebuilding* (Praeger, Westport, Connecticut, 2001), 38.

16. "President Carter States Policy on Northern Ireland" (Department of State bulletin, 77, September 26, 1977).

17. John Kelly, "The Carter Initiative: How the Caucus Got Their Man." *The Sunday Press* (Dublin), Sept. 4, 1977.

18. Irish Caucus Cued Carter: McManus." *The Irish Times*, Aug. 31, 1977.

CHAPTER 11: THE LONG KNIVES OF THE IRISH GOVERNMENT

1. Letter from INC member, INC files.

2. *The New York Times*, Sunday, March 20, 1977.

3. "Dublin Players Get Warning on US Tour," *The Irish Press*, April 21, 1997.

4. Paddy Downey, "GAA tour of United States is on." *The Irish Times*, April 23, 1977.

5. David Nyhan, "Hub Priest Denies He Backs IRA," *Boston Globe*, April 18, 1977.

6. David Nyhan, "Ireland Putting Heat on Me," says priest, *Boston Globe*, May 19, 1977.

7. "Hub Priest Charges Irish Consul with 'Dirty Trick.'"*Boston Herald American*, May 20, 1977.

8. "Consul Accused of 'Dirty Tricks.'" *Irish Post*, June 11, 1977.

9. *The Evangelist*, (Albany, NY). June 9, 1977.

10. Charles H. Gibbons, Jr., Letter of to the editor of *Boston Globe*, June 3, 1977. INC files.

11. "Priest Hits at Bishops over Silence on North," *The Irish Press*, Dec. 30, 1976.

12. "Court Tells Writer to Name Informant," *The New York Times*, Sunday, April 29, 1979.

13. Russell Warren Howe, "Reveal the Name or go to Jail." *Washington Journalism Review*, Jan./Feb. 1991.

14. "Lobby ... Gaining Support in Congress." *The New York Times*, Sept. 21, 1979.

15. "Formation of Ad Hoc Committee for Irish Affairs." INC press release, September 27, 1977; see also "Kinawley-born Rev. Sean McManus Chairs Press Conference in Washington," *Fermanagh Herald*, November 19, 1977; "Irish Get Ear of Congress," *Irish News* (Belfast), September 29, 1977; "U.S. Committee to Consider Injustice," *The Irish Times*, September 29, 1977.

16. "Irish Priest Blasts U.S. Hierarchy." Religious News Service, Sept. 28, 1977.

17. "The Irish National Caucus," Editorials, National Hibernian Digest, September-October 1983.

18. *The Irish Times*, June 29, 1978.

19. "Northern Ireland: A Role for the United States?" Report by two members of the Committee on the Judiciary (Ninety-fifth Congress, U.S. Government Printing Press), vii.

20. *Ibid.*, 219.

21. "Provisionals Disown U.S. Caucus Man." *The Irish Press*, September 27, 1978.

22. INC press release, October 18, 1977; "Caucus to Boycott Provisionals."

CHAPTER 12: MOVE TO WASHINGTON

1. Joseph E. Thompson, *American Policy and Northern Ireland: A Saga of Peacebuilding* (Praeger, Westport, Connecticut, 2001), 52.

2. Sean Cronin, "Blaney Elated at FF Choice." *The Irish Times*, Dec. 8, 1979.

3. "Irish Caucus in the Corridors of Power." *The Irish Times*, Sept. 4, 1979.

4. "The American Connection ... the Men Behind the Mounting Anti-British Chorus in Congress."*Belfast Telegraph*, May 16, 1979.

5. Ken Hartnett, "A Shift on Ulster."*Boston Globe*, March 17, 1979.

6. Garret FitzGerald, *All in a Life: An Autobiography*, (London, Macmillan, 1991), 348.

7. Fr. William D'Arcy, OFM Conv., *The Fenian Movement in the United States: 1858–1886* (The Catholic University of America Press, Washington, DC, 1947), 364.

8. Sean Donlon's letter to Congressman Fish, Nov. 6, 1979, copy in INC files.

9. Leonard Downie, Jr,. "Irish Drop Plans to Replace Envoy," *The Washington Post*, July 9, 1980.

10. "Birmingham Six Case 'Discredited'." *The Irish Press*, Monday, Nov. 4, 1985.

11. "FitzGerald Calls on Haughey to Reject IRA 'Front' Groups." Geraldine Kennedy, *The Irish Times*, July 21, 1980.

12. "FitzGerald Asked for Condemnation." *The Irish Times*, July 28, 1980.

13. FitzGerald, ibid., p. 350.

14. "Report from Capitol Hill: As if Congress Were Not Already Splinter U.S. News and World Report, February 4, 1980.

15. "What's a Boycott Between Friends?" *The NY Times*. May 28, 1980.

16. The Donlon Affair: Irish May Replace Envoy to US in Policy Shift on NI. "Leonard Downey, Jr. and Virginia Hamill, *The Washington Post*, July 8, 1980.

17. "US is reviewing RUC arm sales" *The Irish Press*, August 3. 1979.

18. Letter of State Dept. Counselor Matt Nimetz to Mario Biaggi. *NY Times*, June 7, 1980.

19. "No Guns for Violating Irish Rights: Letter on arms sale to Britain" Mario Biaggi, *New York Times*, June 7, 1980.

20. "Paisley's Visa Revoked by US." *Boston Globe*. Dec. 9, 1981.

21. "Kennedy, O'Neill ask US to bar Paisley "*Boston Globe*. Dec. 9, 1981.

22. "Taking the Bob out of Bob Jones University–Christian Institution Readies For the Next Generation." Peter Carlson, *The Washington Post*. May 5, 2005.

23. Statement, May 30, 1981. INC files.

Chapter 13: The Old Sow That Eats Its Own Farrow

1. Horace, Roman poet, 65 BC–8 BC. 430

2. James Joyce, *Portrait of the Artist as a Young Man* (Modern Library, New York, 1928), 238.

3. "Provos Fall Out with Caucus Priest." *Sunday World*, March 21, 1982.

4. Fr. William Darcy. The Fenian Movement in the United States 185–1886. (Washington, DC: The Catholic University of America. 1947), 218.

5. Gerry Adams Interview, *Hibernia Review*, October 1979.

6. David Lynch, *Radical Politics in Modern Ireland: the Republican Party, 1896–1904* (Dublin, Irish Academic Press, 2005). Irish Socialist. 2.

7. Washington Caucus," editorial, *The Irish People*. October 18, 1980.

8. John Cassidy, "Banished Priest Who Has Ear of All America's Top Politicians." *Sunday World*, March 18, 2007.

9. Telephone conversation, January 24, 2010.

10. Joseph E.Thompson, *American Policyand Northern Ireland: A Saga of Peacebuilding* (Westport, Praeger, Connecticut, 2001), 55.

11. They Change Their Sky, (University of Maine Press. 2002), 23.

12. "Ford Admits Plot to Rewrite MacBride Principles." INC press release. August 29, 1990.

13. "MacBride Campaign Takes Harrisburg by Storm." INC Press Release. Sept. 20, 1989.

14. Caucus Leader Grand marshall in Harrisburg." INC Press Release, March 12, 1990.

15. Letter of Mary Pat Clark, President, Baltimore City Council, Aug. 9, 1993. INC files.

16. "Funeral Guns Mute Ministerial Offennsive, "David Blundy, *The Sunday Times*. July 12, 1981.

CHAPTER 14: CAPITOL HILL STRUGGLE

1. Frederick Douglass, American abolitionist, lecturer, author and slave, 1817–1895. The quote is from the "West India Emancipation" speech he gave on August 3, 1857, at Canandaigua, New York, on the twenty-431 third anniversary of the event.

2. Vincent Browne, "Growing Interest in NI." *Evening Herald*, August 3, 1979.

3. Joseph E. Thompson, *American Policy and Northern Ireland: A Saga of Peacebuilding* (Westport, Praeger, Connecticut, 2001), 80.

4. Ibid., 80.

5. Ibid., 84.

6. Ibid., 229.

7. Kevin McNamara, *The MacBride Principles: Irish-America Strikes Back* (Liverpool University Press, 2009), 15.

8. Ibid., 15.

9. "Kennedy, Donnelly Unveil Visa Proposal," Sen. Edward M. Kennedy and Rep. Brian J. Donnelly yesterday introduced legislation to increase annually by 50,000 the number of visas available to people from Ireland, Italy, some other Western European countries and Canada who wish to immigrate to the United States. Charging that the present system discriminates against countries ..." *Boston Globe*, August 7, 1987.

10. The Sunningdale Agreement, signed on December 9, 1973, led to the establishment of a cross-community, power-sharing Executive to

govern Northern Ireland. The Agreement collapsed six months later because of strenuous opposition from Unionists and Loyalists.

11. Vincent Browne, "The Status of the North: It's not F.F. Policy." *Sunday Independent*, January 29, 1978.

12. Al Hunt "Departure of Two Top O'Neill Aides Marks Loss Of Key Participants in Shaping House Agenda.", *The Wall Street Journal*, December 9, 1985.

13. "Irish Politics." Jack Anderson and Les Whitten, *New York Daily News*, October 21, 1977.

14. "White House Policy." Jack Anderson, *The Washington Post*, June 17, 1978.

15. "Carter Pressured on Northern Ireland." Jack Anderson, *Detroit Free Press*, October 29, 1978.

16. Joseph E. Thompson, *American Policy and Northern Ireland: A Saga of Peacebuilding* (Praeger, Westport, Connecticut, 2001), 57.

17. "Tip O'Neill," *Irish-America*, October 1986.

18. "The Anglo-Irish Agreement Support Act of September 19, 1986 (P.L. 99–415) authorized U.S. contributions to an international fund for economic development projects in Northern Ireland and the Republic of Ireland ... This is the first time the U.S. Government has ever given economic aid to this region," CRS Issue Brief, Northern Ireland and the Republic of Ireland: U.S. Foreign Assistance Facts, October 6, 1989.

19. T. S. Elliot. *Murder in the Cathedral*, (Florida, Harcourt, Brace and Company, 1935).

20. "Irish-American Leader Seeks Roadblocks in Aid to Ireland." *New Hampshire Sunday News* (the Sunday edition of the *Union Leader*), March 9, 1986; of course, I wanted conditions, not "roadblocks"—but Tom Gorey did not write the headline.

21. Garret FitzGerald, "The Most Helpful Ally Ireland Has Ever Had in Washington." *The Irish Times,* January 8, 1994.

22. Kate O'Callaghan, "The Government Strikes Back." *Irish Voice*, May 6, 1989.

23. Ibid.

24. Sean Cronin, "Angry Words at Ireland Fund Hearing." *The Irish Times*, April 26, 1989.

25. "This Week They Said." *The Irish Times*, May 20, 1989.

26. Biden's quote from stenographic transcript of Hearing on August 5, 1985, before the Senate Committee on Foreign Affairs, 34. INC press release,

27. Simon Hoggart, "Britain and Irish in Battle on Capitol Hill." *Observer*, Sept. 15, 1985.

28. "When Irish Eyes Are Frowning." *The Washington Post* National Weekly Edition, October 7, 1985.

29. Christopher Hitchens, "Attacking an IRA Refuge."*Spectator*, October 5, 1985.

30. David Blundy, "Battling Extradition Treaty" *The Sunday Times*, August 11, 1985.

31. "Treaty Stalled." John Robinson, *Boston Globe*, October 23, 1985.

32. Niall O'Dowd, "Caucus Blocks Anti-IRA Move." *The Sunday Press*, July 21, 1985.

33. Fergus Pyle, "Delay in Extradition Law Irks Thatcher." *The Irish Times*, April 28, 1986.

34. Senator Hatch correspondence, INC files.

CHAPTER 15: THE MACBRIDE PRINCIPLES: GENESIS AND HISTORY

1. "An Army of Principles Will Penetrate Where an Army of soldiers cannot." Thomas Paine, *Agrarian Justice*. Pamphlet was written in 1775, published in 1797.

2. The Sullivan Principles are a corporate code of conduct developed by the African American preacher Rev. Leon Sullivan in 1977 for US companies doing business in South Africa to protest agains apartheid.

3. "Caucus in Jobs Blacklist Move: Americans Probe Workers' Religions," *Sunday News*, July 29, 1979.

4. "Irish Caucus Investigates American Firms." *The Irish Times*, July 30, 1979.

5. "Investigating Behavior of American Firms." *The Irish Press*, July 28, 1979.

6. "Investigating Alleged Discrimination." *Belfast Telegraph*, July 28, 1979.

7. "MacBride to Head New Irish Caucus group." *The Irish Times*, August 4, 1979.

8. "Sean MacBride Heads Caucus Liaison Group." *Irish World*, September 15, 1979. 435

9. INC press release, November 4, 1983, INC files.

10. "Irish Embassy Move Angers U.S. Groups." *The Irish Press*, November 4, 1983.

11. "Americans in Ulster Maelstrom." *Daily Telegraph*, August 18, 1983.

12. "Anti-British to the Hilt." *News Letter* (Belfast). August 18, 1983.

13. "Rancid Bigot." *Daily Express* (UK), August 18, 1983.

14. Cardinal Ó Fiaich's Mailgram, April 22, 1987, INC files.

15. "Eccles Not Paid." *Sunday News*, April 2, 1989.

16. Kevin Mc Namara, *The MacBride Principles: Irish-America Strikes Back* (Liverpool University Press, 2009), 103–104.

17. "FEA Man's Firm Lashed Over Bias." *Sunday World* (Dublin), June 3, 1990.

18. "Aer Lingus Covers up for Shorts." INC press release, June 30, 1983.

19. Congressman Shannon's letter, September 2, 1983, INC files.

20. Paddy Devlin, "MacBride Principles Spell Kiss of Death." *Sunday World*, May 11, 1986.

21. "The MacBride Principles a Sham." Paddy Devlin, *Sunday World*, June 7, 1987.

22. "Caucus Proposes New Initiative to Stop Discrimination in Northern Ireland." *Irish Echo* (New York), November 10, 1984.

23. Michael Farrell, "New U.S. Company code endangers NI investment." *Sunday Tribune*, Nov. 4, 1984. Of course, Farrell did not write the headline, and he was one of the first journalists in Ireland to immediately realize the importance of our initiative.

24. "Albanese Urges Bias Bill on US firms in Ulster." *New York Daily News*, January 2, 1985.

25. "Fr. McManus Press Conference." *Irish Echo*, January 2, 1985.

26. "Investment Pressure for NI Catholic Rights." *Chief Leader*, January 11, 1985.

27. Tricia Gallagher, "Pension Fund Proposal." *Catholic New York*, February 7, 1985.

28. Will Ellsworth-Jones, "New York Threat of Ulster Shares Boycott." *The Times*, January 6, 1985.

29. Niall O'Dowd, "US bill on North Bias by Companies." *The Irish Press*, Jan. 4, 1985.

30. "Koch and Goldin Oppose Ulster Investment Ban." *New York Daily News*, Jan. 4, 1985.

31. Patrick Campbell "Campbell's Scoop,"; "Of pension fund investments," *The Irish Echo*, Jan. 19, 1985.

32. Jesus Rangel, "Investment in Ulster Opposed." *The New York Times*, Jan. 4, 1985.

33. "Goldin visit to NI." *New York Daily News*, June 25, 1985.

34. "Goldin's Irish Tenor is Way Off Key." *New York Daily News*, July 19, 1985.

35. "Unfair to Ulster," *The New York Times*, July 5, 1985.

36. "Goldin and Northern Ireland," *New York Post*, June 27, 1985.

37. "Economic Influence Suggested for Ulster." *The Sunday Republican*, Feb. 3, 1985.

38. Tom Gallagher, State Representative, letter to the author, October 1, 1985, INC files.

39. Tiernan MacBride, letter to the author, January 25, 1988, INC files.

40. Caitriona Lawlor, letter to Ken Bertsch, June 28, 1993, INC files.

41. Kevin McNamara, *The MacBride Principles: Irish-America Strikes Back*. Liverpool University Press, 2009), 27.

42. Ibid., 24.

43. Mary Holland, "Agonizing over a few principles." *The Irish Times*, Wednesday, Oct. 7, 1987.

44. Mary Holland's letter, November 15, 1987, INCfiles.

45. Peter Mc Dermott, "Doherty's Way. NYC Aims to Keep Investments Ethical." *Irish Echo*, November 12, 2008.

CHAPTER 16: ANTI-MACBRIDE CAMPAIGN

1. N.E. Sheinwald, letter to Tom Donahue, Secretary-Treasurer, AFL-CIO, March 1, 1985.

2. Kevin McNamara, *The MacBride Principles: Irish-America Strikes Back* (Liverpool University Press, 2009), 89.

3. *Sunday Life* (Belfast), March 22, 1992.

4. "Ulster Leader Assails American Supporters of MacBride Plan. "*The Boston Sunday Globe,* March 8, 1987.

5. "Principles that Burden." *Boston Globe* editorial, March 11, 1987.

6. "Ex-IRA Leader Fights for Jobs." *Boston Globe,* April 25, 1987.

7. "Bishop Opposes Jobs Measures." *Boston Globe,* Nov. 25, 1989.

8. "Bishop Daly Questioned on MacBride." *Irish Voice,* Dec. 9, 1989.

9. "Daly Denies He's Opposed to MacBride." *Irish Echo,* Feb. 12-23, 1993.

10. Bishop McAuliffe, letter to John Carr, August 3, 1993, INC files.

11. INC and Office of Justice and Peace Meeting, INC press release, January 6, 1978, INC files.

12. Letter to Caucus member, dated October 17, 1979. Edward Doherty writing on the official stationery of the United States Catholic Conference, INC files.

13. Archbishop Hickey, letter to author, February 6, 1981; Bishop Kelly's letter to the author, January 29, 1981, INC files.

14. Moderator Dunlop's letter to Sister Regina, May 14, 1993; letter of Josiah Beeman, Chair of the Northern Ireland Working Group of Presbyterian Churches in the United States, to Sister Regina, INC files.

15. "Proposed Church Conference on MacBride Principles Provoke Questions, Suspicions." INC press release, May 26, 1993, INC file.

16. Author, letter to all U.S. Catholic Bishops, May 26, 1993, INC files.

17. "A Call For Fair Employment and Investment in Northern Ireland," statement issued by the four main Churches, January 14, 1993.

18. Garret FitzGerald, "The Path to Peace," remarks by An Taoiseach, Kennedy Library, Boston, May 3, 1985.

19. *Ibid.*, 131.

20. "Dole, GOP Congressional Leaders Meet With Irish Prime Minister." RNC News Release, September 11, 1996.

21. *Ibid.*, 150.

22. *Ibid.*, 131.

23. *Ibid.*, 159.

24. *Ibid.*, 160.

25. Steven Weisman, *Daniel Patrick Moynihan: A Portrait in Letters of an American Visionary.* Public Affairs.(New York. 2 0 1 0) ; "Senator Moynihan afraid he'd be shot by IRA at Saint Pat's Parade"; Patrick Roberts. Irish Central. Jan. 4, 2011. 440

26. *Ibid.*, 23. 26.

27. *Ibid.,* 141.

28. *Ibid.,* 124, 125.

CHAPTER 17: FORCING CLINTON TO SIGN MACBRIDE

1. H.R. 725: "To provide for adherence with the MacBride Principles by United States persons doing business in Northern Ireland. Sponsor: Rep. Fish, Hamilton, Jr. [NY-21] (introduced 1/31/1989). Cosponsors (97). Latest Major Action: May 5,1989. Referred to House subcommittee. Status: Referred to the Subcommittee on Rules of the House.

2. Congressman Lee Hamilton's letter to the author, Aug. 14 1987, INC files.

3. Kevin McNamara. The MacBride Principles: Irish America Strikes Back. (Liverpool University Press, 2009). 159.

4. *Ibid.,* viii.

5. "Capital Hil Reception Huge Success: Gilman Announces MacBride Hearing." INC press release, January 27, 1995, INC files.

6. Hearing before House International Relations Committee, March 15, 1995. (US Government Printing Office, Washington, 1995). 2.

7. *Ibid.,* 74-79.

8. "Clinton Bids to Quell Storm Over MacBride ." Ray O'Hanlon, *Irish Echo,* August 28--September 3, 1996.

9. "Caucus Welcomes Clinton Back to MacBride Fold." INC press release, August 28, 28, 1996, INC files.

10. "Democratic platform renews support for NI peace moves." Joe Carroll, *The Irish Times*. August 27, 1996. 441

11. Author's reviews of Kevin McNamara's book: *The MacBride Principles: Irish America Fights Back*, INC website (www.irishnatioalcaucus.org).

CHAPTER 18: "A PROTESTANT BOY" ON CAPITOL HILL

1. Nuala O'Loan, "*Operation Ballast, A Report on the Police Ombudsman's investigation into matters surrounding the death of Raymond Mc Cord Jr.,*" 2007.

2. "McCord at British Embassy: Deep Disappointment, May 14, 2009, INC press release, INCfiles.

CHAPTER 21: CHANGING MY SKY NOT MY SOUL

1. Michael C. Connolly. *They Change Their Sky: The Irish in Maine*. Edited: The University of Maine. 2002.

2. Thomas Cahill. *How the Irish Saved Civilization*. Anchor Books. New York. 1995.

3. Ibid. 193

4. Angela F. Murphy. *American Slavery: Irish Freedom*. Louisiana State University Press. 2010. 158.

5. On Saturday, December 4, 1971, loyalists from the Ulster Volunteer Force (UVF), under the control of the British military, a no-warning bomb on the doorstep of a family-run bar in north Belfast...killing 15 people, However, the security forces deliberately lied, claiming it was an IRA bomb that had exploded prematurely a it was being constructed inside the bar. Ciaran MacAirt's grandmother, Kathleen

Irvine, was one of the fifteen people killed. www.themcgurksbar-massacre.com

EPILOGUE

1. Marcus Porcius, Cato, (234BC-149BC). Roman statesman, orator and writer, known as Cato the Elder.

2. St. Thomas Aquinas, Summa Theologica. 11-11, 158, 1 and 3.

INDEX

Act of Settlement, 197, 243, 244, 366, 386, 388-390
Adams, Gerry, 66, 99, 158, 186, 187, 203, 210, 301, 359, 431
Ad Hoc Congressional Committee, 150, 152, 179, 205, 218-222, 256, 303, 308, 326, 329, 462
AFL-CIO, v, 103, 163, 272, 276, 336-342, 397
Albanese, Sal, 264, 266-268, 323
Albert, Speaker, 231
Ali, Muhammad, 28
Anderson, Jack Anderson Column, 136, 229
Anderson, John, 34
Anglo-Irish Agreement of 1985, 234, 283
Anti-Partition campaign, 22
AOH, iii, 51, 83, 101, 102, 125, 150, 152, 153, 162, 196-202, 265, 351, 352
Armstrong, Maureen, 105, 110
Armstrong, State Senator Gibson, 199

B

B- Specials, 22, 55, 56
Baggarly, Mary, 110, 118
Ballagh, Bobby, 212, 350
Ballymurphy Massacre, 211, 348, 349, 409, 410
Barr, Glenn, 177, 178
Barry, Kevin, 122
Bateman, Robert J., iii, 154, 174, 224, 346 Beliveau, Severin M., 278
Benelli, Archbishop Giovanni, 125, 126, 147
Berrigan, Fr. Phil, 104-107, 109, 113, 115
Biaggi (D-NY), Mario, vi, 84, 150, 152, 156, 162, 163, 167, 169, 175, 176, 179, 180, 221, 256, 303, 323, 359
Biden, Senator Joe, 181, 239, 434

Big Four, 169
Birmingham Six, 173-175, 233, 299, 305, 326, 430
Black Freedom Struggle, 61, 67, 72, 357
Blair, Prime Minister Tony, 358
Blancato, Bob, 163, 256
Blaney, T. D. M.E.P., Neil, 173, 175, 189, 190, 253, 429
Boland, Kevin, 252, 293
Bonneric, Monsignor, 125
Boxer (D-CA), Congresswoman Barbara, 256
Brady, Fr. Brian, 253, 259, 266
Breheny, John, 199, 200
Brexit, 353, 358, 461-463
Browne, Vincent, iii, xiv, 212, 218, 228, 350, 431, 432
Bulger, Senator Billy, 264, 271
Burke, Dave, 101, 102, 303
Bus Boycott, Montgomery, Alabama, 30
Bush, Vice President George H., 183

C

Cahill, Joe, 85, 112, 126, 154, 157, 197
Carey, Governor Hugh, 142, 143, 169, 175
Carnahan, Rep. Russ, 348
Carn, 5, 6
"The Carn Lintel," 8, 361
Carney, Rep. William, 182 Carr, John, 287, 439
Carron MP, Owen, 181
Carter, Jimmy, 187, 128, 130, 132, 134, 136, 139, 142, 164, 304, 373, 374, 426
Casey (D-PA), Governor Robert, 200
Catholic Conference, 287-291, 439
Chavez, Cesar, 245
Classicism, 42, 43
Clerkin, Fr. Sean, 27, 66
Clifford, Tommy, 129, 346

Clifford, Agnes, 129
Clinton, Bill, 207, 237, 289, 303, 304, 307
Clinton, Hillary, 208, 358
Clonliff, 5, 6, 10, 19, 21, 26, 36, 37, 40, 49, 76, 358, 402
Clough, George, 201
Coleman, Gerry, 237
Collins, Michael, 256
Collins, Michael, (Irish Leader), 52
Congressional Friends, 222, 223, 308
Connolly O' Brien, Nora, 129
Conte (R-MA), Silvio O., 98
Conway, Neil, 346
Coogan, Tim Pat, 135, 426
Cooper, Bob, 278
Cooper, Tom, 350
Corish, Eddie, 49
Craigavon factory, 251
Corkery, Brendan, 217
Cromwell, Oliver, 230
Cronin, Sean, 22, 25, 82, 84, 160, 168, 179, 186, 238, 429, 434
Croke Park, 144
Crowley (D-NY), Congressman Joe, 329
Cullen, Hugh, 15
Cummings (D–MD), Congressman Elijah E., 223
Curran, Joe, 202
Currie, H.J. Chief Inspector RUC, 61

D

Dailey, Bishop Thomas V., 145-147 Daley, Mayor, 133
Daly, Bishop Edward, 90
Daly, Bishop Cathal, 260, 285, 288
De Valera, Eamon, 52, 123, 186, 187
De Concini, Senator, 303

Delahunt, Bill, 329, 348
Delaney, Jim, 193, 194
Dennehy, Dan, 352
Derryrealt, 23
Devlin, MP, Bernadette, 69, 73, 80
Devoy, John, ii, xiii, 319, 320, 326, 404
Doherty, Carmel, 58
Doherty, Edward, 288, 439
Doherty, Joe, 242, 359
Doherty, Pat, 269, 270, 274, 314
Dole, Bob, 294, 317
Donahue, Tom, 276, 439
Donaldson, Denis, 195, 197, 379
Donlon, Sean, 139, 171, 175, 190, 218, 219, 236, 263, 301, 305, 356, 430
Donnelly, Congressman Brian, 223
Donelly, Donal, 213
Dorr, Noel, 305
Downes, Larry, 244, 313
Doyle, John, 278
Drumbroughas National School, 12, 13, 21, 27
Drumm, Jimmy, 188
Drury, Bishop Thomas Drury, 96, 99, 100, 102, 125, 151, 165, 166, 226, 420
Dublin,(Irish)Government, 83, 84, 101, 134, 141, 142, 144, 147, 151,154, 155, 157, 178, 180, 186, 187, 190, 193, 194, 203, 219, 222, 231,233, 235, 240, 262, 263, 265, 277, 282, 284, 302, 311, 312, 355, 367
Dukakis, Governor Michael, 272
Dunlop, Rev. Dr. John, 288, 290, 440

E

East, Fr. Ray, 280
Eccles, James, 259
Eilberg, (D-PA), Joshua, 156
Engel, Elliot L., 223, 359

Extradition Treaty, 238, 241, 434

F

Faul, Fr. Denis, 288 Fee, Tom, 13
Fenians, 45, 66, 173, 186, 275
Fenian Raid, 173
Ferguson, Caroline, 124
Ferguson, Michael, 11, 23, 24, 59
Fine Gael, 176, 228
Finucane, Geraldine (Mrs.), 214, 349
Finucane, John, 313, 348
Finucane, Pat, 307, 326
    Fish (R-NY), Congressman Hamilton, 156, 173, 183, 206, 221
    Fitt, Gerry, 69, 175
FitzGerald, Garrett, 142, 146, 149, 172, 176, 177, 194, 199, 203, 231, 236, 253, 255, 262, 263, 282, 283, 288, 292, 304, 355, 430, 433, 440
    at Corrymeela Reconciliation Center, 177
    Irish-American Partnership, 253
    Jimmy Carter, 142
Flaherty, Barbara J., xx, 216, 217, 334, 337-340, 342, 351, 360, 380, 405
Flaherty, Barbara Maureen, xxx
Flaherty, Martin, 302
Flannery, Michael, 101, 160, 190, 191, 302, 379
Flynn, Bill, iii, 353
Flynn, Mayor Ray, iii, 285
Flynn, State Senator John, 264, 272
Fogarty, Cathy, 118
Foley, Fr. Jim, 145
Foley, Speaker Tom, 221, 237, 305, 307
Ford Motor Company, 196
Foster, Arlene, 214
Four Horsemen, 143
Fox, Fr., 24, 25
Frank (D-MA), Congressman Barney, 222-224

Fraser (D-MN), Congressman Donald M., 99
Friends of Ireland, 221-223, 305, 306, 308, 326, 329

G

GAA (Gaelic Athletic Association), 26, 33, 46, 124, 144, 145, 351, 428
Gallagher, Tom (D-18th Suffolk District), 272, 438
Gallagher, Dermot, 299
Gebre, Tefere, 341
Gibbons, Jr., Charles H., 146, 428
Gildernew, Michelle, 213, 351, 393
Gilman (R-NY), Congressman Ben, ii, xiii, 208, 221, 235, 249, 250, 274, 307, 308, 310, 311, 317, 319, 322, 323, 325, 359, 442
Gilmartin, Fr., 24, 24
Gilmore, Aideen, 348
Gingrich, Newt, 210, 307, 359
Goldin, Comptroller Harrison J., 264, 266, 268, 271, 273-275, 323, 437, 438
Gore, Al, 12, 207
Gorey, Tom, 234, 235, 433
Gormley, Brian, 349
Goulding, Cathal, 54
Guildford Four, 233, 326

H

Haft, Marilyn, 138
Hamilton (D-ID), Congressman Lee, 234, 237, 305, 317, 441
Hannon, Matt, 171, 194
Han, Dr. Min Su, 332-334, 336, 405
Hanton, Fr. Joe, 33, 34
Harding, Rev. David, 115
Haring, Fr. Bernard, 88, 354, 424
Harris, Richard, 121, 209
Harte, T.D, Paddy, 253
Hatch, Senator Orrin, 242, 435

Hastings, Alcee, 223
Haughey, Charlie, 173, 175, 176, 236, 270, 293-295, 298, 300, 304-305, 310, 416, 430
Hawkstone (Redemptorist Major Seminary), 32, 35, 39, 41, 43-48, 51-54, 60, 61, 72, 81, 88, 109, 422
Healy, Cahir, 22
Heaney, Carmel, 145-147, 272, 356 Helms (R-NC), Senator Jesse, 182
Helsinki Commission, 223, 307, 349, 410
Hickey, Archbishop, 289, 439
Hickey, David, 144
Higgins, Michael D., 212, 351, 356
Hill, Paul, 233
Hitchens, Christopher, vii, 240, 434
Hogan, Mary, 352
Holtzman, Elizabeth, 259, 323
Hughes, Francis, 184
Hughes, Oliver, 351
Hume, John, 111, 112, 137, 176, 210, 219, 233, 254, 263, 270, 272, 277, 285-284, 295-297, 302, 317, 427
Hunger Strike, 84, 86, 87, 93, 105, 127, 142, 144, 145, 183, 184, 189, 257, 326, 417
(Portlaoise), 144
(Long Kesh), 70 ,117, 118, 142

I

IFI-International Fund for Ireland, 162, 234, 235, 237, 248, 308, 312, 315, 317, 319
Irish American Unity Conference, 194, 313, 378, 380
Irish Embassy, 99, 100, 129, 134, 136, 137, 138, 145, 147-153, 168, 172-175, 190, 193-195, 218-223, 227-229, 232, 236, 254-256, 262, 263, 289, 292-296, 299, 303, 305, 306, 310, 311, 319, 355, 356, 378, 379, 395, 436

451

Irish Government (Dublin Government), See Dublin Government Irish National Caucus, and the ban on sale of U.S. weapons to RUC, 178-182

and the British Embassy, Washington, 95, 98, 100, 104-106, 108, 111-116, 138, 139, 168, 185, 198, 244-246, 255, 276, 278, 279-281, 288, 290, 303, 319, 328, 330, 374, 377-379, 386, 395

Congressional Reception, 308 Delegation to the Vatican, 125

Donlon and the, 139, 171, 175, 190, 219, 236, 263, 301, 305

FitzGerald and the, 134-139, 142, 146, 149, 172, 176-178, 194, 199, 203, 231, 233, 236, 253, 255, 262, 283, 288, 292-294, 304, 305, 355

Flannery and the, 101, 160, 190, 191 Formation of the, 93-103

Harnett and the, 169, 179

Haughey and the, 173, 175, 176, 236, 270, 293-295, 298, 300, 304, 305, 310, 416

influence on American policy on Northern Ireland, 141-143, 151-153, 169, 174, 176, 178, 271-273

and the MacBride Principles, 170—201 office on Capitol Hill, 98-101

Irish National Congress, 350

Irish Northern Aid (Noraid), 83, 84, 93, 101, 112, 121, 125, 160, 185, 187, 188, 190, 191, 195, 197, 198, 237, 238, 313, 378, 379, 385

Irish Peace Forum, 154

Irish Peace Process, vi, 175, 233, 301, 303, 305, 312, 313, 359, 410 Irish Republican Army (IRA), 18, 21, 23, 24, 27, 31, 48, 52, 54, 59-65, 70, 78, 81, 82, 84-86, 89, 91, 99, 101, 112, 116, 117, 123, 126, 138, 141, 143-150, 154, 157-159, 166, 168-170, 172, 175, 179, 180, 184- 194, 203, 219, 228, 229, 232, 235-238, 241, 284, 299, 301, 302, 350, 358, 367, 369, 374-376, 395, 415, 422, 425, 428, 430, 434, 439, 440, 443

Irish Rights Watch, 348

J

Jackson, Senator Henry, 127, 128, 141

Jay, Peter, 100 Jones, Bob III, 182

Justice in the World (Synod of Bishops), 166, 353, 395, 398, 420

K

Kashkett, Steve, 318, 319
Keane, Jack, 102, 125, 153, 425
Kelly, Bishop, 289, 439
Kelly, Padraig, 23
Kennedy, Bobby, 223, 224, 233
Kennedy, David M., 262
Kennedy (D-MA), Congressman Joe, II 224, 246, 259, 285
Kennedy, (D-MA), Congressman Joe, III, 223, 225
Kennedy, President, 334, 382
Kennedy, Ted, 142, 143, 153, 169, 175, 180, 221, 233, 238, 242, 285, 302, 317
Kerins, Fr. Joseph L., 75, 81, 82, 87, 89, 149
Killaduff Cemetery, 24
Kinawley, iv, 5, 10, 13, 14, 15, 24-26, 28, 29, 34, 46, 54, 59, 61, 66, 159, 194, 224, 232, 241, 280, 330, 354, 355, 360, 382, 383, 399, 402, 421, 429
Kinawley-Swanlinbar team, 14, 25, 26
King Jr., Martin Luther, 3, 30, 67, 71, 73, 83, 88, 92, 120, 121, 286, 304, 310, 322, 357, 359, 391, 392, 410, 420, 422
King, III, Martin Luther, 245
Kipping, 11
Kirkland, Lane, 103
Kissinger, Henry, 80, 232
Koch, Mayor, 268, 269, 437
Ku Klux Klan, 61, 71, 117

L

Lawlor, Caitriona, 273, 438
Lewis (D-GA), Congressman John, 246
Long Kesh, 70, 117, 118, 142
Long March: Baltimore to Washington, 94 Loughinisland Families, 410
Lowey, Nita, 223, 359
Lucas, Fr. George, 40

Lugar, Senator Richard, 241
Lumley-Holmes, Fr. Edward, 91
Lundy, Dr. Patricia, 349
Luther, Martin, 44
Lynch, Taoiseach Jack, 152, 173, 176, 184, 187, 220, 221, 236, 355

M

MI5, 303, 358, 415
MacAirt, Ciaran, 409
MacBride Principles, 177, 196, 199, 200, 201, 205, 234, 235, 247-303, 359, 377, 378, 393
    and Bill Clinton, 135, 207, 303, 304, 306, 307, 309, 310, 312-319
MacBride Principles Contract Compliance Bill, 272 MacBride Hearing, 260, 279, 280, 308, 442
MacBride Principles: Irish America Strikes Back (McNamara's book), 221, 274, 275, 293, 298, 299, 302, 305, 310, 314, 315, 317
MacBride, Seán, 159, 160, 196, 251-254, 264-266, 270, 271, 273-275, 282-284, 295-301, 319, 435, 462
MacBride, Tiernan, 295
MacLua, Brendan, 146
MacManais, Ray, 320
Macrae, Callum, 408, 409
MacStiofain, Sean 84-88
Maguire, Patrick, 8, 27, 29, 361
Maloney, Carolyn, 359
Mallon, Seamus, 297
Mason, Roy, 134
Maulding, Reginald, 69
McAleese, President Mary, 320, 356
McAllister, Malachy, 352
McCarthy, Jack, 84, 96, 144, 160
McCord, Sr., Raymond, 328, 329, 331, 406, 409
McCormack, Speaker John, 227
McCourt, Malachy, 16, 421

McCusker, Brendan, 125
McElwee, Alice (Mrs.), 184 McElwee, Tom, 189
McGrath, Terry, 9, 10
McGuinness, Martin, 66, 213, 301, 351, 359
McGurk's Bar, 349
McKay, John, 350
McKernan, Pádraic, 295, 296, 305
McKittrick, David, 168
(McManus Family Listing)
McManus, Alice (Mrs. Brian Hare), 6, 8, 37, 38, 82, 97
McManus, Arthur, 6, 12 McManus, Aunt Lizzie, 8
McManus, Celia (Mrs. Michael Ferguson), 8, 11, 13, 18, 20, 23, 37, 38, 79, 124, 357
McManus, Celia Mc Mullen (Mother), 5-9, 13-15, 18-21, 25, 26, 32, 37, 41, 47, 76-78, 86
McManus, Frank, 6, 8, 11, 14, 15, 20, 21, 26-30, 35-38, 49, 50, 56-60, 62, 63, 66, 69, 73, 85, 90, 95, 97-99, 116, 144, 294, 327, 350, 351
Congressional Hearing, 99
election as MP for Fermanagh and South Tyrone, 56 shooting of, 97
St. Michael's School, Enniskillen, 27
McManus, Jim, Fr., 6, 8, 13, 19, 24, 25, 32-38, 41, 43, 46, 47, 52, 58, 59, 69, 88
McManus, Mary Kate (Mrs. Milan Ruzicka Anders), 6, 8, 13, 26, 34, 37, 38, 358
McManus, Myles, 6, 8, 11, 14, 15, 20, 27, 35-38, 59-62
McManus, Patrick, XV, 6, 8, 13, 14, 18-26, 36, 65, 82, 91, 99
McManus Memorial Park, 26
McManus, Patrick, Sr. (Father), 5-7, 9, 10, 15, 19-21, 32, 39, 40
McManus, Terence, 6
McManus, Terence (the second) ,6, 8, 13, 14, 19, 24, 36, 37, 50, 58-60*
McManus, Thomas, 6, 8, 13, 36, 37, 82 **(End of McManus Family Listing)**
McLaughlin, George, 346

McNabb, Tom, 102, 151,
McNamara, Kevin, 221, 293, 299, 310, 314, 317, 432, 439, 441
McNamee, Eoin,193 Meany, George, 103, 163
Meehan, Barty, 61
Merton, Thomas, 89, 424
Miami Show Band Massacre, 412, 413, 416
Mission Church, Boston, 122-124, 128, 146, 166, 188, 227
Mitchell, Joe, 105, 110
Moakley (D-MA), Congressman Joe, 99
Molloy, John, 105, 149, 231
Morrison, Matt, 352
Mother Teresa, vii, 240
Mowlam, Mo, 358
Moynihan, Senator, 142, 143, 169, 175, 221, 238, 296-302, 440
Mullan, Rita, 168
Mullen, Michael, 252
Murphy, Charles, 11, 39
Murphy, Liam, 101, 102
Murphy, Patrick, 13
Murphy, Phil, 31
Murray, Fr. Raymond, 173, 174
Mythen, Fr. James, 34

N

Nadler (D–NY), Congressman Jerrold, 223,
Neal (D-MA), Congressman Richard E., 204, 222, 223, 329
Neeson, Sean, 279, 280
Neo-Scholasticism, 41, 42
New York GAA Board,
144 Nimetz, Matthew, 180
Nixon, Richard, 130, 156, 231 *No Stone Left Unturned*, 410
Nolan, Fr., 48, 52
Northern Ireland Bureau, 329, 330
Nyhan, David, 145-147, 181, 182, 428

O

Ó Brádaigh, Ruairí, 99, 126, 154, 157, 158, 190, 192, 328
O'Brien, Edna, 45
O'Brien, Fred, 98, 100, 125, 154, 157-159, 168
O'Brien, Jack, 106
O'Brien, Martin, 59
O'Connell, Dave, 65, 85, 86, 99, 154, 157
O'Donnell, Kirk, 221, 228
O'Dowd, Niall, vii, 232, 241, 256, 268, 352, 434
O'Dwyer, Paul, 136, 137, 149, 292, 426
O'Fiaich, Cardinal Thomas, 260, 261
O'Hanlon, Ray, vi, 139, 216, 316, 373, 442
O'Hare, Rita, 348
O'Kennedy, Dan, 193, 194
O'Kennedy, Michael, Foreign Minister, 228
O'Loan, Nuala, 328, 442
O'Malley TD, Desmond, 228
O'Malley, Martin, 202
O'Meara, Dr. Thomas F., 42
O'Muilleoir, Martin, 351
O'Neill, Tip (Thomas P.), v, 99, 142, 143, 151, 161, 162, 167-169, 175, 179, 182, 184, 219, 221, 229-232, 235, 236, 238, 307, 317, 359, 432, 433
    and Congressional Hearings on Northern Ireland, 162, 205, 229, 231
    and Friends of Ireland, 221
    and Saint Patrick's Day Appeal for Peace in Northern Ireland, 141
        O'Reilly-McAuliffe, Bernadette, 168
O'Shea, Master, 34
O'Siochain, Sean, 144
Orange Order, 175, 389, 390
Orangemen, 86, 243, 301, 366, 386, 389, 390
Ottinger (D–NY), Congressman Dick, I, i, 254-257, 264, 272, 274, 322, 359,

P

Paisley, Reverend Ian, 154, 179, 181, 182, 199, 255
Parnell, 186, 188
Patton, Father Gerry, 260
Payne (D-NJ), Congressman Don, 308, 323, 329, 359
Pearse, Patrick, 122
Pelosi, Speaker Nancy, 211, 359
Pilkington, Fr. Liam, 52
Pope Benedict XVI, 92, 397
Pope John Paul II, 35, 333, 335, 345, 397, 410
Pope Leo XIII, 42, 396
Pope Pius IX, 45, 66
Power, Professor Paul, 127, 139, 426, 427

Q

Quinn, Peter, 351

R

Ramsbotham, Sir Peter, 231
Ratzinger, Joseph, 92
Reagan, President, 105, 182-184, 234, 238, 258, 270, 271, 289
Red Hand Commandos, 154
Redemptorists, i, 2, 12, 19, 24, 27, 32, 33, 39, 41, 49, 54, 56, 58, 61, 62, 67, 70, 72, 74, 80-88, 146, 165, 240, 257, 367, 368, 370
    Hawkstone Seminary, 32, 35, 39, 41, 43-48, 51-54, 60, 61, 72, 81, 88
Reilly, Clara, 351
Reilly, Francie, 9
Reilly, Mattie, 160, 346
Relatives for Justice, 349, 351
Republican Movement, 23-25, 85, 141, 155, 157, 158, 185-191, 194, 386
Resolution, 152-154, 248, 269
Reynolds, Paddy, 155
Reynolds, Taoiseach Albert, 135, 304, 355
Robb, Senator John, 266

Rodgers, Owen, 352
Rodino (D-NJ), Peter,156
Royal Ulster Constabulary (RUC), 21, 22, 24, 55, 59-62, 80, 143, 153, 177, 180, 250, 252, 257, 288, 289, 326, 424

S

Saint Patrick's Day 1977, 117
Sands, Bobby, 142, 181, 183, 184, 257, 326, 417
Schumer, Senator Chuck, 359
Sfikas, Perry, 201
Shakespeare, 34
Sheehan, Gene, 123
Sheehan, Tricia, 124
Sheinwald, N.E., 276, 277, 439
Shepherd, Fr. Charles, 2-4, 39, 44, 45, 50, 51, 66, 69, 73, 74, 81, 82, 88, 89, 152, 419
Short Brothers, 257, 258, 263
Shuler, Liz, 342
Sidway, Shawn, 346
Sinn Fein, 23, 63, 66, 99, 154, 157, 158, 166, 186, 191, 194, 195, 197, 213, 215, 232, 244, 270, 271, 301, 328, 348, 352, 367, 376
Smith, Congressman (R-NJ) Chris, 206, 307, 349
Smith, Howard, 167
Smith, Howard, K., 118-121, 167
Snyder, Mitch, 105, 115
Special Ministry of Justice and Peace for Ireland, 126, 166, 167, 394
Spring, Dick, 277
Stanton, Dick, 346
Stagg, Frank, 127, 128, 141
Stanley, Christopher, 349
Stern, Al, 129, 135, 426
Supplemental Extradition Treaty, 238

T

Teddy Boys, 28
Teggart, John, 211, 349
Thant, U, 232
Thatcher, Margaret, 2, 88, 138, 182, 183, 199, 238, 241, 242, 301, 374, 415
Thompson, Professor Joseph E., I, VI, i, xiii, 93, 165, 192, 218-220, 231, 424, 425, 427, 431, 433
Thompson, Mark, 349, 351
Thurmond (R-SC), Senator Strom, 182, 223
Timilty, Senator Joe, 128
Travers, Stephen, 412-416
Trumka, Richard L., 337, 338, 397
Turkel, Ann, 121, 209
Tyrie, Andy, 177

U

Ulster Defense Regiment (UDR), 31, 424
United Irishman, 22, 422
United Nations, 130, 138, 232

V

Vatican I, 43, 147, 165
    Second Vatican Council, 42, 72, 76
Visa Issue, 156

W

Walsh, Congressman Jimmy, 222, 308
Walsh, Sean, 118, 125
Warfield, Derek, III, iv, 224, 351
Weinfeld, Judge, 150
Weiss, Ari, 228
Weston, Fr. Gerry, 71

Wheelwright, Fr. Thomas, 123
Winter, Jane, 348
Wolfe Tone, 22, 385
Wolff, Lester, 359
Wordsworth, 34
Wright, Jim, 237
Wright, Sir Oliver, 239, 240, 262

Y

Young, Andrew, 138
Young Wolfe Tones, iv, 351

Z

Zablocki, Congressman Clement, 226, 229

FR. MCMANUS ON GERMAN TV REGARDING A BREXIT HARD BORDER.

And fielding other media questions

CAPITOL HILL. Friday, August 2, 2019—There has been a flurry of international media attention to Brexit and its danger to the Good Friday Agreement, and to the reaction of the Irish National Caucus.

In the past three days, the Capitol Hill-based Irish National Caucus has received calls from London BBC radio; from BBC's leading news and current affairs TV show "Newsnight"; from Euronews-NBC, the English language TV channel based in France; and from ZDF German Television, Washington Studio, a news program covering most of Europe.

Fr. Sean McManus, Caucus president, explained: "I guess they were aware of our famous Irish Congressional Briefings with which we inundate the Congress and thousands of Irish-Americans almost daily on Brexit and other key issues. The former three media programs wanted me to put them in touch with our Congressional Friends. Unfortunately, the House of Representatives is in recess, so Congressman Ritchie Neal (D-MA) and Congressman Brendan Boyle (D-PA) were not available. German TV wanted to interview me on the Irish National Caucus' campaign against a hard Border and because I am the only leader of an Irish-American organization who was born and reared beside England's imposed 1920 Border. That damn Border not only divided my country, but also my parish that has essentially existed since the 6th Century: the proud parish of Kinawley, County Fermanagh, placing the other part of the parish in County Cavan—then declared by England to be in a foreign country! ... So, my parents, uncles, aunts and all their contemporaries—and their neighbors in Swanlinbar, County Cavan—were born in Ireland, but, hey presto, since 1920, Fermanagh and County Cavan are in two different countries/states/jurisdictions. How deeply offensive, undemocratic, and ridiculous is that? Fr. McManus continued: "In the German TV interview, I emphasized that Speaker Nancy Pelosi—God bless her good Italian soul and great American heart—has stated recently that Britain will not get a trade deal with the United States if the London government destroys the Good Friday Agreement and erects a hard Border. I also stressed that such a trade deal has to go through the House Ways and Means Committee, which is Chaired by Congressman Ritchie Neal (D-MA) the top Congressional defender and supporter of the Good Friday Agreement and Irish Peace Process."

Barbara Flaherty, Executive Vice President of the Irish National Caucus, said: "And, thus, it has been for almost 50 years: when the British, Irish and international media want to make contact with an authoritative source on Irish affairs in America and especially in Washington, Fr. McManus is the go-to man. The media and others know that nobody knows the issue better, has worked harder and longer than he has, and that he always speaks truth to power. In the words of a major newspaper: 'Fr. Sean McManus is the man who put Northern Ireland on the map in America. As head of Washington-based lobby group the Irish National Caucus, which he founded in 1974, he continues to fight the fight over sectarianism and justice—British governments have been and gone, Fr. Sean is still here. He famously championed the MacBride Principles, which called on US companies investing in Northern Ireland to operate a fair employment practice. It made him a hate figure for Unionists and a constant prick in the side of the British.'(Richard Sullivan. Sunday World. Belfast. January 4, 2018.)"

She concluded: "And the late, great Congressman Ben Gilman (R-NY), former Chairman of the House Foreign Affairs Committee, memorably and authoritatively stated: 'No one has done more than Father McManus to keep the U.S. Congress on track regarding justice and peace in Ireland. Indeed, I believe historians will record that no one since John Devoy (1842–1928) has done more to organize American pressure for justice in Ireland.' And Congressman Gilman was in a unique position to know."

Made in the USA
Middletown, DE
05 November 2019